COMMENTING AND COMMENTARIES

COMMENTING AND COMMENTARIES

A Reference Guide to the Best Bible Study Books

New Updated Edition

Charles H. Spurgeon

Includes
"A Classic Bible Study Library For Today"
by Warren W. Wiersbe, Cyril J. Barber,
David W. Brookman, Wilbur M. Smith, and others

KREGEL PUBLICATIONS
Grand Rapids, Michigan 49501

Commenting and Commentaries by Charles H. Spurgeon,
revised 1988. Includes *A Classic Bible Study Library for
Today*, by C. H. Spurgeon, et. al. Copyright © 1988 and
published by Kregel Publications, a division of Kregel,
Inc. P. O. Box 2607, Grand Rapids, Michigan 49501. All
rights reserved.

Library of Congress Cataloging-in-Publication Data

Spurgeon, C. H. (Charles Haddon), 1834-1892.
   Commenting and Commentaries.

  Includes indexes.

   1. Bible—Commentaries—Bibliography.
   I. Classic Bible Study Library for Today.
   II. Title.
Z7770.S72 1988   [BS482]   016.2207   88-8921
ISBN 0-8254-3749-0

1 2 3 4 5 Printing/Year 92 91 90 89 88
Printed in the United States of America

CONTENTS

PUBLISHER'S PREFACE

The layperson or student with a small but growing library, as well as the pastor possessing an extensive one, will profit greatly from this new edition of Spurgeon's catalog of biblical commentaries and expositions. With the increased number of titles now available in reprint editions, this new revised format of Spurgeon's classic will be more valuable than ever before.

The entire volume has been reset in new type. Spurgeon's recommendations are denoted by the number of asterisks after each title. You will find helpful instructions on using this catalog on pages 35 and 36. Where reprint editions are available, contemporary publishers are listed. However, the comments and entire list of titles cataloged by Spurgeon remains as he compiled it. *A Classic Bible Study Library for Today* has been included to provide you with many additional recommended resources for your life and ministry.

Cataloged titles which are in print may be secured through your favorite bookseller. Kregel's Bookstore, P. O. Box 2607, Grand Rapids, Michigan 49501, carries one of the largest (over 100,000 titles) and finest selections of used religious and theological books in the country and will be happy to assist you in securing any out-of-print and oftentimes difficult-to-locate titles that you may desire. Titles published by Kregel Publications may be obtained through your favorite bookseller or ordered directly from Kregel Publications at the above address.

SECTION ONE

A CHAT ABOUT COMMENTARIES

In order to be able to expound the Scriptures, and as an aid to your pulpit studies, you will need to be familiar with the commentators: a glorious army, let me tell you, whose acquaintance will be your delight and profit. Of course, you are not such wiseacres as to think or say that you can expound Scripture without assistance from the works of divines and learned men who have labored before you in the field of exposition. If you are of that opinion, pray remain so, for you are not worth the trouble of conversion, and like a little coterie who think with you, would resent the attempt as an insult to your infallibility. It seems odd that certain men who talk so much of what the Holy Spirit reveals to them, should think so little of what he has revealed to others. My chat this afternoon is not for these great originals, but for you who are content to learn of holy men, taught of God, and mighty in the Scriptures. It has been the fashion of late years to speak against the use of commentaries. If there were any fear that the expositions of Matthew Henry, John Gill, Thomas Scott and others, would be exalted into Christian Targums, we would join the chorus of objectors, but the existence or approach of such a danger we do not suspect. The temptations of our times lie rather in empty pretensions to novelty of sentiment, than in a slavish following of accepted guides. A respectable acquaintance with the opinions of the giants of the past might have saved many an erratic thinker from wild interpretations and outrageous inferences. Usually, we found the despisers of commentaries to be men who have no sort of acquaintance with them. In their case, it is the opposite of familiarity which has bred contempt.

It is true there are a number of expositions of the whole Bible which are hardly worth shelf space. They aim at too much and fail altogether; the authors have spread a little learning over a vast surface, and have badly attempted for the entire Scriptures that which they might have accomplished for one book with tolerable success. But who will deny the preeminent value of such expositions of those of John Calvin, Christopher Ness, Matthew Henry, John Trapp, Matthew Poole, and John Bengel, which are as deep as they are broad? Yet further, who can pretend to biblical learning who has not made himself familiar with the great writers who spent a life in explaining some one sacred book? Joseph Caryl on Job will not exhaust the patience of a student who loves every letter of the Word; even John Collinges, with his 909 pages on one chapter of the Song of Solomon, will not be too full for the preacher's use; nor will Thomas Manton's long–meter edition of the hundred and nineteenth Psalm be too profuse. No stranger could imagine the vast amount of real learning to be found in old commentaries like the following: James Durham on Solomon's Song, Thomas Wilcocks on Psalms and Proverbs, Michael Jermin on Ecclesiastes and Proverbs, William Greenhill on Ezekiel, Jeremiah Burroughs on Hosea, Henry Ainsworth on the Pentateuch, John King on Jonah, George Hutcheson on John, Peter Martyr on Romans, etc.; and in Andrew Willett, Richard Sibbes, Paul Bayne, Edward Elton, Nicholas Byfield, Jean Daillé, John Adams, Thomas Taylor, John Barlow, Harvey Goodwin, and others, on the various epistles. Without attempting to give in detail the names of all, I intend in a familiar way to mention the more notable ones who wrote on the whole Bible, or on either Testament, and I especially direct your attention to the titles, which in Puritan writers, generally give in brief the run of the work.

First among the mighty for general usefulness we are bound to mention the man whose name is a household word, MATTHEW HENRY[1]. He is the most pious and pithy, sound and sensible, suggestive and sober, terse and trustworthy. You will find him to be glittering with metaphors, rich in analogies, overflowing with illustrations and superabundant in reflections. He delights in apposition and alliteration; he is usually plain, quaint, and full of pith; he sees right through a text directly. Apparently he is not critical, but he quietly gives the result of an accurate critical knowledge of the original fully up to the best critics of his time. He is not versed in the manners and customs of the East, for the Holy Land was not so accessible as in our day. But he is deeply spiritual, heavenly, and profitable; finding good matter in every text, and from all deducing the most practical and judicious lessons. His is a kind of commentary to be placed where I saw it, in the old meeting house at Chester—chained to the vestry for anybody and everybody to read. It is the poor man's commentary, the old Christian's companion, suitable to everybody, instructive to all. His own account of how he was led to write his exposition affords us an example of delighting in the Law of the Lord.

> If any desire to know how so mean and obscure a person as I am, who in learning, judgment, felicity of expression, and all advantages for such a service, am less than the least of all my Master's servants, came to venture upon so great a work, I can give no other account of it but this. It has long been my practice, what little time I had to spare in my study from my constant preparations for the pulpit, to spend it in drawing up expositions upon some parts of the New Testament, not so much for my own use, as purely for my own entertainment, because I know not how to employ my thoughts and time more to my satisfaction. *Trahit sua quemque voluptas;* every man that studies has some beloved study which is his delight above any other, and this is mine. It is that learning which was my happiness from a child to be trained up in by my ever-

---

1. Matthew Henry, *A Commentary on the Whole Bible.* 6 vols., Fleming H. Revell Publishers. Abridged edition, 1 vol., Zondervan Publishing House.

honored father, whose memory must always be very dear and precious to me. He often reminded me that a good textuary is a good divine; and that I should read other books with this in my eye, that I might be the better able to understand and apply the Scripture.

You are aware, perhaps, that the latter part of the New Testament Commentary was completed by other hands, the good man having gone the way of all flesh. The writers were Messrs. Evans, Brown, Mayo, Bays, Rosewell, Harriss, Atkinson, Smith, Tong, Wright, Merrell, Hill, Reynolds, and Billingsley—all dissenting ministers. They have executed their work exceedingly well, having worked in much of the matter which Henry had collected, and have done their best to follow his methods, but their combined production is far inferior to Matthew Henry himself, and any reader will soon detect the difference. Every minister ought to read Matthew Henry entirely and carefully through once at least. I recommend that you get through it in the next twelve months after you leave college. Begin at the beginning, and resolve that you will traverse the goodly land from Dan to Beersheba. You will acquire a vast store of sermons if you read with your notebook close at hand. And as for thoughts, they will swarm around you like twitching swallows around an old gable towards the close of autumn. If you publicly expound the chapter you have just been reading, your people will wonder at the novelty of your remarks and the depth of your thoughts, and then you may tell them what a treasure Matthew Henry is.

Mr. Jay's sermons bear indubitable evidence of his having studied Matthew Henry almost daily. Many of the quaint things in Jay's sermons are either directly traceable to Matthew Henry or to his familiarity with that writer. I have thought that the style of Jay was founded upon Matthew Henry: Matthew Henry is Jay writing, Jay is Matthew Henry preaching. What more could I say in commendation either of the preacher or the author?

It would not be possible for me too earnestly to press upon you the importance of reading the expositions of that prince among men, JOHN CALVIN![2] I am afraid that scant purses may keep you from their purchase, but if it be possible, procure them. I have often felt inclined to cry out with Father Simon, a Roman Catholic: "Calvin possessed a sublime genius," and with Scaliger, "Oh! how well Calvin has reached the meaning of the prophets—no one better." You will find 42 or more goodly volumes worth their weight in gold. Of all commentators I believe John Calvin to be the most candid. In his expositions he is not always what some would call Calvinistic. That is to say, where Scripture maintains the doctrine of predestination and grace he flinches in no degree, but inasmuch as some

2. John Calvin, *Calvin's Commentaries*, 45 vols. in 22 bindings, Baker Book House. *Calvin's New Testament Commentaries*, edited by David and Thomas F. Torrance, 12 vols. Wm. B. Eerdmans Publishing Co. Calvin's *Institutes of the Christian Religion*, translated by Henry Beveridge, 2 vols., Wm. B. Eerdmans Publishing Co. Calvin's *Institutes of the Christian Religion*, edited by John T. McNeil, 2 vols., Westminster Press. *The Institutes of the Christian Religion*, edited by Tony Lane and Hilary Osborne, 1 vol., Baker Book House.

Scriptures bear the impress of human free action and responsibility, he does not shun to expound their meaning in all fairness and integrity. He was no trimmer and pruner of texts. He gave their meaning as far as he knew it. His honest intention was to translate the Hebrew and the Greek originals as accurately as he possibly could, and then to give the meaning which would naturally be conveyed by such Greek and Hebrew words. He labored, in fact, to declare, not his own mind upon the Spirit's words, but the mind of the Spirit as couched in those words. Dr. King very truly says of him:

> No writer ever dealt more fairly and honestly by the Word of God. He is scrupulously careful to let it speak for itself, and to guard against every tendency of his own mind to put upon it a questionable meaning for the sake of establishing some doctrine which he feels to be important, or some theory which he is anxious to uphold. This is one of his prime excellences. He will not maintain any doctrine, however orthodox and essential, by a text of Scripture, which to him appears of doubtful application, or of inadequate force. For instance, firmly as he believed the doctrine of the Trinity, he refuses to derive an argument in its favor from the plural form of the name of God in the first chapter of Genesis. It were easy to multiply examples of this kind, which, whether we agree in his conclusion or not, cannot fail to produce the conviction that he is at least an honest commentator, and will not make any passage of Scripture speak more or less than, according to his view, its divine Author intended to speak.

The edition of John Calvin's works which was issued by the Calvin Translation Society, is greatly enriched by the remarks of the editors, consisting not merely of notes on the Latin of Calvin, and the French translation, or on the text of the original Scriptures, but also of weighty opinions of eminent critics, illustrative manners and customs, and observations of travelers. By the way, gentlemen, what a pity it is that people do not, as a rule, read the notes in the old Puritan books! If you purchase old copies of such writers as Brooks, you will find that the notes in the margin are almost as rich as the books themselves. They are dust of gold, of the same metal as the ingots in the center of the page. But to return to Calvin. If you needed any confirmatory evidence as to the value of his writings, I might summon a cloud of witnesses, but it will suffice to quote one or two. Here is the opinion of one who is looked upon as his great enemy, namely, Arminius: "Next to the perusal of the Scriptures, which I earnestly inculcate, I exhort my pupils to peruse Calvin's Commentaries, which I extol in loftier terms than *Helmich* [3] himself; for I affirm that *he excels beyond comparison in the interpretation of Scripture, and that his commentaries ought to be more highly valued than all that is handed down to us by the Library of the Fathers;* so that I acknowledge him to have possessed above most others, or rather above all other men, what may be called an eminent gift of prophecy."

Quaint Robert Robinson said of him, "There is no abridging this sententious commentator, and the more I read him, the more does he become a favorite expositor with me." Richard Baxter wrote, "I know no man since

---

3. Werner Helmich, a Dutch Protestant divine, A.D. 1551—1608.

the apostles' days, whom I value and honor more than Calvin, and whose judgment in all things, one with another, I more esteem and come nearer to."

If you are well enough versed in Latin, you will fine in MATTHEW POOLE's *Synopsis*,[4] a marvellous collection of all the wisdom and folly of the critics. It is a large cyclopedia worthy of the days when theologians could be cyclopean, and had not shrunk from 12 x 15" to 6 x 9" books. Query—a query for which I will not demand an answer—has one of you ever beaten the dust from the venerable copy of Poole which loads our library shelves? Yet as Poole spent no less than ten years in compiling it, it should be worthy of your frequent notice—ten years, let me add, spent in Amsterdam in exile for the truth's sake from his native land. His work was based upon an earlier compilation entitled *Critici Sacri*, containing the concentrated light of a constellation of learned men who have never been excelled in any age or country.

MATTHEW POOLE also wrote *Annotations*[5] upon the whole Word of God, in English, which are mentioned by Matthew Henry as having passed through many impressions in his day, and he not only highly praises them, but declares that he has in his own work all along been brief upon that which Mr. Poole has more largely discussed, and has industriously declined what is to be found there. The three volumes are necessities for your libraries. On the whole, if I must have only one commentary, and had read Matthew Henry as I have, I do not know but what I should choose Poole. He is a very prudent and judicious commentator, and one of the few who could honestly say, "We have not willingly balked any obvious difficulty, and have designed a just satisfaction to all our readers; and if any knot remains yet untied, we have told our readers what has been most probably said for their satisfaction in the untying of it." Poole is not so pithy and witty by far as Matthew Henry, but he is perhaps more accurate, less a commentator, and more an expositor. You meet with no ostentation of learning in Matthew Poole, and that for the simple reason that he was so profoundly learned as to be able to give results without a display of his intellectual crockery. A pendant who is forever quoting Ambrose and Jerome, Piscator and Oecolampadius, in order to show what a copious reader he has been, is usually a dealer in small wares, and quotes only what others have quoted before him, but he who can give you the result and outcome of very extensive reading without sounding a trumpet before him is the really learned man. Mind you do not confound the *Annotations* with the *Synopsis*; the English work is not a translation of the Latin one, but an entirely distinct performance. Strange to say, like the other great Matthew, he did not live to complete his work beyond Isaiah 58; other hands united to finish the design.

---

4. Matthew Poole, *Synopsis Criticorum aliorumque S. Scripturae Interpretum.* Operâ Matthaei Poli. London, 1669.
5. Reprinted as *A Commentary on the Holy Bible,* 3 vols., The Banner of Truth. Wherein the sacred text is inserted, and various readings annexed, together with the parallel Scriptures. The more difficult terms in each verse explained; seeming contradictions reconciled; questions and doubts resolved; and the whole text opened.

Would it be possible to eulogise too much the incomparably sententious and suggestive work of JOHN TRAPP?[6] Since Mr. Dickinson has rendered them accessible,[7] I trust most of you have bought them. Trapp will be most valuable to men of discernment, to thoughtful men, to men who only want a start in a line of thought, and are then able to run alone. Trapp excels in witty stories on the one hand, and learned allusions on the other. You will not *thoroughly* enjoy him unless you can turn to the original, and yet a mere dunce at classics will prize him. His writings remind me of himself: he was a pastor, hence his holy, practical remarks; he was the head of a public school, and everywhere we see his profound scholarship; he was for some time amid the guns and drums of a parliamentary garrison. He gossips and tells queer anecdotes like a man used to soldier-life; yet withal, he comments as if he had been nothing else but a commentator all his days. Some of his remarks are far-fetched, and like the far-fetched rarities of Solomon's Tarshish, there is much gold and silver, but there are also apes and peacocks. Some of his criticisms would be the cause of amusement in these days of greater scholarship; but for all that, he who shall excel Trapp had need rise very early in the morning. Trapp is my special companion and treasure; I can read him when I am too weary for anything else. Trapp is salt, pepper, mustard, vinegar, and all the other condiments. Put him on the table when you study, and when you have your dish ready, use him by way of spicing the whole thing. Yes, gentlemen, read Trapp certainly, and if you catch the infection of his consecrated humor, so much the better for your hearers.

A very distinguished place is due DR. JOHN GILL.[8] Beyond all controversy, Gill was one of the most able Hebraists of his day, and in other matters no mean proficient. When an opponent in controversy had ventured to call him "a botcher in divinity," the good doctor, being compelled to become a fool in glorying, gave such a list of his attainments as must have covered his accuser with confusion. His great work on the

---

6. John Trapp, *Annotations on the Old and New Testaments,* in five distinct vols. The first is on the five Books of Moses, and on the following books, of Joshua, Judges, Ruth, Samuel, Kings, and Chronicles. The second is on Ezra, Nehemiah, Esther, Job, and Psalms. The third is on Proverbs, Ecclesiastes, Solomon's Song, and the four major prophets, with a treatise called, "The Righteous Man's Recompense." The fourth is on the twelve minor prophets, the fifth and last is on the whole New Testament, with a Decade of Divine Discourses, or Commonplaces, thereunto annexed. By John Trapp, M.A., pastor and preacher of the Word of God at Weston-upon-Avon, in Gloucestershire, 1662.

7. The reprint by R. D. Dickinson is edited by Rev. W. Webster and Rev. Hugh Martin, with a memoir of the author by Rev. A. B. Grosart, 5 vols.

8. John Gill, *An Exposition of the Old Testament,* in which are recorded the origin of mankind, of the several nations of the world, and of the Jewish nation in particular; the lives of the patriarchs of Israel; the journey of that people from Egypt to the land of Canaan, and their settlement in that land: their laws, moral, ceremonial, and judicial; their government and state under judges and kings; their several captivities, and their sacred books of devotion. In this exposition, it is attempted to give an account of their several books and the writers of them; a summary of each chapter, and the genuine sense of each verse, and, throughout the whole, the original text and the versions of it, are inspected and compared;

Holy Scriptures is greatly prized at the present day by the best authorities, which is conclusive evidence of its value, since the set of the current of theological thought is quite contrary to that of Dr. Gill. No one in these days is likely to be censured for his Arminianism, but most modern divines affect to sneer at anything a little too highly Calvinistic. However, amid the decadence of his own rigid system, and the disrepute of even more moderate Calvinism, Gill's laurels as an expositor are still green. His ultraism is discarded, but his learning is respected: the world and the church take leave to question his dogmatism, but they both bow before his erudition. Probably no man since Gill's days has at all equaled him in the matter of Rabbinical learning. Say what you will about that teaching, it has its value. Of course, a man has to rake among perfect dunghills and dustheaps, but there are a few jewels which the world could not afford to miss. Gill was a master cinder-sifter among the Targums, the Talmuds, the Mishna, and the Gemara. Richly did he deserve the degree of which he said, "I never bought it, nor thought it, nor sought it."

He was always at work; it is difficult to say when he slept, for he wrote 10,000 pages of theology. The portrait of him which belongs to this church, and hangs in my private vestry, and from which all the published portraits have been engraved, represents him after an interview with an Arminian gentleman, turning up his nose in a most expressive manner, as if he could not endure even the smell of free will. In some such a vein he wrote his commentary. He hunts Arminianism throughout the whole of it. He is far from being so interesting and readable as Matthew Henry. He delivered his comments to his people from Sabbath to Sabbath, hence their peculiar mannerism. His frequent method of criticizing is, "This text does not mean this," nobody ever thought it did; "It does not mean that," only two or three heretics ever imagined it did; and again it does not mean a third thing, or a fourth, or a fifth, or a sixth absurdity; but at last he thinks it does mean so-and-so, and tells you so in a methodical, sermon-like manner. This is an easy method, gentlemen of filling up the time, if you are ever short on titles for a sermon. Show your people firstly, secondly, and thirdly, what the text does not mean, and then afterwards you can go back and show them what it does mean. It may be thought, however, that one such a teacher is enough, and that what was tolerated from a learned doctor would be scouted in a student fresh from college. For good, sound, massive, sober sense in commenting, who can excel Gill? Very seldom does he allow himself to be run away with by imagination, except now and then when he tries to open up a parable, and finds a meaning in every circumstance and minute detail; or when he falls upon a text which is not

interpretation of the best note, both the Jewish and Christian, consulted; difficult places at large explained, seeming contradictions reconciled, and various passages illustrated and confirmed by testimonies of Gentile as well as Jewish. *An Exposition of the New Testament,* in which the sense of the sacred text is taken; doctrinal and practical truths are set in a plain and easy light, difficult passages explained; seeming contradictions reconciled; and whatever is material in the various readings and several Oriental versions is observed. The whole illustrated with notes taken from the most ancient Jewish writings. Reprinted as *An Exposition of the Old and New Testaments,* 10 vols. Primitive Baptist Library.

congenial with his creed, and hacks and hews terribly to bring the Word of God into a more systematic shape. Gill is the Coryphaeus of hyper-Calvinism, but if his followers never went beyond their master, they would not go very far astray.

I have placed next to Gill in my library ADAM CLARKE,[9] but as I have no desire to have my rest broken by wars among the authors, I have placed Doddridge between them. If the spirits of the two worthies could descend to the earth in the same mood in which they departed, no one house would be able to hold them. Adam Clarke is the great annotator of our Wesleyan friends; and they have no reason to be ashamed of him, for he takes rank among the chief of expositors. His mind was evidently fascinated by the singularities of learning, and hence his commentary is rather too much of an old curiosity shop, but it is filled with valuable rarities, such as none but a great man could have collected. Like Gill, he is one-sided, only in the opposite direction to our friend the Baptist. The use of the two authors may help to preserve the balance of your judgments. If you consider Clarke wanting in unction, *do not read him for savor but for criticism*, and then you will not be disappointed.

The author thought that lengthy reflections were rather for the preacher than the commentator, and hence it was not a part of his plan to write such observations as those which endear Matthew Henry to the million. If you have a copy of Adam Clarke, and exercise discretion in reading it, you will derive immense advantage from it, for frequently by a sort of sidelight he brings out the meaning of the text in an astonishingly novel manner. I do not wonder that Adam Clarke still stands, notwithstanding his peculiarities, a prince among commentators. I do not find him so helpful as Gill, but still from his side of the question, with which I have personally no sympathy, he is an important writer, and deserves to be studied by every reader of the Scriptures. He very judiciously says of Dr. Gill, "He was a very learned and good man, but has often lost sight of his better judgment in spiritualizing the text." This is the very verdict which we pass upon himself, only altering the last sentence a word or two: "He has often lost sight of his better judgment in following learned singularities." The monkey, instead of the serpent, tempting Eve, is a notable instance.

As I am paying no sort of attention to chronological order, I shall now wander back to old master JOHN MAYER,[10] a rare and valuable author. I have been in London a long time now, but I have only of late been able to

---

9. Adam Clarke, *Adam Clarke's Commentary on the Whole Bible*. 1 vol., condensed by Ralph Earle. Beacon Hill Press.

10. John Mayer, *A Commentary Upon the Whole Old Testament*, added to that of the same author upon the whole "New Testament," published many years before, to make a complete work upon the whole Bible. Wherein the several translations and expositions, *Literal* and *Mystical*, of all the most famous commentators, both ancient and modern, are propounded, examined, and judged of, for the more full satisfaction of the studious reader in all things, and many most genuine notions inserted for edification in the grace of our Lord Jesus Christ. A work, the like unto which has never yet been published by any man, yet very necessary, not only for students in divinity, but also for every Christian that loveth the knowledge of divine things. London, 1753.

complete my set. The first volume especially is rare in the extreme. The six volumes, folio, are a most judicious and able digest of former commentators, enriched with the author's own notes, forming altogether one of the fullest and best of learned English commentaries; not meant for popular use, but invaluable to the student. He is a link between the modern school, at the head of which I put Poole and Henry, and the older school, who mostly wrote in Latin and were stained with the conceits of those schoolmen who gathered like flies around the corpse of Aristotle. He appears to have written before Diodati and Trapp, but lacked opportunity to publish. I fear he will be forgotten, as there is but little prospect of the republication of so diffuse, and perhaps heavy, an author. He is a very Alp of learning, but cold and lacking in spirituality; hence his lack of popularity.

In 1653, ARTHUR JACKSON,[11] preacher of God's Word in Wood Street, London, issued four volumes upon the Old Testament, which appear to have been the result of his pulpit expositions to his people. Valuable his works would be if there were no better, but they are not comparable to others already and afterwards mentioned. You can do without him, but he is a reputable author. Far more useful is CHRISTOPHER NESS's *History and Mystery of the Old and New Testament*,[12] a grand repository of quaint remarks upon the historical books of Scripture. You will find it contained in four volumes, and you will have a treasure if you procure it.

Need I commend BISHOP JOSEPH HALL's *Contemplations*,[13] to your affectionate attention? What wit! What sound sense! What concealed learning! His style is as pithy and witty as that of Thomas Fuller, and it has a sacred unction about it to which Fuller has no pretension.

THEODORE HAAK's *Annotations*[14] come to us as the offspring of the famous Synod of Dort, and the WESTMINSTER *Annotations*,[15] as the produc-

11. Arthur Jackson, *A Help for the Understanding of the Holy Scriptures.* Intended chiefly for the assistance and information of those that read some part of the Bible, and would gladly always understand what they read if they had some man to help them. *The first part.* Containing certain short notes of exposition upon the five books of Moses, etc.
12. Christopher Ness, *A Complete History and Mystery of the Old and New Testament* (3 vols.), logically discussed, and theologically improved. The first volume beginning at the Creation of the world, and ending at Moses. The second continuing the History from Joshua till the birth of Christ. The third from the birth of Christ, to the death of the last and longest living apostle, John the Divine. The like undertaking (in such a manner and method) being never attempted before.
13. Joseph Hall, *Contemplations on the Historical Passages of the Old and New Testament.* Numerous editions; the one before us has a memoir of the author by James Hamilton.
14. Theodore Haak, *The Dutch Annotations Upon the Whole Bible;* or, all the Holy Canonical Scriptures of the Old and New Testament, together with, and according to, their own translation of all the text: as both the one and the other were ordered and appointed by the Synod of Dort, 1618, and published by authority, 1637. Now faithfully communicated in English, 1657, 2 vols.
15. *Annotations Upon the Books of the Old and New Testaments.* This third, above the first and second, edition so enlarged, as they make an entire commentary on the sacred Scriptures, the like never before published in English. Wherein the

tion of a still more venerable assembly. If, with my hat off, bowing profoundly to those august conclaves of master minds, I may venture to say so, I would observe that they furnish another instance that committees seldom equal the labors of individuals. The notes are too short and fragmentary to be of any great value.

Among entire commentators of modern date, a high place is usually awarded to THOMAS SCOTT,[16] amd I shall not dispute his right to it. He is the expositor of evangelical Episcopalians, even as Adam Clarke is the prophet of the Wesleyans, but to me he has seldom given a thought, and I have almost discontinued consulting him. The very first money I ever received for pulpit services is London was invested in Thomas Scott, and I neither regretted the investment nor became exhilarated thereby. His work has always been popular; is very judicious, thoroughly sound and gracious; but for suggestiveness and pith it is not comparable to Matthew Henry. I know I am talking heresy, but I cannot help saying that for a minister's use, Scott is mere milk and water—good and *trustworthy*, but not solid enough in matter for full-grown men. In the family, Scott will hold his place, but in the study you want condensed thought, and this you must look for elsewhere.

To all young men of light purses let me recommend THE RELIGIOUS TRACT SOCIETY's *Commentary*,[17] in six volumes, which contains the marrow of Henry and Scott, with notes from a hundred other authors. It is well executed, and for poor men a great Godsend.

Gentlemen, if you want something full of marrow and fatness, cheering to your own hearts by way of comment, and likely to help you in giving to your hearers rich expositions, buy ROBERT HAWKER's *Poor Man's Commentary*.[18] Dr. Hawker was the very least of commentators in the matter of criticism; he had no critical capacity, and no ability whatever as an interpreter of the letter; but *he sees Jesus*, and that is a sacred gift which is most precious whether the owner be a critic or no. It is to be confessed that he occasionally sees Jesus where Jesus is not legitimately to be seen. He allows his reason to be mastered by his affections, which, vice as it is, is not the worst fault in the world. There is always such a savor of the Lord Jesus Christ in Dr. Hawker that you cannot read him without profit. He has the peculiar idea that Christ is in every Psalm, and this often leads him totally astray, because he attributes expressions to the Savior which really shock the holy mind to imagine our Lord's using. However, not as a

text is explained, doubts resolved, Scriptures paralleled, and various readings observed. 1657.

16. Thomas Scott, *The Holy Bible, Containing the Old and New Testaments*, according to the Authorized Version, with explanatory notes, practical observations, and copious marginal references. A new edition, with the author's last corrections and improvements, with 10 maps. 1827.

17. The Religious Tract Society, *The Holy Bible*; the text according to the Authorized Version; and a commentary from Henry and Scott, with numerous observations and notes from other authors; also, the marginal references, maps of the countries mentioned in Scripture, and various useful tables. 6 vols.

18. Robert Hawker, *The Poor Man's Commentary on the Bible*. 3 vols., 1822.

substantial dish, but as a condiment, place the Plymouth vicar's work on the table. His writing is all sugar, and you will know how to use it, not devouring it in lumps, but using it to flavor other things.

"ALBERT BARNES," say you, "what do you think of Albert Barnes?" Albert Barnes is a learned and able divine, but his productions are unequal in value. The gospels are of comparatively little worth, but his other comments are extremely useful for Sunday school teachers and persons with a narrow range of reading, endowed with enough good sense to discriminate between good and evil. If a controversial eye had been turned upon Barnes' *Notes* years ago, and his inaccuracies shown up by some unsparing hand, he would never have had the popularity which at one time set rival publishers advertising him in every direction. His Old Testament volumes are to be greatly commended as learned and laborious, and the epistles are useful as a valuable collection of the various opinions of learned men. Placed by the side of the great masters, Barnes is a lesser light, but taking his work for what it is and professes to be, no minister can afford to be without it, and this is no small praise for works which were only intended for Sunday school teachers.[19]

Upon the New Testament, PHILIP DODDRIDGE's *Expositor* [20] is worthy of a far more extensive reading than is nowadays accorded to it. It is all in the form of a paraphrase, with the text in italics; a mode of treatment far from satisfactory as a rule, but exceedingly well carried out in this instance. The notes are very good, and reveal the thorough scholar. Our Authorized Version is placed in the margin, and a new translation is the paraphrase. The four evangelists are thrown into a harmony, a plan which has its advantages but is not without its evils. The practical improvements at the end of each chapter generally consist of pressing exhortations and devout meditations, suggested by the matter under discussion. It is sadly indicative of the Socinianism of the age in which this good man lived, that he feels called upon to apologize for the evangelical strain in which he has written. He appears to have barely finished this work in shorthand at the time of his death, and the later books were transcribed under the care of Job Orton. No life insurance society should accept the proposals of a commentator on the whole of either Testament, for it seems to be the rule that such students of the Word should be taken up to their reward before their task is completed.

Then, of course, gentlemen, you will economize rigidly until you have accumulated funds to purchase JOHN KITTO's *Pictorial Bible*. You mean to take that goodly freight on board before you launch upon the sea of married life. As you cannot visit the Holy Land, it is well for you that there is a work like the *Pictorial Bible*, in which the notes of the most observant travellers are arranged under the texts which they illustrate. For the geography,

19. Albert Barnes, *Barnes' Notes on Old and New Testaments*, edited by Robert Frew, 14 vols., Baker Book House. *Barnes' Notes on the New Testament*, unabridged edition in 1 vol., Kregel Publications.

20. Philip Doddridge, *The Family Expositor*; or a paraphrase and version of the New Testament; with critical notes, and a practical improvement of each section, to which is prefixed a life of the author, by Andrew Kippis. 4 vols. 1840.

zoology, botany, and manners and customs of Palestine, this will be your counselor and guide. Add to this noble comment, the two volumes of KITTO's *Daily Bible Illustrations*.[21] They are not exactly a commentary, but what marvellous expositions you have there! You have reading more interesting than any novel that was ever written, and as instructive as the heaviest theology. The matter is quite attractive and fascinating, and yet so weighty, that the man who shall study those volumes thoroughly, will not fail to read his Bible intelligently and with growing interest.

The Gnomon of the New Testament, by JOHN ALBERT BENGEL,[22] is the scholar's delight. He selected the title as modest and appropriate, intending it in the sense of a pointer or indicator, like the sundial; his aim being to point out or indicate the full force and meaning of the words and sentences of the New Testament. He endeavors to let the text itself cast its shadow on his page, believing with Luther that "the science of theology is nothing else but grammar exercised on the words of the Holy Spirit." The editor of the translation says in his preface:

> It is quite superfluous to write in praise of the *Gnomon* of Bengel. Ever since the year in which it was first published, A.D.1742, up to the present time, it has been growing in estimation, and has been more and more widely circulated among the scholars of all countries. Though modern criticism has furnished many valuable additions to our materials for New Testament exegesis, yet, in some respects, Bengel stands out still "*facile princeps*" among all who have labored, or who as yet labor in that important field. He is unrivalled in felicitous brevity, combined with what seldom accompanied that excellence, namely, perspicuity. Terse, weighty, and suggestive, he often, as a modern writer observes, "condenses more matter into a line, than can be extracted from pages of other writers".... In the passages which form the subject of controversy between Calvinists and Arminians, Bengel takes the view adopted by the latter, and in this respect I do not concur with him. But while he thus gives an undue prominence, as it would seem to me, to the responsibility and freedom of man in these passages, yet, in the general tenor of his work, there breathes such a holy reverence for God's sovereignty, and such spiritual unction, that the most extreme Calvinist would, for the most part, be unable to discover to what section of opinions he attached himself, and as to the controverted passages would feel inclined to say, "*Quum talis sis, utinam noster esses.*"

Men with a dislike for thinking had better not purchase the precious volumes, for they will be of little use to them; but men who love brainwork will find fine exercise in spelling out the deep meaning of Bengel's excessively terse sentences. His principles of interpretation stated in his "Essay on the Right Way of Handling Divine Subjects," are such as will make the lover of God's Word feel safe in his hands:

21. John Kitto, *Kitto's Daily Bible Illustrations*, being original readings for a year, on subjects from sacred history, biography, antiquities, and theology. Especially designed for the family circle. Kregel Publications.

22. John Albert Bengel, reprinted as *New Testament Commentary*, 2 vols. Kregel Publications. First translated into English, with original notes explanatory and illustrative. Revised and edited by Andrew R. Fausset, of Trinity College, Dublin.

> Put nothing *into* the Scriptures, but draw everything *from* them, and suffer nothing to remain hidden, that is really *in* them.... Though each inspired writer has his own manner and style, one and the same Spirit breathes through all, one grand idea pervades all.... Every divine communication carries (like the diamond) its own light with it, thus showing whence it comes; no touchstone is required to discriminate it.... The true commentator will fasten his primary attention on the *letter* (literal meaning), but never forget that the *Spirit* must equally accompany him; at the same time we must never devise a more spiritual meaning for Scripture passages than the Holy Spirit intended.... The *historical* matters of Scripture, both narrative and prophecy, constitute, as it were, the *bones* of its system, whereas the *spiritual* matters are as its muscles, blood vessels, and nerves. As the *bones* are necessary to the human system, so Scripture *must* have its *historical* matters. The expositor who nullifies the *historical* groundwork of Scripture for the sake of finding only spiritual truths everywhere, brings death on all correct interpretations. Those expositions are the safest which keep closest to the text.

His idea of the true mode of dying touched me much when I first saw it. He declared that he would make no spiritual parade of his last hours, but if possible continue at his usual works, and depart this life as a person in the midst of business leaves the room to attend to a knock at the door. Accordingly he was occupied with the correction of his proofsheets as at other times, and the last messenger summoned him to his rest while his hands were full. This reveals a calm, well-balanced mind, and unveils many of those singular characteristics which enabled him to become the laborious recensor of the various manuscripts, and the pioneer of true biblical criticism.

The Critical English Testament [23] is "a New Testament, so compiled as to enable a reader, unacquainted with Greek, to ascertain the exact English force and meaning of the language of the New Testament, and to appreciate the latest results of modern criticism." Such is the professed aim of this commentary, and the compilers have very fairly carried out their intentions. The whole of Bengel's *Gnomon* is bodily transferred into the work, and as 120 years have elapsed since the first issue of that book, it may be supposed that much has since been added to the wealth of Scripture exposition; the substance of this has been incorporated in brackets, so as to bring it down to the present advanced state of knowledge. We strongly advise the purchase of this book, as it is *multum in parvo,* and will well repay an attentive perusal. Tischendorf and Alford have contributed largely, with other German and English critics, to make this one of the most lucid and concise commentaries on the text and teachings of the New Testament.

HENRY ALFORD's *Greek New Testament,* [24] "for the use of theological students and ministers," is an invaluable aid to the critical study of the text of the New Testament. You will find in it the ripened results of a matured

---

23. John Bengel, *The Critical English Testament.* Being an adaptation of Bengel's *Gnomon,* with numerous notes, showing precise results of modern criticism and exegesis. Edited by Rev. W. L. Blackley and Rev. James Hawes. 3 vols.

24. Henry Alford, *The Greek Testament,* with critical revised text, a digest of

scholarship, the harvesting of a judgment, generally highly impartial, always worthy of respect, which has gleaned from the most important fields of biblical research, both modern and ancient, at home and abroad. You will not look here for any spirituality of thought or tenderness of feeling; you will find the learned Dean does not forget to do full justice to his own views, and is quite able to express himself vigorously against his opponents; but for what it professes to be, it is an exceedingly able and successful work. The later issues are by far the most desirable, as the author has considerably revised the work in the fourth edition.

What I have said of his Greek Testament applies equally to ALFORD's *New Testament for English Readers,*[25] which is also a standard work.

I must confess also a very tender side towards BLOOMFIELD's *Greek Testament,*[26] and I am singular enough to prefer it in some respects to Alford. At least, I have got more out of it on some passages, and I think it does not deserve to be regarded as superseded.

The *Commentary* by PATRICK, LOWTH, ARNALD, WHITBY and LOWMAN,[27] is said by Darling to be of standard authority, but you may do without it with less loss than in the case of several others I have mentioned. The authors were men of great learning, their association in one commentary is remarkable, and their joint production has a place in all complete libraries.

DR. WORDSWORTH's *Holy Bible, With Notes and Introductions,*[28] is a valuable addition to our stores, but it is rendered much more bulk and expensive than it needed to be by the printing of the text at large. It gives many precious hints, and much of the choicest thought of medieval writers, besides suggesting catchwords and showing connections between various passages although it is occasionally marred by the characteristic weaknesses of the Bishop, and has here and there foolishnesses at which one cannot but smile. It is a great work, such as only an eminent scholar could have produced.

I am not so enamored of the German writers as certain of my brethren appear to be, for they are generally cold and hard, and unspiritual. As Dr. Graham says:

> There are about 20 or 30 names in the literary world who have gained a conspicuous place in theological circles; and in German commentaries

---

various readings, marginal references to verbal and idiomatic usage, prolegomena, and a critical and exegetical commentary. 4 vols.

25. Henry Alford, *The New Testament for English Readers,* containing the Authorized Version, with a revised English text, marginal references, and a critical and explanatory commentary. 4 vols., Baker Book House.

26. Bloomfield, *The Greek Testament,* with English notes, critical, philological and explanatory; partly selected and arranged from the best commentators, ancient and modern but chiefly original. 2 vols., 1841.

27. Patrick, Lowth, Arnald, Whitby, and Lowman, *A Critical Commentary and Paraphrase on the Old and New Testament and the Apocrypha.*

28. Charles Wordsworth, *The Holy Bible, With Notes and Introductions* [Old Testament only]. 6 vols. *The New Testament in the Original Greek,* with notes, introductions, and indexes. 2 vols.

these are perpetually introduced. In some of them the bulk of the work is made up of these authoritative names, and quotations from their works. This gives their writings the appearance of prodigious learning and research. Every page is bristling with hard words and strange languages, and the eye of the common reader is terrified at the very appearance, as the peaceful citizen is at the pointed cannon of a fortress.

I do, however, greatly prize the series produced by DR. JOHN PETER LANGE.[29] These volumes are not all of equal value, but, as a whole, they are a grand addition to our stores. The American translators have added considerably to the German work, and in some cases these additions are more valuable than the original matter. For homiletical purposes these volumes are so many hills of gold, but alas, there is dross also, for baptismal regeneration and other grave errors occur.

The Speaker's Commentary [30] is issued (August, 1875) as far as the Lamentations. It is a great work, and contains much which tends to illustrate the text; but if you had it you would not turn to it for spiritual food, or for fruitful suggestion, or if you did so, you would be disappointed. The object of the work is to help the general reader to know what the Scriptures really say and mean, and to remove some of the difficulties. It keeps to its design and in a measure accomplishes it.

I must also add to the list *A Commentary on the Old and New Testaments.* [31] It is the joint work of ROBERT JAMIESON, A. R. FAUSSET, and DAVID BROWN, and is to some extent a compilation and condensation of other men's thoughts, but it is sufficiently original to claim a place in every minister's library. Indeed, it contains so great a variety of information that if a man had no other exposition he would find himself at no great loss if he possessed this and used it diligently.

Several other works I omit, not because they are worthless, or unknown to me, but because for scant purses the best will be best. I must not omit upon the New Testament the goodly volume of WILLIAM BURKITT.[32] He is the celebrated "Rector" of whom Benjamin Keach "rectified" in the matter of infant baptism. Burkitt is somewhat pithy, and for a modern, rather rich and racy, but he is far from deep, and is frequently commonplace. I liked him well enough till I had read abler works and grown older. Some books grow upon us as we read and re-read them, but Burkitt does not. Yet, so

29. John Peter Lange, *A Commentary on the Holy Scriptures,* critical, doctrinal, and homiletical, with special reference to ministers and students, in connection with a number of eminent European divines. Translated from the German, and edited, with additions, by Phillip Schaff, D.D., in connection with American scholars of various evangelical denominations. 1868, ff.

30. F. C. Cook, ed., *The Holy Bible,* according to the Authorized Version, with an explanatory and critical commentary, and a revision of the translations by bishops and other clergy of the Anglican Church, 1871.

31. Robert Jamieson, A. R. Fausset, David Brown, *A Commentary on the Old and New Testaments.* 3 vols., Wm. B. Eerdmans Publishing Co. *Commentary on the Whole Bible.* 1 vol., Zondervan Publishing House.

32. William Burkitt, *Expository Notes,* with practical observations, on the New Testament of our Lord and Savior Jesus Christ.

far from depreciating the good man, I should be sorry to have missed his acquaintance, and would bespeak for him your attentive perusal.

The best commentators, after all, are those who have written upon only one book. Few men can comment eminently well upon the whole Bible. There are sure to be some weak points in colossal works; prolixity in so vast an undertaking is natural, and dullness follows at its heels—but a life devoted to one of the inspired volumes of our priceless Bible must surely yield a noble result. If I find myself able to do so, at some future time I will introduce you to a selection of the great one-book writers. For the present this much must suffice.

SECTION TWO

ON COMMENTING

Having introduced you to the commentators, I must now press upon you one of the most practical uses of them, namely, your own public commenting upon the Scriptures read during worship service. Preaching in the olden time consisted very much more of exposition than it does now. I suppose that the sermons of the primitive Christians were for the most part expositions of lengthy passages of the Old Testament; and when copies of the Gospels, and the Epistles of Paul, had become accessible to the churches, the chief work of the preacher would be to press home the apostolical teachings by delivering an address, the backbone of which would be a complete passage of Scripture. There would probably be but faint traces of divisions, heads and points, such as we employ in modern preaching, but the teacher would follow the run of the passage which was open before him, commenting as he read.

I suppose this to have been the case, because some of the early Christian modes of worship were founded very much upon that of the synagogue. I say some of the modes, since I suppose that as the Lord Jesus left His disciples free from rubrics and liturgies, each church worshiped according to the working of the free Spirit among them: one with the open meeting of the Corinthians, and another with a presiding minister, and a third with a mixture of the two methods. In the synagogue, it was the rule of the Rabbis that never less than 22 verses of the law should be read at one time, and the preaching consisted of notes upon a passage of that length. Such a rule would be a mere superstition if we were slavishly bound by it, but I could almost wish that the custom were re-established, for the present plan of preaching from short texts, together with the great neglect of commenting publicly upon the Word is very unsatisfactory. We cannot expect to deliver much of the teaching of Holy Scriptures by picking out verse by verse, and holding these up at random. The process resembles that of showing a house by exhibiting separate bricks. It would be an astounding absurdity if our friends used our private letters in this fashion, and interpreted them by short sentences disconnected and taken away from the context. Such expositors would make us out to say in every letter all we ever thought of, and a great many things besides far enough from our minds; while the real intent of our epistles would probably escape attention. Nowadays since expository preaching is not so common as it ought to be, there is the more necessity for our commenting during the time of our reading the Scriptures. Since topical preaching, hortatory preaching, experimental preaching, and so on—all exceedingly useful in their way—have almost pushed proper expository preaching out of place, there is the more need that we should, when we read passages of Holy Writ, habitually give running comments upon them.

I support my opinion with this reason, that *the public reading of the hard-to-understand parts of Scripture is of exceedingly little use to the majority of the people listening.* I can recollect hearing in my younger days long passages out of Daniel, which might have been exceedingly instructive to me if I had obtained the remotest conception what they meant. Take again parts of the prophecy of Ezekiel, and ask yourselves what profit can arise from their perusal by the illiterate, "unless some man shall guide them"? What more edification can come from a chapter in English which is not understood than from the same passage in Hebrew or Greek? The same argument which enforces translation demands exposition. If but a few explanatory words are thrown in by a judicious reader, it is wonderful how luminous obscure portions may be made. Two or three sentences will often reveal the drift of a whole chapter; the key of a great difficulty may be presented to the hearer in half-a-score words, and thus the public reading may be made abundantly profitable. I once saw a school of blind children among the charming ruins of York Abbey, and could not help pitying their incapacity to enjoy so much beauty. How willingly would I have opened their eyes! Are ignorant people wandering among the glories of the Scriptures much less to be pitied? Who will refuse them the light?

Abundant evidence has come before me that *brief comments upon Scripture in our ordinary services are most acceptable and instructive to our people.* I have often heard from working men, and their wives, and from merchants and their families, that my own expositions have been most helpful to them. They testify that when they read the Bible at home in the family, the exposition makes it doubly precious to them; and the chapter which they had unprofitably read at family devotions, when they peruse it the next time, recollecting what their minister has said upon it, becomes a real delight to them. The mass of our hearers, in London at least, do not, to any appreciable extent, read commentaries or any other books which throw a light upon the Scriptures. They have neither the money nor the time to do so, and if they are to be instructed in the Word of God in things which they cannot find out by mere experiences, and are not likely to have explained to them by their associates, they must get that instruction from us, or nowhere else. Nor do I see how we are to give them such spiritual assistance except through the regular practice of exposition.

Besides, if you are in the habit of commenting, *it will give you an opportunity of saying many things which are not of sufficient importance to become the theme of a whole sermon,* and therefore would probably remain unnoticed, to the great loss of the Lord's people and others. It is astounding what a range of truth, doctrinal, practical, and experimental,

Holy Scripture brings before us; and equally worthy of admiration is the forcible manner in which that truth is advanced. Hints given in the way in which the Word of God offers them are always wise and opportune; as, for instance, the rebukes which the Word administers might have seemed too severe had they been made by the pastor, unsustained by the Word and unsuggested by it, but arising out of the chapter they cannot be resented. You can both censure sins and encourage virtues by dilating upon the histories which you read in the inspired records, whereas you might never have touched upon them had not the chapter read brought the matter before you. If you want to make full proof of your ministry and leave no single point of revelation untouched, your easiest mode will be to comment upon Scripture habitually. Without this, much of the Word will be utterly unknown to many of your people. It is a very sad fact that they do not read so much as they should at home; the ungodly, in England, scarcely read the Bible at all; and if only that part which we preach upon be expounded to them, how little of the Bible can they ever know! If you will mark your Bibles with lines under the texts from which you have spoken, as I have always done with an old copy, which I keep in my study, you will discover that in twelve or fourteen years very little of the book has been gone through; a very large proportion of it remains unmarked like a field unploughed. Try, then, by exposition to give your people a fair view of the entire compass of revelation. Take them as it were to the top of Nebo, and show them the whole land from Dan to Beersheba, and prove to them that everywhere it floweth with milk and honey.

Earnestly do I advocate commenting. It is unfashionable in England, though somewhat more usual beyond the Tweed River. The practice was hardly followed up anywhere in England a few years ago, and it is very uncommon still. It may be pressed upon you for one other reason, namely, that *in order to execute it well, the commenting minister will at first have to study twice as much as the mere preacher,* because he will be called upon to prepare both his sermons and his expositions. As a rule, I spend much more time over the exposition than over the discourse. Once start a sermon with a great idea, and from that moment the truth naturally consolidates and crystalizes itself around the main subject like sweet crystals around a string hung up in syrup; but as for the exposition, you must keep to the text, you must face the difficult points, and must search into the mind of the Spirit rather than your own.

You will soon reveal your ignorance as an expositor if you do not study; therefore, diligent reading will be forced upon you. Anything which compels the preacher to search the grand old Book is of immense service to him. If any are jealous lest the labor should injure their constitutions, let them remember that mental work up to a certain point is most refreshing, and where the Bible is the theme, toil is delight. It is only when the mind becomes enfeebled by it, and this is not usually reached except by injudicious persons, or men engaged on topics which are unrefreshing and disagreeable; but our subject is a recreative one, and to young men like ourselves the vigorous use of our faculties is a most healthy exercise. Classics and mathematics may exhaust us, but not the volume of our Father's grace, the charter of our joys, the treasure of our wealth.

A man to comment well should be able to *read the Bible in the original.* Every minister should aim at a tolerable proficiency both in the Hebrew and the Greek. These two languages will give him a library at a small expense, an inexhaustible thesaurus, a mine of spiritual wealth. Really, the effort of acquiring a language is not so prodigious that brethren of moderate abilities should so frequently shrink from the attempt. A minister ought to attain enough of these tongues to be able at least to make out a passage by the aid of a lexicon, so as to be sure that he is not misrepresenting the Spirit of God in his sermons, but is, as nearly as he can judge, giving forth what the Lord intended to reveal by the language employed. Such knowledge would prevent his founding doctrines upon expressions in our version when nothing at all analogous is to be found in the inspired original. This has been done by preachers time and again, and they have shouted over an inference drawn from a *shall,* or an *if* gathered out of the translation, with as much assurance of infallibility and sense of importance as if the same language had occurred in the words which the Holy Spirit used. At such times, we have been reminded of the story told by the late beloved Henry Craik, in his book on the Hebrew language. At one time, the Latin Vulgate was constantly spoken of as the very Word of God, that a Roman Catholic theologian thus commented upon Genesis 1:10: "The gathering together of the waters called he seas." The Latin term for seas is *María.* On this ground, the writer asks, "What is the gathering together waters but the accumulation of all the graces into one place, that is, into the Virgin Mary *(María)*? But there is this distinction, that *María (the seas)* has the (i) short, because that which the seas contain is only of a transitory nature, while the gifts and graces of the blessed Virgin *(María)* shall endure for ever." Such superlative nonsense may be indulged in if we forget that translations cannot be verbally inspired, and that to the original is the last appeal.

Fail not to be expert in the use of your *Concordance.* Every day I live I thank God more and more for that poor half-crazy Alexander Cruden [1]. Of course, you have read his life, which is prefixed to the concordance. It exhibits him as a man of diseased mind, once or twice the inmate of a lunatic asylum, but yet for all that successfully devoting his energies to producing a work of absolutely priceless value, which never has been improved upon, and probably never will be; a volume which must ever yield the greatest possible assistance to a Christian minister, being as necessary to him as a plane to the carpenter, or a plough to the farmer. Be sure you buy a genuine unabridged Cruden, and none of the modern substitutes; good as they may be at the price, they are a delusion and a snare to ministers, and should never be tolerated in the manse library. To consider cheapness in purchasing a concordance is folly. You need only one: have none but the best. At the head of each notable word, Cruden gives you its meaning, and very often all its particular shades of meaning, so that he even helps you in sermonizing. When you have read his head-

---

1. Alexander Cruden, *Cruden's Unabridged Concordance* with notes and comments, Baker Book House. *Cruden's Complete Concordance,* Zondervan Publishing House.

ings, by following out the concordance, you will observe connections in which the word occurs, which most advantageously and correctly fix its meaning. Thus will the Word of God be its own key. A good textuary is a good theologian; be then well-skilled in using Cruden's *Concordance*.

I make but small account of most *reference Bibles*; they would be very useful if they were good for anything; but it is extremely easy to bring out a reference Bible which has verbal and apparent references, and nothing more. You will often turn to a reference, and will have to say, "Well, it is a reference, certainly, in a way, for it contains the same word, but there is no reference in the sense that the one text will explain the other." The useful reference cuts the diamond with a diamond, comparing spiritual things with spiritual; it is a thought-reference, and not a word-reference. If you meet with a really valuable reference Bible, it will be to you what I once heard a countryman call "a reverence Bible," for it will lead you to prize more and more the sacred volume. The best reference Bible is a thoroughly good concordance. Get the best, keep it always on the table, use it hourly, and you will have found your best companion.

Need I after my previous lectures commend to you the judicious reading of *commentaries*! These are called "dead men's brains" by certain knowing people, who claim to give us nothing in their sermons but what they pretend the Lord reveals direct to themselves. Yet these men are by no means original, and often their supposed inspirations is but borrowed wit. They get a peep at John Gill on the sly. The remarks which they give forth as the Spirit's mind are very inferior in all respects to what they affect to despise, namely, the mind of good and learned men. A batch of poems was sent me some time ago for *The Sword and the Trowel*, which were written by a person claiming to be under the immediate influence of the Holy Spirit. He informed me that he was passive, and that what was enclosed was written under the direct physical and mental influence of the Spirit upon his mind and hand. My bookshelves can show many poems as much superior to these pretended inspirations as angels are to blue-bottles; the miserable doggrel bore on its face the evidence of imposture. So, when I listen to the senseless twaddle of certain wise gentlemen who are always boasting that they alone are ministers of the Spirit, I am ashamed of their pretensions and of them. No, my dear friends, you may take it as a rule that the Spirit of God does not usually do for us what we can do for ourselves, and that if religious knowledge is printed in a book, and we can read it, there is no necessity of the Holy Spirit to make a fresh revelation of it to us in order to screen our laziness. Read, then, the admirable commentaries which I have already introduced to you. Yet, be sure you use your own minds too, or the expounding will lack interest. One is filled artificially by water brought in barges from a distance, and few care for its insipid contents; the other is a refreshing natural well, cool and delicious, and the people contend for every drop of it. Freshness, naturalness, life, will always attract, whereas mere borrowed learning is flat and insipid. Mr. Cecil says his plan was, when he laid a hold of a Scripture, to pray over it, and get his own thoughts on it, and then, after he had so done, to take up the ablest divines who wrote upon the subject, and see what their thoughts were. If you do not think and think much, you will become slaves and mere copyists. The exercise of your own mind is most healthful to you, and by perseverance, with divine help, you may expect to get at the meaning of every understandable passage. So to rely upon your own abilities as to be unwilling to learn from others is clearly folly; so to study as not to judge for yourselves is imbecility.

What should be the manner of your public commenting? One rule should be always to *point out very carefully wherever a word bears a special sense*; for rest assured, in Holy Scripture the same word does not always mean the same thing. The Bible is a book meant for human beings, and therefore it is written in human language; and in human language the same word may signify two or three things. For instance, "a pear fell from the tree;" "a man fell into drunken habits." There the meaning of the second word, "fell," is evidently different from the first, since it is not literal, but metaphorical. Again, "the cabman mounted the box;" "his lordship is staying at his shooting box." In each case there is the same word, but who does not see there is a great difference of meaning? So it is in the Word of God. You must explain the difference between a word used in a peculiar sense, and the ordinary meaning of the word, and thus you will prevent your people falling into mistakes. If people will say that the same word in Scripture always means the same thing, as I have heard some assert publicly, they will make nonsense of the Word of God, and fall into error through their own irrational maxims. To set up canons of interpretation for the Book of God which would be absurd if applied to other writings is egregious folly: it has a show of accuracy, but inevitably leads to confusion.

The obvious literal meaning of a Scripture is not always the true one, and ignorant persons are apt enough to fall into the most singular misconceptions—a judicious remark from the pulpit will be of signal service. Many persons have accustomed themselves to misunderstand certain texts; they have heard wrong interpretations in their youth, and will never know better unless the correct meaning be indicated to them.

We must make sure in our public expositions that *obscure and involved sentences are explained.* To overleap difficulties, and only expound what is already clear, is to make commenting ridiculous. When we speak of obscure sentences, we mean such as are mostly to be found in the prophets, and are rendered dark through their intrinsic weight of meaning. Involved sentences mostly abound in the writing of Paul, whose luxuriant mind was not to be restrained to any one line of argument. He begins a sentence, and does not finish it perhaps until eight verses further on, and all the space between the commencement and the end of the sentence is packed full of compressed truth, which it is not always easy to separate from the general argument. Hints consisting of but two or three words will let your hearers know where the reasoning breaks off, and where it is taken up again. In many poetical parts of the Old Testament, the speakers change; as in Solomon's Song, which is mostly a dialogue. Here perfect nonsense is often made by reading the passage as if it were all spoken by the same person. In Isaiah the strain often varies most suddenly, and while one verse is addressed to the Jews, the next may be spoken to the Messiah or to the Gentiles. Is it not always well to notify this to the congregation? If the chapters and verses had been divided with a little common sense, this might be of less importance, but as our version is so clumsily chopped into fragments, the preacher must insert the proper paragraphs and divisions as he reads aloud.

In essence, your business is to make the Word plain. In Lombardy I observed great heaps of huge stones in the fields, which had been gathered out from the soil by diligent hands to make room for the crops. Your duty is to "gather out the stones," and leave the fruitful field of Scripture for your people to till. There are Orientalisms, metaphors, peculiar expressions, idioms, and other verbal memorabilia which arise from the Bible having been written in the East; all these you will do well to explain. To this end be diligent students of Oriental life. Let the geography of Palestine, its natural history, its fauna and its flora, be as familiar to you as those of your own native village. Then as you read you will interpret the Word, and your flock will be fed thereby.[2]

The chief part of your commenting, however, *should consist in applying the truth to the hearts of your hearers,* for he who merely comprehends the meaning of the letter without understanding how it bears upon the hearts and consciences of men, is like a man who causes the bellows of an organ to be blown, and then fails to place his fingers on the keys; it is of little service to supply men with information unless we urge upon them the practical inferences therefrom. Look, my brethren, straight down into the secret chambers of the human soul, and let fall the divine teaching through the window, and thus light will be carried to the heart and conscience. Make remarks suitable to the occasion, and applicable to the cases of those present. Show how a truth which was first heard in the days of David is still forcible and pertinent in these modern times, and you will thus endear the Scriptures to the minds of your people, who prize your remarks much more than you imagine. Clean the grand old pictures of the divine masters; hang them up in new frames; fix them on the walls of your people's memories, and their well-instructed hearts shall bless you.

Is a caution needed among intelligent men? Yes, it must be given. Be *sure to avoid being dull.* Avoid it everywhere, but especially in this. Do not be long in your notes. If you are supremely gifted, do not be long. People do not appreciate too much of a good thing; and if your comments are only second-rate, why, then be shorter still, for men soon weary of inferior talking. Very little time in the service can be afforded for reading the sessions. Do not rob the prayer and the sermon for the sake of commenting. This robbing Peter to pay Paul is senseless. Do not repeat common-place things which must have occurred even to a Sunday school child. Do not remind your hearers of what they could not possibly have forgotten. Give them something weighty if not new, so that an intelligent listener may feel when the service is over that he has learned at least a little.

---

2. For suggestions as to interpretation the student is referred to the *Bible Handbook* by Dr. Joseph Angus. From page 150 of that work and onwards, the most valuable hints will be met with. Much that we would otherwise have inserted in this volume is admirably stated by our learned friends.

Again, *avoid all pedantry.* As a general rule, it may be observed that those gentlemen who know the least Greek are the most sure to air their rags of learning in the pulpit. They miss no chance of saying, "The Greek is so-and-so." It makes a man an inch and a-half taller by a foolometer, if he everlastingly lets fall bits of Greek and Hebrew, and even tells the people the tense of the verb and the case of the noun, as I have known some do. Those who have no learning usually make a point of displaying the pegs on which learning ought to hand. Brethren, the whole process of interpretation is to be carried on in your study. You are not to show your congregation the process, but to give them the result; like a good cook who would never think of bringing up dishes, pans, rolling pin, and spice box into the dining hall, but without ostentation sends up the feast.

Never strain passages when you are expounding. Be thoroughly honest with the Word. Even if the Scriptures were the writing of mere men, conscience would demand fairness of you; but when it is the Lord's own Word, be careful not to pervert it even in the smallest degree. Let it be said of you, as I have heard a venerable hearer of Mr. Simeon say of him, "Sir, he was very Calvinistic when the text was so, and people thought him an Arminian when the text was that way, for he always stuck to its plain sense." A very sound neighbor of ours once said, by way of depreciating the grand old reformer, "John Calvin was not half a Calvinist," and the remark was correct as to his expositions, for in them, as we have seen, he always gave his Lord's mind and not his own. In the church of St. Zeno, in Verona, I saw ancient frescoes which had been plastered over, and then covered with other designs. I fear many do this with Scripture, daubing the text with their own glosses, and laying on their own conceits. There are enough of these plasterers abroad, let us leave the evil trade to them and follow an honest calling. Remember Cowper's lines:

> A critic on the sacred text should be
>
> Candid and learn'd, dispassionate and free;
>
> Free from the wayward bias bigots feel,
>
> From fancy's influence and intemperate zeal;
>
> For of all arts sagacious dupes invent,
>
> To cheat themselves and gain the world's assent,
>
> The worst is-Scripture warped from its intent.

Use your judgment more than your fancy. Flowers are well enough, but hungry souls prefer bread. To allegorize with Origen may make men stare at you, but your work is to fill men's mouths with truth, not to open them with wonder.

Do not be carried away with new meanings. Some brethren delight to fish up some hitherto undiscovered tadpole of interpretation, and cry it round the town as a rare dainty. Let us be content with more ordinary and more wholesome fishery. No one text is to be exalted above the plain analogy of faith, and no solitary expression is to shape our theology for us. Other men and wiser men have expounded before us, and anything undiscovered by them, it were well to put to test and trial before we boast too loudly of the treasure-trove.

Do not needlessly amend our Authorized Version. It is faulty in many places, but still it is a grand work taking it for all in all, and it is unwise to be making every old lady distrust the only Bible she can get at, or what is more likely, mistrust you for falling out with her cherished treasure. Correct where correction must be for truth's sake, but never for the vainglorious display of your critical ability. When reading short Psalms, or connected passages of the other books, *do not split up the author's utterances by interjecting your notes.* Read the paragraph through, and then go over it again with your explanations; breaking it up as you may think fit at the second reading. No one would dream of dividing a stanza of a poet with an explanatory remark. It would be treason to common sense to do so; sound judgment will forbid your thus marring the Word of God. Better far never to comment than to cut and carve the utterances of inspiration and obscure their meaning by impertinently thrusting in untimely remarks of your own. Upon many passages comments would be gross folly. Never think of painting the lily or gilding refined gold; leave the sublime sentences alone in their glory. I speak as unto wise men; prove your wisdom in this thing also.

If I were bound to deliver a sermon upon the subject in hand, I could not desire a better text than Nehemiah 8:8: "So they read in the book in the law of God distinctly, and gave the sense, and caused them to understand the reading." Here is a hint for the reader as to his *reading.* Let it always be distinct. Aim to be good readers, and be the more anxious about it because few men are so, and all preachers ought to be so. It is as good as a sermon to hear our best men read the Scriptures; they bring out the meaning by their correct emphasis and tone. Never fall into the idea that the mere utterance of the words before you is all that is required of you in reading; good reading is a high, but rare attainment. Even if you do not comment, yet read the chapter previously, and become familiar with it; it is inexcusable for a man to betray the fact that he is out of his latitude in the reading, traversing untrodden ground, floundering and picking his way across country, like a huntsman who has lost his bearings. Never open the Bible in the pulpit to read the chapter for the first time, but go to the familiar page after many rehearsals. You will be doubly useful if in addition to this you *"give the sense."* You will then, by God's blessing, be the pastor of an intelligent, Bible loving people. You will hear in your church that delightful rustle of Bible leaves which is so dear to the lover of the Word; your people will open their Bibles, looking for a feast. The Word will become increasingly precious to yourself, your knowledge will enlarge, and your aptness to teach will become everyday more apparent. Try it, my brethren, for even if you should see cause to discontinue it, at least no harm will come of the attempt.

In all that I have said I have given you another reason for seeking the aid of the Holy Spirit. If you do not understand a book by a departed writer, you are unable to ask him his meaning, but the Spirit, who inspired Holy Scripture, lives forever, and he delights to open up the Word to those who seek his instruction. He is always accessible: "He dwelleth with you and shall be in you." Go to Him for yourselves and cry, "Open thou mine eyes that I may behold wondrous things out of thy law;" and, this being granted you, entreat him to send forth His light and power with the Word when you expound it, that your hearers also may be led into all truth. Commentaries, expositions, interpretations, are all mere scaffolding; the Holy Spirit Himself must edify you and help you to build up the church of the living God.

SECTION THREE
CATALOG OF BIBLE COMMENTARIES AND EXPOSITIONS

REMARKS UPON THE CATALOG OF COMMENTARIES

This catalog is compiled for the use of ministers, and the brief reviews are written from that standpoint. Other useful lists have been published, specially those by Darling, Orme, and Hartwell Horne, but these are not easily procurable and are not quite what is needed; and therefore as the furnishing of the Pastor's College Library necessitated a catalog, and afforded an opportunity for purchasing books, the present work has been produced. Few can conceive the amount of toil which this compilation has involved, both to myself and my industrious secretary, Mr. J. L. Keys. In almost every case books have been actually examined by myself, and my opinion, whatever it may be worth, is an original one. A complete list of all comments has not been attempted. Numbers of volumes have been left out because they were not easily procurable, or were judged to be worthless, although some of both these classes have been admitted as specimens, or as warnings.

The reader will please observe that the books *most heartily recommended* are listed with *** after the books. *Good,* but more ordinary works are with **, and the *least desirable* with *. Thus, we hope the eye will be caught at once by volumes most worthy of attention.

Latin authors are not inserted, because few can procure them, and fewer still can read them with ease. We are not, however, ignorant of their value. Hosts of family Bibles, discourses, and paraphrases are omitted, because they would have wasted our limited space, and we could only have omitted them by raising the price of our book, which we resolved not to do, lest it should be out of the reach of men of slender incomes. The first volume of this series[1] has had so excellent a circulation that we are able to issue this

---

1. Charles H. Spurgeon, *Lectures to My Students,* a selection from addresses delivered to the students of the Pastor's College, Metropolitan Tabernacle. Baker Book House and Zondervan Publishing House.

second one, although we know from the nature of the work that its sale will, in all probability, never cover the cost of production. We *give* the labor to our brethren freely, only wishing that we could with it confer upon our poorer friends the means of purchasing the choicest of the comments here mentioned.

It is to be specially noted, that *in no case do we endorse all that any author has written in his commentary.* We could not read the works through; it would have needed a Methuselah to do that. Nor have we thought it needful to omit a book because it contains a measure of error, provided it is useful in its own way; for this catalog is for thoughtful, discerning men, and not for children. We have not, however, knowingly mentioned works whose main drift is skeptical or Socinian, except with a purpose. Where we have admitted comments by writers of doubtful doctrine, because of their superior scholarship and the correctness of their criticisms, we have given hints which will be enough for the wise. It is sometimes very useful to know what our opponents have to say.

The writers on the prophetical books have completely mastered us, and after almost completing a full list we could not in our conscience believe that a tithe of them would yield anything to the student but bewilderment, and therefore we reduced the number to small dimensions. We reverence the teaching of the prophets, and the Apocalypse, but for many of the professed expounders of those inspired books we entertain another feeling.

May God bless this laborious endeavor to aid His ministers in searching the Scriptures. If biblical studies shall be in any measure promoted, we shall be more than repaid.

COMMENTARIES ON THE WHOLE BIBLE

1 **Allen, John** – **A SPIRITUAL EXPOSITION OF THE OLD AND NEW TESTAMENTS;** or, The Christian's Gospel Treasure. 3 vols., 1816. *
Spiritual reflections after the high calvinistic school. Some preachers cannot see Christ where He is, but Allen finds Him where He is not. There is in these reflections much godly savor, but very little exposition.

2 **Assembly of Divines, Westminster** – **ANNOTATIONS.** 2 vols., 1657. **
Contain valuable remarks, but are somewhat out of date. The work is probably less esteemed than it should be (see page 17).

3 **Barth, C. G.** – **PRACTICAL COMMENTARY ON THE BOOKS OF HOLY SCRIPTURE.** Arranged in chronological order, being a Bible manual for the use of students of the Word of God. ***
Helpful in showing the historical position of the books, and in assisting to illustrate them by the circumstances under which they were written. We have referred to it with benefit.

4 **Benson, Joseph** (1748-1821) – **NOTES, CRITICAL, EXPLANATORY, AND PRACTICAL.** 6 vols. **
Adopted by the Wesleyan Conference as a standard work, and characterized by that body as marked by "solid learning, soundness of theological opinion, and an edifying attention to experimental and practical religion."

5 **BIBLICAL MUSEUM, by James C. Gray,** Revised edition reissued as **GRAY AND ADAMS' BIBLE COMMENTARY.** 6 vols. ***
We can only speak of the New Testament; it is surpassingly useful, sententious and sensible. Buy the work at once.

6 **Bonar, Horatius** – **LIGHT AND TRUTH; or BIBLE THOUGHTS AND THEMES.** 5 vols. ***
One volume is rather short space in which to bring out the "light and truth" of the Old Testament. If Dr. Bonar required four volumes for the New Testament, we wish he had felt the same need for the Old. The passages selected are popularly expounded, but the thought is not deep. The volumes will be more prized by the ordinary reader than by the minister.

7 **Boothroyd, Benjamin** – **FAMILY BIBLE.** 1824, 1853 **
Good, but may now be dispensed with, now that the East has been more fully explored.

8 **Brown, John** (1722-1787) – **SELF-INTERPRETING BIBLE. ****
Useful in its day, and still popular. Notes on the New Testament an undisguised plagiarism from Guyse. Not a student's book.

9 **Burder, Samuel** – **THE SCRIPTURE EXPOSITOR.** A New Commentary, Critical and Practical. 4 vols., 1811. ******
Well–selected notes. Those upon Eastern manners, geography, etc., are collected very judiciously.

10 **Calvin, John** – **THE WORKS OF JOHN CALVIN.** Reprint edition, 45 vols. in 22 bindings. Baker Book House. *******
Of priceless value. See pages 11 – 13 of this work.

11 **Chalmers, Thomas** (1780-1847) – **DAILY SCRIPTURE READINGS.** 3 vols., and, **SABBATH SCRIPTURE READINGS**, 2 vols. These are volumes 1 to 4 of the "Posthumous Works" of Dr. Chalmers, edited by Rev. W. Hanna. *******
Those acquainted with the writings of Chalmers will know what to expect from his pen when guided by fervent devotion.

12 **Clarke, Adam** – **ADAM CLARKE'S COMMENTARY.** 3 vols., Abingdon Press. 1 vol., Baker Book House, Beacon Hill Press. *******
Despite some few oddities, this is one of the most learned of English expositions. See page 16.

13 **Clarke, Samuel** – **THE OLD AND NEW TESTAMENT,** with annotations and parallel Scriptures. 1690. ******
Notes very brief, but judicious. Author one of the ejected ministers, an exceedingly learned man. This work was highly commended by Owen, Baxter, Howe, and others, but is now superseded.

14 **THE CLASS AND THE DESK, by James C. Gray** and C. Stokes Carey. 4 vols. *******
Condensed thought. Suited for teachers and local preachers.

15 **Cobbin, Ingram** – **A CONDENSED COMMENTARY ON THE BIBLE.** 1839. ******
An excellent makeshift for a poor man.

16 **Cobbin, Ingram** – **EVANGELICAL SYNOPSIS.** The Holy Bible with notes explanatory and practical, selected from the writings of the most esteemed divines and biblical critics. 3 vols. ******
An admirable collection of notes. Men with small means will find it a miniature library. We have heard brethren who have had no commentary but Cobbin's speak of the work with much enthusiasm.

17 **Coke, Thomas** – **A COMMENTARY ON THE OLD AND NEW TESTAMENT.** 6 vols., 1803. *****
A Wesleyan comment. Too big; ought to have been put in half the space. Moreover, it is next door to a fraud, for it is "in the main a reprint of the work of Dr. Dodd," without that author's name. Ah, Dr. Coke, this is a burning shame!

18 **COMMENTARY WHOLLY BIBLICAL.** An exposition in the very words of Scripture. 3 vols. Published later under the title: *The Bible Self-Explained.* Moody Press. ******
It is very handy to have explanatory passages thus presented to the eye. In

general the work is excellently done; but ministers with scanty purses can make a biblical exposition for themselves.

19 **THE COMPREHENSIVE BIBLE.** W. Greenfield, ed. The Old and New Testaments, with the various readings and marginal notes, parallel passages systematically arranged, numerous philological and explanatory notes, etc. **
Generally used as a pulpit Bible. Said to contain 4,000 notes and 500,000 parallel passages, being all those of Blayney, Scott, Clarke, and others. The tables, notes, introductions, etc. are of standard value.

20 **Diodati, John –ANNOTATIONS PLAINLY EXPOUNDING THE MOST DIFFICULT PLACES.** 1651 **
Edward Bickersteth says: "The spiritual and evangelical remarks are of much value." Diodati's notes are short and worth consulting.

21 **Dodd, William – A COMMENTARY ON THE BOOKS OF THE OLD AND NEW TESTAMENT.** Inserted are the notes and collections of John Locke, Daniel Waterland, the Earl of Claredon and other learned persons with practical improvements. 1770. *
An almost forgotten production of the unhappy Dodd. It is founded on the manuscript collections of Cudworth, Waterland, Clarendon, and others. Not very likely to quicken piety, or inspire spiritual thought; yet, as Adam Clarke thought very highly of it, and Dr. Coke appropriated it, it must have some value.

22 **D'Oyly, George and Mant, R. – NOTES.** Taken principally from the Church of England writers. 3 vols., 1845. **
Of moderate value. More fitted for the family than the study. A compilation most appreciated among Episcopalians.

23 **DUTCH ANNOTATIONS** upon the whole Bible. As ordered by the Synod of Dort, 1618, and published in English by Theodore Haak. 2 vols., 1657. **
Similar to the Westminster Assembly's *Annotations* (see page 17).

24 **Fausset, A. R.** (also Jamieson, Robert and Brown, David) – **A COMMENTARY ON THE OLD AND NEW TESTAMENTS.** 3 vols., Wm. B. Eerdmans Publishing Co.; 1 vol. abridged edition, Zondervan Publishing House. ***
A really standard work. We consult it continually, and with growing interest. Mr. Fausset's portion strikes us as being of the highest order. See page 23.

25 **FOURFOLD UNION COMMENTARY;** Containing:
   I. Parallel Texts, in full
   II. Matthew Henry's Commentary
   III. Scott's Commentary
   IV. Commentary by Jamieson, Fausset, and Brown to which is added the *Biblical Cyclopaedia* by Dr. John Eadie, a Biblical Atlas, etc. 2 vols., 1872. ***
A Christian man wishing for the cream of expository writers could not make a better purchase. Ministers, as a rule, should not buy condensations, but get the works themselves.

26 **Fraser, Donald – SYNOPTICAL LECTURES ON THE BOOKS OF HOLY SCRIPTURES. *****
First Series–Genesis to Song of Solomon
Second Series–Isaiah to Acts
Dr. Fraser has observed, like many others of us, the mischief which results from cutting the Bible into fragments, and using it piecemeal. In these volumes he discourses the Bible at large, indicates the scope of each book, and furnishes a brief digest of its contents. He has compressed rigorously. The design was in itself most laudable, and it has been well carried out.

27 **Gill, John – AN EXPOSITION OF THE OLD AND NEW TESTAMENT. 9 vols. Primitive Baptist Library. *****
Invaluable in its own line of things. For extended remarks, see pages 14 - 16.

28 **Haak, Theodore.** See *Dutch Annotations* (No. 23). **

29 **Hall, Joseph – CONTEMPLATIONS.** The edition has a memoir of the good Bishop by the late Dr. James Hamilton. 1844. ***
The work can be readily procured; but if its price were raised in proportion to its real value, it would become one of the most costly books extant. (See page 17.)

30 **Hall, Joseph – A PLAIN AND FAMILIAR EXPLICATION**, by way of paraphrase, of all the hard texts of the whole divine Scriptures. 1633. **
Not so pithy as the *Contemplations;* nor, indeed, could it be expected to be so. It is not necessary to the student, but might be useful.

31 **Haweis, Thomas – THE EVANGELICAL EXPOSITOR. 2 vols., 1765-66. ***
Partakes of the author's character; for of him it has been said, that "he was rather useful than eminent." The work is mainly an abridgment of Matthew Henry.

32 **Hawker, Robert – THE POOR MAN'S COMMENTARY. 3 vols., 1843. ****
Full of devotion and sweetness. See pages 18 and 19.

33 **Henry, Matthew – A COMMENTARY OF THE WHOLE BIBLE.** 6 vols., Fleming H. Revell Company. 1 vol. abridged edition, Zondervan Publishing House. ***
For remarks, see pages 10 and 11.

34 **Holden, George – CHRISTIAN EXPOSITOR. 2 vols., 1837. ****
Notes highly spoken of; we consider them the most ordinary of platitudes.

35 **Jamieson, Robert, Fausset, A. R. and Brown, David – A COMMENTARY ON THE OLD AND NEW TESTAMENTS. 3 vols.,** Wm. B. Eerdmans Publishing Co.; 1 vol. abridged edition, Zondervan Publishing House. ***
A really standard work. We consult it continually, and with growing interest. Mr. Fausset's portion strikes us as being of the highest order. (See page 23.)

The following are different forms or abridgments of the same work, each of which we can highly recommend:

36 **Jamieson, Robert – THE COMPLETE COMMENTARY. ***** (2 vols.) See No. 25 and 35.

37 **Jamieson, Robert – THE STUDENT'S COMMENTARY. ***** (4 vols.)

38 **Jamieson, Robert – THE PORTABLE COMMENTARY. ***** (2 vols.)

39 **Kitto, John –THE PICTORIAL BIBLE.** 4 vols., 1855. *******
A work of art as well as learning. See page 20.

40 **Kitto, John – THE ILLUSTRATED COMMENTARY OF THE OLD AND NEW TESTAMENTS.** A reproduction of the notes, etc. of *The Pictorial Bible.* 5 vols., 1840. *******
The omission of the text renders the work cheaper.

41 **Kitto, John – KITTO'S DAILY BIBLE ILLUSTRATIONS,** being original readings for a year, on subjects relating to sacred history, biography, geography, antiquities, and theology. New edition, edited and revised by F. L. Porter. Kregel Publications. See page 20. *******

42 **LANGE'S COMMENTARY ON THE HOLY SCRIPTURES.** Phillip Schaff, ed., 12 vols. *******
The volumes greatly differ in excellence, yet none could be spared. We have nothing equal to them as a series. See page 23.

43 **Lees, Fred R.** and **Burns, Dawson – THE TEMPERANCE BIBLE COMMENTARY.** 1872. ******
Readers will probably estimate the value of this work according to their views upon total abstinence. This question appears to be one which renders both advocates and opponents too warm either to give or accept a cool, impartial verdict; we shall not therefore offer one.

44 **Leigh, Edward – ANNOTATIONS FROM JOB TO CANTICLES.** 1657. ******

ANNOTATIONS UPON ALL THE NEW TESTAMENT Philological and theological. 1650. ******
Frequently associated with *Richardson* on the Old Testament. See No. 71. Good, brief notes. Antique, but still prized.

CRITICA SACRA. In two parts: 1) "Observations on all the primitive Hebrew words of the Old Testament." 2) "Philological and theological observations on all the Greek words of the New Testament." 1662. ******
Horne says this is "a very valuable help to the understanding of the original languages." Parkhurst valued it.

45 **Mant, R.** See D'Oyly. ******

46 Mayer, John – A COMMENTARY ON THE WHOLE OLD TES-
TAMENT. 6 vols., and 1 vol., 1653. The seventh volume, containing
the Catholic Epistles and Revelation. For remarks, see pages 16-17. **
Laborious writing and heavy reading.

47 Millington, Thomas S. – THE TESTIMONY OF THE HEATHEN
TO THE TRUTHS OF HOLY WRIT. Compiled almost exclusively
from Greek and Latin authors of the classical ages of antiquity.
1863. **
It was a capital idea to lay the heathen under contribution. The author is at
home in the classics, and has performed his work well.

48 Ness, Christopher – HISTORY AND MYSTERY. 4 vols., 1690-96.
***
Quaint, pithy, suggestive. Full of remarks such as are to be found in Thomas
Fuller and Bishop Hall. See page 17.

49 THE NEW BIBLE COMMENTARY – Sometimes spoken of as
THE SPEAKER'S BIBLE COMMENTARY. F.C. Cook, editor.
See page 23. 1871. **
The proverb concerning too many cooks applies also to commentators. The
work is good, but it might have been better.

50 Patrick and Lowth – A CRITICAL COMMENTARY. Corrected by
the Rev. F. R. Pitman, 6 vols., 1822. ***
There are other editions, but some of them do not contain the whole of the
commentary; the above is one of the best. Good edition in smaller type. 4 vols.
See page 22.

51 Poole, Matthew – COMMENTARY ON THE WHOLE BIBLE.
The Banner of Truth. ***
See title and remarks on page 13.

52 Purver, Anthony – A NEW AND LITERAL TRANSLATION. 2
vols., 1764. *
A Quaker translation. Often ungrammatical and unintelligible. Not without
its good points, but much more curious than useful.

53 RELIGIOUS TRACT SOCIETY'S COMMENTARY. From Henry
and Scott, with numerous observations from other writers. With the
text and maps, 6 vols. **
The abridgements are carefully executed.

54 Scott, Thomas – COMMENTARY ON THE HOLY BIBLE. 6 vols.
Thomas Nelson Publishers. For remarks, see page 18. ***
F. M. Neale says of Scott's practical observations, "They are such as some men
would not take the trouble of even thinking, many would not be at the pains of
speaking, and—one should have imagined, were not the fact as it is—such as
no man would have condescended to write down." This judgment is far too
severe, and reveals the High churchman; it raises Scott in our esteem.

55 Simeon, Charles – EXPOSITORY OUTLINES ON THE WHOLE
BIBLE. (Previously entitled *Horae Homileticae*.) Discourses digested into one continued series, and forming a comment upon every
book of the Old and New Testament. 21 vols. 1845. **

Not commentaries, but we could not exclude them. They have been called "a valley of dry bones": be a prophet and they will live.

56 THE SPEAKER'S BIBLE COMMENTARY. See *New Bible Commentary*, No. 49. **

57 Sutcliffe, Joseph – A COMMENTARY. Containing copious notes. **
To comprise the whole Bible in one volume necessitated notes few and brief. *Sutcliffe*, though an Arminian, is in general so good that we wish we had more of him; his style is vivacious and forcible.

58 THE TEMPERANCE BIBLE COMMENTARY. See Fred Lees, No. 43. **

59 Trapp, John – COMMENTARY. 5 vols., 1654. ***
Oh, rare John Trapp! See page 14.

60 Wall, William – CRITICAL NOTES ON THE OLD AND NEW TESTAMENT. 3 vols., 1730-34. *
Dr. Wall was the greatest champion of infant baptism against the learned Gale. His notes are good, but out of date.

61 Wells, Edward – HELP FOR THE MORE EASY AND CLEAR UNDERSTANDING OF THE HOLY SCRIPTURES. 6 vols., 1724. **
Seldom to be met with complete, but need not be regretted, for though somewhat useful, it is not of primary importance.

62 Wesley, John – NOTES ON OLD AND NEW TESTAMENT, 4 vols., London, 1764. EXPLANATORY NOTES UPON THE NEW TESTAMENT, 2 vols., Beacon Hill Press; Baker Book House. **
The notes on the New Testament are esteemed, but Dr. Clark say that those on the Old are meagre and unsatisfactory. He is quite right.

63 Wilson, Thomas – THE HOLY BIBLE WITH NOTES. Various Renderings, by the Rev. C. Crutwell, 3 vols., 1785. *
The good Bishop's notes are brief hints, only intended for the explanation or practical improvement of certain passages; their value to biblical students is inconsiderable. Crutwell's various readings are numerous.

64 Wordsworth, Christopher. See page 22. ***

65 Young, Robert – COMMENTARY ON THE BIBLE, as literally and idiomatically translated. *
Too small to be of any use. You cannot put the sea into a tea cup.

OLD TESTAMENT OR CONSIDERABLE PORTIONS

66 Ainsworth, Henry – ANNOTATIONS UPON THE FIVE BOOKS OF MOSES, THE BOOK OF PSALMS AND THE SONG OF SONGS; wherein the Hebrew words and sentences are compared with the Greek and Chaldee versions, 1627 and 1639. ***
"Ainsworth was a celebrated scholar and an excellent divine. His uncommon skill in Hebrew learning, and his excellent commentaries on the Scriptures are held in high reputation to this day."— Brook's *Lives of the Puritans*.

67 **Hengstenberg, E. W. – CHRISTOLOGY OF THE OLD TESTAMENT:** A Commentary on the Messianic Predictions. 4 vols. condensed into 1. Kregel Publications. **
This great work deals with a most vital theme in a masterly manner; it has always been held in high esteem. We confess, however, that we can only read it as a task, for the dry scholastic style repels us, and it seems to us that in answering a number of skeptical doctors, whose opinions are ridiculous, the author has made much ado about nothing.

68 **Horsley, Samuel – BIBLICAL CRITICISM** on the first fourteen historical books of the Old Testament; also on the Prophetical Books. Second edition, 2 vols., 1844. **
These criticisms will be of more interest to the scholar than of value to the minister. Horsley was far too ready to invent new readings; yet he was a master in his own line. He writes very dogmatically and with a violent bias toward a theory of interpretation which, with all its excellencies, cannot be everywhere maintained. Numbers of other writers have followed in his track, but none with equal footsteps.

69 **Jackson, Arthur – A HELP FOR THE UNDERSTANDING OF THE HOLY SCRIPTURES.** Genesis to Isaiah, 4 vols., 1643. **
Rather tame, but will repay quiet reading. His works are now somewhat rare. See page 17.

70 **Orton, Job – EXPOSITION OF THE OLD TESTAMENT,** with devotional and practical reflections, from the author's manuscripts, by Robert Gentleman. 6 vols., 1788. Reprinted, 1822. **
A sort of paraphrase, after the manner of Doddridge's *Family Expositor,* which it was intended to accompany. Not a very able production.

71 **Richardson, John – CHOICE OBSERVATIONS AND EXPLANATIONS UPON THE OLD TESTAMENT,** containing in them many remarkable matters, additional to the large annotations made by some of the Assembly of Divines. 1655. **
Of secondary importance, and very short; yet good. Frequently bound up with *Leigh* (No. 44).

THE PENTATEUCH

72 **Ainsworth, Henry – ANNOTATIONS ON THE PENTATEUCH.** See also No. 66. 1616. ***
Thoroughly learned. Though old, not out of date.

73 **Alexander, William – THE PENTATEUCH WITH NOTES.** *
A book of no importance.

74 **Babington, Gervase –** In Babington's **WORKS,** 1622, there are "Certain plain, brief, and comfortable notes" upon the first five books of Moses. *
Our copy is in the old Black Letter. It contains little to repay the student for toiling through the old-fashioned expressions.

75 **Barrett, R. A. – A SYNOPSIS OF CRITICISMS** upon those passages of the Old Testament in which modern commentators have differed from the Authorized Version. 2 vols. in 2 parts each, and vol.

3, part 1, 1847. (Only extends from Genesis to Esther.) **
The object of this work is to lay before the reader the principal alterations
which modern critics have proposed in the Authorized Version, together with
the reasons for or against such emendations. Many of the notes are in Latin.
Of small use to the average minister.

76 **Bate, Julius – NEW LITERAL TRANSLATION OF THE PEN-
TATEUCH AND HISTORICAL BOOKS TO END OF 2 KINGS.**
With notes, 1773. *
We greatly grudge the four shillings which we gave for it.

77 **BIBLE TEACHINGS; or Remarks on Genesis, Exodus, and Leviticus. With recommendatory preface by Rev. W. B. Mackenzie,
1855. ***
This book was written by the three Misses Bird, of Taplow. The remarks are
very plain and practical, and a spirit of earnest piety and fervent prayer
pervades them throughout.

78 **Blunt, Henry – FAMILY EXPOSITION OF PENTATEUCH.** 3
vols., 1844. *
See remarks under each separate volume (Nos. 109, 167, and 228).

79 **Brightwell, T. – NOTES**, selected from the exegetical parts of
Rosenmüller's *Scholia,* and of Dathe's *Notes* to his Latin version. Also
from Schrank, Michaelis, Le Clerc, Ainsworth, Poole, and other authors, 1840. **
This writer worked very industriously at the almost impossible task of
condensing the 28 volumes of Rosenmüller's *Notes.* Besides the remarks from
authors mentioned in the text, there are observations from the manuscripts of
Joseph Kinghorn, of Norwich. It is not a didactic or spiritual work, but almost
entirely explanatory and illustrative.

80 **CHRIST IN THE LAW;** or The Gospel Foreshadowed in the Pentateuch. Compiled by a priest of the Church of England. **CHRIST IN
THE PROPHETS** – Joshua to Kings, 2 vols., 1872 and 1873. *
Of the High Church order, and praised by the *Saturday Review.* What worse
need be said? Yet will we add that the savor of Christ in these books saves them
from unqualified condemnation.

81 **Delgado, Isaac – NEW TRANSLATION.** 1789. *
The author modestly says, that his work is *highly useful.* This is another
instance of paternal partiality, and of "great cry and little wool."

82 **Etheridge, J. W. – THE TARGUMS** of Onkelos and Jonathan Ben
Uzziel on the Pentateuch, with the fragments of the Jerusalem Targum.
Leviticus, Numbers, and Deuteronomy, 1865. *
Comparatively few of our readers will set much store by the Targums of
Onkelos and Jonathan Ben Uzziel; but those who desire to read them will find
here a good literal version.

83 **Geddes, Alexander – TRANSLATION FROM CORRECTED
TEXTS WITH VARIOUS READINGS AND NOTES.** (Genesis to
Ruth only published.) 3 vols., 1792-1800. *
The author was a Hebraist of considerable repute, but treated the inspired word
far too flippantly. His style of criticism is essentially skeptical.

84 **Von Gerlach, Otto** (1801-1849) – **PENTATEUCH.** Translated by
    the Rev. Henry Downing. ******
    Very different from other German authors. Plain, clear, and instructive. Not
    choked up with metaphysical bewilderments and long lists of skeptical authors
    whose names defile the pages which bear them.

85 **Hävernick, H. A.** – **HISTORICO-CRITICAL INTRODUCTION
    TO THE PENTATEUCH.** Translated by A. Thomson. 1850. *****
    Almost entirely occupied with a discussion upon the genuineness of the Pen-
    tateuch. A check to the rationalistic and infidel spirit. Those who have never
    taken the poison do not need the antidote.

86 **Hengstenberg, E. W. – GENUINENESS OF THE PENTATEUCH.**
    Translated by J. E. Ryland. 2 vols., 1847. ******
    This great author contends ably for the Pentateuch, but the perusal of his book
    reminds of the king who
            Fought all his battles o'er again,
            And thrice he routed all his foes,
            and thrice he slew the slain.

87 **Hengstenberg, E. W. – EGYPT AND THE BOOKS OF MOSES;** or
    The Books of Moses Illustrated by the Monuments of Egypt. 1845. ******
    Dr. Hengstenberg, as Professor at Berlin, had access to the rich collection of
    Egyptian antiquities in the Museums, and he has made noble use of his
    advantages.

88 **Howard, E. J.** –1857.
    1. **GENESIS ACCORDING TO THE LXX.** Translated into English,
    with notes on the passages in which it differs from our Authorized
    Version. *****
    2. **EXODUS AND LEVITICUS. ***
    3. **NUMBERS AND DEUTERONOMY. ***
    Of no particular use to preachers; but the *Guardian* says, "It is an excellent
    introduction to the comparative study of God's word in those three languages
    with which an ordinary English student is mainly concerned."

89 **Jamieson, J.** – **THE PENTATEUCH,** with notes, etc. 1748. *****
    Published anonymously. Mainly a compilation, in which more industry was
    shown in the collection than discretion in the selection.

90 **Kalisch, M. M.** – **HISTORICAL AND CRITICAL COMMEN-
    TARY ON THE OLD TESTAMENT;** with a new translation. 1858.******
    Vol. 1 – Genesis
    Vol. 2 – Exodus
    Vol. 3 – Leviticus, part 1
    Vol. 4 – Leviticus, part 2
    Contains a large amount of historical illustration, shedding new light upon the
    letter of the Word. The author has used the fresh information which has come
    to us from the Euphrates and the Nile. At the same time he sows skepticisms
    and we cannot recommend him.

91 **Keil, Carl Friedrich** – **THE PENTATEUCH.** Wm. B. Eerdmans
    Publishing Co. ******
    A work for the learned. It has received the highest commendations from
    competent scholars. But it is somewhat dull and formal.

92 **Kelly, William** – INTRODUCTORY LECTURES ON THE PENTATEUCH. Believer's Bookshelf, Inc. *
By a leading writer of the exclusive Plymouth school. Not to our mind.

93 **Kidder, Richard** – FIVE BOOKS OF MOSES. 2 vols., 1694. *
Of no importance: a chip in the porridge: mild as a modern bishop.

94 **Kingsley, Charles** – THE GOSPEL OF THE PENTATEUCH. (18 sermons). 1875. **
A small volume of Kingsley's usual sort. Not over-freighted with what is usually known as the Gospel; but plain and practical with common sense remarks for common people.

95 **Law, Henry** – "CHRIST IS ALL:" The Gospel of the Old Testament. 4 vols. ***
Deservedly popular. Simple, instructive, full of Christ. Law abounds in gospel.

96 **MacDonald, Donald** – INTRODUCTION AND AN ENQUIRY into the genuineness, authority and design of the mosaic writings. 2 vols., 1861. **
"A full review of the evidence, external and internal, for the genuineness, authenticity, and Divine character of the Pentateuch. Its special attention is devoted to the connection between the Pentateuch and the great scheme of revelation, of which it forms the basis."— *Guardian.*

97 **Morison, James** – INTRODUCTORY KEY TO THE FIRST FOUR BOOKS OF MOSES; being an attempt to show that the great design of the things recorded therein was the sufferings of Christ and the following glory. 1810. *
Plain, forcible, and instructive remarks, realizing the title–an Introductory Key.

98 **Parker, Samuel** – BIBLIOTHECA BIBLICA. A commentary gathered out of the writings of fathers and ecclesiastical historians, etc. (Anonymous.) 5 vols. (Genesis to Deuteronomy only completed,) 1720. *
Darling says that this is "a commentary of profound learning and research;" but it seems to us to be mainly filled with that archaic learning which is now out of date.

99 **Pierce, Samuel Eyles** – DISCOURSES on the several revelations of the Lord Jesus, from the fall to Moses. 1815. *
Dr. Hawker says that "these discourses carry with them testimonies of being written under Divine teaching." Sweet, but not very expository.

100 **Pyle, Thomas** – PARAPHRASE WITH NOTES. 4 vols., 1717-28. (Genesis to Esther only). *
A pile of paper, valuable to housemaids for lighting fires.

101 **Robertson, James** – CLAVIS PENTATEUCHI. Analysis of the Hebrew words in the Pentateuch, with notes. 1824. *
Almost entirely in Latin, and therefore useful only to those who can readily read that language. The work was in good repute in its day.

**102 Saurin, James – DISSERTATIONS ON THE MOST MEMO-
RABLE EVENTS OF THE BIBLE.** Volume 1, *The Books of Moses*,
was all that was ever published in English. 1723. *
More eloquent than accurate. Florid rather than solid.

103 Shepheard, H. – TRADITIONS OF EDEN; or Proofs of the Historical Truth of the Pentateuch, from existing facts, and from the customs
and monuments of all nations. **
A very interesting and curious work. Good lectures might be gathered from
it for week–night instruction. Not a commentary.

**104 Stanley, Arthur Penrhyn – LECTURES ON THE HISTORY OF
THE JEWISH CHURCH.** 3 vols. 1870. **
Part 1- Abraham to Samuel.
Part 2- Samuel to the Captivity.
Part 3- Captivity to the Christian Era
A fascinating book, which no one can read without being the better able to
realize the scenes of Scripture history. The author's broad views are known
and deplored: that he has equal breadth of learning we cheerfully admit.

105 Thistlewaite, W. – EXPOSITORY SERMONS. 4 vols., 1837-38. *
Sermons as good as these are plentiful as blackberries. Why were they printed?

**106 Townsend, George – THE PENTATEUCH AND THE BOOK OF
JOB.** Arranged in chronological order with prayers and notes. 2 vols.,
1849. *
A singular combination of family prayers, essays, and notes, by an able but
singular writer.

107 Wright, Abraham – A PRACTICAL COMMENTARY, wherein
the text of every chapter is practically expounded, in a way not usually
trod by commentators. 1662. **
An extremely rare book. The style and matter are after the manner of
Christopher Ness. Wright does not comment upon every verse, but after
indicating the run of the chapter gives little sermons upon the more salient
points. He is very quaint and pithy.

GENESIS

**108 Alford, Henry – THE BOOK OF GENESIS AND PART OF THE
BOOK OF EXODUS (Chapters 1-25).** A revised version, with
commentary. Klock and Klock (Kregel Publications). ***
The works of this eminent scholar are too well–known and appreciated to need
even a word from us.

109 Blunt, Henry – GENESIS. (Vol. 1 of a *Family Exposition of the
Pentateuch,* 1841). **
Simple expositions for family reading. Good, but not brilliant.

110 Burroughs, W. K. – LECTURES ON GENESIS. 1848 *
Useful to grocers and buttermen. Worth nothing to students.

111 Bush, George – NOTES ON GENESIS. 2 vols. Klock and Klock
(Kregel Publications). **
Bush has in the most barefaced manner taken copious verbatim extracts from

Andrew Fuller, without acknowledgment, and he has also plagiarized Lawson on *Joseph* by wholesale, without even mentioning his name. For such a scholar to be guilty of wholesale plunder is inexcusable. It is one of the worst cases of robbery we have ever met with, and deserves a far stronger denunciation than our gentle pen and slender space will permit.

112 **Calvin, John – GENESIS.** Baker Book House; The Banner of Truth. *******
Participates in the general excellencies of Calvin's works.

113 **Candlish, Robert S. – STUDIES IN GENESIS.** 2 vols. in 1. Kregel Publications. *******
We venture to characterize this as THE work upon Genesis, so far as lectures can make up an exposition; we have greatly profited by its perusal. It should be in every biblical library.

114 **Close, Francis – HISTORICAL DISCOURSES.** 1828. *****
A course of smoothly-flowing, respectable, quiet, evangelical sermons. Nobody could be so wicked as to call them sensational.

115 **Coghlan, C. L. – GENESIS TO ST. MATTHEW.** 2 vols., 1832. *****
Consists entirely of parallel and illustrative passages of Scripture printed in full; it is superseded by the *Commentary Wholly Biblical*. (See No. 18.)

116 **Cumming, John – SCRIPTURE READINGS ON GENESIS.** 1853. ******
Dr. Cumming's works are not very original, but his style is flowing, his teachings are always evangelical, and he puts other men's thoughts into pleasing language.

117 **Dawson, Abraham – NEW TRANSLATION OF GENESIS (1-17),** with notes. 1763. *****
Tainted with infidelity. A writer of the Geddes school.

118 **Dimock, Henry – NOTES.** 1804. *****
Chiefly taken up with the various readings of Hebrew manuscripts. The young student will not value it. The same author has written on Exodus and the Prophets.

119 **Franks, James – SACRED LITERATURE;** or Remarks on Genesis. 1802. *****
This writer collected notes from various authors. As the sources from which he drew his extracts are within reach, we can select for ourselves.

120 **Fuller, Andrew** (1754-1815) **– EXPOSITORY DISCOURSES ON GENESIS.** One small vol. (Also in Fuller's *Works*.) *******
Weighty, judicious, and full of Gospel truth. One of the very best series of discourses extant on Genesis, as Bush also thought.

121 **Gibbens, Nicholas – QUESTIONS AND DISPUTATIONS CONCERNING THE HOLY SCRIPTURE: GENESIS.** 1602. *****
In his own fashion this antique writer tries to answer curious questions which are suggested by Genesis. His day is over.

122 **Greenfield, William – GENESIS IN ENGLISH AND HEBREW,** with an interlinear translation, notes, and gramatical introduction, 1862. ******

This work will not only enable the student to get at the literal meaning of the text, but may be used as an introduction to the Hebrew language. The plan is most admirable, and we earnestly commend it to the attention of those uninstructed in the sacred tongue.

123 **Groves, Henry Charles – COMMENTARY ON GENESIS,** for readers of the English version, 1861. **
Physical science, the discoveries of travelers, and the results of criticism, so far as they bear on Genesis, are here brought within the reach of the general reader.

124 **Harwood, T. – ANNOTATIONS. 1789. *
The author professed to offer his work with great diffidence, and he had just cause to do so: he had better have burned his manuscript.

125 **Hawker, John – BIBLE THOUGHTS IN QUIET HOURS: GENESIS.** 1873. **
Deeply spiritual reflections, not without learning and critical power. The preacher will find here many hints for sermons.

126 **Head, F. A. – THE WORLD AND ITS CREATOR.** 1847. *
One of the many *good* books which from lack of vigor are only "born to die."

127 **Hughes, George – ANALYTICAL EXPOSITION OF GENESIS, AND OF 23 CHAPTERS OF EXODUS.** 1672. ***
The deductions which Hughes draws from the text are of the nature of homiletical hints, and for this reason he will be a treasure to the minister. He belongs to the noble army of Puritans.

128 **Jacobus, Melancthon W. – NOTES.** 2 vols., 1866. ***
A very valuable work, in which Colenso is boldly met and answered. It contains much Gospel teaching, and aids the preacher greatly. Not easily to be obtained. It ought to be reprinted.

129 **Jervis-White-Jervis, John – GENESIS.** A new translation collated with the Samaritan, Septuagint, and Syriac, with notes. 1852. **
Brings out very vividly the oriental character of Genesis, and although we cannot reconcile ourselves to *Abh-rauhaum, Is' hauk, and Y' aakobh,* and find it hard to believe in *Saurauh* and *Haughaur,* we have been glad of the light which the East and its languages have here afforded.

130 **Jukes, Andrew – TYPES IN GENESIS.** Kregel Publications. **
In many places far too forced, and therefore to be read with caution; but in its own spiritualizing way very masterly. Jukes dives deep.

131 **Lange, J. P. –** *Commentary on Genesis,* in **LANGE'S COMMEN-TARY ON THE HOLY SCRIPTURES,** edited by Philip Schaff. ***
The best of the series, and in all respects beyond price.

132 **Mackintosh, C. H. – NOTES ON GENESIS.** Loizeaux Brothers. ***
Precious and edifying reflections marred by peculiarities.

133 **MacGregor, Sir C. Bartholomew – NOTES FOR STUDENTS IN DIVINITY.** Part 1 (Chapters 1-11), 1853. **
Contains a great deal of learning; of small use to the preacher. Many curious and knotty points which arise in the first 11 chapters of Genesis are discussed with considerable ability.

134 Murphy, James G. – COMMENTARY ON GENESIS, with a new translation. 1863. ***
"A work of massive scholarship, abounding in rich and noble thought, and remarkably fresh and suggestive."— *Evangelical Magazine*

135 Osburn, William – ISRAEL IN EGYPT; or, The Books of Genesis and Exodus Illustrated With Existing Monuments, 1856. **
Not a commentary; but a volume full of interest, which should be studied by all who would understand this portion of history.

136 Paul, William – ANALYSIS AND CRITICAL INTERPRETA-TION OF THE HEBREW TEXT, preceded by a Hebrew Grammar, 1852. *
Designed to promote the study of Hebrew. Not a comment, but rather a grammatical exercise. Useful to students of the sacred tongue.

137 Preston, Theodore – PHRASEOLOGICAL NOTES ON THE HEBREW TEXT. 1853. *
Intended to explain and illustrate the most remarkable peculiarities and anomalies of matter, style, and phrase in the Book of Genesis. It may interest Hebraists, but can little aid the preacher.

138 Sibthorpe, Richard Waldo – GENESIS WITH BRIEF OBSERVA-TIONS. 1835. *
Mere platitudes. Paper spoiled.

139 Turner, Samuel H. – A COMPANION TO GENESIS. 1851. **
In Horne's *Introduction* we read: "Though not designed to be a commentary, this valuable work furnishes the biblical student with abundant aid for the exact and literal interpretation of the Book of Genesis."

140 Warner, Richard – EXPOSITION. 1840. *
Common place remarks; intended to be used at family worship. Likely to send the servants to sleep.

141 Whateley, William – PROTOTYPES; or, the Primarie Precedent Presidents out of the Booke of Genesis. Showing the good and bad things they did and had. Practically adapted to our information and reformation. 1640. **
A queer old book. The oddity of the title is borne out by the singularity of the matter. It does not expound each verse; but certain incidents are dwelt upon.

142 Willet, Andrew – HEXAPLA. A sixfold exposition of Genesis. 1605. **
This work is called by its author a *Hexapla*, because he treats his subject under six heads, giving "a sixfold use of every chapter, showing: 1. The method, or argument. 2. The divers readings. 3. The explanation of difficult questions and doubtful places. 4. The places of doctrine. 5. Places of confutation. 6. Moral observations." Willet is tedious reading; his method hampers him. In all his commentaries he lumbers alone in his six-wheeled wagon.

143 Wright, C. H. H. – BOOK OF GENESIS IN HEBREW, with various readings, notes, etc. *
Intended to assist the student who has mastered the elements of Hebrew grammar to acquire a better knowledge of that language. Rather a class-book than a commentary.

GENESIS: EARLY CHAPTERS AND PATRIARCHS

144 **Bonar, Horatius – THOUGHTS ON GENESIS: EARTH'S MORN-ING.** 1875. ***
An exposition of the first six chapters only. The author endeavors "to investigate the meaning of each verse and word; that, having done so, the exact revelation of God in these may be brought out, and the spiritual truth evolved." He has in a great measure attained his object. What more could be said in his praise?

145 **Bunyan, John – TEN FIRST CHAPTERS OF GENESIS AND PART OF THE ELEVENTH.** *
Allegorical and spiritual. Bunyan's characteristics are very manifest.

146 **Edersheim, Alfred – WORLD BEFORE THE FLOOD, AND HISTORY OF THE PATRIARCHS.** 1875. **
The author has mainly aimed at giving instruction to the Sunday school teacher, and the Bible class student. He may be read with profit by students of a higher grade. The work is not a commentary, but is full of instruction.

147 **Henry, Philip – EXPOSITION OF THE FIRST ELEVEN CHAPTERS OF GENESIS.** 1839. **
Interesting as the exposition of Matthew Henry's father, taken down from his lips at family prayer by Matthew, his son. This probably suggested the famous commentary.

148 **Hurdis, James – SELECT CRITICAL REMARKS,** upon the first English version of the first ten chapters of Genesis. 1793. *
"Judicious observations"; but it is so easy to be *judicious*. Unimportant.

149 **Luther, Martin – ON THE FIRST FIVE CHAPTERS OF GENESIS.** Translated by Dr. Henry Cole, 1858. **
Cole made a choice selection. Luther left four volumes upon Genesis in Latin. How these Reformers worked!

150 **MacDonald, D. – CREATION AND THE FALL.** The first three chapters of Genesis. **
"We do not hesitate to designate this volume as the most complete examination of the literature and the exegesis of the creation and the fall which has appeared in England."— *Journal of Sacred Literature.*

151 **Needler, Benjamin – EXPOSITORY NOTES,** with observations towards the opening of the first five chapters of Genesis. 1655. *
Needler was one of the eminent divines who took part in the famous Morning Exercises. The little work is a curiosity, but nothing more.

152 **Rosse, Alexander – EXPOSITION OF THE FOURTEEN FIRST CHAPTERS OF GENESIS.** 1626. *
A very scarce catechism by that Scotch divine who is mentioned in Hudibras in the lines:
>   There was an ancient sound philosopher
>   That had read Alexander Ross over.

153 **White, John – THE FIRST CHAPTERS OF GENESIS.** 1656. **
A book on three chapters! There were giants in those days. Manton says, "To speak of the worth of the author is needless, his praise being already in all the

churches," and he adds that he had been greatly refreshed by the perusal of this book.

154 Williams, Isaac – BEGINNING OF GENESIS, with notes. 1861. *******
A very remarkable work by a high churchman, opening up in a masterly manner the mystical teachings of the early chapters of Genesis. To be read *cum grano salis.*

(The following works are placed in chronological order)

155 Bonnet, L. – THE EXILE FROM EDEN. Meditations on the third chapter of Genesis, translated from the French, by the Rev. W. Hare. 1839. ******
After the French manner. In nine meditations the salient points in the all-important story of the Fall are touched upon. One of the best separate treatises upon the subject.

156 Olmstead, J. – NOAH AND HIS TIMES. *
One of the dreariest works ever written. We have often wondered why it was reprinted, or even printed at all. It is as dry as Noah in the ark.

157 Blunt, Henry – TWELVE LECTURES ON THE HISTORY OF ABRAHAM.

EIGHT LECTURES ON THE HISTORY OF JACOB. 1842. ******
Like the rest of this author's lectures. Good, plain addresses.

158 Shute, Josias – SARAH AND HAGAR; or, Genesis 16 Opened in 20 Sermons. 1649. ******
In shape, the editor tells us, "this book is somewhat slender, like the encouragements of learning." He informs us that the author was "one of the five famous brother-preachers, somewhat like the five fingers on the right hand of fellowship;" and that Chrysostom did so much lie in his bosom that he became like him in his flowing style and golden eloquence. He writes like a learned man, and treats the Scriptures as if "each book were a course, each chapter a Benjamin's mess, and every verse a morsel of the food of angels."

159 Bouchier, Barton – HISTORY OF ISAAC. **
A charming book, in Bouchier's gracious style.

160 Rollinson, Francis – TWELVE PROPHETICAL LEGACIES; or 12 Sermons upon Jacob's Last Will, recorded in the 45th chapter of Genesis. 1612. *****
Old-fashioned learning, and singular remarks; its rarity is no great calamity.

161 Cumming, John – THE LAST OF THE PATRIARCHS; or, Lessons From the Life of Joseph. 1856. ******
Fitted for popular reading; ministers need more thought.

162 Gibson, T. – LECTURES ON JOSEPH. 1848. *****
Very respectable sermons, bringing out the gospel of Joseph's history.

163 Lawson, George – LECTURES ON JOSEPH. 2 vols., 1807 and 1812. *******
Dr. Lawson had a fertile mind, and a heart alive both to the human and divine side of truth. He writes with pleasing simplicity of style. One of the highest compliments to this book is found in the fact that a distinguished American scholar issued much of it as his own.

164   Smith, Thornley – HISTORY OF JOSEPH, viewed in connection
      with the antiquities of Egypt. 1875. ***
      "Written under the full light of the most recent archaeological discoveries,
      modern scholarship, and theological science, it is THE book on the subject.
      Now we have it, we cannot dispense with it."— *Homilist.*

165   Wardlaw, Ralph – LIFE OF JOSEPH AND THE LAST YEARS
      OF JACOB. 1845. **
      Wardlaw, though rather wordy, is always instructive.

Exodus

166   Birks, T. R. – THE EXODUS OF ISRAEL: Its Difficulties Ex-
      plained, and its Truth Confirmed. 1863. **
      A reply to Dr. Colenso's famous assault upon the Pentateuch. The great
      abilities of the author are known to all.

167   Blunt, Henry – *Exodus and Leviticus.* Vol. 2 of A FAMILY
      EXPOSITION OF THE PENTATEUCH. 1842. **
      Profitable for household and private reading: not very striking.

168   Bush , George – NOTES ON EXODUS. 2 vols., 1856. **
      Of considerable value. We do not know that it is a plagiarism.

169   COTTAGE READINGS ON THE BOOK OF EXODUS. **
      Not at all a student's book; yet many preachers might learn from it how to put
      things plainly. There is a similar volume on Genesis.

170   Cumming, John – SABBATH MORNING READINGS ON
      EXODUS. 1853. **
      Dr. Cumming's style is a model, but his matter seldom verges upon originality.
      He always gives you the gospel when he is not prophesying.

171   Exell, Joseph S. – *Homiletic Commentary on Exodus.* Included in
      THE PREACHER'S HOMILETIC COMMENTARY.   31 vols.
      Baker Book House. **
      It excels, so far as we have seen.

172   Hughes, George. See No. 127. **

173   Jackson, Thomas – PARAPHRASE ON THE ELEVEN FIRST
      CHAPTERS OF EXODUS, with annotations, etc. 3 vols. *
      George Herbert set great score by Dr. Jackson's writings, for he said, "I bless
      God for the confirmation Dr. Jackson has given me in the Christian religion,
      against the atheist, Jew and Socinian, and in the Protestant against Rome." It
      would hardly repay a student to purchase three volumes to obtain the small
      portion allotted to his paraphrase. So far as commenting is concerned, it is not
      important.

174   Mackintosh, C. H. – *Exodus*, in NOTES ON THE PENTATEUCH.
      Loizeaux Brothers. ***
      Not free from Plymouth errors, yet remarkably suggestive.

175   Millington, Thomas S. – SIGNS AND WONDERS IN THE LAND
      OF HAM. A description of the 10 plagues of Egypt. 1873. ***
      It has been an intellectual treat to read this interesting work. On the same
      subject there is an old work by James Bryant, 1794, but Millington is enough.

176 **Murphy, James G. – COMMENTARY ON THE BOOK OF EXODUS.** Klock and Klock (Kregel Publications). ***
The result of laborious study by a scholar of ripe learning.

177 **Willet, Andrew – HEXAPLA; or Sixfold Commentary Upon Exodus.** 1608. **
See No. 142. Full, exhaustive, and exhausting.

LIFE OF MOSES

178 **Hamilton, James** (1814-1867) – **MOSES: THE MAN OF GOD.** ***
Beautiful as a poem, like everything which fell from Dr. Hamilton's pen. It would be impossible to study it without profit.

179 **Van Oosterzee, J. J. – THE LIFE OF MOSES.** **

180 **Smith, Thornley – HISTORY OF MOSES.** Viewed in connection with Egyptian Antiquities, and the times in which he lived. 1862. ***
Of the same class as John Kitto's Daily Readings: well executed.

181 **Spong, James – MOSES, THE HERO OF THE DESERT.** *
A book for the public. Not for students.

JOURNEYINGS OF THE CHILDREN OF ISRAEL

182 **Buddicom, R. P. – THE CHRISTIAN EXODUS.** In a series of discourses. 2 vols., 1826. **
Able discourses, using the Exodus spiritually and wisely.

183 **Cardall, William – ISRAEL'S JOURNEYS, ILLUSTRATIVE OF THE DIVINE PILGRIMAGE.** 1848. *
Twenty evangelical lectures manifesting respectable ability.

184 **Forster, Charles – ISRAEL IN THE WILDERNESS;** or Gleanings from the scenes of the wanderings. 1865. **
If the author's renderings of the desert inscriptions are indeed correct, this is a wonderful book. That, however, is a question for the learned, and they have pronounced against him.

185 **JOURNEYINGS OF THE CHILDREN OF ISRAEL,** and their settlement in the promised land. (Anonymous.) 1832. *
Useful to the young, but the engravings are of almost pre-Adamite antiquity, and nearly as ugly as the profoundest master of the ridiculous could have made them.

186 **Krummacher, Gottfried Daniel – ISRAEL'S WANDERINGS.** 2 vols., 1837. **
Written by the uncle of the author of *Elijah the Tishbite*. A good, thought-breeding work.

187 **Osburn, W.** See under "GENESIS," No. 135. **

188 **Seaton, W. – CHURCH IN THE WILDERNESS.** 2 vols., 1821. Enlarged, 2 vols. ***
Of the thoroughly evangelical school, fraught with much experimental truth and sound doctrine soberly discussed.

189 **Wagner, George – PRACTICAL TRUTHS FROM ISRAEL'S WANDERINGS.** Kregel Publications. ***
A book which we have read with great pleasure and profit, and very heartily recommend.

THE DECALOGUE

(This list does not include comments contained in bodies of divinity, etc., but those forming separate volumes. In many theological works there are lengthy portions set apart for the Commandments.)

190 **Andrewes, Lancelot – THE PATTERN OF CATECHISTICAL DOCTRINE AT LARGE;** or A Learned and Pious Exposition of the Ten Commandments. 1675. ***
This is a book indeed. It is a joy to read it, for it flashes with thought and illustration, and sparkles with ingenious remarks. Profound learning did not lead the Bishop into the depths of dullness, as it has done many another divine; he manifests the happy quaintness of Latimer side–by–side with great scholarship. He was highly esteemed by his contemporaries; but we can hardly believe that his death:
> Left the dim face of our dull hemisphere
> All one great eye all drown'd in one great tear.

191 **Barker, Peter – A LEARNED AND FAMILIAR EXPOSITION.** 1624. **
Old-fashioned, remarkably quaint, and even coarse in places. Barker's work abounds in scriptural illustrations, but it is almost forgotten.

192 **Dale, R. W. – THE TEN COMMANDMENTS.** 1873. **
Written in a clear, bold, and trenchant style. We could not subscribe to all the author's views, but we admire his practical remarks, and their outspoken manner.

193 **Dod, John and Cleaver, Robert – FAMILIAR EXPOSITION.** 1632. **
This work was published by John Dod and Robert Cleaver, with an intimation that the name of the author was purposely suppressed. Our edition, dated 1632, is the eighteenth, so that work enjoyed a rare popularity in its own time. It has been frequently reprinted since. The book has been long held in high esteem.

194 **Downame or Downham, George – ABSTRACT** of the duties, commandments, and sins forbidden in the Law of God. 1635. *
A sort of catalog of sins, arranged in a tabular form under the Ten Commandments. These are the heads and divisions of a larger treatise, which does not appear to have been published. These mighty men could afford to leave in the oblivion of manuscript works which would cost modern weaklings half a lifetime to write.

195 **Durham, James – EXPOSITION** with a resolution of several monumentous questions, and cases of conscience. 1675. ***
Whatever Durham has written is very precious. He has the pen of a ready writer, and indites good matter.

196 Elton, Edward – GOD'S HOLY MIND, TOUCHING MATTERS MORAL; which He Himself uttered in Ten Commandments. 1648. *
This work discusses the Decalogue in question and answer, in a somewhat dull manner; but touches many cases of conscience, and deals wisely with them. Belief in witchcraft comes out very strongly in some passages.

197 Fisher, Edward – MARROW OF DIVINITY. A plain, pithy and spiritual exposition of the Ten Commandments. **
This exposition is part of the work which occasioned the famous Marrow Controversy. One fails to see anything calculated to stir up such strife. Fisher might have said that the lines had fallen to him in troubled waters.

198 Hooper, John – A DECLARATION of the ten holy Commandments of Almighty God. 1548, 1550, etc. **
After the manner of the English Reformers. The style is harsh to the modern ear, and the matter too much occupied with the controversies in the author's times to be very interesting now.

199 Hopkins, Ezekiel – AN EXPOSITION OF THE TEN COMMANDMENTS. 1692. **
Hopkins in this exposition searches the heart thoroughly, and makes very practical application of the Commandments to the situations and circumstances of daily life. His homely eloquence will always make his works valuable.

200 Knewstub, John – LECTURES ON EXODUS 20. 1584. *
More valuable for its antiquity than for anything else.

201 McCaul, Joseph B. – THE TEN COMMANDMENTS; the Christian's rule of daily life. 1861. **
The author says, "There is nothing deep in the following pages except their subject". A modest estimate.

202 Newton, Richard – THE KING'S HIGHWAY. ***
Though intended for children, ministers will find it useful, for it teems with illustration, and brings up little points of conduct worth touching upon. Dr. Newton is the prince of preachers to children.

203 Tudor, Richard – DECALOGUE VIEWED AS THE CHRISTIAN'S LAW. 1860. **
The author attempts to give the Christian's sense of the Decalogue in its application to present needs and questions. With much moderation he discusses many of the disputed points of the day, such as the legislative enforcement of the Sabbath, marriage with a deceased wife's sister, etc. He usually takes the view which is natural to a clergyman; but he says some capital things.

204 Weemse, John – THE MORAL LAWS. In vol. 1 of *Works*, 1632. **
Solid, sober, weighty. Orme says of Weemse: "He was well acquainted with the original Scriptures, with Jewish manners and antiquities, and with the best mode of interpreting the Bible. The style is quaint, but always intelligible." (See No. 225.)

205 Whateley, William – A PITHY, SHORT, AND METHODICAL OPENING OF THE TEN COMMANDMENTS. 1622. **
Exceedingly scarce, but as rich as it is rare.

THE TABERNACLE

(Of works on this subject it is not possible to give more than a selection.)

206 Brown, W. – THE TABERNACLE and its service in relation to Christ and the Church. 1874. **
An instructive interpretation of the types of the Tabernacle.

207 Garratt, S. – SCRIPTURE SYMBOLISM. 1848. **
Most unexceptionable in doctrine and style. It deals mainly with the sacred vessels.

208 Kitto, John – TABERNACLE AND ITS FURNITURE. 1849. **
Artistic illustrations with a little letter-press. Soltau well supplies the place of this rare work.

209 Mudge, William – THE TABERNACLE IN THE WILDERNESS. 1861. **
The writer, a thoroughly evangelical second-advent clergyman, makes some very admirable remarks in these lectures, which were delivered in his parish church. Our copy is in the third edition. We are not surprised to find the work thus popular.

210 Soltau, Henry W. – THE HOLY VESSELS AND FURNITURE OF THE TABERNACLE OF ISRAEL. (With ten full-color illustrations.) Kregel Publications. **
A series of sumptuous pictures, executed in the best style of art, impressing the mind far more vividly than any letter-press could do.

211 Soltau, Henry W. – THE TABERNACLE, THE PRIESTHOOD AND THE OFFERINGS. Kregel Publications. ***
Richly suggestive. Exceedingly well worked out in details; but not so wire-drawn as to prevent thought on the reader's part.

212 White, Frank H. – CHRIST IN THE TABERNACLE, with some remarks on the offerings. Illustrated with twelve chromo-lithographs. 1873. **
Written for the private Christian. Full of instruction and devotion.

LEVITICUS

213 Bonar, Andrew A. – LEVITICUS, with notes. The Banner of Truth. ***
Very precious. Mr. Andrew Bonar has a keen eye for a typical analogy, but he always keeps the rein upon his imagination, and is therefore safe to follow. He is a master in Israel.

214 Bush, George – NOTES ON LEVITICUS. Klock and Klock (Kregel Publications). ***
The author read extensively to produce this volume. In his later years, he became a Swedenborgian, but there is no trace of that learning in this or his other comments. He inserts the notes of the *Pictorial Bible*, but handsomely acknowledges them.

215 Cumming, John – SABBATH MORNING READINGS ON
LEVITICUS. 1854. **
For popular reading. The author wrote too much to be profound.

216 Cumming, John – THE GREAT SACRIFICE; or the Gospel According to Leviticus. **
A companion to the volume last mentioned.

217 James, Horatio – SERMONS ON THE LEVITICAL TYPES.
1847. *
Very attenuated. These sermons, like the lean kine, have eaten up the fat kine
of the types and are never the fatter.

218 Jukes, Andrew – THE LAW OF THE OFFERINGS. (Leviticus,
chapters 1-7). Kregel Publications. ***
A very condensed, instructive, refreshing book. It will open up new trains of
thought to those unversed in the teaching of the types.

219 Mackintosh, C. H. – NOTES ON LEVITICUS. Loizeaux Brothers. **
We do not endorse the Plymouthism which pervades these notes, but they are
frequently suggestive. Should be read cautiously.

220 Mather, Samuel – THE FIGURES OR TYPES OF THE OLD
TESTAMENT. 1705. **
Though this is a work upon all the types, it contains so much instructive matter
upon the Levitical sacrifices that we cannot forbear mentioning it here. It is
one of the old standard books of our fathers.

221 Keach, Benjamin – PREACHING FROM THE TYPES AND
METAPHORS OF THE BIBLE. Kregel Publications. **
This is a vast cyclopaedia of types and metaphors of all sorts, and was once very
popular. It is a capital book, though too often the figures not only run on all-
fours but on as many legs as a centipede. It is not strictly upon Leviticus, but
we felt bound to insert it in this place.

222 Michaelis, John David – THE LAWS OF MOSES. Translated by Alexander Smith. 4 vols., 1814. *
However much of learning there seems to be here, we are not prepared to
recommend a work which treats so sacred a subject with levity and coarseness.

223 Newton, Benjamin Wills – THOUGHTS ON PARTS OF
LEVITICUS. 1857. **
This touches only the first six chapters; but it treats of the offerings in a manner
deeply spiritual and helpful. This writer has some peculiarities of style and
thought; but in matter and spirit he is far removed from the Darby school.

224 Seiss, Joseph A. – THE GOSPEL IN LEVITICUS. Kregel Publications. **
Twenty-one very admirable lectures, founded upon Bush and Bonar, but containing much original matter. The work deserves attention.

225 Weemse, John – EXPOSITION OF THE LAWS OF MOSES,
MORAL, CEREMONIAL, JUDICIAL. 2 vols., 1632. *
This contains many useful and curious things, together with fancies and

rabbinical trifles. Weemse may generally be bought very cheap, and we should think his work is very little read or cared for. (See Orme's opinion, No. 204.)

226 Willet, Andrew – HEXAPLA; *Leviticus*. 1631. **
Plodding along with his six-fold load, Willet gives us a comparison of 10 versions, "handles well nigh 2,000 theological questions," and quotes "above 40 authors, old and new." He sums up all preceding commentaries, both Protestant and Romish.

NUMBERS

(Seaton, Wagner, and other writers whom we have placed under Exodus are equally upon Numbers, and should be referred to.)

227 Attersoll, William – A COMMENTARY UPON NUMBERS. 1618. **
A stupendous work, well fitted to make a headstone for the author's grave. It is so huge that it might have been the work of a lifetime, and yet the same writer also gave us *Philemon*. Think of 1,271 large pages on Numbers!

228 Blunt, Henry – *Numbers and Deuteronomy*. (Vol. 3, FAMILY EXPOSITION OF PENTATEUCH). 1843. **
Intended for families, but not without value for the preacher.

229 Bush, George – NOTES ON NUMBERS. 1858. ***
Although Bush is indebted to many authors, he is by no means a mere collector; his remarks repay you for consultation, and we hope that in this case they are his own.

230 Cumming, John – READINGS ON NUMBERS. 1855. **
Good, as usual.

231 Mackintosh, C. H. – NOTES ON NUMBERS. Loizeaux Brothers. **
Like the other notes of C. H. M., they need filtering. Good as they are, their Darbyism gives them an unpleasant and unhealthy savor.

DEUTERONOMY

(As so few expositions have been written upon Deuteronomy alone, the reader will do well to use the commentaries upon the Pentateuch and the whole Old Testament.)

232 Calvin, John – SERMONS UPON DEUTERONOMY. Translated out of the French by A. Golding. 1583. ***
This is not the same as that which is contained in *Calvin's Commentaries*. Everything that Calvin wrote by way of exposition is priceless; even those who differ from him in theology admit this.

233 Cumming, John – SABBATH MORNING READINGS ON THE BOOK OF DEUTERONOMY. Reprinted as THE BOOK OF DEUTERONOMY. Klock & Klock (Kregel Publications). **
Pretty, popular, profitable.

JOSHUA

234 Blackwood, Stevenson A. – HEAVENLY PLACES. Addresses. 1873. **

Mr. Blackwood has illustrated passages from the first five chapters only. He has a beautifully quiet way of saying very sweet things. This little book will be useful if it shows the young preacher how to expound Scripture with unction and power.

235 Bush, George – NOTES. 1852. ***

Bush is a careful illustrator of the Word, and apt at giving the practical lesson. His works are well compiled.

236 Calvin, John – *Commentary Upon Joshua,* translated by W. F.; in **CALVIN'S COMMENTARIES.** Baker book House. ***

We have said enough upon Calvin in general. His expositions are more equal in excellence than those of other men; other men rise and fall, but he is almost uniformly good.

237 CHRIST IN THE PROPHETS – Joshua, Judges, Samuel, Kings. Anonymous. 1873. *

See *Christ in the Law,* No. 80. Needs well-sifting. There is much rubbish.

238 Cumming, John – READINGS IN JOSHUA AND JUDGES. 1857. **

Dr. Cumming keeps up to his average of value.

239 Groser, W. H. – JOSHUA AND HIS SUCCESSORS. An Introduction to Joshua, Judges, Ruth, and I Samuel, with notes. Parts 1 and 2. 1874. **

A very useful condensed book for teachers.

240 Keil, Karl Friedrich – *Joshua, Judges and Ruth.* Part of vol. 2, Keil and Delitzsch, **COMMENTARY ON THE OLD TESTAMENT.** Wm. B. Eerdmans Publishing Co. **

"Let our biblical students not only master the facts and logic, but catch the spirit of these commentaries, and we can have no fear for the issue of that conflict with rationalism and popery united, by which Protestantism in this country seems to be threatened."— *Wesleyan Methodist Magazine*

241 Kelly, William – INTRODUCTORY LECTURES to the study of the earlier historical books (Joshua to 2 Samuel). 1874. *

After the manner of Plymouth commenting in general; quite sufficiently taken up with spiritualizing and nice points; but yet, read with half a ton of salt, a book likely to arouse thought, and suggest topics.

242 LANGE'S COMMENTARY ON THE HOLY SCRIPTURES. *Joshua,* by F. R. Fay; *Judges, Ruth,* by P. Cassel. Edited by Philip Schaff. ***

This is a standard work. No minister's library is furnished without the whole set. Joshua however is inferior to Judges.

243 Marchant, F. G. – COMMENTARY ON JOSHUA. (Part 3 of *Preacher's Commentary.*) 1875. **

While writing this we have only one number before us, but it promises well, and we feel sure its quality will be sustained, for we know the author's industrious habits.

244 THE GOSPEL IN THE BOOK OF JOSHUA. Anonymous 1867. *
Pious remarks, such as anyone would make.

245 Seaton, W. – THE CHURCH IN CANAAN; or, Heirs in Possession
Receiving the Promises. Vol. 1., 1823. **
A sequel to No. 188.

246 Smith, Thornley – THE HISTORY OF JOSHUA, viewed in connection with the topography of Canaan, and the customs of the times in
which he lived, 1870. ***
Although not a commentary, it will answer the same purpose; for almost every
event is fully illustrated. A capital work.

JUDGES
See also "JOSHUA".

247 Bush, George – NOTES ON JUDGES. 1852. ***
Like other works of this author—of considerable value.

248 Dods, Marcus – ISRAEL'S IRON AGE: Sketches from the Period of
the Judges. 1874. *
Dr. Dods considers that to find in Samson and other judges types of our Lord
Jesus is mere fancy, and he interprets upon "a rational principle" which renders
his book dry and unspiritual; at the same time his sketches are not without
value.

249 Hengstenberg, E. W. – TIME OF THE JUDGES. (See No. 86.) **

250 Kitto, John – *Judges*, in KITTO'S DAILY BIBLE ILLUSTRA-
TIONS. See No. 41. Kregel Publications. ***
Exceedingly meritorious. Refer to it frequently.

**251 Martyr, Peter – MOST FRUITFUL AND LEARNED COMMEN-
TARY UPON THE BOOK OF JUDGES.** 1560. Rare. *
This would seem to be a profound work. Rogers says of Peter Martyr: "Few
private men can understand his works, and few ministers who understand them
can obtain them; nor if they can will they find in them much that will benefit
their simple hearers." This has not been our experience with Peter Martyr's
works. On the contrary, we have read them with interest.

252 Nobel, Samuel – SERMONS on the singular histories recorded in the
first eleven chapters. 1856. *
Swedenborgian mysticism. Exposition in a trance.

253 Rogers, Richard – THE WHOLE BOOK OF JUDGES. (103
sermons.) 1615. ***
This for the Puritan period is THE work upon Judges. It is thoroughly plain and
eminently practical.

254 Wiseman, Luke H. – PRACTICAL TRUTHS FROM JUDGES.
Kregel Publications. ***
Mr. Wiseman in this work tells "of Gideon and Barak, of Samson and of
Jephthah", and he does it in a powerful style. He was one of the best preachers
in the Wesleyan body. A man of fulness and judiciousness; in fact, a wise man.

255 Bruce, John – THE LIFE OF GIDEON. 1870. **
The author deserves attention, both for matter and style. Note Hugh Miller's high opinion of his *Biography of Samson* (No. 259). Gideon is a better work, but both are overestimated.

256 Elwin, Fountain – SERMONS ON THE CHARACTER OF GIDEON. 1844. *
Seven sermons, containing nothing remarkable.

257 Howard, Lady – GIDEON, THE MIGHTY MAN OF VALOR. 1841. *
Of small use to the preacher.

258 Rogers, George Albert – THE VALOR OF FAITH; or The Gospel in the Life of Gideon. 1859. ***
A thoroughly lively little book, each of the eight chapters is full of thought.

259 Bruce, John – THE BIOGRAPHY OF SAMSON. 1870. **
Hugh Miller said: "There is a poetic richness in the style, which at one time reminds us of Chalmers, and at another of Jeremy Taylor, but which in reality is Dr. Bruce's own, that does not seem poor or bald beside even the blank verse of the great master of English song." We think this eulogy is greatly overdone.

260 Quarles, Francis – THE HISTORIE OF SAMSON. 1631. **
This queer, quaint, odd volume of rhymes is far from despicable. Kitto frequently quotes Quarles upon Samson, and says of him that he was a poet of no mean order. We are glad to have his testimony to confirm our own opinion. Refined tastes will be offended, but those who wish for quaint thought will be gratified. The book is very rare.

RUTH
See also "JOSHUA"

261 Bernard, Richard – RUTH'S RECOMPENSE. 1628. **
Mr. Grosart is enthusiastic in his praise of this work, and says "that it abounds with apophthegms and compressed thoughts." We defer to so high an authority, but we are not much fascinated by the book.

262 Fuller, Thomas – A COMMENT ON RUTH, with two sermons. 1650. **
Not one of Fuller's best; but still quaint and pithy, and lit up with flashes of his irrepressible wit. The above works of Bernard and Fuller have been reprinted in *Nichol's Series of Commentaries*, in one vol., 1865.

263 Braden, William – THE BEAUTIFUL GLEANER. 1874. **
Mr. Braden is an able preacher. His sermons upon Ruth are popular and practical, though not very remarkable.

264 Lavater, Lewis – RUTH EXPOUNDED. In 28 sermons, translated from the Latin by E. Pagett, 1586. *
Lavater was a Reformer of high repute, son-in-law of Bullinger. He wrote a curious work on specters, and made a catalogue of comets, thus showing himself to be both philosopher and divine. His book is seldom met with.

265 **Lawson, George** – LECTURES ON THE BOOK OF RUTH. 1805. ***
By a man of great genius. Simple, fresh, and gracious. Nothing critical or profound may be looked for, but wise and sound teaching may be gleaned in these pages.

266 **Macartney, H.B.** – OBSERVATIONS ON RUTH. 1842. *
A nice little book, little in all ways.

267 **MacGowan, John** – DISCOURSES ON RUTH, and other important subjects. 1781. **
MacGowan, the author of *Dialogue of Devils*, is well–known for originality and force. In this case his sermons are full of Gospel truth, but the texts are too much accommodated and spiritualized. The discourses are good reading.

268 **Oxenden, A.** – STORY OF RUTH. *
A very tiny affair, of no great moment to the expositor.

269 **Philpot, B.** – SIX LECTURES. *
A very small book, containing good, simple lectures; not an exposition.

270 **Price, Aubrey C.** – SIX LECTURES ON THE BOOK OF RUTH. 1869. **
Sermons of remarkable power, both of doctrine and diction. Not so expository as practical. Mr. Price is an earnest and large-hearted clergyman of the thoroughly evangelical school.

271 **Topsell, Edward** – THE REWARD OF RELIGION: Lectures upon Ruth. 1613. ***
A very choice old work. Attersol in his rhyming preface says of it:
Go little Booke, display thy golden title,
(And yet not little though thou little bee);
Little for price and yet in price not little,
Thine was the Paine, the gaine is ours I see:
(Although our gaine thou deem'st no paine to thee).
If then, O reader, little paine thou take,
Thou greatest gaine with smallest paine shall make.

272 **Tyng, Stephen** – THE RICH KINSMAN, or, The History of Ruth. 1856. *
Written for young people, and suitable for their reading, though none too lively.

273 **Wright, C.H.H.** – RUTH, IN HEBREW, with grammatical and critical commentary. 1864. **
For Hebraists only. The author has selected the book of Ruth as a study for beginners in the Hebrew tongue, because of the simplicity of the language.

FIRST AND SECOND SAMUEL

(Expositions upon these books being few, the student should consult works on Scripture characters, and also comments on the Old Testament as a whole.)

274 **Keil, C.F.** and **Delitzsch, F.** – *The Books of Samuel.* Part of vol. 2, COMMENTARY ON THE OLD TESTAMENT. Wm. B. Eerdmans Publishing Co. **

Like most of Clark's series, Keil's works are valuable helps towards obtaining the meaning of the text; but for spiritual reflections and fruitful hints we must look elsewhere.

275 Lindsay, Henry – LECTURES ON THE HISTORICAL BOOKS. (1 and 2 Samuel only.) 2 vols., 1828. *
Practical sermons on a few of the more prominent events.

276 Willet, Andrew – AN HARMONIE upon the First Booke of Samuel, and an Harmonie upon the Seconde Booke of Samuel. 1614. ***
The work continues the Hexapla to which we have referred in Nos. 142 and 177. It is unusually brief for the age of its composition, and full of variety. Under every verse, and often clause of a verse, the learned author proposes a question, and proceeds to answer it. These are such as the following: "What a daughter of Belial is?" "Whether any may be said to sin with the will of God?" "What doors of the house of Jehovah Samuel opened?" "What is to be thought of Eli's state before God?"

277 Guild, William – THE THRONE OF DAVID. An exposition of the 2nd Samuel, wherein is set down the pattern of a pious and prudent prince. 1659. **
The manuscript of this rare book was sent to Dr. John Owen by the widow of the author, with a letter of her own, informing him that her dying husband desired it to be so forwarded. Dr. Owen says that he found the treaties "written with perspicuity and clearness, handling a subject of great and delightful variety, with a choice mixture of spiritual, moral, and political observations, tempered by a good and sound judgment unto common capacities." We do not presume to criticize where Owen commends, but we should not have originated such a commendation.

SAMUEL, SAUL, DAVID

278 Kitto, John – *Samuel, Saul, and David,* in **KITTO'S DAILY BIBLE ILLUSTRATIONS,** Kregel Publications. See No. 41. ***
Should always be consulted.

279 Plumptre, Helen – THE HISTORY OF SAMUEL. 1842. ***
A children's book, and childlike men will be thankful for the many very useful hints which it throws out. We have got more out of it than we have found in huge and learned tomes.

280 Steel, Robert – SAMUEL, THE PROPHET. 1861. ***
The author has done his work well, and has shown an evident desire to excite others to a greater knowledge of the subject than he could impart. Hence he gives a list of the writers upon Samuel, and such accounts of them as were within his reach. Young readers will find this book a great help to them.

281 Miller, J.A. – SAUL, THE FIRST KING OF ISRAEL. 1866. ***
Eminently thoughtful, useful, practical sermons. We do not see how Saul's life-failure could be more profitably set forth.

282 Blaikie, William G. – DAVID, KING OF ISRAEL. The divine plan and lessons of his life. 1861. ***
Dr. Blaikie is a good writer. This life of David has supplied a great lack.

283 Chandler, Samuel – A CRITICAL HISTORY OF THE LIFE OF DAVID. 2 vols., 1766; 1 vol., 1853. ******
This is a masterpiece as a critical history, and the best of Chandler's productions. Many of the Psalms are explained with commendable learning, but the spiritual element is absent.

284 Delany, Patrick – AN HISTORICAL ACCOUNT OF THE LIFE AND REIGN OF DAVID. 2 vols., 1745. *****
Delany was a friend of Swift, no great recommendation for a commentator. He defends David in a way which David would have sternly repudiated. Chandler is far preferable to Delany, but both are devoid of the evangelical spirit.

285 Kingsley, Charles – DAVID. Four sermons. ******
In his usual free and easy manner, Kingsley speaks of David's strength and his weakness, his anger and his deserts. The character of this writer is supposed to be well understood, but we question if many have formed a true estimate of him. For commenting purposes these sermons are of small value; they are plain, practical discourses.

286 Krummacher, F.W. – DAVID, THE KING OF ISRAEL. ******
Anything by Krummacher is worthy of patient reading.

287 Lawson, George – DISCOURSES ON THE HISTORY OF DAVID. 1833. *******
Here the life of David is piously turned to practical use. Delany and Chandler are but bones, and Lawson the marrow.

288 Marbeck, John – THE WHOLE HISTORY OF KING DAVID. 1579. *****
This is in English meter, and was written by the famous organist of the Royal Chapel in Windsor, in the reign of Henry VIII. He narrowly escaped martyrdom. His work entitled *Booke of Common Praier Noted*, is the ground work of the plain-song used in our Cathedrals from the Reformation to the present day. Marbeck's *History of David* is very rare. We cannot therefore set a price.

289 Rogers, Mrs. – THE SHEPHERD KING. 1856. ******
This authoress writes well for the young, and her book will be useful to those who teach them.

290 Smith, George – THE LIFE AND REIGN OF DAVID. 1867. ******
David's life is here concisely written, with such of the Psalms interwoven as can be referred to special periods. It cannot be read without ministering instruction.

291 Taylor, William M. – DAVID: His Life, and Its Lessons. 1875. *******
A grand work which should be in every library.

292 Thompson, Henry – DAVIDICA. Twelve sermons on the life and character of David. 1827.*****
Discourses of the kind which are usually published by subscription; rather pretentious, but with nothing in them. The process of subscribing to print sermons is one suggested by kindness, but seldom directed by reason.

293 Vince, Charles – LIGHTS AND SHADOWS IN THE LIFE OF KING DAVID. 1871. *******
Sermons of the highest order upon a few incidents in David's life, they are models of chaste, subdued, but powerful preaching.

FIRST AND SECOND KINGS

294 Geneste, Maximillian – THE PARALLEL HISTORIES OF JUDAH AND ISRAEL. 2 vols., 1843. **
The explanatory notes are mostly from other authors. The work has a very noble appearance, and may be useful as showing the run of biblical history; but Barth's *Bible Manual* (No. 3) would answer every purpose.

295 Jukes, Andrew – THE MYSTERY OF THE KINGDOM, traced through the books of Kings. Part 1, 1858. **
This author is more mystical than we could wish, but never writes without being instructive.

296 Keil, K. F. – COMMENTARY ON THE BOOKS OF KINGS. Translated by James Murphy. Supplemented by a *Commentary on the Books of Chronicles* by Ernst Bertheau. Translated by James Martin. 2 vols., 1857. **
Distinguished by careful investigation of the meaning of the text. This is a most important help to the expositor. The student will not, however, find much in the way of reflections and doctrines.

297 Keil, C.F. and Delitzsch, F. – *The Books of the Kings.* Translated by James Martin. Part of volume 3, **COMMENTARY OF THE OLD TESTAMENT.** Wm. B. Eerdmans Publishing Co. **
This appears to be another form of the work mentioned above. At least there can be no necessity for purchasing both. This is the better.

298 Kitto, John – *Solomon and the Kings*, in **KITTO'S DAILY BIBLE ILLUSTRATIONS.** Kregel Publications. See No. 41. ***
Full of deeply interesting matter.

299 LANGE'S COMMENTARY ON THE HOLY SCRIPTURES. *Commentary on the Books of Kings,* by Bahr. Edited by Philip Schaff. ***
It must have cost great effort to make the homiletical part of this volume as good as it is. It is a treasury to the preacher, and is all the more precious because we have next to nothing upon the Books of the Kings. See No. 42.

SOLOMON'S TEMPLE

300 Bunyan, John – SOLOMON'S TEMPLE SPIRITUALIZED. 1688. **
A marvellous display of allegorizing genius: full of Gospel truth. Bunyan hammers away at each type, but no one may call it tinkering.

301 Edersheim, Alfred – THE TEMPLE: Its Ministry and Services. Wm. B. Eerdmans Publishing Co. ***
This will supply the student with all that he needs upon the subject in hand.

302 Lee, Samuel – ORBIS MIRACULUM, or, The Temple of Solomon Portrayed by Scripture Light. 1659. **
Of course, as will be inferred from its date, this work is of the antique order,

but it is profoundly learned, and goes into architectural and ritualistic details, explaining them spiritually with much sweetness and suggestiveness.

ELIJAH, ELISHA, ETC.

303 Anderson, James – DISCOURSES ON ELIJAH. 1835. *
Ordinary sermons by a "Chaplain in Ordinary to the Queen." Rhetorical and grandiose, but not expository.

304 Bayne, Peter – THE DAYS OF JEZEBEL. An Historical Drama. 1872. **
A fine poetic drama, worthy of quotation by preachers; but hardly in the line of works contemplated by this catalog.

305 Edersheim, Alfred – ELISHA THE PROPHET, A TYPE OF CHRIST. 1873. **
This author is always interesting, showing close acquaintance with Jewish customs, and knowing how to utilize his information.

306 Howat, H.T. – ELIJAH, THE DESERT PROPHET. 1868. **
Very picturesque and poetical. A work to be read for enjoyment.

307 Krummacher, F.W. – ELIJAH THE TISHBITE. Translated from the German. ***
Too well–known and approved to need any commendation from us.

308 MacDuff, J. R. – THE PROPHET OF FIRE. 1863. ***
Dr. MacDuff writes popularly, yet he is by no means weak or shallow. He is to the young minister all the more useful, because he has worked out the problem of making sound thought intelligible to the multitude.

309 Mackintosh, C.H. – REFLECTIONS ON THE LIFE AND TIMES OF ELIJAH. *
Strongly Plymouthistic. A small affair.

310 Blunt, Henry – LECTURES ON THE HISTORY OF ELISHA. 1839. **
We like Blunt better upon Elisha than upon any other portion of Scripture. He says that, had he known of Krummacher's having written upon the subject, he should not have attempted it himself. A wise observation. What shall he do that cometh after a King, or after a Krummacher?

311 Dothie, W.P. – THE HISTORY OF THE PROPHET ELISHA. 1872. **
Sketchy. Not very deep, but interesting.

312 Glyn, George L. – LIFE OF ELISHA. In eleven plain discourses. 1857. **
Evangelical and simple. Ministers do not need it.

313 Krummacher, F.W. – ELISHA. Translated from the German, 1838. ***
Of this we may say as we did of the same author's *Elijah*, it needs no commending from us.

314 **Bullock, Charles – THE SYRIAN LEPER. 1862. ****
Telling in style, and earnestly evangelical, these chapters are good specimens of popular expounding.

315 **MacDuff, J.R. – THE HEALING WATERS, or, The Story of Naaman.** An Old Testament chapter on providence and grace. 1873. *******
In Dr. MacDuff's best manner: the story of Naaman is admirably handled, and made to teach the gospel with much freshness.

316 **Rogers, Daniel – NAAMAN THE SYRIAN,** his disease and cure; discovering lively to the reader the spiritual leprosy of sin and self-love; together with the remedies, viz., self-denial and faith. 1642. *******
A huge volume of 898 pages, almost large enough to have loaded one of Naaman's mules. It is a work which exhausts the subject and turns it to earnest evangelical uses.

317 **Woodward, Henry – THE SHUNAMITE. 1863. ***
We scarcely remember a more flagrant case of high-sounding verbiage. Here is the author's way of describing a hen which has hatched ducklings: "That much tired bird, whose hard allotment it has been to hatch and rear a brood of aliens, and who seems as if melancholy had marked her for her own, when her charge, with unanimous consent, hurry to some tempting pool of water, and violate her feelings and shock her instincts, by casting themselves upon that hostile element."

FIRST AND SECOND CHRONICLES

318 **Bertheau, E.** See Keil and Bertheau, No. 296. *******

319 **Keil, K. F. –** *The Book of the Chronicles,* in **COMMENTARY ON THE OLD TESTAMENT.** Translated from the German by Andrew Harper. Wm. B. Eerdmans Publishing Co. ******
Without indicating either the spiritual lesson or the moral of the history, Keil simply explains the facts, and in so doing aids the reader to realize them. We confess we should like something more.

EZRA, NEHEMIAH, AND ESTHER

320 **Keil, K. F. –** *Commentary on Ezra, Nehemiah, and Esther,* in **COMMENTARY ON THE OLD TESTAMENT.** Translated by Sophia Taylor. Wm B. Eerdmans Publishing Co. ******
Just the kind of book in which Keil's method of commenting appears to the best advantage. He gives much needful information, and thus supplements more didactic works. We cannot read Keil with pleasure, for we want spiritual meat, but yet it is most desirable for us to know what the text really means.

321 **Pilkington, James – A GODLIE EXPOSITION UPON CERTEINE CHAPTERS OF NEHEMIAH.** 1585. Reprinted in the Parker Society's edition of Pilkington's Works, 1842. ******
Very old fashioned and singular, somewhat in the style of Latimer and perhaps a little coarser. Pilkington's downright onslaughts upon the vices and follies of his times are fine instances of personal, faithful preaching. They are,

however, so minutely descriptive of the manners which then prevailed that they are the less useful now. The style is cramped, and even grotesque in places, yet Pilkington is a grand old author. He has only written upon five chapters.

322 Randall, J. Montague – NEHEMIAH, THE TIRSHATHA: His Life and Lessons. 1874. ******
The substance of thirteen Sunday evening addresses to a village congregation, "dictated by the author, who is nearly blind, on the following Monday." These familiar and almost chatty discourses are full of gospel teaching, and while they give a fair idea of Nehemiah and his times, they are also enlivened by anecdote, and made exceedingly interesting. Students will not learn much from these sermons, but they may see how rustic preaching should be done.

323 SCENES FROM THE LIFE OF NEHEMIAH, or, Chapters for Christian Workers. Anonymous. ******
The heads of these chapters would serve exceedingly well for the key-notes of a series of sermons.

324 Stowell, Hugh – A MODEL FOR MEN OF BUSINESS, or, Lectures on the Character of Nehemiah. 1855. ******
The author does not attempt a full exposition, but aims at furnishing a plain, practical handbook for men of business and others whose time is limited. He gives fourteen good, sensible lectures on the Book.

325 Woodward, Henry – THOUGHTS ON THE CHARACTER AND HISTORY OF NEHEMIAH. 1849. *****
Words, and only words.

ESTHER

326 Cooper, Thomas – THE CHURCHES DELIVERANCE; containing meditations and short notes upon the Book of Esther. 1609. *****
We have not been able to meet with this work.

327 Davidson, Alexander D. – LECTURES ON ESTHER. 1859. ******
Helpful lectures. The Book of Esther is here used for instruction in doctrine and practice. The work is not so much for the study as for the family.

328 Hughes, John – ESTHER AND HER PEOPLE. Ten sermons, 1842. ******
Good evangelical discourses, but nothing very special.

329 Lawson, George – DISCOURSES ON ESTHER. 1804. *******
Intended for the general reader, the discourses are as spiritual and unaffected as their excellent author. Dr. John Brown, in commending all the Lawson books, says that "he has rendered subjects, apparently barren, full of instruction."

330 McCrie, Thomas – LECTURES ON ESTHER. 1838. *******
Dr. Davidson says of Dr. McCrie: "There is an ancient fable of a king who was gifted with the power of turning everything he touched into gold; and this eminent divine and historian possessed remarkably the gift of rendering every subject he handled so precious, as at least to discourage any one from attempting to follow in his track. In his lectures upon the Book of Esther, he has certainly left little for any to say who may come after him."

331 **Morgan, R. C. – THE BOOK OF ESTHER TYPICAL OF THE KINGDOM.** 1885 *
An allegorical interpretation, which commences with these words: "The true scene of this beautiful book opens in heaven." Is heaven under the dominion of Ahasuerus? Who then is Vashti?

THE POETICAL BOOKS

332 **Durell, D. – CRITICAL REMARKS ON THE BOOKS OF JOB, PROVERBS, PSALMS, ECCLESIASTES, AND CANTICLES.** 1772. *
A critic who is forever mending the text, who contends for the modern origin of Job.of Job, thinks the Canticles to be a love song, and considers the imprecatory Psalms to be ebullitions of passion, is not one whom our readers need consult.

333 **Holden, Lawrence – PARAPHRASE ON THE BOOKS OF JOB, PSALMS, PROVERBS AND ECCESIASTES,** with notes. 1763. *
An atrocious instance of bombastic verbosity, Job 2 is thus expanded: "Heaven and earth's great Lord and guardian, the instant Satan appeared observed, and thus demanded of him: 'from what quarter proceedest thou? or in what district, and to what purpose hast thou lately employed thy perverted, and subtle, wicked abilities and arts?' To whom the destroyer answers: 'my last station, or rather, unsettled, wandering motion, has been upon earth; various districts whereof I have made short visits to, being sometimes with the inhabitants of one region or climate, sometimes with those of another.'" Paraphrases generally mean the text padded out with superfluous words, and this is an emphatic instance.

334 **Kitto, John –** *Job and the Poetical Books***,** in **KITTO'S DAILY BIBLE ILLUSTRATIONS.** See No. 41. Kregel Publications. ***
Worthy of attentive reading.

335 **Leigh, Edward.** See under "WHOLE BIBLE," No. 44. **

336 **Wilcocks, Thomas – THE WORKS** of that reverend and learned divine, Mr. Thomas Wilcocks, minister of God's Word; containing an exposition upon the whole Book of David's Psalms, Solomon's Proverbs, the Canticles, and part of the eighth chapter of St. Paul's Epistle to the Romans. 1589, 1620 and 1624. **
Very old. The notes are brief, but furnish many hints for sermons.

JOB

337 **Abbot, George – THE WHOLE BOOK OF JOB PARAPHRASED,** or made easy for any to understand. 1640. *
This is not by Archbishop Abbot, neither is the work of any value. This Abbot was a member of Parliament, and his paraphrase is better than we could have expected from an M.P.; but still it is a heavy performance.

338 **American Bible Union – THE BOOK OF JOB.** A translation from the original Hebrew; on the the basis of the common and earlier English versions. By Thomas J. Conant. 1867. **

An excellent translation. The design did not allow of more than slender notes, but those notes are good.

339 **Barnes, Albert** – *Notes on Job,* in BARNES' NOTES ON THE OLD TESTAMENT. Edited by Robert Frew, 2 vols. Baker Book House. ***
Exceedingly good. One of the best of this author's generally valuable productions. The student should purchase this work at once, as it is absolutely necessary to his library.

340 **Bellamy, D.** – PARAPHRASE, with observations. 1748. *
A collection of notes from other authors. Original works are far better.

341 **Beza, Theodore** – JOB EXPOUNDED. 1590. **
Beza was the great friend and assistant of Calvin. As a commentator he lacked the profound insight and comprehensive grasp of Calvin, but as a critical scholar he is said to have been his equal if not his superior. The work on Job is rare.

342 **Blackmore, R.** – PARAPHRASE on the Book of Job, the Songs of Moses, Deborah, and David, four select Psalms, some chapters of Isaiah, and the third chapter of Habakkuk. 1700. *
Grandiose poetry. Pope speaks of the power of Blackmore's numbers "to soothe the soul in slumbers." The worthy knight is not the worst of the poetical expositors, but he is bad enough. Miserable paraphrases are ye all, ye brethren of jingling rhyme and doubtful measure.

343 **Calvin, John** – SERMONS ON THE BOOK OF JOB. ***
Not the same as the *Commentary*, but equally rich.

344 **Carey, Cateret Priaulx** – BOOK OF JOB, translated, explained by notes and illustrated by extracts from works on Antiquities, Science, etc. 1858. **
Purely critical and exegetical. The author has grappled manfully with all difficulties, and has stored up a mass of precious materials with which to illuminate a book from its antiquity.

345 **Caryl, Joseph** – EXPOSITION, WITH PRACTICAL OBSERVATIONS. 12 vols., 1648-1666; also in 2 vols. ***
Caryl must have inherited the patience of Job to have completed his stupendous task. It would be a mistake to suppose that he is at all prolix or redundant; he is only full. In the course of his expounding he has illustrated a very large portion of the whole Bible with great clearness and power. He is deeply devotional and spiritual. He gives us much, but none too much. His work can scarcely be superseded or surpassed.

346 **Caryl, Joseph** – AN ABRIDGMENT OF CARYL'S EXPOSITION. 1836. ***
We do not believe in abridgments of a book which is good throughout. Think of 12 large volumes condensed into 1 small one! An ox in a gallipot is nothing to it.

347 **Chappelow, Leonard** – A COMMENTARY, in which is inserted the Hebrew text and English translation, 2 vols. 1752. *
Chappelow is great upon Arabic etymologies, but he is dreadfully verbose, and really says nothing of any consequence. Chappelow and several other authors follow Schultens in the belief that the Hebrew can only be read in light of the Arabic; they even imagine that the Book of Job was originally composed in

Arabic by Job himself and then translated by someone else into the Hebrew tongue. This opened a fine field for parading their learning.

348 **Coleman, J. Noble – THE BOOK OF JOB.** From the Hebrew with notes. 1869. **
We do not value this so much as the same author's "Psalms," but it is serviceable in its own way.

349 **Conant, T. J.** See *American Bible Union*, No. 338. **

350 **Davidson, A. B. – A COMMENTARY GRAMMATICAL AND EXEGETICAL,** with a translation. vol. 1, 1862. **
Strict grammatical treatment of Scripture is always commendable, and in this case the results are highly valued by advanced scholars.

351 **Delitzsch, Franz –** *Job*, in **COMMENTARY ON THE OLD TESTAMENT.** Wm. B. Eerdmans Publishing Co. **
"Unquestionably the most valuable work on this inexhaustibly interesting Scripture that has reached us from Germany."— *Nonconformist.*

352 **Durham, James – EXPOSITION OF JOB.** 1659. ***
This is a small book, and we have been unable to procure it. Orme only mentions it upon the authority of Watt's *Bibliotheca*. It is certain to be good, for Durham is always admirable.

353 **Evans, Alfred Bowen – LECTURES ON THE BOOK OF JOB.** 1856. **
Discourses from 14 single verses from different parts of the patient partriarch's history. They are quite out of the usual run of Church of England preaching, and are full of thought and originality. They would have been all the better for a little gospel, for even if his text does not look that way, we do expect a Christian minister to have something to say about his Master.

354 **Fenton, Thomas – ANNOTATIONS ON JOB AND THE PSALMS,** collected from several commentators, and methodized and improved. 1732. **
All that will be found here is taken from others, but well selected.

355 **Fry, John – NEW TRANSLATION AND EXPOSITION,** with notes. 1827. ***
Written in a devout, enquiring spirit, with due respect to learned writers, but not with a slavish following of their fancies. Fry's work is somewhat of the same character as Good's (No. 358). We greatly esteem this exposition for its own sake, and also for the evangelical tone which pervades it.

356 **Garden, Charles – AN IMPROVED METRICAL VERSION,** with preliminary dissertation and notes. 1796. *
This author has not attempted a commentary, but he has consulted a vast array of authors, and from them gathered a large number of notes. His work is of very moderate value.

357 **Garnett, John – A DISSERTATION ON THE BOOK OF JOB.** 1749. *
Rubbish. This Bishop ascribes the authorship of Job to Ezekiel!

358 **Good, John Mason – THE BOOK OF JOB LITERALLY TRANSLATED,** with notes. 1812. **
A very valuable contribution to sacred literature. Dr. Good's learning was,

however, more extensive than accurate, and it would be dangerous to accept his translations without examination.

359 **Gregory the Great – ON THE BOOK OF JOB.** (The *Magna Moralia.*) Translated with notes and indices. *Library of the Fathers,* 4 vols. **
The Fathers are of course beyond criticism, and contain priceless gems here and there; but they spiritualize at such a rate, and also utter so many crudities and platitudes, that if they were modern writers they would not be so greatly valued as they are. Antiquity lends enchantment.

360 **Heath, Thomas – ESSAY TOWARDS A NEW ENGLISH VERSION OF THE BOOK OF JOB.** With a commentary, 1756. *
All that is good in this book is marred by its utterly untenable conjectures. It treats Job with slender reverence. Do not lumber your shelves with it.

361 **Hodges, Walter – ELIHU: An Enquiry Into the Scope and Design of the Book of Job.** 1750. *
Based on the absurd supposition that Elihu was the Son of God Himself, and Job a type of the Savior. Poor Job's book has been the subject of trials as numerous as those of its hero, and Hodges has given the finishing stroke. The course of dreaming can no further go. Hodge, the village Methodist, could never have raved at the rate of Dr. Hodge, Provost of Oriel College, Oxford.

362 **Hengstenberg, E. W.** See under "ECCLESIASTES." **

363 **Hulbert, Charles Augustus – THE GOSPEL REVEALED IN JOB.** Thirty lectures with notes, 1853. ***
An unusually good book; exceedingly comprehensive and helpful in many ways. The author aimed at usefulness and has succeeded wonderfully. We wonder that his work has not been better known.

364 **Hutcheson, George – AN EXPOSITION ON JOB,** being the sum of 316 lectures. 1669. ***
Whenever the student sees a commentary by Hutcheson let him buy it, for we know of no author who is more thoroughly helpful to the minister of the Word. He distills the text, and gives his readers the quintessence, ready for use.

365 **Hutchinson, R. E. – THOUGHTS ON THE BOOK OF JOB.** *

366 **Kitto, John – *Job* and *The Poetical Books*, in KITTO'S DAILY BIBLE ILLUSTRATIONS.** See No. 41, Kregel Publications. ***
Exceedingly instructive. Most charming reading.

367 **LANGE'S COMMENTARY ON THE HOLY SCRIPTURES.** *The Book of Job,* by Otto Zöckler. Translated from the German, with additions by professor L. J. Evans. Edited by Philip Schaff. ***
Contains a large collection of available material, and, if within a minister's means, should be a foundation book in his library. We are very far from endorsing all Zöckler's remarks, but the volume is an important one.

368 **Lee, Samuel – THE BOOK OF JOB.** Translated with introduction and commentary. 1837. **
Barnes says, "This work is not what might have been expected from the learning and reputation of Professor Lee. It abounds with Arabic learning, which is scattered with ostentatious profuseness through the volume, but which often contributes little to the elucidation of the text. It is designed for the critical scholar rather than the general reader.

369 Noyes, G. R. – A NEW TRANSLATION, with notes. **
We have been informed that Dr. Noyes belongs to the Unitarian body, but we fail to see any trace of Arian or Socinian views in this volume. We do no not agree with all he says, but he strikes us as being an honest, able, and accurate translator and commentator, worthy to stand in the foremost rank.

370 Peters, Charles – A CRITICAL DISSERTATION ON THE BOOK OF JOB. Wherein the account in that book by the author of *The Divine Legation of Moses Demonstrated*, is particularly considered; and a future state shewn to have been the popular belief of the ancient Hebrews. 1751. ***
Of a controversial character; mainly written against Warburton and Le Clerc, and as those authors are now almost forgotten, answers to them have lost their interest. Peters was an eminently learned man, and well–versed in argument; but his work is of very small use for homiletical purposes.

371 Quarles, Francis – JOB MILITANT, with meditations, divine and moral. 1624. **
A Poem in Quarles' usual inflated, but withal instructive, manner.

372 Robinson, T. – A HOMILETIC COMMENTARY ON JOB. Part 4 of the *Preacher's Commentary*. Baker Book House. ****
This we hope will be of use to preachers, but we have hardly enough before us to judge of it.

373 Scott, Thomas – THE BOOK OF JOB IN ENGLISH VERSE, with remarks. 1771. ***
Here we have Job in rhyme:
> There lived an Arab of distinguish'd fame,
> In Idumean Uz; and Job his name.
> Of spotless manners, with a soul sincere,
> Evil his hate, and God alone his fear.

This will hardly do. To translate Job in meter needed a Pope or a Dryden, and Thomas Scott was neither: he has, however, done his best, the best could have done no more. This is not Thomas Scott the great expositor, but a dissenting minister at Ipswich.

374 Senault, J. F. – A PARAPHRASE. 1648. *
Senault was a famous preacher of the Oratory in Paris, who, from the character of his works, would seem to have been almost a Protestant. His writings were highly esteemed in their day, and translated into English.

375 Smith, Elizabeth – THE BOOK OF JOB, translated from the Hebrew with annotations. 1810. ****
"A good English version of Job, produced chiefly by the aid of Parkhurst's *Lexicon*."— Orme.

376 Stather, W. C. – THE BOOK OF JOB, in English verse, with notes. 1859. ***
We do not like Job in rhyme. We know of no rhyming version of any part of Scripture, except the Psalms, which can be called a success. Certainly this is not one. The author's notes deserve consideration.

377 Stock, Joseph – THE BOOK OF JOB, metrically arranged, and newly translated, with notes. 1805. ***
The work of six weeks! Well may Magee say that it is full of "precipitances, mistakes, and mutilations." This was a bishop and a Doctor of Divinity! It

takes a great man to perpetuate a very great folly. A metrical translation of Job with notes in six weeks! In that time stocks bloom to perfection. Perhaps the fact operated on our author. Let this blundering haste serve as a warning to young divines.

378 **Umbreit, Friedrich** (1795-1860) – **A NEW VERSION OF THE BOOK OF JOB,** with notes. Translated by the Rev. John Hamilton Gray, 2 vols. **
Useful philologically; but Barnes would supply far more in that direction, and spiritual exposition besides.

379 **Van Hagen, Mrs. Henry** – **EVENINGS IN THE LAND OF UZ.** A comment on Job. 1843. **
Isaac Taylor commends this volume as one which, "disclaiming all purpose of critical exposition, aims only under the guidance of Christian feeling and experience to follow and to unfold the spiritual intention of this rich portion of Holy Scripture." Such an introduction must have helped to sell the work and carry it speedily to the second edition.

380 **Wagner, George** – **SERMONS ON THE BOOK OF JOB.** 1863. **
Wagner's sermons are simple and plain, devout and instructive. We have here nothing very fresh, but everything is sound and good.

381 **Wemyss, Thomas** – **JOB AND HIS TIMES.** New version with notes. 1839. **
Albert Barnes says: "This is designed to be a popular work. It is not so much of the nature of a commentary as a collection of fragments and brief essays on various topics referred to in the Book of Job. It is chiefly valuable for its illustration of the religion of the time of Job, the arts and sciences, the manners and customs, etc." It lacks lucid arrangement, and furnishes comparatively little illustration of the difficulties of the text.

PSALMS

382 **Abbot, George** – **BRIEF NOTES,** being a pithy and clear opening of the scope and meaning of the text, to the capacity of the weakest. 1651. **
An experimental exposition by a Member of Parliament under the Commonwealth. Though not of the first order, many of his remarks are good. Abbot was nephew to the Archbishop of the same name.

383 **Alexander, Joseph Addison** – **THE PSALMS,** translated and explained. 1864. ***
Occupies a first place among expositions. It is a clear and judicious explanation of the text, and cannot be dispensed with.

384 **Alexander, William Henry** – **THE BOOK OF PRAISES.** The Psalms with notes. 1867. *
The notes are mostly from other authors, and are selected with discretion. They do not appear to have been designed by their collector for use beyond his own family circle, and they were published after his death by his friends. We question the wisdom of this publication.

385 **Augustine** – **EXPOSITIONS,** translated with notes. 6 vols., 1847. **
As a Father, he is beyond ordinary criticism, or we would venture to say that he is too frequently mystical and confounds plain texts. No theological library

is complete without this work, for there are grand thoughts in it like huge nuggets of Australian gold.

386 Baker, Richard – THE PSALMS EVANGELIZED. 1811. *
Very pious; but if the work should ever disappear from literature its absence will not leave a very great gap. Bishop Horne and Dr. Hawker between them more than cover the space.

387 Barnes, Albert – *Psalms*, in BARNES' NOTES ON THE OLD TESTAMENT. Edited by Robert Frew. Baker Book House. *******
Thoroughly good. Using these notes constantly, we are more and more struck with their value. For the general run of preachers this is probably the best commentary extant.

388 Bellarmine, Robert – A COMMENTARY, translated from the Latin by the Ven. John O'Sullivan. 1866. ******
Popish, but marvelously good for a Cardinal. He is frequently as evangelical as a Reformer. He follows the Vulgate text in this comment.

389 Bellet, J. G. – SHORT MEDITATIONS ON THE PSALMS, chiefly in their prophetic character. 1871. *****
Mere fragments in a style which we do not admire, which seems to be peculiar to certain brethren. Only the inflated can understand what such writers mean.

390 Binnie, William – THE PSALMS: Their History, Teachings, and Use. 1870. *******
A highly valuable work. It is not an exposition, but can readily be used as such, for it possesses a good index to the passages treated. Dr. Binnie reviews with great skill and intense devotion the various sacred poems contained in the Book of Psalms, and gives the general run and character of each one. His work is unlike any other, and supplies a great desideratum.

391 Bonar, Andrew A. – CHRIST AND HIS CHURCH IN THE BOOK OF PSALMS. 1859. *******
Of the highest order of merit. The author does not strain the text, but gives its real meaning. His remarks are always weighty, spiritual, and suggestive; we only wish there were more of them. He has cultivated brevity.

392 Bouchier, Barton – MANNA IN THE HEART; or, Daily Comments on the Psalms, for the use of families. 2 vols., 1856. ******
Among the best books ever written for family reading. Evangelical, devotional, and expository. Preachers will find good thoughts here.

393 Burton, John – THE BOOK OF PSALMS IN ENGLISH VERSE. 1871 *****
The Psalms rhymed in a New Testament spirit; they are better in prose.

394 Bush, G. – A COMMENTARY ON THE BOOK OF PSALMS. With a new literal version. 1838. ******
Does not appear to have been reprinted in England.

395 Bythner, Victor – THE LYRE OF DAVID; or, An Analysis of the Psalms, Critical and Practical; to which is added a Hebrew and Chaldee grammar. To which is added by the translator a praxis of the first eight Psalms. Translated by the Rev. Thomas Dee, 1836. *******
We agree with the statement found in the preface of this work: "Nearly two centuries have passed away, since Bythner, uncertain of its reception, first committed his *Lyra* to public light; during which time, instead of sinking, it has

advanced in estimation; being admitted by all the learned to be the very best work on the Psalms in Hebrew. The number of Hebrew radical words is 1,867; of these, 1,184 occur in the Psalms. It follows then, that a thorough knowledge of the Psalms very nearly amounts to a thorough knowledge of the language, and that Bythner's *Lyra*, in being the best work on the Psalms, must be the best work on Hebrew in general." Our readers will scarcely need us to add that Bythner's work is only useful to those who study the Hebrew.

396 **Calvin, John** – THE PSALMS OF DAVID and others, with commentaries. Translated by Arthur Golding, 2 vols., 1571. *******

397 **Calvin, John** – *A Commentary on the Psalms*, in CALVIN'S COMMENTARIES. Baker Book House. **** ***
Calvin is a tree whose "leaf also shall not wither"; whatever he has written lives on, and is never out of date, because he expounded the Word without bias or partiality.

398 **Carter, Charles** – THE PSALMS, newly translated from the Hebrew. 1869 ******
The emendations are carefully made by the translator, who has been for many years engaged upon the Singalese version. A helpful book.

399 **Cayley, C. B.** – THE PSALMS IN METRE, with notes. 1860. ******
We do not think much of the metrical rendering, which often jars on the ear. There are a few good notes at the end.

400 **Champney, H. N.** – A TEXTUAL COMMENTARY ON THE PSALMS. 1852. *****
Merely a collection of parallel texts. Make one for yourself.

401 **Chandler, Samuel.** See No. 283. ******

402 **Clay, William Keatinge** – EXPOSITORY NOTES, on the prayer book version of the Psalms. 1839. ******
Commendable in its way, but not important. Most of its matter is to be found elsewhere.

403 **Coleman, John Noble** – PSALTERIUM MESSIANICUM DAVIDIS REGIS ET PROPHETAE. A revision of the Authorized Version, with notes, original and selected; vindicating the prophetic manifestations of Messiah in the Psalms. 1865. ******
Useful for its quotations from the Fathers and ancient writers. The large type swells out a small quantity of material to a needless size, and so puts purchasers to an unnecessary expense.

404 **Conant, Thomas J.** – THE PSALMS. The common version revised for the American Bible Union. 1871. ******
A trustworthy translation with a few notes.

405 **Congleton, Lord** – THE PSALMS. A new version with notes. 1875. *****
The translation is mainly that of Rogers (see No. 464), and the notes refer the Psalms to historic and prophetic subjects. We see no use whatever in this production.

406 **Cowles, Henry** – THE PSALMS, with notes. 1872. *******
Always repays for consulting, though it does not contain much that is new, original, or profound.

407 **Cresswell, Daniel – PSALMS OF DAVID,** according to the Book of Common Prayer, with notes. 1843. **

The explanatory notes are neither prolix nor commonplace, but show much clear insight. They are deservedly held in esteem.

408 **A CRITICAL TRANSLATION OF THE PSALMS,** in Meter. **

The author has labored hard to arrive at the correct meaning of the Hebrew, and to versify it. The work is very carefully done.

409 **Dallas, A. R. C. – THE BOOK OF PSALMS,** arranged in daily portions for devotional reading. 1860. *

A new arrangement: the old one is good enough for us.

410 **Darby, J. N. – PRACTICAL REFLECTIONS.** 1870. *

Too mystical for ordinary minds. If the author would write in plain English his readers would probably discover that there is nothing very valuable in his remarks.

411 **De Burgh, William – COMMENTARY:** Critical, Devotional, and Prophetical. 2 vols. 1860. **

A second-advent interpreter, and one of the best of his class. Highly esteemed by those who are enthusiastic upon prophetical subjects.

412 **Delitzsch, Franz – *Psalms*,** in vol. 5 of **COMMENTARY ON THE OLD TESTAMENT.** Wm. B. Eerdmans Publishing Co. **

Thoroughly learned, but wants unction. Not adapted for common readers, but scholars will prize greatly. The *Princeton Review* says of it: "We commend this commentary as a valuable aid to preachers and exegetes in elucidating the Psalms."

413 **Dickson, David – A BRIEF EXPLANATION OF THE PSALMS.** 1655. ***

A rich volume, dropping fatness. Invaluable to the preacher. Having read and re-read it, we can speak of its holy savor and suggestiveness. We commend it with much fervor.

414 **Dimock, H. – NOTES,** critical and explanatory, on the Book of Psalms. 1791. *

The notes mainly concern the various readings, and exhibit considerable learning; but we do not think much of a homiletical kind can be got out of them.

415 **Dunwell, F. H. – PAROCHIAL LECTURES ON THE PSALMS** from the Fathers of the Primitive Church. 1855. **

This author spiritualizes far too much. His metaphors are overdone.

416 **Edwards, Joseph – DEVOTIONAL EXPOSITIONS.** 1850. *

A paraphrase of no great value.

417 **Edwards, T. – NEW TRANSLATION,** with notes. 1755. *

The writer was an able man, but his book is of small worth.

418 **Ewart, J. – LECTURES ON THE PSALMS.** 3 vols., 1826. *

The author was a Presbyterian minister of the time of the Pretender, and we suspect that he was a high and dry moderate. His comments were given at the public reading of the Scriptures, and although destitute of spirituality and Gospel clearness, they are not without a measure of originality.

419 **Exton, Richard Brudenell** – SIXTY LECTURES ON THE
PSALMS, as appointed to be read in the services of the Church of
England. 1847. *
Very poor and prosy. We pity the hearer who sat out these 60 lectures.

420 **Fenton, Thomas** – ANNOTATIONS ON JOB AND PSALMS, from
several commentators. 1732. **
The annotations are choice, but will be found in easily accessible works.

421 **Fenwick, George** – THOUGHTS ON THE HEBREW TITLES OF
THE PSALMS. 1749. **

422 **Fenwick, George** – THE PSALTER IN ITS ORIGINAL FORM,
with arguments and notes. 1789. **
These two works are praiseworthy in design, but they are too fanciful.

423 **Forbes, Granville** – THE VOICE OF GOD IN THE PSALMS. *
Sermons by a Northamptonshire Rector of the broad school. They do not strike
us as being anything very wonderful; certainly "the voice of God" is not
remarkably audible in them.

424 **"Four Friends."** – THE PSALMS OF DAVID CHRONOLOGI-
CALLY ARRANGED, with notes. By Four Friends. 1867. *
Here the Psalms are thrust out of their usual order and treated after the manner
of the broad school of thought. We do not attach any great value to this
production. With some persons perversity passes for profundity, and if a man
differs from everybody else they are persuaded that he must be an original
genius: the "four friends" will stand high in the esteem of such critics. We
neither believe in their chronology, their theology, nor their philology.

425 **French, William** and **Skinner, George** – TRANSLATION, with
notes. 1842. **
A version of high esteem. Notes very short.

426 **Fry, John** – A TRANSLATION AND EXPOSITION OF THE
PSALMS; on the principles adopted in the posthumous work of Bishop
Horsley; viz., that those sacred oracles have, for the most part, an
immediate reference to Christ and to His first and second advents.
1842. **
Fry follows Bishop Horsley and looks much to the Second Advent. The work
is not fair either as a translation or as an exposition. It is useful in its own
direction, as showing how a peculiar theory has been supported by an able
man; but it must not be implicitly relied upon.

427 **Fysh, Frederic** – A LYRICAL, LITERAL VERSION, with notes. 2
vols., 1851. **
A valuable literal version. Notes scant, but scholarly.

428 **Geddes, Alexander** – NEW TRANSLATION, with various readings
and notes. 1807. *
This is said to be "a careful rendering, aiming at the primary meaning of the
psalmists." Dr. Henderson speaks of Geddes as flagrantly disfiguring his
biblical labors with profanity. He was a singular mixture of Romanist and free-
thinker.

429 **Good, John Mason** – HISTORICAL OUTLINE OF THE BOOK
OF PSALMS. Edited by the Rev. John Mason Neale, 1842. ***
This is not a commentary, but may be regarded as an introduction to the work

next mentioned, by the same author. Historical light is frequently the very best which can be cast upon a passage, and Dr. Good has known how to apply it. He may sometimes be thought fanciful, but he is never really speculative, and he almost always says something worth noting.

430 **Good, J. M. – THE BOOK OF PSALMS;** a new translation, with notes. Edited by the Rev. E. Henderson, 1854. *******
Dr. Good was a medical gentleman with a large practice, and yet he managed to produce this learned volume. "I save every quarter of an hour for it," says he, "for my heart is in it." He was a man of great attainments and genuine piety. The progress made in Hebrew philology and exegesis since his day has been great; but his work has not been altogether superseded. It is of a high class, from a literary point of view, but must not be blindly followed.

431 **Green, William – A TRANSLATION** with notes. 1762. *****
A translation with meagre notes.

432 **Hammond, Henry – PARAPHRASE AND ANNOTATIONS.** 1659, 1850. ******
Much esteemed, and deservedly so. Hammond's weighty tome is somewhat dry, and many of his remarks are rather those of a linguist than of a divine, but he touches on many matters which others omit, and is, upon the whole, an expositor of singular merit.

433 **Hapstone, Dalman – THE PSALMS IN APPROPRIATE METERS.** A strictly literal translation with notes, 1867. *****
We prefer our own version, and do not think many of Mr. Hapstone's stanzas successful as attempts at poetry.

434 **Hengstenberg, E. W. – COMMENTARY.** 3 vols., 1845-8. ******
A masterly work; but about as dry as Gideon's unwetted fleece.

435 **Hiller, O. Prescott – NOTES ON THE PSALMS (1-77).** Explanatory of their spiritual sense. 1869. *****
Swedenborgian, and frequently absurd. The author confounds rather than expounds.

436 **Horne, George** (1730–1792) – **COMMENTARY.** (Numerous editions: among others a Glasgow edition, 3 vols. with an Introductory Essay by Edward Irving, which is one of Irving's best efforts. Tegg's edition, 1 vol.) *******
It has been said that this author had no qualification for a commentator except piety. This is not true, for he had natural poetry in his soul; and even if it were true, his work would go far to show how abundantly piety compensates for other deficiencies. He is among the best of our English writers on this part of Scripture and certainly one of the most popular.

437 **Horsley, Samuel – THE BOOK OF PSALMS,** with notes explanatory and critical. 1833. ******
Vigorous writing, with a propensity to indulge in new readings, and a persistent twist in one direction. The notes show the hand of a master, and have exerted much influence in directing thoughtful minds to the subject of the Second Advent, as foreshadowed in the Old Testament, but they must be used with extreme caution.

438 **Jebb, John – LITERAL TRANSLATION;** with dissertations on the word Selah, and on the authorship, order, titles, and poetry of the Psalms. 2 vols., 1846. ******

Jebb takes for his motto in translating that saying of Hooker: "I hold it for an infallible rule in expositions of sacred Scripture, that where a literal construction will stand, the farthest from the letter is commonly the worst." His notes are scant, but his dissertations in the second volume are most admirable.

439 **Jennings, A. C.** and **Lowe, W. H.** – **THE PSALMS,** with introductions and critical notes. Books III and IV (Psalms 73 to 106). 1874 ******
Learned, but more occupied with mere verbal criticisms than with any useful suggestions which could be turned to account by a preacher.

440 **Jones, Joseph** – **THE PSALMS;** with reflections. 1846. *****
Pious, but poor.

441 **Kay, William** – **THE PSALMS TRANSLATED FROM THE HEBREW,** with notes, chiefly exegetical. 1871. *******
A refreshing book; the notes being out of the ordinary run, and casting much light on many passages. To thoroughly appreciate this author one should be a Hebrew scholar.

442 **Keble, John** – **THE PSALTER IN ENGLISH VERSE.** 1869. ******
A poet's version of a grand series of poems.

443 **LANGE'S COMMENTARY ON THE HOLY SCRIPTURES.** *Psalms,* by various authors. Edited by Philip Schaff. ******
Comparatively feeble. Not up to the usual standard of this admirable series. Still, it is among the best of the modern commentaries.

444 **Linton, Henry** – **THE PSALMS OF DAVID AND SOLOMON EXPLAINED.** 1871. *****
A small affair in all ways.

445 **Luther, Martin** – **A MANUAL OF THE BOOK OF PSALMS;** or The Subject-contents of all the Psalms. Translated by Rev. Henry Cole, 1823. ******
Fragmentary, a mere table of contents, but truly Lutheran.

446 **Mant, Richard** – **THE BOOK OF PSALMS IN AN ENGLISH METRICAL VERSION,** with notes. 1824. *******
A bold version, with important notes. In this instance we confess that there may be real poetry in a metrical version, and though the flame does not in each composition burn with equal brilliance, yet in some verses it is the true poetic fire. Mant is no mean writer.

447 **Marsh, Edward Garrard** – **THE BOOK OF PSALMS,** translated into English verse, with notes. 1832. *****
Contains nothing of any consequence to an expositor, though the verse is considerably above the average of such productions.

448 **Merrick, James** – **THE PSALMS PARAPHRASED IN ENGLISH VERSE.** 1766. *****

Merrick, James – **ANNOTATIONS ON THE PSALMS.** 1778. *****
These two works are scarce. They are rather more suited for the admirers of poetry than for ministers of the Word. It is said that some of the notes are by Archbishop Secker, and that Lowth also aided in the exposition; but the combined result is of no great value to the preacher.

449 Morison, John – EXPOSITION OF THE BOOK OF PSALMS, explanatory, critical and devotional. 2 vols., 1829. 3 vols., 1832. *******
The first volume is the best. There is nothing very original, but it is an instructive exposition, and ought to be better known.

450 Mudge, Zachary – AN ESSAY TOWARDS A NEW ENGLISH VERSION. 1744. *****
Elegant in taste rather than sound in scholarship. Mudge was highly esteemed by Dr. Johnson, and he was no doubt a very worthy man; but his exposition can be dispensed with.

451 Murphy, James G. – A CRITICAL AND EXEGETICAL COMMENTARY. 1875. *******
This may be called a volume of compressed thought. The author has aimed at neither being too long nor too short. He has succeeded in producing a very useful and usable work, with many points of unusual value. Dr. Murphy is well–known as an accomplished Hebraist and a lucid expositor. We have noticed his works on Genesis (No. 134) and Exodus (No. 176).

452 Neale, John Mason and Littledale, R. F. – A COMMENTARY, from primitive and medieval writers. 4 vols., 1860-74. ******
Unique, and to very high churchmen most precious. We admire the learning and research; but the conceits, the twistings, and allegorical interpretations surpass conception. As a collection of medieval mysticisms it is unrivalled.

453 Nicholson, William – DAVID'S HARP STRUNG AND TUNED; or, An Easy Analysis of the Whole Book of Psalms. 1662. ******
"Wholly practical and explanatory. In his explications the author steers between the two extremes of literal and spiritual interpretation. Dr. Adam Clarke has inserted Bishop Nicholson's analysis in his commentary on the Psalms, omitting his prayers"— Horne.

454 Noyes, G. R. – A NEW TRANSLATION WITH NOTES. 1831 and 1846. ******
Dr. Noyes was the Hebrew Professor in Harvard University. His introduction is full of information; the new translation is useful, and the notes are brief and pertinent.

455 Oxenden, Ashton – A SIMPLE EXPOSITION. 2 vols. *****
For reading at family prayers. Alas, poor families! Ye have need of patience.

456 Perowne, J. J. Stewart – THE BOOK OF PSALMS; a new translation with introductions and notes. 1864-68. *******
A masterpiece of extraordinary learning and critical skill, although not altogether what we would desire. The *"Saturday Review"* said: "Mr. Perowne is probably as capable as anyone in England of doing all that Hebrew scholarship can do towards a better knowledge of the Psalms. The learning which he has brought together gives a value of its own to his book and makes it an important contribution to a department of biblical scholarship in which we are at present rather poorly furnished."

457 Pierce, Samuel Eyles – THE BOOK OF PSALMS. 2 vols., 1817, very rare. ******
This author is held in high esteem for the "sound and savoury" character of his works. On the Psalms he writes for comfort and edification. The work is regarded as super-excellent by our extra-calvinistic friends, but we do not think it quite the fancy price which is now asked.

458 Phillips, George – THE PSALMS IN HEBREW, with commentary. 2 vols., 1846. ******
This commentary will be valued by Hebrew scholars; but it is beyond the general attainments of those for whom this Index is compiled.

459 A PLAIN COMMENTARY ON THE BOOK OF PSALMS. (P. B. Version), chiefly grounded on the Fathers. 2 vols., 1859. *******
Of the High Church school, and rather strained in places, but abounding in sweet spiritual thoughts. We have read it with pleasure and profit, though with some caution.

460 Plumer, William S. – STUDIES IN THE BOOK OF PSALMS. 1867. ******
A huge volume, compiled from such works as were accessible to the author in the United States. Full of instructive comment, but not very original, or remarkably learned.

461 A PRACTICAL ILLUSTRATION OF THE BOOK OF PSALMS. By the author of *The Family Commentary on the New Testament.* 2 vols., 1826. *****
For families. Consisting of remarks which would occur to any motherly person.

462 Pridham, Arthur – NOTES AND REFLECTIONS ON THE BOOK OF PSALMS. 1869. ******
Spiritual reflections of an excellent kind, but not very striking.

463 REMARKS UPON THE PSALMS AS PROPHETIC OF THE MESSIAH. 1843. *****
Mere outlines; of no consequence.

464 Rogers, J. – THE BOOK OF PSALMS IN HEBREW, metrically arranged; with selections from the various readings of Kennicott and De Rossi, and from the ancient versions. 2 vols., 1833. *****
For the Hebrew scholar only.

465 Rosenmüller, Ernest F. C. – ANNOTATIONS ON THE MESSI- ANIC PSALMS. Translated, 1841. ******
It may be altogether our own fault, but we cannot make any use of this volume. No doubt these scholastic notes have a value; but commentaries upon inspired Scripture written in the same style as one might write upon Ovid or Horace are not to our taste. Gesenius praises this work for its criticisms. We wish there had been a little religion in it, but perhaps if there had been it would have been the religion of neology.

466 Ryland, R. H. – THE PSALMS RESTORED TO MESSIAH. 1853. ******
Written with an admirable design. Good, but not very able. The subject still demands the pen of a master.

467 Sheriffe, Mrs. – PRACTICAL REFLECTIONS. 2 vols., 1820. *****
We hope they benefited the printer; they will not help the reader much.

468 Spurgeon, Charles Haddon – THE TREASURY OF DAVID con- taining an original exposition of the Book of Psalms; a collection of illustrative extracts from the whole range of literature; a series of homiletical hints upon almost every verse; and lists of writers upon each Psalm. *Spurgeon on the Psalms,* edited by David Otis Fuller, 1 vol., Kregel Publications. *The Treasury of David,* 7 vols., Pilgrim Publications; 2 vols., Baker Book House. **

Reviewers have handled this book with remarkable kindness, and the public have endorsed their judgment by largely purchasing the volumes already issued. It would not become us to say more.

469 **Street, Stephen** – A NEW LITERAL VERSION, with a preface and notes. 2 vols., 1790. *

One hardly desires a rigidly literal translation of a poetic book, for the beauty and spirit are lost. The notes are purely critical and are superseded by later works.

470 **Tholuck, Augustus** – A TRANSLATION AND COMMENTARY, translated from the German by J. Isidor Mombert. 1856. **

Tholuck is one of the most spiritual of the German interpreters. Though we cannot say that this is equal to some others of his works, yet he is a great writer, and always deserves attention.

471 **Thrupp, Joseph Francis** – AN INTRODUCTION TO THE STUDY AND USE OF THE PSALMS. 2 vols., 1860. **

Though not the best, it is still a learned and helpful work of its class.

472 **Tucker, William Hill** – THE PSALMS, with notes, showing their prophetic and Christian character. 1840. **

The writer refers all the Psalms to Christ, and writes many weighty things, but we cannot place him in the front rank among expositors.

473 **Wake, W. R.** – A LITERAL VERSION OF THE PSALMS INTO MODERN LANGUAGE, according to the Liturgy translation. 2 vols., 1793. *

Think of a translation of a translation. The author was Wake, but not awake, or he would never have wasted so much good paper.

474 **Walford, William** – A NEW TRANSLATION, with notes, explanatory and critical. 1837. **

Contains some useful notes, good, but not specially remarkable.

475 **Weiss, Benjamin** – A NEW TRANSLATION, EXPOSITION, AND CHRONOLOGICAL ARRANGEMENT OF THE BOOK OF PSALMS, with critical notes. 1852 *

The Psalms are arranged in a new order, and are very hard to find. The author is dogmatic to the last degree. Our estimate of his work is not so high as his own.

476 **Wilcocks, Thomas** – A VERY GODLY AND LEARNED EXPOSITION UPON THE WHOLE BOOK OF PSALMS. See No. 336. **

Short spiritual remarks, followed by many doctrinal inferences, calculated to suggest topics to preachers.

477 **Wilson, W.** (1549-1608) – THE PSALMS; with an exposition, typical and prophetical of the Christian dispensation. 2 vols., 1860. ***

We have consulted Wilson with advantage and often quoted from him in the *Treasury of David.* He is a clear, gospel expositor, and has written much that is weighty and precious.

478 **Woodford, Samuel – A PARAPHRASE. 1667. ***
Poor rhymes; though the preface says of the author:
> At length the skilful way you found,
> With a true ear judg'd the melodious sound,
> And with a nimble hand run descant on the Hebrew ground.

It would seem from this that the poem scrambles on all-fours, and we think it does.

479 **Wright, Abraham – A PRACTICAL COMMENTARY,** wherein the text of every Psalm is practically expounded, according to the doctrine of the Catholic Church, in a way not usually trod by commentators; and wholly applied to the life and salvation of Christians. 1661. ******
Wright selects the more remarkable verses, and comments upon them in a deeply spiritual, quaint, and suggestive manner.

480 **Zillwood, J. O. – THE PSALMS ARRANGED IN PARALLELISMS,** with notes, chiefly from Bishops Horne and Horsley. 2 vols., 1855. *****
The student had better get Horne and Horsley for himself, and he will have no need of this.

PORTIONS OF THE PSALMS

481 **Baker, Sir Richard – MEDITATIONS AND DISQUISITIONS ON THE FIRST AND SEVEN PENITENTIAL PSALMS,** viz., the 6, 32, 38, 51, 102, 130 and 143. 1640. *******

MEDITATIONS AND DISQUISITIONS ON THE SEVEN CONSOLITARY PSALMS, viz., the 23, 27, 30, 34, 84, 103, and 116. 1640 *******
O rare Sir Richard Baker! Knight of the flowing pen. His *Meditations and Disquisitions* are altogether marrow and fatness. We have often tried to quote from him and have found ourselves so embarrassed with riches that we have been inclined to copy the whole book. Why it has not been reprinted, and made to pass through 50 editions, we cannot tell. Poor man, he became a surety and smarted, dying in poverty in the Fleet. Were there any Christians alive in those days?

482 **Barker, Frederick – THIRTY-SIX PSALMS,** with commentary and prayer for use in families. 1854. *****
What platitudes people will write for the use of families. Families will best use these commentaries and prayers by lining their cake tins with them.

483 **Bertram, R. A. – THE IMPRECATORY PSALMS.** Six lectures, 1867. ******
Contains some very sensible remarks upon a subject which no doubt bewilders certain of the weaker sort.

484 **Bowman, Hetty – STUDIES IN THE PSALMS. 1869. ***
Outlines of teaching upon a few Psalms. The authoress begs that these "Studies" may not in any sense be considered as a commentary. We do not so consider them.

485 **Boys, John** – WORKS. An exposition of the proper Psalms used in our English liturgy. 1629. ***
One of the richest of writers. From his golden pen flows condensed wisdom. Many of his sentences are worthy to be quoted as gems of the Christian classics.

486 **Cope, Anthony** – MEDITATIONS ON TWENTY SELECT PSALMS. Reprinted from the edition of 1547. 1848. *
More curious than valuable. The style is scholastic and pointless.

487 **Didham, R. Cunningham** – PSALMS 1-36. New translation made by means of Arabic lexicons, Syriac New Testament words, the ancient versions, Bishop Lowth's parallelisms, and parallel places whereby the scriptural Messianic Canon that our Lord Jesus Christ is the key to the Psalms is upheld. 1870. *
Principally consists of denunciations of others writers.

488 **Luther, Martin** – SELECT WORKS OF LUTHER, a commentary on Psalms 1—11; and on Psalm 51, in vol. 3, and on Psalm 2 in vol. 4. Translated by Rev. H. Cole, 4 vols., 1824. **

A COMMENTARY ON THE PSALMS, commonly called the Psalms of Degrees [120-134]. 1823. **
Luther needs no trumpeter.

489 **Pitman, J. R.** – A COURSE OF SERMONS on some of the chief subjects in the book of Psalms, abridged from eminent divines of the established church. 1846. *
We have seldom obtained much from these sermons. A far better selection might have been made; at the same time, some of the discourses are admirable.

490 **Rollock, Robert** – AN EXPOSITION ON SOME SELECT PSALMS. 1600. **
Rollock's works are rare. He wrote in Latin, and his language is made more dull than need be by the translator. All his writings are masterly.

491 **Strigellius, Victorinus** – HARMONY OF KING DAVID'S HARP. Translated by R. Robinson. In four parts. 1582 to 1596. **
This volume the expositor is not at all likely to see, and there is, therefore, the less need for us to speak of. Strigellius was the friend of Luther and Melancthon, and a man of sound sense and vast learning.

492 **Williams, Isaac** – THE PSALMS INTERPRETED OF CHRIST. (Vol. 1., Psalms 1-26.) 1864. ***
This writer is of the High Church school, but he is very spiritual and deep, and we seldom turn to him without profit.

THE PENITENTIAL PSALMS

(The Penitential Psalms are seven in number. Psalms 6, 32, 38, 51, 102, 130, and 143. For 102 some substitute 25.)

493 **Baker, R.** See No. 481. ***

494 Donne, John – SERMONS ON THE PENITENTIAL PSALMS. In vols. 2 and 3 of his *Works*. 6 vols., 1839. ***
A right royal writer, whose every line is a pearl.

495 Fisher, John – FRUITFUL SAYNGES OF DAVID. 1509, reprinted 1714. *
Dry and tedious; in the stiff antique style.

496 Hayward, John – DAVID'S TEARS. On Psalms 6, 32 and 130 only. 1623. **
After the Puritanic method: full of point and pith.

497 Oxenden, Charles – SERMONS ON THE SEVEN PENITENTIAL PSALMS. Preached during Lent. 1838. *
To listen to these sermons must have afforded a suitable Lenten penance to those who went to church to hear them. There their use began and ended.

498 Symson, Archibald – A SACRED SEPTENARIE; or, A Godly and Fruitful Exposition on the Seven Psalms of Repentance. 1638. ***
A marrowy author, full of instruction.

SEPARATE PSALMS

(The following works are arranged according to the order of the Psalms, to assist reference. We have not attempted to include all writers in this list.)

499 (1) Smith, Samuel – DAVID'S BLESSED MAN. Ninth edition, 1635. Reprinted in Nichol's *Commentaries,* with Pierson (see no. 527); and Gouge (see no. 560). **
Very popular in its day, and worthily so.

500 (1) Stonham, Matthew – A TREATISE ON THE FIRST PSALM. 1610. **
Somewhat dry, scholastic, and out of date; but still an interesting and instructive piece of old divinity.

501 (2, 45, 110) Harpur, George – CHRIST IN THE PSALMS. A series of discourses. 1862. **
Discourses of a high order as to ability, but the historico-prophetic interpretations here given do not commend themselves to us.

502 (2) Pitcairn, David – ZION'S KING. 1851. **
This author does not err on the side of conciseness. His book is a meritorious effort, but we have found it somewhat heavy reading.

503 (4, 42, 51, 63) Horton, Thomas – CHOICE AND PRACTICAL EXPOSITIONS. 1675. ***
A marvellous homiletical exposition. Horton's discourses are very full of diversions, but then he always has plenty of solid matter to divide. Ministers will find teeming suggestions here.

504 (15) Cartwright, Christopher – COMMENTARY. 1658. **
A learned and weighty work; not readily met with.

505 (15) Downame, George – LECTURES. 1604. **
Lectures by one of the race of giant divines.

506 **(15) Turnbull, Richard – FOUR SERMONS ON PSALM 15.** 1606.
Forming last part of volume on James and Jude. **
By a popular and edifying preacher of the olden times.

507 **(16) Dale, Thomas – THE GOLDEN PSALM.** 1847. *
Good, simple discourses; the headings might suggest a course of sermons.

508 **(16) Frame, James – CHRIST IN GETHSEMANE.** 1858. **
A sterling, well-intentioned and well-executed comment. The text has to be a
little twisted to suit the theory of the interpreter, but we do not suppose that Mr.
Frame is conscious of it. He is one of the best of modern discoursers upon the
Pslams.

509 **(18) Brown, John – THE SUFFERINGS AND GLORIES OF THE
MESSIAH.** 1853. ***
Like all Dr. Brown's productions, this is a work of the highest order. Clear,
full, and, in the best manner, exegetical.

510 **(19) Reeve, J. W. – LECTURES ON THE NINETEENTH PSALM.**
1863. ***
By one of the ablest preachers among the evangelical Episcopalians. Scriptural, thoughtful, and original.

511 **(19) Richardson, J. Wilberforce – ILLUSTRATIONS OF THE
NINETEENTH PSALM.** 1870. **
Sound in doctrine, but verbose and commonplace.

512 **(20, vv.1-6) Bownd, Nicholas – MEDICINES FOR THE PLAGUE.**
Twenty-one sermons. 1604. **
Racy, quaint, extremely rare.

513 **(22) Frame, James – THE SONG OF THE CROSS.** 1872. **
This is valuable, as Mr. Frame's books generally are.

514 **(22) Stevenson, John – CHRIST ON THE CROSS.** An exposition of
Psalm 22. **
The best of Dr. Stevenson's books. Exceedingly precious in its unveiling of
the Redeemer's sorrows. We have derived personal spiritual benefit from the
perusal of this gracious exposition, and are unable to judge it critically.

515 **(23) Stevenson, John – THE LORD OUR SHEPHERD.** An exposition of Psalm 23. **
Too wire-drawn, but it is golden wire.

516 **(23) Baker, R.** See No. 481. ***

517 **(23) Dale, Thomas – THE GOOD SHEPHERD AND THE CHO-
SEN FLOCK.** 1847. **
Somewhat ordinary evangelical discourses.

518 **(23, 62, 73-77) Hooper, John – CERTAIN COMFORTABLE EX-
POSITIONS.** *
The cramped style and antiquated matter repel the reader.

519 **(23, 84) Miller, Andrew – MEDITATIONS ON TWENTY-THIRD
AND EIGHTY-FOURTH PSALMS.** **
Discursive, but devout; more useful to the heart than the head.

520 (23) Paton, James – THE CHILDREN'S PSALM. 12 meditations and 12 spiritual songs. 1870. **
Worthy of much commendation. It is unfortunate that the title leads the reader to expect a book for children, whereas the author intended to edify the children of God of an older growth.

521 (23) Sedgwick, Obadiah – THE SHEPHERD OF ISRAEL. 1658. **
Sedgwick was one of the most eminent preachers of the time of the Commonwealth. His commenting is solid and lively.

522 (23) Smith, Samuel – THE CHIEFE SHEPHEARD; or An Exposition on Ye 23rd Psalme. 1625. **
All the writings of Samuel Smith are good, but not so full of memorable sentences and pithy sayings as certain others of their date.

523 (23) Stoughton, John – THE SONG OF CHRIST'S FLOCK. 1860. **
Devout practical meditations, but we don't see how a flock can sing.

524 (23) Thornton, J. – THE SHEPHERD OF ISRAEL. 1826. *
We need no longer wonder how spiders make such long threads with such little material, for here is an equally amazing instance of spinning. Plentiful quotations of Scripture, and venerable anecdotes are here used as substitutes for thoughts, not as aids to it.

525 (25) Halket, Lady Anne – MEDITATIONS. 1778. **
This lady was eminent for medicine as well as theology; she left 21 volumes. This and another book of meditations appear to be all that have been reprinted.

526 (25) Mossom, Robert – THE PREACHER'S TRIPARTITE. Contains divine meditations upon Psalm 25. 1657. ***

527 (27, 84, 85, 87) Pierson, Thomas – EXCELLENT ENCOURAGEMENTS AGAINST AFFLICTIONS. 1647. Reprinted in *Nichol's Commentaries,* with Smith, No 499; and Gouge, No. 560. **
Pierson was not the richest or most overflowing of the old divines, but yet one who stood in the front rank.

528 (32) Bingham, Charles H. – LECTURES. 1836. *
Tame sermons. Faultlessly feeble. Good, but no good.

529 (32) Leighton, Robert – PSALM 32. ***
In some editions of Leighton's collected works will be found choice meditations on this Psalm, and also on Psalms 4 and 130. Everything that fell from his pen is worth its weight in diamonds.

530 (32) Taylor, Thomas – DAVID'S LEARNING, or Way to True Happiness. 1617. Also in his *Works.* 1660. **
On account of Taylor's great knowledge of the Scriptures, he was commonly called "the illuminated Doctor." Fuller calls him "a grave divine, a painful preacher, and a profitable writer." He is one of the richest in matter of all the Puritans.

531 (32) Reeve, J. W. – LECTURES. 1859. **
Orthodox, spiritual, and suggestive lectures, by an evangelical clergyman.

532 (32) Willard, Samuel – THE TRULY BLESSED MAN. Rare. **
One of the first books printed in the United States. An old-fashioned exposition.

533 **(40) Frame, James – CHRIST AND HIS WORK.** 1869. ******
Well–done. Though differing from the author at times, we are grateful for such real help.

534 **(42) MacDuff, J. R. – THE HART AND THE WATERBROOKS.** 1860 ******
See remarks on other books by this copious writer: Nos. 308, 315, etc.

535 **(42, 43) March, H. – SABBATHS AT HOME.** 1823. ******
Profitable reading, rendered all the more pleasing by the introduction of very choice poetry. Not important to the expositor.

536 **(42) Sibbes, Richard – THE SOUL'S CONFLICT AND VICTORY OVER ITSELF BY FAITH.** 1635. *Works, Vol. I.,* Nichol's edition. *******
Mainly upon verses 5 and 11. Sibbes never wastes the student's time; he scatters pearls and diamonds with both hands.

537 **(45) Bennett, Thomas – SERMONS ON THE FORTY-FIFTH PSALM.** 1781. ******
Twenty-four sermons after the manner of Ralph Erskine, in which Jesus is all in all. What more be said in their praise?

538 **(45) Pennefather, William – THE BRIDEGROOM KING.** A meditation on the Forty-fifth Psalm. ******
Rather a meditation than an exposition. A fitting book for a sick bed. The little chapters might lie, like wafers made with honey, upon the praiseful tongue of the suffering believer. The beloved writer has now gone to see the King in His beauty, of whom he had those glimpses here which enabled him to pen this tiny volume.

539 **(45) Troughton, W. – THE MYSTERY OF THE MARRIAGE SONG.** 1656. *****
An old work with nothing new or striking in it. Remarkably tame and meagre for a work of that exuberant period. Let it alone.

540 **(45) Pitcairn, David – THE ANOINTED SAVIOR.** 1846. ******
Contains an exposition of part of Psalm 45, as applied to Messiah's first and second advents. Good, yet it reads rather wearily to us.

541 **(51) Alexander, Thomas – THE PENITENT'S PRAYER.** 1861. ******
Our friend the late Dr. Alexander of Chelsea handled this Psalm well.

542 **(51) De Coetlogon, Charles Edward – THE PORTRAITURE OF THE CHRISTIAN PENITENT.** 2 vols., 1775. *****
Very proper. We see nothing in the book but platitudes decorously expressed.

543 **(51) Biddulph, Thomas T. – LECTURES ON PSALM 51.** 1830. ******
Lectures far above the average of such lucubrations, making up a very fair exposition.

544 **(51) Bull, John – SERMONS ON THE FIFTY-FIRST PSALM.** 1824. *****
Another specimen of sermons published by subscription. The poor curate was no doubt the better for the profits, and nobody was any the worse. Clipston church was not set on fire by the flaming eloquence of the preacher, nor was the country disturbed by any fanatical excitement produced by his excessive zeal.

545 (51) Hieron, Samuel – DAVID'S PENITENTIAL PSALM OPENED. 1617. **
Hieron was a conforming Puritan. His works were once exceedingly popular and they are still esteemed.

546 (51) Hildersham, Arthur – ONE HUNDRED AND FIFTY-TWO LECTURES ON PSALM 51. 1635 and 1642. ***
Hildersham was one of the most tried of the nonconforming ministers, and at the same time one of the most able. He is copious and discursive, we had almost said long-winded. Both Willet and Preston speak of him in the highest terms.

547 (51) Morgan, James – THE PENITENT. 1855. ***
The excellent doctor first wrote this exposition for his own spiritual benefit, then preached it for the edification of his flock, and lastly published it for the good of us all. This is a worthy pedigree for a book, and the book itself is worthy of the pedigree.

548 (51) Page, Samuel – DAVID'S BROKEN HEART. 1637 and 1646. ***
Every page is like a bank note for value. Here are homiletical materials in abundance.

549 (51) Smith, Samuel – DAVID'S REPENTANCE. 16th edition, 1655. See Nos. 499 and 522. **
It will be seen from the numerous editions that this work was well–received in its author's lifetime. He tells us that he spent the spare hours of a long sickness in publishing this short exposition, and thus the world is all the healthier for his illness.

550 (68, 110) Dixon, Richard – A NEW INTERPRETATION OF THE SIXTY-EIGHTH PSALM, with an exposition of Psalm 110. 1811. **
This author, in a most interesting manner, traces out the analogy between this Psalm and the Song of Deborah. Those who like choice pieces of writing upon the literature of Scripture will be gratified by the perusal of this exposition.

551 (73) Parry, Edward – DAVID RESTORED; or, An Antidote Against the Prosperity of the Wicked and the Afflictions of the Just. 1660 **
Not super-excellent, nor free from blemishes, but containing much of sterling value.

552 (82) Hall, Thomas – THE BEAUTY OF MAGISTRACY. An exposition of Psalm 82. 1660. **
This exposition has always nestled in the bosom of Swinnock's works. We agree with Dr. Jenkyn's criticism: "The style is terse and clear, though grave and theological, and the matter is solid and judicious."

553 (82) Heminge, Nicholas – THE FAITH OF THE CHURCH MILITANT. 1581. *
A Danish divine of high repute in his own day. Some of his works were turned into English; but the translations, like the originals, are now left in undeserved oblivion.

554 (90) Smith, Samuel – MOSES, HIS PRAYER. 1656. **
See our notes on Nos. 499, 522 and 549.

555 **(99, 101, 102) Edersheim, Alfred – THE GOLDEN DIARY OF HEART CONVERSE WITH JESUS.** Contains expositions of Psalms 99, 101, and 102. 1873. **
Sweet and spiritual; worth purchasing.

556 **(103) Stevenson, John – GRATITUDE.** An exposition of Psalm 103. **
Somewhat diffuse, but at the same time too good to be criticized.

557 **(107) Hyperius, Andrew Gerard – A SPECIAL TREATISE OF GOD'S PROVIDENCE AND COMFORT** against all kinds of crosses and calamities, to be drawn from the same; with an exposition of Psalm 107. From the Latin, 1602. **
This author has written in Latin upon many subjects, but his works are now little known. He was a learned Lutheran.

558 **(107) Romaine, William – A PRACTICAL COMMENT ON PSALM 107.** Fifth edition. 1767. Also in *Works, 4*. **
Romaine's doctrine and style of writing are well-known. He could not be accused of overlaying the truth with much learning. The thought is gracious, sound, and practical, but the style is just a little dull.

559 **(110) Reynolds, Edward – EXPLICATION OF THE ONE HUNDRED AND TENTH PSALM.** 1632 and 1635; 1837. Also in *Works*. ***
Surpassingly clear and elaborate. Reynolds was a man of vast learning and thoroughly evangelical spirit.

560 **(116) Gouge, William – THE SAINTS' SACRIFICE.** 1632, Scarce. Reprinted in Nichol's *Commentaries*, with Smith, No. 499; and Pierson, No. 527. **
Gouge's method of cutting up his exposition into sections and discussing everything in propositions, is very tedious to the reader, but we judge it to be advantageous to the preacher. At any rate Gouge has often given us a hint. He was a man of great learning.

561 **(119) Bridges, Charles – EXPOSITION.** Twenty-second edition. 1857. ***
Worth its weight in gold. Albeit that the work is neither learned nor very original we praise it for its surpassing grace and unction.

562 **(119) Cowper, William – A HOLY ALPHABET FOR SION'S SCHOLARS.** A commentary on Psalm 119. 1613; and in *Works*. 1629. **
Dr. M'Crie gives a high character to all Cowper's works, and says that a vein of practical piety runs through them, while the style is remarkable for ease and fluency. This remark applies emphatically to the *Holy Alphabet*. We have found it very delightful reading.

563 **(119) Greenham, Richard – AN EXPOSITION OF THE 119 PSALME.** *Works*. 1612. **
We regret that this comment is not published separately, and is only to be procured by purchasing the rest of Greenham's works. The style, however, is antique and cramped, and Manton and Bridges are quite enough.

564   (119) Manton, Thomas – ONE HUNDRED AND NINETY SER-
      MONS ON THE ONE HUNDRED AND NINETEENTH PSALM.
      1725; 3 vols., 1842; 3 vols., (with life). 1845. ***
      Fully up to Manton's highest mark, and he is well known to have been one of
      the chief of the Puritan brotherhood. The work is long, but that results only
      from the abundance of matter.

565   (119) Sanderson, R.B. – LORD'S DAY LITERATURE: or, Illustra-
      tions of the Book of Psalms from Psalm 119, consecutively. 1842. *
      We cannot call this an exposition. Its title far more accurately describes it. The
      author takes occasion from the text to plead for those points of doctrine and
      practice into which he had been led by the Spirit of God. He was an eminently
      conscientious man, a bold believer, and a Baptist.

566   (120-134) Armfield, H.T. – THE GRADUAL PSALMS: A Treatise
      on the Fifteen Songs of Degrees, with commentary, based on ancient
      Hebrew, Chaldee, and Christian authorities. 1874. **
      A wonderfully interesting book from a literary point of view; perhaps more
      singular than profitable; but in many respects a publication which we should
      have been sorry to have missed. The homiletical student will not be able to
      make much use of it.

567   (120-134) Cox, Samuel – THE PILGRIM PSALMS; an exposition
      of the Songs of Degrees. Klock and Klock (Kregel Publications). ***
      This will be greatly valued by intelligent readers. A noble series of sermons
      would be pretty sure to grow out of its attentive perusal. Mr. S. Cox is a great
      expositor.

568   (120-134) Luther, Martin. See No. 488. **

569   (120-134) M'Michael, N. – THE PILGRIM PSALMS. 1860. ***
      A capital work, full of sound doctrine perfumed with devotion.

570   (120-134) Nisbet, Robert – THE SONGS OF THE TEMPLE
      PILGRIMS. 1863. **
      Dr. Nisbet regards the "Songs of Degrees as affording so complete an
      exhibition of the phases of religious sentiment, as to make these short poems
      a transcript of the feelings of the whole Church; a miniature Bible for the use
      of all." He has expounded in this spirit, with well–chosen language, and
      produced a very valuable and instructive book.

571   (122) Willet, Andrew – In Willet's HARMONIE AND EXPOSI-
      TION OF THE BOOKS OF SAMUEL there is "a brief exposition of
      Psalm 122." *
      Willet ought to have known better than to twist a psalm to the honor and glory
      of James I. As a learned man he says good things, and as a courtier foolish
      things.

572   (130) Hutcheson, George – FORTY-FIVE SERMONS ON PSALM
      130. 1691. ***
      We have already advised the purchase of anything and everything by Hutche-
      son. Be sure not to confound this with Hutchinson.

573   (130) Leighton, Robert. See No. 529. ***

574 (130) Owen, John – A PRACTICAL EXPOSITION ON THE ONE HUNDRED AND THIRTIETH PSALM. 1669 and 1680. ***
One of the best–known and most esteemed of John Owen's works. It is unnecessary to say that he is the prince of divines. To master his works is to be a profound theologian. Owen is said to be prolix, but it would be truer to say that he is condensed. His style is heavy because he gives notes of what he might have said, and passes on without fully developing the great thoughts of his capacious mind. He requires hard study, and none of us ought to grudge it.

575 (130) Sibbes, Richard – THE SAINTS' COMFORTS. 1638. *Works*, Vol. 6. Nichol's edition. **
Notes on five verses only. Published without the author's sanction, it is incomplete, but very full as far as it goes, and considering its brevity.

576 (130) Winslow, Octavius – SOUL-DEPTHS AND SOUL-HEIGHTS; an exposition of Psalm 130. 1874. **
Not very deep nor very high, but pleasant spiritual reading.

BOOKS OF SOLOMON

577 Keil and Delitzsch – *Proverbs—Song of Solomon,* translated by M. G. Easton. Volume 6 of COMMENTARY ON THE OLD AND NEW TESTAMENT. Wm. B. Eerdmans Publishing Co. **

578 LANGE'S COMMENTARY ON THE HOLY SCRIPTURES. *Proverbs*, by Otto Zockler. Edited by Philip Schaff. ***
We cannot say that we admire Zockler's interpretation of the Song of Solomon. The volume contains much that we do not like, but its value is considerable. It is a pity that the value of the volumes in this series varies so much.

579 Noyes, G.R. – A TRANSLATION OF PROVERBS, ECCLESIASTES, AND CANTICLES. With notes. 1846. **
Of Noyes upon Ecclesiastes, Dr. Hamilton says: "This interpretation is clear and straightforward, but the American professor gives to the book an air of theological tenuity and mere worldly wisdom which carries neither our conviction nor our sympathy." Noyes is a good literary expositor, but his theological views render him a very poverty-stricken commentator from a spiritual point of view.

PROVERBS

580 Allen, Robert – CONCORDANCES OF THE PROVERBS AND ECCLESIASTES. 1612. *
An ordinary concordance will answer the purpose far better; but the wonderfully wise, half-crazy Cruden had not complied his invaluable work in Allen's days.

581 Arnot, William – STUDIES IN PROVERBS: Laws from Heaven for Life on Earth. Kregel Publications. ***
We wish Dr. Arnot had gone steadily through the whole book, for his mind was of an order peculiarly adapted for such a task. Those passages which he dilates

upon are set in a clear and beautiful light. For a happy blending of illustrative faculty, practical sound sense, and spirituality, Dr. Arnot was almost unrivalled.

582 **Bridges, Charles – PROVERBS.** The Banner of Truth. *******
The best work on the Proverbs. The scriptural method of exposition so well carried out by Bridges renders all his writings very suggestive to ministers. While explaining the passage in hand, he sets other portions of the work in new lights.

583 **Brooks, J. W. – A NEW ARRANGMENT OF THE PROVERBS OF SOLOMON.** 1860. *****
We do not see the use of the arrangement; but those who want the Proverbs classified have the work done for them here.

584 **Case, R. J. – A COMMENTARY.** 1822. *****
The Proverbs themselves are plainer than this author's exposition of them.

585 **Day, William – A POETICAL COMMENTARY.** 1862. *****
The author says, he has "a taste for building rhymes," and he has here gratified it. That is all we can say for his book.

586 **Delitzsch, Franz** *– Proverbs — Song of Solomon,* translated by M. G. Easton. Vol. 6 of COMMENTARY ON THE OLD TESTAMENT. Wm. B. Eerdmans Publishing Co. ******

587 **Dod, John – A PLAINE AND FAMILIAR EXPOSITION OF PROVERBS, CHAPTERS 4 TO 17.** 1608-9. (The commentary in Chapters 13 and 14 appears to have been the work of Robert Cleaver. In our copy, containing Chapters 28-30, the names of both Dod and Cleaver are given, and the last chapter was "penned by a Godly and learned man, now with God.") ******
Both Dod and Cleaver were popular as preachers, and their joint works were widely circulated. This book can rarely be met with entire.

588 **French, W. and Skinner, G. – A NEW TRANSLATION,** with explanatory notes. 1831. ******
These translators endeavor to produce faithful renderings of the text, giving to each word the same sense in all places. They are calm, dispassionate, judicious, and able.

589 **Hodgson, Bernard – THE PROVERBS OF SOLOMON.** With notes. 1788. *****
Darling says: "A good translation; the notes are chiefly philological." We set no store by this mass of letter-press, and we question whether any one else does.

590 **Holden, George – AN ATTEMPT TOWARDS AN IMPROVED TRANSLATION.** With notes. 1819. *****
Horne says of this work: "It is one of the most valuable helps to the critical understanding of this book." It is certainly one of the best of Holden's productions. We may be wrong, but we could not conscientiously subscribe to Horne's opinion.

591 **Jacox, Francis – SCRIPTURE PROVERBS, ILLUSTRATED, ANNOTATED, AND APPLIED.** 1874. ******
This work illustrates many of the proverbs scattered throughout the Scriptures,

and some of those collected by Solomon. Mr. Jacox seems to have read everything good and bad, and hence he pours forth a medley of fact and fiction more entertaining than edifying. He reminds us of the elder Disraeli and his *Curiosities of Literature.*

592 **Jermin, Michael – PARAPHRASTICAL MEDITATIONS ON THE BOOK OF PROVERBS.** 1638. **
Very antique, and full of Latin quotations. Jermin does not err in excessive spirituality, but the reverse. Those who can put up with his style will be repaid by his quaint learning.

593 **Lange, J.P.** See No. 578. ***

594 **Lawson, George – EXPOSITION OF PROVERBS.** Kregel Publications. **
A thoroughly sound and useful commentary. Lawson wrote popularly and vigorously.

595 **Miller, John – A COMMENTARY,** with a new translation, and with some of the original expositions re-examined. 1875. *
This author's interpretations are new, and in our judgment very far removed from accuracy. Certainly the old interpretations are better in many ways. His theory that the Proverbs are spiritual and not secular will not hold water. He needs reading with very great discrimination, if read at all. "Too great innovation" is the author's own suspicion of his work, and we quite agree with him, only we go beyond mere suspicion.

596 **Muffet, Peter – A COMMENTARY ON THE WHOLE BOOK OF PROVERBS.** 1596. Reprinted, with Cotton's *Commentaries on Ecclesiastes and Song of Solomon,* in one of the vols. of Nichol's series. 1868. **
Homely, but not very striking. Mr. Nichol's choice of commentators for reprinting was not a wise one.

597 **Newman, William – PROVERBS.** An improved version. 1839. *
Merely the corrected text. A very small affair.

598 **Nicholls, Benjamin Elliott – THE BOOK OF PROVERBS,** explained and illustrated from Holy Scripture. 1858. **
Conatins very sensible suggestions for the interpretation of proverbs, and gives instances of explanations by geography, natural history, etc. It is a somewhat helpful work.

599 **Noyes.** See No. 579. **

600 **Stuart, Moses – A COMMENTARY ON THE BOOK OF PROVERBS.** 1852. **
We have not met with any English reprint of this useful volume. Dr. Stuart purposely adapted his work to beginners in Hebrew study. He has set himslf to prepare a commentary of explanation only, believing that a hortatory and practical comment every minister ought to be able to make for himself. Stuart's introductory matter is highly instructive, though no reader should blindly accept it all.

601 **Taylor, Francis – OBSERVATIONS UPON THE THREE FIRST CHAPTERS OF PROVERBS.** 1645. An exposition (as above) upon chapters 4, 5, 6, 7, 8, 9. 1657. ***
Two volumes (in one) of rich, old-fashioned Puritan divinity.

602 Thomas, David – THE PRACTICAL PHILOSOPHER. 1873. **
Dr. Thomas of the "Homilist" is a well-known writer, and a man capable of great things. This work does not equal his *Genius of the Gospel.* It contains a large amount of practical comment, written in a rather grandiose style. We can hardly fancy men of business reading this book from day to day as the author proposes.

603 Wardlaw, Ralph – LECTURES. 3 vols., 1861. ***
Wardlaw is diffuse, and his views upon "wisdom" are peculiar; but he always repays the reader, and neither Bridges nor Arnot have rendered him obsolete, for he works a different vein, and expounds in a manner peculiar to himself.

604 Wilcocks, Thomas – A SHORT YET SOUND COMMENTARY. *Works.* See No. 336. **
Wilcocks briefly sums up the teaching of the verses, and so aids in suggesting topics; in other respects he is rather wearying.

ECCLESIASTES

605 ANNOTATIONS ON THE BOOK OF ECCLESIASTES. 1669. *
By no means remarkable, except for extreme rarity.

606 Beza, Theodore – ECCLESIASTES. Solomon's sermon to the people with an exposition. 1594. **
Sure to be weighty and instructive. It is exceedingly rare.

607 Bridges, Charles – ECCLESIASTES. *** The Banner of Truth.
After the manner of other works by this devout author, who is always worth consulting, though he gives us nothing very new.

608 Broughton, Hugh – A COMMENT ON ECCLESIASTES. Framed for the instruction of Prince Henry. 1605. *
Broughton was a far-famed and rather pretentious Hebraist whom Dr. Gill quoted as an authority. His work is nearly obsolete, but its loss is not a severe one.

609 Buchanan, Robert – ECCLESIASTES, Its Meaning and Its Lessons Explained and Illustrated. 1859. ***
Dr. Buchanan has endeavored in every instance to give the true meaning of the text. His explanations were composed for the pulpit and delivered there. The work is most important, but strikes us as lacking in liveliness of style.

610 CHOHELETH, or The Royal Preacher, a Poem. First published in the year 1768; reprinted, 1830. *
This is the work of which Mr. Wesley wrote: "Monday, Feb. 8, 1768. I met with a surprising poem, entitled Choheleth, or the Preacher. It is a paraphrase in tolerable verse on the Book of Ecclesiastes. I really think the author of it (a Turkey merchant) understands both the difficult expressions and the connection of the whole, better than any other, either ancient or modern, writer whom I have seen." We defer to Mr. Wesley's opinion, but it would not have occurred to us to commend so warmly.

611 Coleman, John – ECCLESIASTES. A new translation, with notes. 1867. **
A scholarly translation with important observations.

612 Cotton, John – A BRIEF EXPOSITION WITH PRACTICAL OBSERVATIONS. 1654. Reprinted in Nichol's series of *Commentaries*. See Muffet, No. 596. **

By a great linguist and sound divine. Ecclesiastes is not a book to be expounded verse–by–verse; but Cotton does it as well as anyone.

613 Cox, Samuel – THE QUEST OF THE CHIEF GOOD. Expository lectures. 1868. **

We should find it hard to subscribe to Mr. Cox's views of Ecclesiastes, for, to begin with, we cannot admit that its author was not Solomon, but some unnamed Rabbi: nevertheless, *The Quest of the Chief Good* is full of valuable matter, and abundantly repays perusal.

614 Dale, Thomas Pelham – ECCLESIASTES with a running commentary and paraphrase. 1873. *

This author makes all that he can out of the errors of the Septuagint, which he seems to value almost as much as the correct text itself. The new translation is a sort of stilted paraphrase, which in a remarkable manner darkens the meaning of the wise man's words. Mr. Dale says he is a man of one book, and we are glad to hear it: for we should be sorry for another book to suffer at his hands.

615 Desvoeux, A.V. – A PHILOSOPHICAL AND CRITICAL ESSAY ON ECCLESIASTES. 1760. *

A curious and elaborate production. Neither in criticism, nor in theology, is the author always sound, and his notes are a very ill-arranged mass of singular learning.

616 Ginsburg, Christian D. – COHELETH, OR ECCLESIASTES. Translated with a commentary. 1857. **

The author does not believe that Solomon wrote the book, and his view of its design is not the usual, nor, as we think, the right one. His outline of the literature of the book is very complete.

617 Granger, Thomas – A FAMILIAR EXPOSITION. Wherein the world's vanity and true happiness are plainly deciphered. 1621. **

Very antique, containing many obsolete and coarse phrases; but pithy and quaint.

618 Greenaway, Stephen – NEW TRANSLATION. 1781. *

Confused, eccentric, and happily very rare.

619 Hamilton, James – ROYAL PREACHER: Lectures on Ecclesiastes. 1851. ***

We have had a great treat in reading this prose poem. It is a charming production.

620 Hengstenberg, E.W. – COMMENTARY ON ECCLESIASTES. To which are appended: Treatises on the Song of Solomon; on the Book of Job; on the Prophet Isaiah, etc. 1860. ***

Scholarly, of course, and also more vivacious than is usual with Hengstenberg.

621 Hodgson, Bernard – NEW TRANSLATION. 1791. *

Notes neither long, numerous, nor valuable.

622 **Holden, George** – AN ATTEMPT TO ILLUSTRATE THE BOOK OF ECCLESIASTES. 1822. **
Bridges says Holden "stands foremost for accuracy of critical exegesis," and Ginsburg considers his commentary to be the best in our language. We may, therefore, be wrong in setting so little store by it as we do, but we are not convinced.

623 **Jermin, Michael** – ECCLESIASTES. 1639. **
The school to which Jermin belonged delighted to display their learning, of which they had no small share. They excelled in wise sayings, but not in unction. The fruit is ripe, but lacks flavor.

624 **Keil** and **Delitzsch.** See under "BOOKS OF SOLOMON," No. 577. ***

625 **Lange, J.P.** See under "BOOKS OF SOLOMON," No. 578. ***

626 **Lloyd, J.** – AN ANALYSIS OF ECCLESIASTES. With reference to the Hebrew grammar of Gesenius, and with notes; to which is added the Book of Ecclesiastes, in Hebrew and English, in parallel columns. 1874. **
This will be esteemed by men who have some knowledge of the Hebrew. The repeated references to Gesenius would render the book tedious to the ordinary reader, but they make it all the more valuable to one who aspires to be a Hebraist.

627 **[Luther]** – AN EXPOSITION OF SOLOMON'S BOOKE, CALLED ECCLESIASTES, OR THE PREACHER. 1573. **
Even the British Museum authorities have been unable to find this volume for us, though it is mentioned in their catalog.

628 **MacDonald, James** – THE BOOK OF ECCLESIASTES. Klock and Klock (Kregel Publications). ***
Thoroughly exegetical, with excellent "scopes of argument" following each division. To be purchased if it can be met with.

629 **Morgan, A. A.** – ECCLESIATES METRICALLY PARAPHRASED. With illustrations. 1856. **
This is an article deluxe, and is rather for the drawingroom than for the study. A graphic pencil, first-class typography, and a carefully written metrical translation make up an elegant work of art.

630 **Mylne, G. W.** – ECCLESIASTES; or Lessons for the Christian's Daily Walk. 1859. **
The author in this little publication does not comment upon the whole book; but the passages he touches are ably explained.

631 **Nisbet, Alexander** – AN EXPOSITION, with practical observations. 1694. **
One of those solid works which learned Scotch divines of the seventeenth century have left us in considerable numbers. In our judgment it is as heavy as it is weighty.

632 **Noyes.** See No. 579. **

633 **Pemble, William** – SOLOMON'S RECANTATION AND REPENTANCE; or, The Book of Ecclesiastes Briefly and Fully Explained. 1628. **
Anthony A. Wood calls Pemble "a famous preacher, a skillful linguist, a good

orator, and an ornament to society." Moreover, he was a learned Calvinistic divine. This *Recantation* is a minor production. The style is scholastic, with arrangements of the subjects such as render it hard to read. We confess we are disappointed with it.

634 Preston, Theodore – **A TRANSLATION** of the Commentary of Mendelssohn from the Rabbinic Hebrew. Also a newly arranged English version. 1845. **
A book more prized by linguists than by preachers. We might with propriety have named this *Mendelssohn's Commentary*, for so it is.

635 Proby, W. H. B. – **ECCLESIASTES FOR ENGLISH READERS.** 1874. *
About 45 pages, and these are quite enough. What has come to a man's brain when he prophecies that Antichrist will take away the daily sacrifice, that is, "forbid the eucharistic bread and wine," and then adds: "To this awful time there is probably a mystical reference in the words of our present book (12:6), 'While the silver cord is not loosed, or the golden bowl broken, or the pitcher broken at the fountain, or the wheel broken at the cistern.' For silver and gold signify respectively, in the symbolic language of Scripture, love and truth: thus the loosening of the silver cord will mean failure of truth from the earth; and we understand, then, that in the last awful time there will be no longer any speaking of the truth in love. And as the 'wells of salvation' in Isaiah 12:3, are the sacraments and other means of grace, so the breaking of the pitcher and the wheel may signify the cessation of those ministries by which the sacraments and other means of grace are dispensed."

636 Reynolds, Edward – **ANNOTATIONS.** *Works.* Vol. 4. 1826, 1811. **
See Westminster Assembly's *Annotations* (No. 2), for which Reynolds wrote this. He is always good.

637 Serranus or **De Serres, John** – **A GODLY AND LEARNED COMMENTARY UPON ECCLESIASTES,** newly turned into English, by John Stockwood. 1585. *
Serranus was a Protestant pastor at Nismes, of such moderate opinions, and such objectionable modes of stating them, that he was about equally abhorred by Romanists and Protestants. He is said to have been very inaccurate in his learning.

638 Stuart, Moses – **A COMMENTARY ON ECCLESIASTES.** 1851. ***
Full and minute, with most instructive introductions. It is unnecessary to say that Moses Stuart is a great authority, though not all we could wish as to spirituality.

639 Tyler, Thomas – **ECCLESIASTES.** A contribution to its interpretation. 1875. *
This writer is no doubt a profound thinker, but we do not set much store by the result of his thinkings. He maintains that the writer of Ecclesiastes was a Jew who had traveled abroad, and heard the Stoic philosophers and their opponents at Athens. He seems to think that his point is proved, but it is the merest surmise possible. The work is not at all to our taste.

640 Wardlaw, Ralph – **LECTURES ON ECCLESIASTES.** 2 vols., 1821. Edition in 1 vol., 1871. ***
Wardlaw is always good, though not very brilliant. He may be relied upon, when not critical, and he generally excites thought.

641 Weiss, Benjamin – NEW TRANSLATION AND EXPOSITION. With critical notes. 1856. **

It is pleasing to find a converted Jew engaged upon this book. Mr. Weiss says many good things, but frequently his interpretations and remarks are more singular than wise.

642 Ycard, Fr. – PARAPHRASE. 1701. *

The Dean supposes the Royal Preacher to have been interrupted by an impudent sensualist, and so he gets rid of the difficulty of certain passages by putting them into the scoffer's mouth. The theory is not to be tolerated for a moment.

643 Young, Loyal – COMMENTARY, with introductory notices by Mc Gill and Jacobus. 1865. ***

This American commentary is highly spoken of by eminent judges, and appears to have been carefully executed. It is able and solid, and at the same time, enlivened with originality of thought, vivacity of expression, and practical pungency.

644 Smith, John – KING SOLOMON'S PORTRAITURE OF OLD AGE, wherein is contained a sacred anatomy both of soul and body, with an account of all these mystical and enigmatical symptoms, expressed in the six former verses of the 12th chapter of Ecclesiastes, made plain and easy to a mean capacity. 1666. **

A curious book by a physician, who brings his anatomical knowledge to bear upon the twelfth chapter of Ecclesiastes, and tries to show that Solomon understood the circulation of the blood. Matthew Poole introduced the substance of this treatise into his Synopsis, and in that huge compilation he speaks eulogistically of the author, with whom he resided. We mention it because of its singularity.

SONG OF SOLOMON

645 Ainsworth. See under "PENTATEUCH," No. 72. **

646 Avrillon, John Baptist Elias – THE YEAR OF AFFECTIONS; of sentiments on the love of God, drawn from the Canticles, for every day of the year. 1847. **

One of the series of Romish authors, issued by Dr. Pusey. It is a deeply spiritual work, after the manner of the mystics. It might have been written by Madame Guyon. Despite its occasional Popery and sacramentarianism, it contains much choice devotional matter.

647 Beza, Theodore – SERMONS ON THE THREE FIRST CHAPTERS OF CANTICLES. Translated from the French, by John Harmar. 1587. ***

These 31 sermons are a well of instruction, very precious and refreshing. The unabbreviated title indicates a controversial use of the Song, and we were, therefore, prepared to lament the invasion of the dove's nest of the Canticles by the eagle of debate; but we were agreeably disappointed, for we found much less of argument, and much more of the Well-Beloved, than we looked for.

648 Beverley, T. – AN EXPOSITION OF THE DIVINELY PROPHETIC SONG OF SONGS, which is Solomon's; beginning with the

reign of David, and ending in the glorious Kingdom of our Lord Jesus Christ. 1687. *
This maundering author finds in Canticles the history of the church from David to our Lord, and rhymes no end of rubbish thereon. Truly, there is no end to the foolishness of expositors. We suppose there must be a public for which they cater, and a very foolish public it must be.

649 **Brightman, Thomas – A COMMENTARY ON THE CANTICLES.** Wherein the text is analyzed, the native signification of the words declared, the allegories explained, and the order of times whereunto they relate observed. 1644. See under "DANIEL" and "REVELATION". *
Brightman was a writer of high renown among the prophetic students of the seventeenth century. With singular strength of the visionary faculties he sees in the Canticles "the whole condition of the church from the time of David, till time shall be no more." Expounding on this needs an acrobatic imagination.

650 **Burrowes, George – COMMENTARY.** 1853. ***
Moody Stuart says: "The excellent work of Dr. Burrowes is specially fitted to remove the prejudices of men of taste against the Song of Solomon, as the medium of spiritual communion between the soul and Christ. We welcome it as a valuable contribution to us from our transatlantic brethren."

651 **Bush, Joseph – THE CANTICLES OF THE SONG OF SOLOMON.** A metrical paraphrase, with explanatory notes and practical comments. 1867. **
A good compilation, with a helpful translation. For popular use.

652 **Clapham, Enoch – SOLOMON, HIS SONG EXPOUNDED.** 1603. *
Clapham was a voluminous author of very remarkable attainments. He wrote also on the first 14 chapters of Genesis. This work is rare as angels' visits.

653 **Collinges, John – THE INTERCOURSES OF DIVINE LOVE BETWIXT CHRIST AND HIS CHURH.** Metaphorically expressed by Solomon in Canticles 1 and 2. 2 vols., 1676. ***
909 pages upon one chapter is more than enough. The materials are gathered from many sources and make up a mass of wealth. On the second chapter there are 530 pages. It would try the constitution of many modern divines to read what these Puritans found it a pleasure to write. When shall we see their like?

654 **Cotton, John – A BRIEF EXPOSITION.** Describing the estate of the church in all ages thereof, both Jewish and Christian, and modestly pointing at the gloriousness of the restored state thereof, 1642. Reprinted in Nichol's series. See Muffet, No. 596. *
Cotton explains the sacred love-song historically, and misses much of its sweetness by so doing. We should never care to read his exposition while Durham, and Gill, and Moody Stuart are to be had.

655 **Davidson, William – A BRIEF OUTLINE OF AN EXAMINATION OF THE SONG OF SOLOMON.** 1817. **
A precious work by one whose heart is warm with the good matter. He sees in the Song the history of the Church and Christ.

656 **Dove, John – THE CONVERSION OF SOLOMON, A DIRECTION TO HOLINESS OF LIFE;** handled by way of commentary upon the whole Book of Canticles. Profitable for young men which are not yet mortified, for old men which are decrepit and have one foot in

the grave, and for all sorts of men which have an intent to renounce the
vanities of this world, and to follow Jesus Christ. 1613. *
A quaint old work. The student will do better with the moderns. Moreover,
this dove is rare, and seldom lights on poor men's shelves.

657 **Durham, James – AN EXPOSITION OF THE SONG OF SOLO-
MON.** Klock & Klock (Kregel Publications); The Banner of Truth. *******
Durham is always good, and he is at his best upon the Canticles. He gives us
the essence of the good matter. For practical use this work is perhaps more
valuable than any other key to the Song.

658 **Fenner, Dudley – THE SONG OF SOLOMON,** in verse with an exposition. 1587. *
Moody Stuart says: "This is a faithful and excellent translation, accompanied
by an admirable exposition. There is no poetry in it, but the renderings are
often good, and the comment valuable." We have not met with it.

659 **Fleming, Robert – THE MIRROR OF DIVINE LOVE.** Unveiled in
a poetical paraphrase of the Song of Solomon. 1691. *
The poetry is after the same manner as that of Quarles, and though not without
merit, it is too antiquated to be admired in the present day. This is the Fleming
who interpreted the Apocalyptic vials, and was fortunate enough to hit upon
the date of the French revolution and other events connected with the decline
of Papal power. His prophetic work has been reprinted, but not this limping
poetry.

660 **Francis, Ann – A POETICAL TRANSLATION,** with notes, historical, critical, and explanatory. 1781. *
Framed on a fanciful theory. Verses flowing and feeble. Insignificant.

661 **Fry, John – NEW TRANSLATION,** with notes, and an attempt to
interpret the sacred allegories. 1811. ******
Fry's work may be called the supplement and complement of Dr. Good's. He
divides the Songs into idyls, and gives notes in the same manner as Good; but
he also plunges into the spiritual meaning of the blessed Song, and so far is to
be preferred.

662 **Gifford, Mr. – A DISSERTATION ON THE SONG OF SOLO-
MON.** 1751. *
Worthless rhymes. This man dares to say that the Song is a pastoral, composed
by Solomon for the amusement of his lighter hours, before God had given him
the divine wisdom for which he was afterwards so eminent.

663 **Gill, John – AN EXPOSITION OF THE BOOK OF SOLOMON'S
SONG.** 1728. Not contained in the author's Exposition of the Old and
New Testament *******
The best thing Gill ever did. He could not exhaust his theme, but he went as
far as he could towards so doing. He is occasionally fanciful, but his work is
precious. Those who despise it have never read it, or are incapable of elevated
spiritual feelings.

664 **Ginsburg, Christian D. – A TRANSLATION,** with a commentary,
historical and critical. 1857. *
Written upon an untenable theory, viz., that the Song is intended "to record an
example of virtue to young women who encountered and conquered the
greatest of temptations, and was eventually rewarded." This grovelling

interpretation needed the aid of great liberties with the text, and a few interpolations, and the author has not hesitated to use them. However learned the book may be, this vicious theory neutralizes all.

665 Good, John Mason – SONG OF SONGS; or Sacred Idyls Translated; with notes, critical and explanatory. 1803. *
By a man of great learning. It is not at all spiritual, or even expository, in the theological sense, but treats the Canticles as an Oriental drama, explaining its scenery and metaphors from a literary point of view.

666 Green, William – SONG OF SOLOMON. In "The Poetical Parts of the Old Testament", translated with notes. 1781. *
Critical only. Orme says, "The translations are in general very accurate and elegant specimens of biblical interpretation."

667 Guild, William – LOVE'S INTERCOURSE BETWEEN THE LAMB AND HIS BRIDE. 1658. **
A rare old work; but we prefer Durham. The author was one of the better sort of the Scotch Episcopalians.

668 Gyffard, George – FIFTEEN SERMONS ON THE SONG OF SOLOMON. 1598 to 1612. **
We have several times met with this writer's name coupled with that of Brightman as in his day regarded as a very learned writer, but we cannot procure his work.

669 Harmer, Thomas – OUTLINES OF A NEW COMMENTARY ON SOLOMON'S SONG. Drawn by the help of instructions from the East. 1768. **
"This book is not well arranged, but is otherwise one of the most ingenious, modest, and interesting of all the treatises on the outward sense of the Song."— Moody Stuart.

670 Hengstenberg. See under "ECCLESIASTES," No. 620. ***

671 Hodgson, Bernard – SOLOMON'S SONG, translated from the Hebrew. 1786. **
Moody Stuart says that this is "a good translation," and therefore we suppose it is so, but we do not admire it. It does not even refer to the mystical sense, and it mars the poetry of the Song. Dr. Hodgson renders chapter 9:9: "My pigeon, my undefiled is but one." This is an alteration, but certainly not an emendation. The name of the bride's mother he discovers to have been Talmadni. Wonderful!

672 Homes, Nathaniel – A COMMENTARY ON THE CANTICLES. 1652. **
This goes to the very marrow of spiritual teaching, and uses every word and syllable in a deeply experimental manner with great unction and power. Homes, however, spiritualizes too much, and is both too luscious in expression and too prolix for these degenerate days.

673 Houghton, William – TRANSLATION. 1865. *
Useless. The Song is viewed as a secular poem on chaste love.

674 Ibn Ezra, Abraham – COMMENTARY ON THE CANTICLES, after the first recension. Edited from two manuscripts with a translation, by H. J. Matthews. 1874. *
The original Hebrew of the Song, with a Jewish comment, which conveys but

little instruction. In this small book the student will have a specimen of Jewish exposition.

675 Irons, Joseph – NYMPHAS: A Paraphrastic Exposition . 1844. *******
Outside of his own circle we fear that this work by the late Joseph Irons is little known. It is a paraphrase in blank verse, rendered in a very spiritual manner. We confess that we look upon the little book with admiring eyes, though we know that the critics will sneer both at us and it.

676 Keil and Delitzsch. See under "Books of Solomon," No. 577. *******

677 Krummacher, F. W. – SOLOMON AND THE SHULAMITE. Sermons on the Book of Canticles. 1838. ******
Touches only upon a few portions. Short and Sweet.

678 Lange, J. P. See under "Books of Solomon," No. 578. *******

679 Littledale, R. F. – A COMMENTARY. From ancient and medieval sources. 1869. ******
Littledale is a close follower of John Mason Neale, and here reproduces the beauties and the deformities of medieval spiritualizing. Great judgment will be needed to extract the good and true from the mass of semi-popish comment here heaped together. If discretion be used, jewels of silver and jewels of gold may be extracted.

680 MacPherson, Peter – THE SONG OF SONGS. Shown to be constructed on architectural principles. 1856. *****
"His supposition that this song consists of verses written round an archway, is so entirely gratuitous, that it is only misguiding and deceptive."— Moody Stuart

681 METRICAL MEDITATIONS ON THE CANTICLES. Anonymous. 1856. *******
Exceedingly well–rendered. Noteworthy both from a literary and religious point of view. The author seizes the meaning of the Song, and repeats it in well-chosen words.

682 Miller, Andrew – MEDITATIONS. **
First published in the Plymouthite magazine, *Things New and Old*. Devotional, and glowing with the light of fellowship with Jesus.

683 Moore, Daniel – CHRIST AND HIS CHURCH. A course of Lent lectures on the Song of Solomon. 1875. *******
These lectures treat upon the first chapter only, but they do so in an admirable manner. Moore has evangelized Littledale.

684 Neale, John Mason – SERMONS ON THE CANTICLES. 1857. ******
By that highest of high churchmen, Dr. Neale. These sermons smell of Popery, yet the savor of our Lord's good ointment cannot be hid. Our Protestantism is not of so questionable a character that we are afraid to do justice to Papists and Anglicans, and therefore we do not hesitate to say that many a devout thought has come to us while reading these "sermons by a priest of the Church of England."

685 Newton, Adelaide L. – THE SONG OF SOLOMON COMPARED WITH OTHER PARTS OF SCRIPTURE. 1871. ******
Miss Newton's book is very dear to spiritual minds; it is full of that quiet power

which comes from the Spirit of God through deep experience and precious fellowship with the Well-Beloved.

686 Noyes. See No. 579. **

This author sees in the Canticles nothing but a collection of amatory songs, written without express moral or religious design. Blind!

687 Percy, Thomas – NEW TRANSLATION, with a commentary and annotations. 1764. *

His theory of the sacred Song is dead, and not worthy of a monument in our pages. We trust that not a relic will remain. Percy did very well with his ballads, but he had better have let the Song of Songs alone.

688 Power, Philip Bennet – FAILURE AND DISCIPLINE: Thoughts on Canticles 5. **

Upon the fifth chapter only. Mr. Power always writes attractively. His book is "linked sweetness," but not "long drawn–out."

689 REFLECTIONS ON CANTICLES; or, The Song of Solomon, with Illustrations from Modern Travelers and Naturalists. 1870. **

Has much sweetness, and a fair measure of freshness.

690 Robotham, John – EXPOSITION. 1652. **

Very solid; but not to be compared with Durham, No. 657. It is just a little dull and commonplace.

691 Romaine, William – DISCOURSES UPON SOLOMON'S SONG. 1789. **

Twelve excellent sermons from verses taken out of the Song. They do not summarize the book, nor form a commentary, but are simply a selection of spiritual discourses by one of the most eminent Calvinistic divines of the last century.

692 Sibbes, Richard – BOWELS OPENED; or, A Discovery of the Near and Dear Love Union and Communion Betwixt Christ and His Church. Sermons on Canticles 4, 5, and 6. 1639 (*Works 2*, Nichol's edition). ***

Sibbes never writes ill. His repute is such that we need only mention him. His title is most unfortunate, but in all else his "discovery" is worthy of our commendation.

693 Skinner, John – ESSAYS TOWARDS A LITERAL OR TRUE RADICAL EXPOSITION, *Works 2*. 2 vols., 1809. *

Not very important. The Bishop closes his exposition with the following prayer for those who do not believe in the mystical sense: "God forgive the fools and open their eyes." Pretty strong for a Bishop!

694 Stuart, A. Moody – EXPOSITION, with critical notes. 1860. ***

Although this admirable author expounds the Song upon a theory which we do not quite endorse, we do not know where to find a book of equal value in all respects. He has poetry in his soul, and, beyond that, a heart like that of Rutherford, fired with love to the Altogether Lovely One. We thank him for this noble volume.

695 THE BRIDE OF CHRIST; or, Explanatory Notes on the Song of Solomon. Anonymous. 1861. *

A little book for general use; not for students.

696   THE THREEFOLD MYSTERY. Hints on the Song of Songs, viewed as a prophecy of the double united church of Jew and Gentile. By the author of *The Gathered Lily.* 1869. *

It seems to us to be a wild fancy that all ecclesiastical history is condensed into the Canticles; hence we do not value this book.

697   Thrupp, John Francis – NEW TRANSLATION, with commentary. 1862. ***

We are highly pleased with this work. It defends the usual Christian interpretation by the conclusions of sober criticism, and shows that the spiritual sense is confirmed by the investigations of modern scholarship. In the introduction the author deals heavy blows at the skeptical school, and at those who, like Ginsberg, content themselves with imputing a merely moral meaning to the blessed Canticle of love.

698   Weiss, Benjamin – THE SONG OF SONGS UNVEILED. A new translation and exposition. 1859. *

This author believes that the Song sets forth the history of Israel and her relation to the Covenant Angel from Horeb to Calvary. Beyond a few eastern illustrations, nothing of value is contributed to existing materials. The work is thoroughly evangelical.

699   Wilcocks, Thomas – EXPOSITION. 1624. **

Short, and somewhat in the manner of a paraphrase. This venerable author gives a doctrinal summary of each verse, and from this we have frequently been directed to a subject of discourse.

700   Williams, Thomas – A NEW TRANSLATION, with a commentary and notes, 1801. Second edition, 1828. **

This volume is little known, but its value is above the average of Canticles literature. We have read many of the remarks with pleasure, but most of them are to be found in the standard commentaries.

701   Woodford, Samuel – PARAPHRASE IN VERSE. 1679. *

Better than many poetical paraphrases, but still below the mark of true poetry.

702   Wright, M. – THE BEAUTY OF THE WORD IN THE SONG OF SOLOMON. 1872. **

A purely spiritual commentary, casting no light upon the text, but drawing much from it. More devotional than expository. The figures of the allegory are pressed as far as they should be, perhaps further.

PROPHECY

(Volumes upon this subject are so extremely numerous and so varied in their opinions, that we confine ourselves to the few which follow. The reader is also referred to works upon the Apocalypse.)

703   Davison, John – DISCOURSES ON PROPHECY: Its Structure, Use and Inspiration. 1845. ***

Elliot calls this "Davison's noble work on prophecy." This is one of the Warburtonian lectures, and we would here note that those lectures are all upon prophecy, and are many of them by first-class men, and therefore worthy of study. Of course they greatly vary in value according to the ability of the lecturers.

704 Faber, George Stanley – CALENDAR OF PROPHECY, or, a Dissertation of the Prophecies Which Treat of the Seven Times and Especially of the Latter Three Times and a Half. 3 vols., 1828. **
Faber is one of the greatest rabbis of prophecy. He was a man of almost boundless learning and industry. His characteristics are said to have been "strong masculine sense, extensive classical erudition, and *a hearty love of hypothesis.*" This last quality, no doubt, led him to expound prophecy, and also disqualified him for doing it well.

705 Fairbairn, Patrick – PROPHECY: Its Distinctive Nature, Special Functions and Proper Interpretation. ***
A standard work by one who is at home with the subject.

706 Fleming, Robert – THE FULFILLING OF THE SCRIPTURE. Fifth Edition, 1726. **
This we mention because it is generally placed under this head, but it is not an exposition of prophecy at all. It is an elaborate treatise upon the fact that the Scriptures are fulfilled, and the Word of the Lord is true. As such it deserves the high encomiums so freely showered upon it by the eminent divines of Fleming's own time, and it abundantly justifies the issue of so many editions.

707 Hengstenberg, E. W. – THE MESSIANIC PROPHECIES OF ISAIAH AND THE OTHER PROPHETS. ***
These remarks are contained in Hengstenberg's *Christology of the Old Testament,* which is a standard work on the subject. See No. 67.

708 Keith, Alexander – CHRISTIAN EVIDENCES: Fulfilled Bible Prophecy. Illustrated by the history of the Jews and by the discoveries of recent travelers. Klock & Klock (Kregel Publications). ***
Horne says, "The multiplied editions which have been required within a very few years sufficiently attest the high estimation in which Mr. Keith's work is deservedly held." And we may add that the improvements and additions have increased its value, and that fresh editions have shown that it is still appreciated.

709 Newton, Thomas (1704-1782) – DISSERTATIONS ON THE PROPHECIES WHICH HAVE BEEN FULFILLED, AND ARE FULFILLING. Numerous editions. ***
A standard work of a laborious and learned author; rather laborious reading. The Bishop must not be trusted upon the New Testament prophecy. Theologically his standing is very dubious.

THE PROPHETS

710 Kitto, John – *Isaiah and the Prophets,* in KITTO'S DAILY BIBLE ILLUSTRATIONS. See No. 41. Kregel Publications. ***
Should be consulted wherever the readings touch upon a passage.

711 Lowth, Bishop and others – A LITERAL TRANSLATION OF THE PROPHETS FROM ISAIAH TO MALACHI, with notes by Lowth, Balayney, Newcome, etc. 5 vols., 1836. **
Concerning each of the five volumes, we refer the reader to our notices under the separate books.

712   **Lowth, William – COMMENTARY ON THE PROPHETS. 4 vols., 1714. ****
This is Lowth's part of Patrick (No. 50). He was more spiritual than those with whom he became associated, which is not saying much.

713   **Noyes, George R. – A NEW TRANSLATION OF THE HEBREW PROPHETS. 3 vols., 1849. ****
We are bound to commend this author's learning, taste, and candor, even though we differ widely from him. The reader must not look for savor or spiritual quickening, but use the work as a literary help only.

714   **Williams, Rowland – THE HEBREW PROPHETS DURING THE ASSYRIAN AND BABYLONIAN EMPIRES.** Translated afresh from the original, with illustrations. 2 vols., 1866-71. *
The author does not admit that there are references to the Messiah in the Prophets. Whatever he may have written, this fatal error deprives it of value. A man writing in that fashion should have been a rabbi in the synagogue, and not a minister among professed Christians.

ISAIAH

715   **Alexander, Joseph Addison – PROPHECIES OF ISAIAH,** earlier and later. 2 vols. in 1. ***
Dr. Hodge says of this author: "I regard Dr. Joseph Addison Alexander as incomparably the greatest man I ever knew—as incomparably the greatest man our Church has ever produced." He wastes no space, but gives the essence of exposition.

716   **Alexander, Joseph Addison – ISAIAH TRANSLATED AND EX-PLAINED.** An abridgement of the preceding. 2 vols., 1858. ***
This abridgment of the larger work is by no means a small affair. For all ordinary purposes it is voluminous enough. We cannot too strongly recommend it.

717   **Barnes, Albert – *Notes on Isaiah*, in BARNES' NOTES ON THE OLD TESTAMENT.** Edited by Robert Frew. Baker Book House. ***
A good popular exposition, though not the most learned.

718   **Birks, T. R. – COMMENTARY ON ISAIAH,** and a revised translation, 1871. **
Written for *The Speaker's Commentary*, and, though not inserted therein, it strikes us as being far superior to that work. It is a great treasure to the student of this much neglected prophet.

719   **Calvin, John – COMMENTARY ON ISAIAH.** Translated by C. Cotton. 1609 **
The translation of the Calvin Translation Society will be better.

720   **Cheyne, T. K. – THE BOOK OF ISAIAH CHRONOLOGICALLY ARRANGED.** An amended version. 1870 *
We do not as a rule believe in these rearrangements. The book of Isaiah is best as we have it. The tone of the interpretation in this instance is not such as we can delight in. What the evangelical teacher has a right to expect is totally absent. The work is of the broad school. The notes are, however, learned and somewhat suggestive.

721 Cheyne, T. K. – NOTES AND CRITICISMS ON THE HEBREW TEXT OF ISAIAH. *
The *Westminster Review* speaks of it as "a piece of scholarly work, very carefully and considerably done." It may be so.

722 Cowles, Henry – ISAIAH, with notes. 1869. ***
Cowles writes more popularly than Alexander, and though he is not so profound an authority, we have read him with pleasure.

723 Day, William – AN EXPOSITION OF THE BOOK OF ISAIAH. 1654. *
Day does not throw much light upon the text. He says he wrote for his children, and certainly he is childish enough.

724 Delitzsch, Franz – *Isaiah*, in COMMENTARY ON THE OLD TESTAMENT. Wm. B. Eerdmans Publishing Co. **
"The author has long been honorably distinguished among the scholars of Germany. He occupies, indeed, a position always peculiar to himself; for whilst his attainments in Hebrew philology and Talmudical lore are of the highest order, he unites with these a genuine appreciation of evangelical truth and godliness." So says the *Literary Churchman*. For our own part, we are not enraptured with Delitzsch.

725 Ewald, H. – THE PROPHET ISAIAH. Chapters 1—33. From the German, by Octavius Glover. 1869. *
Decidedly skeptical; but yet it may be useful as leading the reader to appreciate the poetic beauty of the book. Question if the good to be gained equals the risk incurred. Our verdict is to the contrary.

726 Fraser, Alexander – PARAPHRASE, with notes. 1800. *
Of very small value.

727 Galloway, William Brown – ISAIAH'S TESTIMONY FOR JESUS. A series of discourses. 1864. **
A congregation which would listen to such lectures as these must be a very select one indeed. The writer goes most throughly and learnedly into his subject.

728 Henderson, Ebenezer – ISAIAH. Translated from the Hebrew, with a commentary. 1840. Second and best edition, 1857. **
The author has given no doctrinal or practical observations, as he conceived that others had furnished these in abundance; he has confined himself to eliciting the real meaning of the words, and has thereby rendered great service to all expositors who have wit enough to make use of his critical assistance. To the less instructed reader, Dr. Henderson's work will appear to be dull and savorless; but to those who only need to have the language translated, and are able to supply reflections for themselves, it will be of much service.

729 Govett, R. Jr. – ISAIAH UNFULFILLED. Exposition with new version and critical notes. Schoettle Publishing Company. **
We have not met with this publication.

730 Jenour, Alfred – THE BOOK OF ISAIAH. Translated with notes and practical remarks. 2 vols. 1830. **
This appears to us to be a faithful translation; the commentary and practical reflections are instructive and gracious.

731 **Keith, Alexander** – ISAIAH AS IT IS; or, Judah and Jerusalem, the Subjects of Isaiah's Prophesying. 1850. **
The student will consult with benefit this valuable contribution to the explanation of a most important, but neglected book.

732 **Kelly, William** – LECTURES ON ISAIAH. 1871. *
This eminent divine of the Brethren school sometimes expounds ably, but with a twist towards the peculiar dogmas of his party.

733 **Lowth, Robert** – ISAIAH. Translation with notes. See No. 711. **
Smith's *Dictionary* remarks that Bishop Lowth's incessant correction of the Hebrew text is constantly to be mistrusted. This seriously diminishes Lowth's value, but his is a grand work notwithstanding.

734 **Lyth, John** – HOMILETICAL TREASURY. 1868. *
This should have been to the preacher of a book of the utmost value, for it consists wholly of outlines and hints for sermons, but these are frequently poor and commonplace. The design is superlatively practical, and, had the execution been better, we should have rejoiced in it.

735 **MacCulloch, Robert** – LECTURES ON ISAIAH. 4 vols., 1791-1805. **
In these days we need consideration. This author would have been far more valued if he had compressed his matter into one volume. He is good, but verbose. Some authors toil not, but they spin; MacCulloch both toils and spins.

736 **MacLachlan, Mrs.** – NOTES ON THE UNFULFILLED PROPHECIES OF ISAIAH. 1868. *
This authoress treats Isaiah as a Jewish book only, and refers all the prophecies to that nation. We do not agree with her fundamental principle.

737 **Montague, George** – SHORT NOTES ON ISAIAH, chapters 5—12. 1852. *
We confess that we cannot enjoy the very singular style of the Duke's prelections, but there are some who set great store by them. We wonder why.

738 **Noyes, G. R.** See No. 713. ***

739 **Stock, Joseph** – ISAIAH IN HEBREW AND ENGLISH, with notes. 1852. **
The notes are few, but are said by the *British Critic* to be "uncommonly valuable for their depth and acuteness." We should have thought so. Stock alters the renderings of Lowth, but seldom improves them. We judge him to be overestimated.

740 **Smith, R. Payne** – THE AUTHENTICITY AND MESSIANIC INTERPRETATION OF THE PROPHECIES OF ISAIAH VINDICATED, in sermons before the University of Oxford. 1862. **
A work which would be invaluable in a discussion with Jews. It meets their objections, and also those advanced by neologians.

741 **Verney, Lady** – PRACTICAL THOUGHTS on the first 40 chapters of Isaiah. 1858. **
Some sensible spiritual hints will be found in these remarks. As an exposition it is one of the least.

742 **Whish, J. C. – A PARAPHRASE OF THE BOOK OF ISAIAH,** with notes. 1862. **
Somewhat helpful. The paraphrasing is not prolix, and it does, as a rule, aid the reader in getting at the literal sense. With the spiritual teaching Mr. Whish has not intermeddled.

743 **White, Samuel – COMMENTARY ON ISAIAH,** wherein the literal sense is briefly explained. 1709. **
This author keeps to the literal sense and is very severe upon spiritualizers, of whose vagaries he gives specimens. In aiming at one excellence he misses others, and fails to see Christ where he certainly is, thus rendering his remarks less valuable to the Christian mind.

PARTS OF ISAIAH

(There are many works upon separate chapters of this book, but it does not fall in with our plan to go so much into detail as to enumerate them all. We thought it would be useful to our readers if we mentioned a few.)

744 **MacDuff, J. R. – "COMFORT YE, COMFORT YE."** God's words of comfort addressed to His Church in the last 27 chapters of Isaiah. 1872. **
Dr. MacDuff translates into popular language the teachings of great expositors, and does it to perfection. For an hour's pleasant reading and holy reading commend us to Dr. MacDuff.

745 **Calvert, Thomas – MEL COELI, MEDULLA EVANGELII; or,** The Prophet Isaiah's Crucifix. An exposition of the fifty-third chapter of Isaiah. 1867. ***
Precious and practical. Just what the title would lead us to expect—marrow and fatness; honey from the Rock, Christ Jesus.

746 **Durham, James – CHRIST CRUCIFIED; or the Marrow of the Gospel, holden forth in 72 sermons on Isaiah 53. ***
This is marrow indeed. We need say no more: Durham is a prince among spiritual expositors.

747 **MacDonogh, T. M. – MESSIAH AS REVEALED IN ISAIAH 53.** Founded upon Manton (748). 1858. **
This is a serving up of the next work in the form of lectures. We do not admire abridgments and especially those which make alterations and additions; still it is likely that many have read MacDonogh's Manton who might never have fallen with Manton's Manton.

748 **Manton, Thomas – A PRACTICAL EXPOSITION** on the whole Fifty-Third Chapter of Isaiah. 1703. ***
Manton needs no praise from us. Whatever he does is done in a style worthy of a chief among theologians. He is, however, seldom too brief, and his own bulk hinders his being read. Preachers of long sermons should take a hint from this.

749 **Margoliouth, Moses – SIX LECTURES ON ISAIAH 53. 1846. **
Well worth a careful reading.

750 **Stewart, James Haldane – LECTURES UPON ISAIAH 55. 1846. **
Nine sweet evangelical discourses, in a lively, impressive style.

JEREMIAH AND LAMENTATIONS

(We would call special attention to the volume of the *Speaker's Commentary*, 49, upon this book. It is by Dr. Payne Smith, Dean of Canterbury, and deserves much praise.)

751 **Blayney, Benjamin – JEREMIAH AND LAMENTATIONS.** New translation with notes, 1836. See No. 711. **
Blayney belonged to a past school of clever men, too apt to suggest new readings, and more able to appreciate literary beauties than spiritual teachings. He was a zealous follower of Lowth, but he lacked the fine taste and poetic genius of his master.

752 **Broughton, Hugh – THE LAMENTATIONS OF JEREMY,** translated, with explications. 1608 *
Incomprehensible. One of Broughton's wilder pieces. It may as well die.

753 **Hull, John – EXPOSITION UPON PART OF LAMENTATIONS.** 1618. ***
Full of quietness. Marrow throughout.

754 **Keil, K. F. –** *Jeremiah and Lamentations,* 2 vols., in **COMMENTARY ON THE OLD TESTAMENT.** Wm. B. Eerdmans Publishing Co. **
We have already indicated the direction in which Keil is servicable. For exact interpretation he is esteemed, but he is too cold and formal ever to be a favorite.

755 **LANGE'S COMMENTARY ON THE HOLY SCRIPTURES.** *Jeremiah and Lamentations,* by C. W. Nägelsbach. Edited by Philip Schaff. ***
"Whoever becomes possessed of this great work will have, in a comprehensive form, the results of all ancient and modern exegesis, with an apparatus criticus of surprising copiousness."— *British Quarterly Review.*

756 **Lowth, William – A COMMENTARY ON JEREMIAH AND LAMENTATIONS.** 1718. See Nos. 50 and 712. **
This forms a part of what is known as *Bishop Patrick's Commentary.* Orme says that Lowth is "one of the most judicious commentators on the prophets, and *he never prophesies himself.*" We wish we could say this of all writers on prophetic subjects.

757 **Smith, Thornley – THE PROPHET OF SORROW;** or Life and Times of Jeremiah. 1875. **
Not a commentary; but as it cast light on the character and times of the prophet it deserves a place here.

758 **Swift, Daniel – ZION'S SUFFERINGS:** An Exposition of Lamentations. 1654. **
Strong, rough, coarse. Excessively rare.

759 **Udall, John – A COMMENTARY ON THE LAMENTATIONS OF JEREMY.** 1599. **
In this extremely rare work the author has labored after brevity, and has given the abridgment of many discourses; hence, to those who can procure it, it is all the more useful.

EZEKIEL

760 Alleine, William – THE NINE LAST CHAPTERS OF EZEKIEL UNFOLDED. 1679. **
Very rare; will interest interpreters of prophecy.

761 Cowles, Henry – EZEKIEL AND DANIEL. With critical, explanatory, and practical notes. 1867. ***
In his own way, this author is one of the most instructive of American writers; he is clear and definite, and leaves his meaning impressed upon the mind. His scholarship is respectable.

762 Fairbairn, Patrick – EZEKIEL. Exposition with new translation. 1851. ***
This exposition has passed through three editions, and has gained for its author a high place among elucidators of difficult parts of Scripture. Dr. Fairbairn has a cool judgment and a warm heart; he has cast much light upon Ezekiel's wheels, and has evidently felt the touch of the live coal, which is better still.

763 Greenhill, William – EXPOSITION OF EZEKIEL. 5 vols., 1645-1667. Reprinted in Nichol's *Commentaries.* 1863. ***
We always get something out of Greenhill whenever we refer to him. He had not, of course, the critical skill of the present, but his spiritual insight was keen. He rather commented on a passage than expounded it.

764 Guthrie, Thomas – THE GOSPEL OF EZEKIEL. 1864. **
Very little of Ezekiel, and a great many of those flowers of eloquence which rendered Dr. Guthrie so famous. We can hardly regard it as an exposition. It only dwells upon the latter part of the 36th chapter.

765 Henderson, Ebenezer – EZEKIEL. With commentary. 1855. ***
Valuable condensed notes.

766 Hengstenberg, E. W. – THE PROPHECIES OF EZEKIEL ELUCIDATED. 1869. **
We have frequently characterized this author's writings. They are clear, cold, and dry, like a fine moonlight night in the middle of winter. A man needs a peculiar mind to *enjoy* Hengstenberg; but all educated students can profit by him.

767 Keil, K. F. – *Ezekiel,* in vol. 9 of **COMMENTARY ON THE OLD TESTAMET.** Wm. B. Eerdmans Publishing Co. **

768 LANGE'S COMMENTARY ON THE HOLY SCRIPTURE. *Ezekiel,* by Wilhelm Julius Schröder, and *Daniel,* by Otto Zöckler. Edited by Philip Schaff. ***

769 Newcome, William – NOTES ON EZEKIEL. Improved version, metrical arrangement, and explanation, 1728, 1836. See Lowth and others, No. 711. **
Dr. Fairbairn says: "The notes are of a very brief description, chiefly explanatory of the meanings given in the translation; and both the translation and the notes proceed to a large extent on the vicious principle, very prevalent at the time, of getting rid of difficulties in the sense by proposed emendations of the text." Yet Newcome showed both learning and diligence in this improved version.

DANIEL

770 **Amner, R. – ESSAY TOWARDS INTERPRETATION.** 1776. *
Written on the absurd hypothesis that the prophecies were all fulfilled before
the death of Antiochus Epiphanes.

771 **Auberlen, Carl August – THE PROPHECIES OF DANIEL AND
THE REVELATION.** Translated by Adolph Saphir. 1856. **
Not a textual commentary, but a treatise upon the mysterious prophecies.
Auberlen's spirit is reverential and his views are evangelical, or we should not
have found Mr. Saphir translating it. He acknowledges his indebtedness to
Roos, No. 799. We must leave the interpretations to be judged by those who
are learned in such objects.

772 **Barnes, Albert – *Daniel*, in BARNES' NOTES ON THE OLD TES-
TAMENT.** Edited by Robert Frew. Baker Book House. ***
Dr. Wardlaw said of this work: "I have examined the 'Notes' of the Rev. Albert
Barnes on a considerable variety of testing passages; and, so far as my
examination has gone, I feel confident in pronouncing them to be characterized, in no ordinary degree, by discriminative judgment, sound theology,
unostentatious learning, practical wisdom, and evangelical piety."

773 **Birks, T. R. – EXPOSITION OF THE FIRST TWO VISIONS OF
DANIEL.** 1845. **

774 **Birks, T. R. – THE TWO LATER VISIONS OF DANIEL HIS-
TORICALLY EXPLAINED.** 1846. **
We must leave judgment upon this work and the preceeding one to those
skilled in prophetic interpretation.

775 **Brightman, Thomas – A MOST COMFORTABLE EXPOSITION**
of the last and most difficult part of the prophecy of Daniel from the
26th verse of the 11th chapter to the end of the 12th chapter, wherein
the restoring of the Jews and their calling to the faith of Christ after the
utter overthrow of their three last enemies is set forth in lively colors.
1644. *
The exposition and the author's commentary on Canticles are appended to his
work on Revelation, and do not appear to have been published separately. In
his title page Brightman is called a bright and worthy man, and in the preface
we are told that "he shined every way and was a Brightman indeed." His work
is rather a curiosity than a treasure.

776 **Broughton, Hugh – DANIEL'S CHALDEE VISIONS.** 1662. *
This author was pendantic and eccentric, but yet a man of real learning. His
works have almost disappeared. In his own day some considered him a sage
and others a quack. He was a little of both.

777 **Calvin, John – *Daniel*, in CALVIN'S COMMENTARIES.** Baker
Book House. ***
Also in *Calvin's Complete Works*.

778 **Coleman, Thomas – DECISION, EXEMPLIFIED IN DANIEL.**
1858. *
This is by the author of *Memorials of Independent Churches*. It is intended for
children and is suitable for them.

779 Cowles, Henry. See under "EZEKIEL", No. 761. ***

780 DANIEL: Statesman and Prophet. Anonymous. **
A valuable popular addition to the literature of the book of Daniel. Objections to its authenticity and inspiration are met, and the assaults of infidels are made to bring out the evidences of divine authority with all the greater clearness. We are delighted with the volume, which is beautifully got up. Every student and minister should have a copy.

781 Darby, John Nelson – STUDIES IN DANIEL. *
The name of the writer sufficiently indicates the character of the book.

782 Desprez, Philip S. – DANIEL; or, The Apocalypse of the Old Testament. 1865. *
This work is of the Essays and Reviews schools. The author cannot see the Messiah in Daniel. It is worse than useless.

783 Elliott, C. B. See under "REVELATION". ***

784 Frere, James Hatley – A COMBINED VIEW OF THE PROPHECIES OF DANIEL, EZRA, AND ST. JOHN. 1826. *
This has been esteemed by many in its day, but we do not recommend its purchase.

785 Gaussen, S. R. Louis – DANIEL EXPLAINED FOR YOUNG PERSONS. 2 vols., 1874. ***
This is a work for children only. We hope it will not set our Sunday school teachers explaining to their little ones the image and its toes, the he-goat, and all the other marvels. If they do attempt it we wish them as well through their task as professor Gaussen.

786 Harrison, Benjamin – PROPHETIC OUTLINES of the Christian church and the Antichristian power, as traced in the vision of Daniel and John. 1849. ***
We like the manner of this book. The author has been content throughout to trace the true outline of interpretation without entering on a detailed examination of counter–theories; and he has done this in the spirit of Bishop Ridley, who said upon a kindred subject, "Sir, in these matters I am so fearful, that I dare not speak further than the very text doth, as it were, lead me by the hand."

787 Hengstenberg, E. W. – DISSERTATIONS ON THE GENUINENESS OF DANIEL AND THE INTEGRITY OF ZECHARIAH. 1848. **
Much valuable matter is brought out by the discussion; but few of us have time to go into it, or any need to do so; for we are fully persuaded of the integrity of all the prophets, and of their books too.

788 Huit, Ephraim – THE WHOLE PROPHECY OF DANIEL EXPLAINED. 1643. **
Huit's short doctrinal summaries of the verses will bring useful subjects before the preacher's mind; otherwise Huit is not very remarkable.

789 Irving, Edward – BABYLON AND INFIDELITY FORDOOMED OF GOD. A discourse on Daniel and the Apocalypse. 1826. **
More of rolling sound than anything else.

790 Keil, K. F. – Daniel, in vol. 9 of COMMENTARY ON THE OLD TESTAMENT. Wm. B. Eerdmans Publishing Co. ***

"We have just had occasion to make ourselves acquainted with Keil's book on Daniel, and we can speak of it in very high terms. It is marked by great erudition, rare accuracy, and much spiritual thoughtfulness."— *Evangelical Magazine*

791 **Kelly, William – NOTES ON DANIEL. 1870. ****
It needs minds of peculiar organization to enjoy Plymouth writings. They abound in peculiar phraseology, which only the initiated can understand. We are sorry to such a mind as Mr. Kelly's so narrowed by party bounds.

792 **Knox, J. – REFLECTIONS ON DANIEL. 1849. ****
This book is unknown to us.

793 **Montague, George – THE TIMES OF DANIEL, CHRONOLOGICAL AND PROPHETICAL. 1845. ***
This work has received the most enthusiastic praise from German writers, who dwell with pleasure upon his being "erudite and illustrious." The duke's writing is certainly *sui generis*. He is by no means a favorite author with us.

794 **Miles, Charles Popham – LECTURES ON DANIEL, with notes.** Chapters 1-7. 2 vols., 1840- 41. **
Commendable sermons and good notes.

795 **More, Henry – A PLAIN AND CONTINUED EXPOSITION** of the several prophecies of Daniel. 1681. *
If a man had no more than More on Daniel he would certainly long for more, and need a work more spiritual and more suggestive.

796 **Newton, Sir Isaac – OBSERVATIONS ON DANIEL AND THE APOCALYPSE. 1733. ****
The author's name will always keep this book in repute. The spiritual student will not glean much from it. Sir Isaac's fame does not rest in his expositions. The following extract we cannot forbear inserting in this place: "The folly of interpreters has been, to foretell times and things by this prophecy (the Apocalypse), as if God designed to make them prophets. By this rashness they have not only exposed themselves, but brought the prophecy also into contempt. The design of God was much otherwise. He gave this and the prophecies of the Old Testament, not to gratify men's curiosities by enabling them to foreknow things, but that after they were fulfilled they might be interpreted by the event; and His own providence, not the interpreter's wisdom, be then manifested thereby to the world."

797 **Parker, Thomas – DANIEL EXPOUNDED. 1646. ***
This learned book is enough to perplex and distract any ordinary mortal, but probably Dr. Cumming and brethren of his school would revel in it. We had sooner read a table of logarithms.

798 **Pusey, Edward – DANIEL THE PROPHET.** Klock & Klock (Kregel Publications). ***
To Dr. Pusey's work on Daniel all subsequent writers must be deeply indebted, however much they may differ from him in other departments of theological study.

799 **Roos, Magnus Frederick – EXPOSITION OF SUCH OF THE PROPHECIES OF DANIEL** as receive their accomplishment under the New Testament. Translated by E. Henderson. 1811. ***
Dr. Henderson gently chides those who are not sufficiently intent upon prophetical interpretation. There would be fewer of such delinquents if

expositors were more reasonable. Roos, however, is dull to a dreadful degree: we should say that nobody ever read him through, except his translator. He is very devout, and this is the saving point about his book. We cannot tell whether the views of Roos are correct or not, for we cannot keep awake while reading him. As far as we have gone we have seen some reason to question.

800 **Rule, William Harris – HISTORICAL EXPOSITION OF DANIEL. 1869. *****
A notably interesting exposition, bringing historical facts and memorials to bear upon the prophecy. It is not merely readable, but attractive.

801 **Strong, Leonard – LECTURES ON DANIEL. 1871. ****
Notes of instructive lectures.

802 **Stuart, Moses – A COMMENTARY ON THE BOOK OF DANIEL. 1850. ****
Stuart gives quite an independent interpretation, and fails to see the Pope and his Cardinals in Daniel, for which we like him all the better. We do not accept his conclusions, but he is always worthy of respect.

803 **Tregelles, S. Prideaux – REMARKS ON THE PROPHETIC VISIONS OF DANIEL. 1852. ****
Tregelles is deservedly regarded as a great authority upon prophetical subjects.

804 **Wells, Edward – DANIEL EXPLAINED. 1716. ***
This is a different work to that mentioned in No. 61. It is of no great value.

805 **Willet, Andrew – HEXAPLA IN DANIELEM. 1610. ****
Dr. Williams says that this is a work of much information, as it contains the "opinions of many authors on each point of difficulty." He adds that in none of his expositions does Willet "discover more skill and judgment than in the present work."

806 **Wilson, Joseph – HORAE PROPHETICAE; or Dissertation on the Book of Daniel. 1824 ****
We consider this to be of more than average worth.

807 **Wintle, Thomas – DANIEL, AN IMPROVED VERSION, with notes. 1792, 1836. See No. 711. ***
Learned notes, mainly philological, with a translation on the plan of Lowth.

808 **Wodrow, Robert – DESTINY OF ISRAEL, as unfolded in the eighth and succeeding chapters of Daniel. 1844. ***
This devout author follows the system of Sir Isaac Newton and Bishop Newton. His calculations as to the year 1843 were disproved by history.

809 **Wood, William – LECTURES ON THE FIRST SEVEN CHAPTERS OF DANIEL. 1847. ***
Plain sermons of no great expository value.

MINOR PROPHETS

810 **Barlee, Edward – EXPLANATORY VERSION OF THE MINOR PROPHETS. 1839. ****
One of the best paraphrases we have ever met with.

811   Cowles, Henry – THE MINOR PROPHETS, with notes. 1867. **
      "This work is designed for both pastor and people. It embodies the result of
      much research, and elucidates the text of sacred Scripture with admirable force
      and simplicity."— *New York Christian Intelligencer.*

812   Danaeus or Daneau, Lambert – A FRUITFUL COMMENTARY
      ON THE TWELVE SMALL PROPHETS. Translated by John
      Stockwood, Minister at Tunbridge. 1594. *
      A translation of a work famous in its day, but of small service now.

813   Henderson, Ebenezer – THE TWELVE MINOR PROPHETS.
      1845. **
      A learned critical work, not spiritually or doctrinally suggestive, but simply
      explanatory of the text. This author denounces the theory of a double sense in
      prophecy; we, none the less, believe it to be a fact.

814   Hutcheson, George – BRIEF EXPOSITION OF THE TWELVE
      SMALL PROPHETS. 3 vols., 1655. ***
      Get it, Hutchenson is always rich. He resembles Dickson.

815   Keil, K. F. – *The Minor Prophets*, vol. 10 of COMMENTARY ON
      THE OLD TESTAMENT. Wm. B. Eerdmans Publishing Co. ***
      "Dr. Keil is at his best in this commentary; and to all who have ventured on this
      obscure region we can promise an intelligent guide and a serviceable light in
      this work. We ourselves, under his guidance, have resumed the study of these
      beautiful and instructive Scriptures with renewed vigor and growing de-
      light."—*Nonconformist.*

816   Kelly, William – LECTURES ON THE MINOR PROPHETS.
      1871. *
      Mr. Kelly finds in the Minor Prophets a great many things which we cannot
      see a trace of. For instance, he here discovers that we shall lose India. It is a
      pity that a man of such excellence should allow a very superior mind to be so
      warped.

817   LANGE'S COMMENTARY ON THE HOLY SCRIPTURES.
      The Minor Prophets, by various authors. Edited by Philip Schaff. ***
      The commentaries on the different prophets are by various authors; hence their
      value differs. As a whole the volume is excellent, but not so good as Keil.

818   Newcome, William D. – THE MINOR PROPHETS. Improved ver-
      sion with all the principal notes of Horsley on Hosea, and Blayney on
      Zechariah. 1836. See No. 711. **
      A celebrated critical work of a past age, but not expository. Newcome was too
      fond of new readings to be safely followed.

819   Pusey, Edward B. – THE MINOR PROPHETS. With a commen-
      tary. Baker Book House. ***
      All authorities speak of this work with great respect and so would we; but it
      is evident that Dr. Pusey is far too much swayed by patristic and medieval com-
      mentators.

820   Randall, James–SERMONS ON THE BOOKS OF JOEL, JONAH,
      NAHUM, MICAH AND HABAKKUK. 1843. **
      Superior sermons; but what are they among so many prophets.

821 **Stokes, David** – PARAPHRASE. 1659. **
Of no importance.

HOSEA

822 **Burroughs, Jeremiah** – EXPOSITION OF THE PROPHECY OF HOSEA. 4 vols., 1643-1651 (The original work does not include chapter 14, upon which there is a exposition by Sibbes, and another by Bishop Reynolds. The reprint, by James Sherman, contains the exposition completed by Hall and Reynolds. Nichol's series of *Commentaries*. 1 vol.) 1863. ***
Masterly. A vast treasure-house of experimental exposition. With the exception of Adams, we prefer it to any other of the expositions reprinted under the editorship of Mr. Sherman.

823 **Horsley, Samuel** – HOSEA. Translated from the Hebrew; with notes, 1804. And in vol. 2 of *Biblical Criticism*. **
Horsley occasionally succeeds in elucidating obscurities, but frequently his treatment of the text reminds one of the old army surgeons who cut and hacked their patients without mercy. This translation is still valued, but is to be followed with discretion.

824 **Downame, John** – LECTURES ON THE FIRST FOUR CHAPTERS OF HOSEA. 1608. ***
An exposition of the richest kind. Get it by all means, if you can.

825 **Drake, William** – NOTES CRITICAL AND EXPLANATORY ON THE PROPHECIES OF JONAH AND HOSEA. 1853. *
For Hebraists only.

826 **Neale, James** – HOSEA. Translation, commentary, and notes. 1850. **
We do not think many ministers will value it for homiletical purposes.

827 **Pocock, Edward** – COMMENTARY ON HOSEA. In vol. 2 of his *Works*; 2 vols., 1740. **
Orme says Pocock was "one of the finest Oriental scholars, and certainly the first Arabic scholar of his age." His book is a treasury filled with the products of laborious research.

828 **Wolfendale, J.** – HOMILETICAL COMMENTARY ON HOSEA. (In progress; being part 5 of the *Preacher's Homiletic Commentary*.) 1875. **
On an excellent plan, and moderately well executed. With Burroughes and others to quarry from, and so good a method to work by, Mr. Wolfendale ought to have produced a better book; but even as it is he deserves a measure of commendation.

829 **Smith, Samuel** – AN EXPOSITION ON THE SIXTH CHAPTER OF THE PROPHECY OF HOSEA. 1616. ***
In Smith's usual quiet, rich, expository manner.

830 **Margoliouth, Moses** – GENUINE REPENTANCE AND ITS EFFECTS. Exposition of Hosea 14. 1854. **
Respectable discourses.

831 Reynolds, Edward – AN EXPLICATION OF THE FOURTEENTH
CHAPTER OF HOSEA. In seven sermons, 1649. See also under
Burroughes, No. 822. ***
Reynolds was one of the greatest writers in an age of great divines. He worthily
takes place with Burroughes.

832 Sibbes, Richard – THE RETURNING BACKSLIDER, or a commentary on Hosea 14. 1639. Also in vol. 2 of his *Works*, Nichol's
edition. ***
Manton says of Sibbes, that he had a peculiar gift in unfolding the great
mysteries of the Gospel in a sweet and mellifluous manner, and therefore he
was by his hearers, usually termed the "Sweet Dropper," "sweet and heavenly
distillations usually dropping from him with such a native elegance as is not
easily to be imitated." This commentary on Hosea is a fair specimen of his
style.

JOEL

833 Chandler, Samuel – PARAPHRASE AND CRITICAL COMMEN-
TARY ON JOEL. 1735. **
Chandler makes very few remarks of a spiritual kind, but explains the letter of
the word with considerable skill. In writing upon Joel he does not appear to
the same advantage as in his *Life of David*. He does not effect much in clearing
up "the things hard to be understood" in the prophet, and he is of the old broad
school.

834 Hughes, Joseph – THE PROPHECY OF JOEL. The Hebrew text
metrically arranged, with a new translation and critical notes. *
A purely literary treatise, useful to Hebraists only.

835 Pocock, Edward – A COMMENTARY ON JOEL. *Works*, vol. 2,
1691. (The same volume contains his commentaries on Micah and
Malachi.) **
Full of antique learning. Holds a high place among the older comments, but
will never again be popular.

836 Rowley, Adam Clarke – JOEL. Metrical translation. 1867. **
The translation has been carefully executed. The notes are illustrative and
literary only; they do not profess to open up the moral and spiritual teaching
of the prophet. Could Adam Clarke rise from the dead, he would rejoice to find
his grandson following in his footsteps.

837 Topsell, Edward – TIMES LAMENTATIONS; or, An Exposition
on the Prophet Joel. 1599. ***
Among the old English commentaries Topsell is the writer on Joel. He has the
usual force, homeliness, piety, and fulness of the Puritan period.

838 Udall, John – THE TRUE REMEDY AGAINST FAMINE AND
WARS. Five sermons on the first chapter of the prophecy of Joel.
1586. **
We gave so high a price for this small volume that we should like to make it
profitable to our brethren, and therefore we commend to the more starchy of
them the following extract, which will also serve to show how the old
preachers lashed with vigor the fashions of the times. Udall says: "For the
feeding of our monstrous humor of vanity, how many thousands of quarters of
the finest wheat, which God ordained for the food of man, are yearly converted

into that most devilish device of starch. A sin so abominable that it doth cry
so loudly in the Lord's ears for vengeance, as his justice must needs proceed
against us for it, without speedy repentance."

AMOS

**839 Benefield, Sebastian – A COMMENTARY ON THE FIRST CHAP-
TER OF THE PROPHECY OF AMOS.** Delivered in 21 sermons,
1629. Upon the second chapter, in 21 sermons, 1620. Upon the third
chapter, in 17 sermons. 1629. **
Dr. Benefield was Lady Margaret Professor in Oxford, a Puritan, and thorough
Calvinist. His volume was, in its time, the standard commentary on Amos. It
is somewhat prolix and plentifully sprinkled with Latin. It only discusses three
chapters in 953 pages.

840 Hall, Thomas – AN EXPOSITION on the fourth, fifth, sixth, eighth
and ninth chapters of Amos. 1661. **
Hall took up Amos where Benefield left off. He says he studied brevity, and
perhaps he succeeded, for he does not quite fill 600 pages with six chapters.
The two volumes make up a complete work, of an antique type, not suitable
to modern tastes, nor up to the mark of present criticism, but still instructive.
What Puritan is not?

841 Ryan, Vincent William – LECTURES ON AMOS. 1850. **
A commendable series of lectures; the more valuable because so few modern
writers ventured to touch the subject.

OBADIAH

842 Marbury, Edward – OBADIAH AND HABAKKUK. Klock &
Klock (Kregel Publications). ***
Far more lively than Rainolds. His spirituality of mind prevents his learning
becoming dull. He says in the preface "all my desire is to do all the good I can,"
and he writes in that spirit.

843 Pilkington, James – In the WORKS OF BISHOP PILKINGTON,
reprinted by the Parker Society, there are commentaries on Haggai,
Obadiah, and Nehemiah. **
Full of the minor as well as the major controversies of the Reformation period,
and therefore the less interesting to us. In its own day it was *the* masterwork
on the two prophets, Haggai and Obadiah.

**844 Rainolds, John – THE PROPHECY OF OBADIAH OPENED
AND APPLIED.** 1613. **
Full of classical stories and learned allusions; but more useful when first
written than now. The author was one of the most learned men the world ever
produced, but he is not likely to be a favorite with modern readers.

JONAH

(This unlovable prophet has found more commentators than any other. Partly
we suppose because the angles of his character excite greater interest, but

mainly because we have some knowledge of his life, and therefore are able to realize his personality. He has received quite as much attention as he deserves in proportion to other prophets.)

845 **Abbott, George – AN EXPOSITION ON THE PROPHET JONAH. 1613. ***
Abbott was a renowned Calvinistic divine, and one of the translators of the present version of the Bible. No set of works on Jonah would be complete without this learned, laborious, and comprehensive exposition. It is, of course, very antique in style; but, like "old wine," it is none the worse for its age.

846 **Benjoin, George – JONAH.** Translation, with notes. 1796. *
Plenty of paper. Horne says this work "is literally good for nothing."

847 **Calvin, John – LECTURES UPON THE PROPHET JONAH.** Translated by N. Baxter. 1578. ***
This, of course, is fuller than the commentary, and, as the work of a revered master, is beyond our criticism.

848 **Cunningham, J. W. – SIX LECTURES ON THE BOOK OF JONAH.** With notes. 1833. **
Good, simple lectures.

849 **Desprez, P. S. – THE BOOK OF JONAH.** Illustrated by discoveries at Nineveh. 1857. **
To make Layard illustrate Jonah was a good idea, and it has been well carried-out by this author.

850 **Drake, William – NOTES ON JONAH AND HOSEA.** 1853. **
Entirely critical. Only useful to Hebrew scholars.

851 **Edwards, Henry – EXPOSITION OF THE BOOK OF JONAH.** 1837. **
Fourteen plain, earnest, practical sermons.

852 **Ephraem, Syrus – A METRICAL HOMILY ON THE MISSION OF JONAH.** Translated from the original Syriac, by Henry Burgess. 1853. *
A literary curiosity—nothing more.

853 **Exell, Joseph S. – PRACTICAL TRUTHS FROM JONAH.** Kregel Publications. ***
Mr. Exell in a very unpretending but able way, brings to light the practical lessons of Jonah. Paxton Hood calls these readings "admirable," and we concur in the verdict.

854 **Fairbairn, Patrick – JONAH:** Life, Character and Mission. 1849 ***
The life and times of the prophet are set in a clear light; and the nature and design of his mission fully explained. The work is well done, and is by far the ablest English treatise on this prophet.

855 **Fuller, Thomas – *Notes on Jonah*, in A COLLECTION OF SERMONS.** 1656. Mr. Tegg has reprinted Fuller's *Commentary on Ruth*, and *Notes upon Jonah*, in 1 small volume, 1868. ***
Full of wisdom and fuller of wit; in fact, too full of the soul of the latter, for they are far too short.

856 Gaussen, Louis – JONAH THE PROPHET. Lessons on his life. *
Addresses to a Sunday school at Geneva.

857 Harding, Thomas – EXPOSITORY LECTURES. 1856. *
What intelligent man in this kingdom could learn anything from these
lectures? The worthy man writes only such self-evident truisms as must have
occurred to anybody and everybody who has read his Bible.

858 Hooper, John – AN OVERSYGHTE AND DELIBERACION
UPPON THE HOLY PROPHET JONAS: Made and Uttered Before
the Kinges Majesty and His Most Honorable Councell by Jhon Hoper,
in Lent last past. Comprehended in seven sermons. Reprinted by the
Parker Society. 1550. *
It would not repay the student to buy Hooper's works for this short piece. The
language is antique, and the thought not of the newest.

859 Jones, Thomas – JONAH'S PORTRAIT. 1827. **
Jonah's Portrait was very popular 50 years ago, and deservedly so, for Mr.
Jones sketches it with considerable power. We should fancy that Jonah's
portrait, as he sat under his withered gourd, was not a thing of beauty, or a joy
forever.

860 King, John – LECTURES ON JONAH. 1600. Reprinted in Nichol's
series of *Commentaries*. See Rainolds, No. 844. **
Quaint and rich, with a little occasional quiet mirth. It was *the* book of its time.
Some will think it out of date, others will, like Grosart, prize the work of "the
Bishop with the royal name."

861 MacPherson, A. – LECTURES ON JONAH. 1849. **
Far superior to the general run of lectures.

862 Martin, Hugh – JONAH. The Banner of Truth. ***
A first-class exposition of Jonah. No one who has it will need any other. It is
not a small treatise, as most of the Jonah books are; but it contains 460 pages,
all rich with good matter.

863 Muir, A. S. – LESSONS FROM JONAH. 1857. **
A lively, popular, and earnest book, in a specially florid style. The author talks
a great deal about "the Son of Amittai;" why not say Jonah? We are tempted
to pull the finery to pieces; but we stay our hand, for there is really something
good in these "lessons."

864 Peddie, James – A PRACTICAL EXPOSITION OF THE BOOK
OF JONAH. 1842. ***
The pungent remarks peculiar to the Ralph Erskine school make the Jonah of
Dr. Peddie a favorite wherever it is known.

865 Preston, Matthew Morris – LECTURES. 1840. *
Ordinary sermons. Better ones can be bought for a penny.

866 Quarles, Francis – A FEAST FOR WORMS. A poem on the history
of Jonah. 1620. **
Quaint and rather bombastic verse, but full of meaning.

867 Raleigh, Alexander – THE STORY OF JONAH. 1875. ***
Dr. Raleigh calls your attention to every touch of the strange picture which
hangs before us in the life of Jonah. Although we do not always endorse the

Doctor's remarks, we can but marvel at the beauty and power of his descriptions and reflections.

868 Tweedie, W. K. – MAN BY NATURE AND GRACE; or, Lessons from Jonah. 1850. **
A good, practical work, expounding the book of Jonah for Christian edification.

869 Simpson, James – DISCOURSES FROM JONAH 1. 1816. *
Very little in the sermons, but their titles are singularly happy, and in themselves enough to afford subjects of discourse to preachers.

MICAH

(Since there is so very little upon this book, the student should refer to works on the Minor Prophets as a whole. There are some excessively rare authors and also works in Latin; but these do not fall within our range.)

870 Pocock, Edward. See No. 835. **

HABAKKUK

871 Marbury, Edward – OBADIAH AND HABAKKUK. Klock & Klock (Kregel Publications). ***
Here Marbury holds the field alone among old English authors, and he does so worthily. There is about him a vigorous, earnest freshness which makes his pages glow.

HAGGAI

872 Grynaeus, John James – HAGGEUS THE PROPHET. A most plentiful commentary. Gathered out of the public lectures of Dr. J. J. Grynaeus. 1586. *
Grynaeus was a voluminous author, and commented on most of the books of Scripture but only this work has been turned into English, and it is now seldom met with.

873 Moore, T. V. –HAGGAI, ZECHARIAH, AND MALACHI. A new translation with notes. 1858. ***
A capital book. Most useful to ministers.

874 Pilkington, James. See under "OBADIAH," No. 843. **

875 Rainolds, John – HAGGAI, INTERPRETED AND APPLIED. 1613 and 1649. For reprint, see No. 844. **
Rainolds was the tutor of Hooker, and had a main hand in our Authorized Version of the Bible. Bishop Hall says, "The memory, the reading of that man were near a miracle." We ought to be enraptured with a commentary from such a divine, but we confess that we are not.

ZECHARIAH

876 Blayney, Benjamin – ZECHARIAH. A new translation with notes. 1787. **

This learned author writes after the manner of Lowth, but has neither Lowth's taste nor poetic vein. His notes will not suggest sermons, but will be philologically useful if cautiously read.

**877 Hengstenberg, E. W. ** **

In his *Christology of the Old Testament* (see No. 67), Hengstenberg has given a thorough and elaborate exposition of the greater part of Zechariah and Malachi. He is too grammatical and dry to be generally interesting.

878 Kimchi, David – COMMENTARY ON ZECHARIAH. Translated from the Hebrew by Rev. A. M. M'Caul. 1837. **

This enables the English reader to see how the Jews themselves understood the Prophets, and this is worth knowing.

879 Moore, T. V. See under "HAGGAI," No. 873. ***

880 Park, I. R. – AN AMICABLE CONTROVERSY WITH A JEWISH RABBI ON THE MESSIAH'S COMING. With an entirely new exposition of Zechariah. 1832. **

The words "entirely new exposition" puts us on our guard, and did not entice us to read. The caution was needful. This author explains the prophecy spiritually, and asserts that "the spiritual is the most literal interpretation." We more than doubt it.

881 Pemble, William – A SHORT AND SWEET EXPOSITION ON THE FIRST NINE CHAPTERS OF ZECHARIAH. In his *Works*. 1659. **

Richard Capel says: "Among the hardest books of Scripture the prophets may have place, and among the prophets, Zechariah is a deep wherein an elephant may swim, and therefore I cannot but commend the wisdom of that man of God (the author of this book), who bestowed his learning and his pains to open the mysteries of this prophecy. Death ended his days ere he could finish his work and great weakness hindered an intended supplement." Pemble was a learned Calvinistic divine, and his writings are highly esteemed, but not very captivating.

882 Stonard, John – COMMENTARY ON ZECHARIAH. With a corrected translation and critical notes. 1824. *

An earnest attempt to expound this prophecy; we do not think the author has succeeded, but he has written some good things.

883 Wardlaw, Ralph – LECTURES ON ZECHARIAH. 1862. ***

Written in the doctor's old age; but we prefer it, in some respects, to other volumes of his lectures. We always consult it.

MALACHI

884 Moore, T. V. See under "HAGGAI," No. 873. **

885 Pocock, Edward. See under "JOEL," No. 835. **

886 Sclater, William – BRIEF AND PLAIN COMMENTARY ON MALACHI. 1650. **
Not equal to the general standard of Puritan comments. The editor of the work rightly says, "The method is, for the chapters themselves, analytical; for the practical observations, synthetical." We are quaintly told that he would start the hare with any man; that is to say, he would suggest thought and leave others to pursue its track.

887 Stock, Richard – A COMMENTARY ON MALACHI, whereunto is added an exercitation upon the same prophecy by Samuel Torshell. 1641. Reprinted, together with Bernard and Fuller on Ruth, 1865. See No. 262. ****
Contains a *stock* of knowledge, and more than a sufficient stock of quotations from the fathers. Torshell printed the book 15 years after Stock's death, and finding it to be written for a popular audience only, he added an examination of the original and a few notes in a more learned style, to make a complete commentary. The authors have thus composed the work upon Malachi.

888 Watson, Thomas – NOTES ON MALACHI 3. 1682. **
This would be a great find if we could only come at it, for Watson is one of the clearest and liveliest of Puritan authors. We fear we shall never see this commentary, for we have tried to obtain it, and tried in vain.

*May God bless this effort to assist His ministers
in the study of the Old Testament*

COMMENTARIES ON THE NEW TESTAMENT

(See also under "WHOLE BIBLE," Nos. 1-65. In many cases the New Testament may be obtained separately.)

889 Alford, Henry – THE GREEK NEW TESTAMENT, with a critically revised text, etc. 1856–61 *******

890 Alford, Henry – THE NEW TESTAMENT FOR ENGLISH READERS. See page 18. Baker Book House. *******

891 Alford, Henry – THE NEW TESTAMENT AUTHORIZED VERSION REVISED. ***

892 Alford, Henry – HOW TO STUDY THE NEW TESTAMENT. Part 1, Gospels and Acts; Part 2, Epistles (first section); Part 3, Epistles (second section) and Revelation. 1868. *******
All critics speak of Alford with respect, though they consider that something better than his Greek Testament is still needed. He is, for the present at any rate, indispensable to the student of the original. With some faults, he has surpassing excellencies. We especially commend No. 892 to the careful reading of young ministers.

893 Ash, Edward – NOTES AND COMMENTS ON THE NEW TESTAMENT. 3 vols. 1849-50. *****
Remarks such as any plain, thoughtful reader would make offhand.

894 Barnes, Albert – BARNES' NOTES ON THE NEW TESTAMENT. Enlarged type edition, edited by Robert Frew. Kregel Publications. Also Barnes' *Notes on the Old and New Testament.* 14 vols. Baker Book House. *******
Everybody has this work, and therefore can judge for himself, or we would both commend and criticize. See page 19.

895 Baxter, Richard – PARAPHRASE ON THE NEW TESTAMENT. With notes. 1810. ******
The notes are in Baxter's intensely practical and personal style, and show the hortatory use of Scripture; but they are not very explanatory.

896 Bengel, John Albert – NEW TESTAMENT COMMENTARY. Formerly published as *Gnomon of the New Testament* with original notes. 2 vols. Kregel Publications. See also No. 909. *******
See our remarks upon pages 20 and 21.

897 Beza, Theodore – NEW TESTAMENT. Translated out of Greek by
Theodore Beza. 1596. ***
The compact marginal notes are still most useful. The possessor of this old
black letter Testament may think himself happy.

898 Gray, James Comper – THE BIBLICAL MUSEUM. Revised
edition reissued as *Gray and Adams Bible Commentary*, 6 vols., 1871-
73. ***
Most helpful in suggesting divisions and furnishing anecdotes. *Multum in
parvo.* Our opinion of it is very high. It is not critical, but popular. The author
has used abbreviations in order to crowd in as much matter as possible. See
No. 5.

**899 Bloomfield, S. T. – THE GREEK TESTAMENT WITH ENG-
LISH NOTES.** Chiefly original. 2 vols., 1841. ***

**900 Bloomfield, S. T. – ADDITIONAL ANNOTATIONS ON THE
NEW TESTAMENT.** 1850. ***
We frequently get more from Bloomfield than from Alford, though he is not
so fashionable. His notes are full of teaching.

**901 Bloomfield, S. T. – RECENSIO SYNOPTICA ANNOTATIONIS
SACRAE.** A critical digest of the most important annotations on the
New Testament. 8 vols., 1826. (A considerable part of this work was
included in recent editions of the editor's *Greek New Testament*.) ***
"It would be impossible to convey to our readers an adequate idea of the mass
of information which the learned author has brought to bear upon the numerous
passages which he has undertaken to illustrate, and we can safely say, that the
enquirer will find very few of which Mr. Bloomfield has not given a complete
and satisfactory exposition."– *Quarterly Theological Review.*

**902 Bowyer, William – CRITICAL CONJECTURES AND OBSER-
VATIONS** on the New Testament. From various authors. 1812. *
According to Orme, the best that can be said for these conjectures is, that they
are ingenious; but who wants conjectures at all?

**903 Boys, John – EXPOSITION OF THE DOMINICAL EPISTLES
AND GOSPELS.** Used in our English liturgy throughout the whole
year. 1638. ***
Racy, rich, and running over. We marvel that it has not been reprinted. English
churchmen ought not to leave such a book in its present scarcity, for it is
especially adapted for their use. Boys is all essence. What a difference between
the John Boys of 1638 and the Thomas Boys of 1827! Note well the name.

904 Boys, Thomas – THE NEW TESTAMENT, with a plain exposition
for the use of families. 1827. *
Ordinary readers might be benefited by the practical observations and evangelical applications and exhortations; but students do not require this *Boys'* exposition.

905 Burkitt, William (1650–1703) – **EXPOSITORY NOTES.** See page
23. **
We liked Burkitt better when we were younger. He is, however, a homely and
spiritual writer, and his work is good reading for the many.

906 Chalmers, Thomas (1780–1847) – **SABBATH SCRIPTURE READINGS.** *Posthumous Works*, vol. 4. See No. 11. *******
The readings are not upon every portion of Scripture, neither can they be viewed as a full exposition of any part thereof. They are precious fragments of immortal thought.

907 Chrysostom – **HOMILIES** on Matthew, 3 vols.; John, 2 vols.; Acts, 2 vols.; Romans, 1 vol.; 1 and 2 Corinthians, 3 vols.; commentaries on Galatians and homilies on Ephesians, 1 vol.; Philippians, Colossians, and Thessalonians, 1 vol.; Timothy, Titus, and Philemon, 1 vol., in *Library of the Fathers.* ******
Enough of solid truth and brilliant utterance will be found here to justify this father's title of "Golden Mouth"; but still all is not gold which fell from his lips, and to modern readers, Chrysostom is not so instructive as he was to his own age.

908 Churton, Edward and **Jones, William Basil** – **THE NEW TESTAMENT,** with a plain explanatory comment. 2 vols., 1869. ******
Meant for private or family reading; with brief notes and well-executed engravings. An elegant work.

909 THE CRITICAL ENGLISH TESTAMENT. An adaptation of Bengel's *Gnomon*, with notes, showing the results of modern criticism and exegesis. 3 vols., 1869. *******
"The editors of this valuable work have put before the English reader the results of the labors of more than 20 eminent commentators. He who uses the book will find that he is reading Bengel's suggestive *Gnomon*, modifying it by the critical investigations of Tischendorf and Alford, and comparing it with the exegetical works of De Wette, Meyer, Olshausen, and others, and adding to it also profound remarks and glowing sayings from Trench and Stier."– *Evangelical Magazine.*
We have heard this opinion questioned; but with all discounts the book is a good one.

910 Cumming, John – **SABBATH EVENING READINGS.** Issued as follows: The four Gospels, in 4 vols.; Acts, Romans, Corinthians, Galatians, Ephesians, and Philippians, James, Peter, and Jude, Revelation. 1853. ******
Dr. Cumming is always evangelical, and his style is very attractive. These works are rather for popular reading than for students; but they are good as a whole, and their spirit is excellent. The doctor has written too fast and borrowed too much; but he interests and edifies.

911 Dallas, Alexander – **THE COTTAGER'S GUIDE TO THE NEW TESTAMENT.** 6 vols., 1839-45. *****
Six volumes for cottagers! How could they ever buy them? If bought, how could they refrain from sleeping while trying to read them? The *Guide* could be of no possible use to a sensible man, except as an opiate.

912 Dalton, W. – **COMMENTARY.** Edited by Rev. W. Dalton, 2 vols., 1848. *****
Not of use to preachers. Prepared for family reading and mainly taken from Henry and Scott. There are quite enough of these compilations.

913 Davidson, David – CRITICAL NOTES. 2 vols., 1834. *
Two small thick volumes; really a pocket commentary. Although the notes are
good, the student had better spend his money on larger and better books.

914 Doddridge, Philip – EXPOSITION OF THE FOUR GOSPELS.
Reprinted in 2 vols., as a Granary Classic (Kregel Publications). **
The late Dr. Barrington, Bishop of Durham, in addressing his clergy on the
choice of books, characterizes this masterly work in the following terms: "I
know of no expositor who unites so many advantages as Doddridge; whether
you regard the fidelity of his version, the fulness and perspicuity of his
composition, the utility of his general and historical information, the impartiality of his doctrinal comments, or, lastly, the piety and pastoral earnestness
of his moral and religious applications." Later interpreters have somewhat
diminished the value of this work.

915 Erasmus, Desiderius – PARAPHRASE. 2 vols., 1548,1551. **
This paraphrase was appointed by public authority to be placed in all churches
in England, and the clergy were also ordered to read it. The volumes are very
rare, and expensive because of their rarity.

916 Gell, Robert – GELL'S REMAINS; or, Select Scriptures Explained.
1676. *
A queer collection of remarks, criticisms, and fancies, in a huge volume Baxter
called Gell "one of the sect-makers." He was, no doubt, a singular man, an
Arminian, and one who had great respect for "the Learned Society of Astrolo-
gers."

917 Gilpin, William – EXPOSITION OF THE NEW TESTAMENT.
1790. Fourth edition, 2 vols., 1811. *
Half a paraphrase, half very free translation. Notes meagre. Useful to
buttermen.

918 Girdlestone, Charles – NEW TESTAMENT. Lectures for families,
2 vols., 1835. **
Profitable household reading.

919 Guyse, John – THE PRACTICAL EXPOSITOR. 3 vols., 1739-52;
6 vols., 1775. *
The day of paraphrase is past. Dr. Guyse was ponderous in style, and we
question if at this date he is ever read. Doddridge's *Expositor* is far better.

920 Hammond, Henry – PARAPHRASE AND ANNOTATIONS. 1675.
Works, vol. 3. Also in 4 vols., 1845. **
Though Hammond gives a great deal of dry criticism, and is Arminian,
churchy, and peculiar, we greatly value his addition to our stores of biblical
information. Use the sieve and reject the chaff.

921 Heylyn, John – THEOLOGICAL LECTURES AT WESTMIN-
STER ABBEY, with an interpretation of the New Testament. 2 vols.,
1749-61. *
Five volumes with absolutely nothing in them beyond a spinning out of the
text.

922 Knatchbull, Sir Norton – ANNOTATIONS UPON SOME DIFFI-
CULT TEXTS. 1693. **
Much valued in its day; but far outdone by more recent critics.

923 LANGE'S COMMENTARY ON THE HOLY SCRIPTURES. 24 vols. Edited by Philip Schaff. ✱✱✱
See under separate books.

924 Leigh, Sir Edward. See No. 44. ✱✱✱

925 Lindsay, John – NEW TESTAMENT, with notes. Selected from Grotius, Hammond, etc, 2 vols., 1736. ✱✱
A condensation of other writers—very well-done.

926 McClellan, John Brown – NEW TESTAMENT. A new translation, analysis, copious references, and illustrations from original authorities, harmony of the gospels, notes, and dissertations. In 2 vols., 1875. ✱✱
This work is what it professes to be, and we need say no more. It is, however, a very expensive luxury at the publishing price.

927 Mayer, John – NEW TESTAMENT. 2 vols. 1631. See pages 16 and 17. ✱✱✱

928 Meyer, Dr. H. A. W. – NEW TESTAMENT COMMENTARY. 11 vols. Hendrickson Publishers. ✱
A very learned commentary, of which Bishop Ellicott speaks in the highest terms. Meyer must be placed in the first class of scholars, though somewhat lower down in the class than his admirers have held. Apart from scholarship we do not commend him. Alford was certainly no very rigid adherent of orthodoxy, yet he says of Meyer that he is not to be trusted where there is any room for the introduction of rationalistic opinions. Whatever credit may be due to him for accurate interpretation, this is a terribly serious drawback. It is well to be warned.

929 Newcome, William – ATTEMPT TOWARDS REVISING OUR ENGLISH TRANSLATION, and illustrating the sense by notes. 2 vols., 1796. ✱
Newcome was a critical scholar whose works enjoyed a high repute. Unhappily, the Unitarians brought out an "Improved Version," professedly based upon Newcome's and this led the public to question Newcome's orthodoxy, but there is little reason for doing so. Few of our readers will care for this cold literal interpretation.

930 Penn, Granville – THE BOOK OF THE NEW COVENANT. A critical revision of the English Version. 1836. ✱

931 Penn, Granville – ANNOTATIONS ON THE BOOK OF THE NEW COVENANT. 1837. ✱

932 Penn, Granville – SUPPLEMENTAL ANNOTATIONS. 1838. ✱
These books are too learned for much to be learned from them; perhaps if they had been more learned still they would have been useful.

933 Platts, John – SELF-INTERPRETING TESTAMENT. 4 vols., 1827. ✱
A sort of biblical commentary. A concordance will answer the purpose.

934 Quesnell, Pasquier – NEW TESTAMENT. 4 vols., 1719-1725. ✱✱
A sweet and simple French writer who says many good things of a very harmless character.

935 Sumner, John Bird – PRACTICAL EXPOSITION OF THE GOS-
PELS, ACTS, EPISTLES OF PAUL, JAMES, PETER, JOHN,
AND JUDE. 9 vols., 1833 to 1851. *
Sumner's expositions are very mild and can generally be bought very cheap.
The public are pretty good judges, and the price indicates the value. The
qualities which procure an archbishopric are not such as qualify a man to be
an eminent expositor.

936 Townsend, George – NEW TESTAMENT, arranged in chronologi-
cal order. Notes. 2 vols., 1838. **
This harmony has always been in repute; but we confess we like the New
Testament best as we find it.

937 Trollope, William – ANALECTA THEOLOGICA. 2 vols., 1830-
35. **
A condensation of the opinions of eminent expositors, very well executed, and
useful except so far as superseded by more modern works.

938 Wall, William – BRIEF NOTES. 1730. *
Explains some difficulties, but it is far surpassed by other annotators.

939 Wesley, John. See No. 62. ***

940 Whedon, D. D. – WHEDON'S NEW TESTAMENT COMMEN-
TARY. Schmul Publishing Co. *
Dr. Whedon lacks common sense, and is no expositor. He is furiously anti-
calvinistic, and as weak as he is furious.

941 Whitby, Daniel. See No. 50.
This is a part of Patrick, Lowth, etc.

942 Wilson, William – EXPLANATION OF THE NEW TESTAMENT,
by the early opinions of Jews and Christians concerning Christ. 1838. **
Follows a deeply interesting line of investigation. It is not a commentary, but
is too good to be omitted.

943 Worsley, John – TRANSLATION, with notes. 1770. *
Translation second rate, criticism none, notes very short.

THE FOUR GOSPELS

944 Adam, Thomas – EXPOSITION OF THE GOSPELS. 2 vols.
1837. **
Short and sweet; but Adam is not the first man as an expositor.

945 Aquinas, Thomas – CATENA AUREA. Commentary collected out
of the Fathers. 6 vols., 1870. **
The Fathers are overestimated, by a sort of traditionary repute, for we question
if they are much read. This collection of extracts we always look into with
curiosity, and sometimes we find a pearl.

946 Bonar, Horatius – LIGHT AND TRUTH. See No. 6. ***

947 **Bouchier, Barton – MANNA IN THE HOUSE.** Vol. 1, Matthew and Mark; Vol. 2, Luke; Vol. 3, John. 1853-4. *
Mr. Bouchier writes sweetly, and his books aid the devotions of many families. Ministers may read them with profit; but they are not exactly intended for them.

948 **Brown, John – DISCOURSES AND SAYINGS OF OUR LORD.** Three large vols., 1852. ***
Of the noblest order of exposition. Procure it.

949 **Burgon, J. W. – PLAIN COMMENTARY FOR DEVOTIONAL READING.** 5 vols., 1870. **
Ryle says: "This is an excellent, suggestive, and devout work; but I connot agree with the author when he touches upon such subjects as the Church, the sacraments, and the ministry."

950 **Campbell, George – THE GOSPELS TRANSLATED,** with notes. 4 vols., 1814. **
Clear and cold. Orme says it is "one of the best specimens of a translation of the Scriptures in any language." The preliminary dissertations are valuable; the notes are purely critical.

951 **CHOICE NOTES ON MATTHEW.** Drawn from Old and New Sources. Also on Mark, Luke, and John. 1868-69. **
These are taken from the grander treasuries of Prebendary Ford (No. 955). We have mentioned them because those who could not afford to buy Ford's books might be able to get these.

952 **Clarke, Samuel – PARAPHRASE,** with notes. 2 vols., 1741. *
We do not care for paraphrases. Clarke was a learned man, but an unsafe guide.

953 **Denton, W. – THE GOSPELS FOR THE SUNDAYS AND OTHER HOLY DAYS OF THE CHRISTIAN YEAR.** 3 vols., 1860-63. **
Curates will find this just the thing they need for sermonizing.

954 **Elsley – ANNOTATIONS ON THE GOSPELS AND ACTS.** 3 vols., 1827. **
Wholly critical and philological.

955 **Ford, James – THE GOSPELS,** illustrated from ancient and modern authors. 4 vols. Matthew, Mark, Luke, John. 1856-72. ***
Those who wish to see what the Fathers said upon the Gospels, and to read the choicest sayings of the early Anglican bishops, cannot do better than consult Ford, who has made a very rich collection. Some of the extracts do not materially illustrate the text, but they are all worth reading.

956 **Forster, John – THE GOSPEL NARRATIVE WITH A CONTINUOUS EXPOSITION.** 1845. **
A paraphrase upon a good system, carefully executed, and instructive. Thoroughly Anglican.

957 **Gilby, William – SPIRIT OF THE GOSPEL.** 1818. *
Interesting remarks on certain texts. All can be found in other writers.

958 **Hall, Charles H. – NOTES FOR THE USE OF BIBLE CLASSES.** 2 vols., 1857. **
This book is full of reverence to Bishops and other Episcopal arrangements as if it had been "appointed to be read in Churches." American Episcopalians can evidently be very thorough. Notes poor.

959 **Jacobus, Melancthon W. – NOTES.** 3 vols., 1868-69. *******
Jacobus is sound and plain, and is therefore a safe guide to Sunday school teachers and others who need to see the results of learning without the display of it.

960 **Jukes, Andrew – FOUR VIEWS OF CHRIST.** Characteristic differences of the Gospels considered, as revealing various relations of the Lord Jesus. 1853. *******
Remarks prompting thought; containing in a small compass a mass of instruction.

961 **Lange, J. P.** See No. 923. *******
The Gospels are among the best of the series.

962 **Lyttleton, Lord George – GOSPELS AND ACTS,** with notes. 1856. *****
Such remarks as most teachers could make for themselves.

963 **Norris, John – KEY TO THE GOSPEL NARRATIVE.** 1871. ******
"Canon Norris writes primarily to help 'younger students' in studying the Gospels. But the unpretending volume is one which all students may peruse with advantage. It is an admirable manual for those who take Bible classes through the Gospels." – *London Quarterly.*

964 **Olshausen, Hermann – COMMENTARY ON THE GOSPELS AND ACTS.** 4 vols., 1848-1860. ******
Olshausen is mentioned by Alford as so rich in original material, that he has often cited him in his *New Testament for English Readers*. He is one of the most devout of the Germans, and a great scholar; but we are not enamored of him.

965 **Oxenden, Ashton – SHORT LECTURES ON THE SUNDAY GOSPELS.** 2 vols., 1869. *****
Why Oxenden's books sell we do not know. We would not care to have them for a gift. "Milk for babies" watered beyond measure.

966 **Pearce, Zachary – COMMENTARY ON THE GOSPELS, ACTS AND 1 CORINTHIANS.** 2 vols., 1777. *****
A huge mass of learning, said by great divines to be invaluable. To most men these volumes will simply be a heap of lumber.

967 **Riddle, J. E. – COMMENTARY.** 1843. *****
Choice extracts selected by the author of the well-known Latin Dictionary. Ministers should make such collections for themselves rather than purchase them.

968 **Ripley, Henry J. – THE GOSPELS,** with notes. 2 vols., 1837. ******
Adapted for Sunday school use. Simple, brief, and practical.

969 **Ryle, John Charles – EXPOSITORY THOUGHTS ON THE GOSPELS.** 3 vols. Attic Press, Evangelical Press. *******
We prize these volumes. They are diffuse, but not more so than family reading requires. Mr. Ryle has evidently studied all previous writers upon the Gospels and has given forth an individual utterance of considerable value.

970 **Stabback, Thomas – GOSPELS AND ACTS.** With annotations. 2 vols., 1809. *****
Very useful in its day, but quite out of date.

971 Stier, Rudolph – THE WORDS OF THE LORD JESUS. 1869. ***

972 Stier, Rudolph – THE WORDS OF THE RISEN SAVIOR. Klock and Klock (Kregel Publications). ***
No one can be expected to receive all that Stier has to day, but he must be dull indeed who cannot learn much from him. Read with care he is a great instructor.

973 Stock, Eugene – LESSONS ON THE LIFE OF OUR LORD. For the use of Sunday school teachers. 1875. ***
A thoroughly commendable book. Teachers and preachers have here more matter given them on the lessons than they are likely to use. Admirable!

974 Townson, Thomas – DISCOURSES ON THE GOSPELS. 2 vols., 1810. **
Bishop Lowth welcomed this as "a capital performance." It is only so from Lowth's point of view.

975 Trapp, Joseph – NOTES. 1748. *
This Trapp, grandson of the famous commentator, is the author of a wretched pamphlet upon "the nature, folly, sin and danger of being righteous over-much." He opposed Whitfield and Wesley with more violence then sense. His work is utterly worthless, and we only mention it to warn the reader against confounding it with the productions of the real old Trapp.

976 Trench, R. Chenevix – STUDIES ON THE GOSPEL. 1874. ***
Masterly studies on important topics. Students will do well to read also Trench's *Sermon on the Mount*. We do not always agree with this author, but we always learn from him.

977 Warren, Israel – SUNDAY SCHOOL COMMENTARY. 1872. *
An American work imported by Hodder and Stoughton. Notes slender.

978 Watson, Richard – EXPOSITION OF MATTHEW AND MARK. **
Arminian views crop up at every opportunity. The notes are meant to elucidate difficulties in the text, and frequently do so.

979 Westcott, Brooke Foss – INTRODUCTION TO THE STUDY OF THE GOSPELS. 1860. ***
Worthy of high commendation. The author knows the German writers, but is not defiled by their scepticism. He is a man of deep thought, but displays no pride of intellect. A man had need be a thorough student to value this *Introduction*. It is not an introduction to the Gospels, or to the reading of them, but to their study.

980 Wieseler, Karl – CHRONOLOGICAL SYNOPSIS OF THE GOSPELS. 1864. *
This important work formed the basis both of the *Synopsis Evangelica* of Tischendorf, and of the *Historical Lectures on the Life of our Lord* by Bishop Ellicott. It is much to be regretted that so many novel interpretations and baseless hypotheses should have marred the book; but, notwithstanding all drawbacks, it must be a masterly work to have received the heartiest commendation of the greatest scholars of the day. Only the more advanced student will care for this *Synopsis*.

981 **Williams, Isaac – DEVOTIONAL COMMENTARY.** 8 vols.
Thoughts on the study of the Gospels, harmony of the evangelists, the
nativity, second year of the ministry, third year of the ministry, the holy
week, the passion, the Resurrection. 1873. **

Anglican popery for quartz, and sparkling grains of precious gospel largely
interspersed as gold. We cannot imagine any spiritual man reading these works
without benefit, if he knows how to discriminate.

HARMONIES OF THE GOSPELS

(As these are somewhat aside from our plan, we mention but few. That they
are very numerous may be gathered from the following list given in Smith's
Dictionary: Osiander, 1537; Jansen, 1549; Stephanus, 1553; Calvin, 1553;
Cluver, 1628; Calov, 1680; Chemnitz, 1593 (continued by Leyser and Ger-
hard, 1704); Calixt, 1624; Cartwright, 1627; Lightfoot, 1654; Cradock, 1668;
Lancy, 1689; Le Clerc, 1699; Tomard, 1707; Burmann, 1712; Whiston, 1702;
Rus, 1727/8-30; Bengel, 1736, Hauber, 1737; Büsching, 1766; Doddridge,
1739-40; Pilkington, 1747; Macknight, 1756; Berthing, 1767; Griesbach,
1776, 97, 1809, 22; Newcome, 1778; Priestly, 1777, in Greek, and 1780 in
English; Michaelis, 1788, in his Introduction; White, 1799; Planck, 1809;
Keller, 1802; Mutschelle, 1806; De Wette and Lücke, 1818; Hess, 1822;
Sebastiani, 1806; Matthaei, 1826; Kaiser, 1828; Roediger, 1829; Clausen,
1829; Greswell, 1830; Chapman, 1836; Carpenter, 1838; Reichel, 1840;
Gehringer, 1842; Robinson, 1845, in Greek, 1846, in English; Stroud, 1853;
Anger, 1851; Tischendorf, 1851.)

982 **Calvin, John –** *A Harmony of Matthew, Mark, and Luke,* in
CALVIN'S COMMENTARIES, Translated by Rev. W. Pringle.
Baker Book House; Wm. B. Eerdmans Publishing Co. ***

There are older translations of this noble work, but they are less suitable to
modern taste than Mr. Pringle's. Calvin only harmonized three of the evangelists, but he did his work in his usual superb manner.

983 **Clarke, George W. – HARMONY,** with notes. 1870. ***

This American author is greatly indebted to other works. He has produced a
very handy book for teachers of youth.

984 **Doddridge, Philip.** See No. 914. **

985 **Dunn, Samuel – GOSPELS HARMONIZED,** with notes, forming a
complete commentary on the evangelists. Chiefly by Adam Clarke.
1838. **

Samuel Dunn has taken Adam Clarke as his basis, and then built thereon with
stones from Lightfoot, Macknight, Doddridge, Greswell, and others. It is, of
course, a Wesleyan harmony, and the reader is not long before he discovers that
fact; but the names of those concerned are a sufficient guarantee that it is by
no means a despicable production.

986 **Greenleaf, Simon – EXAMINATION OF THE TESTIMONY OF
THE EVANGELISTS** by the rules of evidence administered in courts
of justice, with an account of the trial of Jesus. 1847. **

The author is an American lawyer, very learned in his profession. He has
issued a treatise upon the laws of evidence, which is a standard work among

his brethren. It was a happy thought on his part to apply the laws of evidence to the narratives of the evangelists. To thoughtful men of all sorts, but to lawyers especially, this book is commended.

987 Greswell, Edward – DISSERTATIONS ON THE PRINCIPLES AND ARRANGEMENTS OF AN HARMONY OF THE GOSPELS. 4 vols., 1837. *
"The learned writer has greatly distinguished himself as the most laborious of modern harmonists. His work is the most copious that has appeared, at least since the days of Chemintz's folios." So says Dr. S. Davidson. To us it seems to be prolix and tedious.

988 Lightfoot, John – HARMONY, CHRONICLE AND ORDER OF THE NEW TESTAMENT. 1654. **
Lightfoot was a member of the Assembly of Divines, profoundly skilled in scriptural and talmudical lore. He never completed this harmony, for his plan was too comprehensive to be finished in a lifetime.

989 Macknight, James – HARMONY OF THE GOSPELS, with paraphrase and notes. 2 vols,. 1819. *
This author has enjoyed considerable repute and is still prized by many, but we can never bring our soul to like him, he always seems to us to be so graceless.

990 Mimpriss, Robert – THE TREASURY HARMONY OF THE FOUR EVANGELISTS. **
Condensed and compressed. Wonderfully useful.

991 Newcome, William – ENGLISH HARMONY, with notes. 1827. *
Merely the text arranged and a few rather ordinary notes. We do not see what a man can get out of it. But, hush! It is by an archbishop!

992 Robinson, Edward – HARMONY OF THE AUTHORIZED VERSION, following the harmony in Greek, by Dr. E. Robinson. With notes. ***
Robinson's *Harmony* is a work which has met great acceptance, and the Religious Tract Society did well to bring out this work for those unacquainted with Greek. The notes are mainly those of Robinson; but Wieseler, Greswell, and others have also been laid under contribution by the Editor, who has executed his work well.

993 Stroud, William – GREEK HARMONY, with synopsis and diatessaron. 1853. ***
One of the best of the harmonies.

994 Williams, Isaac. See No. 981. **
Merely the text arranged, without note or comment.

LIFE OF JESUS CHRIST
See "GOSPELS,"
especially Nos. 971, 972, 973, and 981.

(Here also we can only mention a few leading works.)

995 Andrews, Samuel – THE LIFE OF OUR LORD ON THE EARTH, in its historical, chronological, and geographical relations. 1863. ***
A good book for a student to read through before taking up larger works. It is a standard work.

996 Beecher, Henry Ward – LIFE OF JESUS, THE CHRIST. Earlier scenes. 1872. **
Here the great genius of Beecher glows and burns; but we are disappointed with his book as a biography of our Lord.

997 Bennett, James – LECTURES ON THE HISTORY OF JESUS CHRIST. Second edition. 2 vols., 1828. **
Lively, popular lectures, full of matter, well-expressed, and possessing sterling excellence.

998 Ellicott, C. J. – HISTORICAL LECTURES. 1869. **
This great author stands in the highest place of honor; but having no sympathy with what he calls "the popular theology," he should be read with considerable caution.

999 Farrar, F. W. – LIFE OF CHRIST. Klock and Klock (Kregel Publications). ***
THE work upon the subject. Fresh and full. The price is very high, and yet the sale has been enormous.

1000 Fleetwood, John – LIFE OF OUR LORD JESUS CHRIST. Also the lives of the apostles and evangelists. *
This has had a great run, and is to be found in farm houses and cottages. Why, we cannot tell, except that the sellers of parts and numbers are fine hands at pushing the trade, and plates and pictures have caught the simple purchasers.

1001 Kitto, John – *Life and Death of Our Lord*, in KITTO'S DAILY BIBLE ILLUSTRATIONS. See No. 41. ***
Abounds in instructive matter.

1002 Lange, J. P. – LIFE OF OUR LORD JESUS CHRIST, with additional notes, by Rev. Marcus Dods. 4 vols., 1864. ***
We constantly read Lange, and though frequently differing from him, we are more and more grateful for so much thoughtful teaching.

1003 Neander, J. A. W. – THE LIFE OF JESUS CHRIST IN ITS HISTORICAL DEVELOPMENT. Translated by professors McClintock and Blumenthal. 1853. **
Good as an answer to Strauss, but unsatisfactory from the standpoint of evangelical theology.

1004 Pressensé, Edmond – JESUS CHRIST: HIS TIMES, LIFE AND WORK. 1875. The above work "abridged by the author, and adapted for general readers." **
There have been many discussions upon the orthodoxy of this work, but it is a noble production, and is written in an adoring spirit. The accomplished author has made a valuable contribution to the cause of truth. Yet we are inclined to agree with the writer who said, "to write a life of Christ is to paint the sun with charcoal." The life of a Christian is the best picture of the life of Christ.

1005 Young, John – THE CHRIST OF HISTORY. Enlarged edition. 1869. **
"A work of great excellence, eloquence, and logical compactness."— *British Quarterly Review.*

MIRACLES OF OUR LORD

(Here, also, we cannot attempt a complete list.)

1006 Collyer, William – LECTURES ON SCRIPTURE MIRACLES.
1812. *
While reading we seem to hear the rustling of a silk gown. The lectures are by
no means to be despised, but they are far too fine for our taste.

1007 Cumming, John – LECTURES ON OUR LORD'S MIRACLES,
as earnests of the age to come. 1851. **
Below the Doctor's usual mark, which is none too high.

1008 Howson, J. S. – MEDITATIONS ON THE MIRACLES. 1871. **
Short, simple, but deeply spiritual and suggestive.

**1009 Knight, James – DISCOURSES ON THE PRINCIPAL
MIRACLES.** 1831. *
Mediocre discourses much appreciated by the clergy who borrow their
sermons.

1010 MacDonald, George – THE MIRACLES OF OUR LORD. 1870. **
Contains many fresh, childlike, and we had almost said, dreamy thoughts. It
suggests sidewalks of meditation.

1011 Maguire, Robert – THE MIRACLES OF CHRIST. 1863. **
We have been agreeably disappointed in this book. The bad paper offends the
eye, but the page bears many living, stirring thoughts. If the author preaches
in this fashion we do not wonder at his popularity.

**1012 Steinmeyer, F. L. – THE MIRACLES OF OUR LORD IN RELA-
TION TO MODERN CRITICISM.** Translated from the German by
L. A. Wheatley. 1875. *
No doubt a very scholarly book, and useful to those whose heads have been
muddled by other Germans, but we are weary of Teutonic answers to Teutonic
skepticisms. We suppose it was needful to hunt down the rationalists, for
farmers hunt down rats, but the game does not pay for the trouble.

1013 Trench, R. C. – NOTES ON THE MIRACLES. Baker Book
House. ***
Brimming with instruction. Not always to our taste in doctrine; but on the
whole a work of highest merit.

PARABLES OF OUR LORD

(A selection from a long list, for which see No. 1024.)

1014 Anderson, Charles – NEW READING OF OLD PARABLES.
1876. *
We paid four precious shillings for this book, and find 70 pages of rubbish and
50 more of advertisements. Our readers will, we hope, profit by our experience.

1015 Arnot, William – PARABLES OF OUR LORD. Kregel Publications.
***
We do not consider this to be up to our lamented friend's usual high mark of
excellence, but it is of great value.

1016 Bourdillon, Francis – THE PARABLES EXPLAINED AND AP-PLIED. *
Sufficiently common and commonplace. Platitudes sleepily worded.

1017 Collyer, William Bengo – LECTURES ON SCRIPTURE PAR-ABLES. 1815. See No. 1006. *

1018 Cumming, John – FORESHADOWS; or, Lectures on our Lord's Parables. 1852. See No. 1007. **
The Doctor evdidently prints his sermons without much revision. They are pleasing, popular, and, of course, rather prophetic.

1019 Greswell, E. – EXPOSITION OF THE PARABLES. 5 vols. in 6, 1834. **
A vast heap of learning and language. The work, though padded out, stilted in style, and often fanciful, is a mine for other writers.

1020 Guthrie, Thomas – THE PARABLES READ IN THE LIGHT OF THE PRESENT DAY. 1874. **
Twelve parables treated in Dr. Guthrie's lively, sparkling manner. Flowers in abundance.

1021 Keach, Benjamin – EXPOSITION OF THE PARABLES. Kregel Publications. **
Although our honored predecessor makes metaphors run on as many legs as a centipede, he has been useful to thousands. His work is old-fashioned, but it is not to be sneered at.

1022 Knight, James – DISCOURSES ON THE PRINCIPAL PARABLES. 1829. See No. 1009. *

1023 Lisco, Frederick Gustav – PARABLES EXPLAINED. 1840. **
Largely composed of citations from Luther and Calvin. The remarks will assist in elucidating the design of the parables.

1024 Trench, R. C. – NOTES ON THE PARABLES. Baker Book House. ***
We do not like Trench's theology in many places, but he is a capital writer. The student will find a very complete list of expositions on the parables in the appendix at the close of Trench's work.

1025 Upjohn, W. – DISCOURSES ON THE PARABLES. 3 vols., 1824. *
Earnestly Calvinistic sermons, full of old-fashioned Gospel. Not very original.

MATTHEW

1026 Abbott, Lyman – NEW TESTAMENT. Vol. 1., Matthew and Mark. 1875. **
Intended for workers, and likely to be useful to them.

1027 Adamson, H. T. – MATTHEW EXPOUNDED. 1871. *
This book reads to us like utter nonsense. We question if anyone except the author will ever be able to make head or tail of it, and he had better be quick about it, or he will forget what he meant.

1028 Alexander, Joseph Addison – MATTHEW EXPLAINED. 1870. ***
Dr. Alexander's last work. He died before it was quite finished. It is complete
to chapter 16. Its value is great.

1029 Beausobre, Isaac de, and **L'Enfant, Jaques – A NEW VERSION
WITH A COMMENTARY.** 1790. **
The brief notes are purely literal or illustrative, and are remarkably pertinent.
The mass of the volume is taken up with an introduction to the New Testament.

1030 Benham, W. – MATTHEW, with notes. 1861. **
With this in his hand a teacher would be much aided in conducting his class.
It is written by a teacher for teachers. The remarks are not very profound, nor
always such as we should endorse, but they are well-fitted for their purpose.

1031 Blackwood, Christopher – AN EXPOSITION on the ten first chapters of Matthew. 1649 **
This learned divine became a Baptist through studying the arguments against
believer's baptism. This proves his candor. His comment is somewhat out-of-
date, but it is still good.

1032 Clarke, George W. – NOTES ON MATTHEW. 1870. **
Good notes for teachers. Well-compiled. A fit companion to No. 983.

1033 Dickson, David – MATTHEW. The Banner of Truth. ***
A perfect gem. The work is, to men of our school, more suggestive of sermons
than almost any other we have met with.

1034 Godwin, John H. – NEW TRANSLATION, with brief notes. 1863. **
Dr. Godwin is a painstaking elucidator of the word, and his plan is an excellent
one. Students in college will value him.

1035 Goodwin, Harvey – COMMENTARY. 1857. **
An important work, which may be consulted with advantage.

1036 Kelly, William – LECTURES ON THE GOSPEL OF MATTHEW.
Believer's Bookshelf, Inc. *
We cannot accept the forced and fanciful interpretations here given.

1037 Marloratus, Augustine [Marlorat] – EXPOSITION. Translated by
Thomas Tymme. 1570. **
Marlorate was an eminent French reformer, preacher, and martyr. His commentaries contain the cream of the older writers, and are in much esteem, but
are very rare. He wrote on the whole New Testament, but we have in English
only the Gospels and Jude.

1038 Morison, James – THE GOSPEL ACCORDING TO MATTHEW.
Klock & Klock (Kregel Publications). ***
We differ greatly in doctrinal views from Dr. Morison, but we set a great price
upon his Matthew and Mark, which deserves the utmost praise.

1039 Overton, Charles – EXPOSITORY PREACHER. Course of lectures on Matthew. 2 vols., 1850. *
Solid, sound, soporific sermons; intended for lay helpers to read, with the
prayers appended. They will not make the hearers lie awake at nights, or cause
them palpitations of heart through excess of original and striking thought.

1040 Parker, Joseph – HOMILETIC ANALYSIS. Matthew. 1870. **
Dr. Parker is an able though somewhat—. But stop, he is a near neighbor of ours.

1041 Penrose, John – LECTURES ON MATTHEW. 1832. *
The author says of his work, "No novelty of any kind, no originality either of thought or research will be found in it." Why, then, did he print it?

1042 Thomas, David – GENIUS OF THE GOSPEL. Homiletical commentary. 1873. ***
We hardly know a more suggestive book.

1043 Ward, Richard – THEOLOGICAL QUESTIONS, dogmatical observations, and evangelical essays on the Gospel According to Matthew. About 2,650 profitable questions are discussed; and 580 points of doctrine noted, etc. 1640. **
A hugh mass of comment, in which are thousands of good things mostly set forth by way of question and answer. Few could ever read it through; but to a wise minister it would be a mine of wealth.

MARK

1044 Alexander, Joseph Addison – COMMENTARY ON MARK. Klock & Klock (Kregel Publications). ***
Alexander expounds Mark as an independent record, and does not constantly tell us to "see Matthew and Luke." Hence, the book is complete in itself, and the author's learning and care have made it invaluable.

1045 B., G. – PRACTICAL COMMENTARY ON MARK, in simple and familiar language. 1863. **
The different paragraphs are treated under most suggestive headings, which are the most useful parts of the book. Infant baptism is far too prominent, but the little work is likely to be very helpful.

1046 Godwin, John H. – MARK. A new translation with notes and doctrinal lessons. 1869. **
We like the brief doctrinal lessons, which are rather a new feature. They will serve admirably well as sermon-hints. The notes and translation are really good.

1047 Goodwin, Harvey – COMMENTARY. 1860. **
Contains much very helpful comment. Produced in connection with the Cambridge Working Men's College.

1048 Morison, James – GOSPEL ACCORDING TO MARK. Klock & Klock (Kregel Publications). ***
A deeply learned work. We know of none more thorough. Differing as we do from this author's theology, we nevertheless set a high price upon this production.

1049 Petter, George – COMMENTARY ON MARK. 2 vols., 1661. **
J. C. Ryle says of this work: "For laborious investigation of the meaning of every word, for patient discussion of every question bearing on the text, for fulness of matter, for real thoughtfulness, and for continued practical applica-

tion, there is no work on Mark which, in my opinion, bears comparison with Petter's. Like Goliath's sword, there is nothing like it." We have found far less fresh thought in it than we expected, and think it rather tedious reading.

LUKE
See also "GOSPELS"

(Oostersee in Lange is excellent.)

1050 Foote, James – LECTURES ON LUKE. 2 vols., 1858. *******
We frequently consult this work, and never without finding in it things new and old. To preachers who will not steal the lectures, but use them suggestively, they will be extremely serviceable.

1051 Godet, Frederick – COMMENTARY ON LUKE. Translated by E. W. Shelders and M. D. Cusin. Kregel Publications. *******
Dr. Meyer says: "To an immense erudition, to a living piety, Godet unites a profound feeling of reality; there is here a vivifying breath, an ardent love for the Savior, which helps the disciple to comprehend the work, the acts, the words of his Divine Master."

1052 Goodwin, Harvey – COMMENTARY ON LUKE. 1865. ******
This writer endeavors to give the results of learning in such a manner that working men may understand them. He says many good things.

1053 Major, J. R. – LUKE, with English notes. 1826. *****
Notes compiled with a view to the divinity examinations at Cambridge, containing a considerable amount of information.

1054 Thomson, James – EXPOSITION OF LUKE. A series of lectures. 3 vols., 1849. *******
Eminently instructive. Clear, good sense, freshness, and earnestness are well-combined. We have had great pleasure in examining these lectures.

1055 Van Doren, W. H. – THE GOSPEL OF LUKE. Formerly entitled *Suggestive Commentary on St. Luke*. Kregel Publications. *******
Well-named "suggestive;" it is all suggestions. It teems and swarms with homiletical hints.

JOHN

1056 Anderson, Robert – PRACTICAL EXPOSITION OF JOHN. 2 vols., 1841. ******
By an evangelical clergyman. Sound, but not very original.

1057 Augustine – COMMENTARY ON JOHN. 2 vols. of *Works of Augustine*. ******

1058 Augustine – HOMILIES ON THE GOSPEL AND FIRST EPISTLE OF JOHN. 2 vols. of the *Library of the Fathers*. ******
To the wise, a mine of treasure. Augustine is often fanciful; but even his fancies show a mastermind. Much that passes for new is stolen from this prince of theologians.

1059 Beith, Alexander – EXPOSITORY DISCOURSES. 1857. ******
Discourses which must have been very profitable to the hearers. Students will do better with works which are more condensed.

1060 Besser, Rudolph – BIBLICAL STUDIES ON JOHN. Translated from the German by M. G. Huxtable. 2 vols., 1861-62. **
"The character of this commentary is practical and devotional. There are often very exquisite devotional passages, and a vein of earnest piety runs through the whole work."— *Literary Churchman.*

1061 Brown, George – LECTURES FORMING A CONTINUOUS COMMENTARY. 2 vols., 1863. **
The plan of this work will prevent its being widely used; but its execution strikes us as being uncommonly able. It is a gathering up of other men's materials and an amalgamation, yet it brings a good deal of light to bear on the Gospel of John.

1062 Drummond, D. T. K. – EXPOSITION OF THE LAST NINE CHAPTERS OF JOHN. 1850. **
Good, but not very striking.

1063 Dunwell, Francis Henry – COMMENTARY ON THE AUTHORIZED VERSION OF JOHN, compared with the Sinaitic, Vatican, and Alexandrian manuscripts, and also with Dean Alford's revised translation. 1872. *
The notes from various authors are good, and the various readings are useful; but we fail to see any very special value in the volume. The interpretation of the Third of John is eminently unsatisfactory; Mr. Dunwell teaches baptismal regeneration.

1064 Fawcett, John – EXPOSITION OF JOHN. 3 vols., 1860. **
Good, evangelical sermons.

1065 Hengstenberg, E. W. – COMMENTARY ON JOHN. 2 vols. Klock & Klock (Kregel Publications). **
Like others of this author's works: solid, but dry.

1066 Hutcheson, George – JOHN. The Banner of Truth. ***
Excellent; beyond all praise. It is a full-stored treasury of sound theology, holy thought, and marrowy doctrine.

1067 Meyer, H. A. W. See No. 928. **

1068 O'Conor, W. A. – COMMENTARY. 1872. *
In this translation, the first verse runs thus: "In origin the Word was, and the Word was the Deity, and the Word was Deity." Who likes this, or understands it? The notes do not charm us.

1069 Shepherd, R. – NOTES ON THE GOSPEL AND EPISTLES OF JOHN. 1769. *
Though the author opposed Socinianism, we cannot but regard his views as an introduction to that heresy. The spirit of the book is vicious.

1070 Tholuck, Augustus – COMMENTARY ON JOHN. 1860. ***
More spiritual than is usual with German theologians, and quite as scholarly as the best of them.

1071 Tittmann, K. C. – COMMENTARY ON JOHN. 2 vols., 1844. **
Horne, in speaking of this work in the German, without endorsing all Tittmann's opinions, declares it to be the most valuable commentary on John extant in so small a form. Our judgment is less commendatory.

1072 Traheron, Bartholomew – AN EXPOSITION OF A PART OF ST. JOHN'S GOSPEL made in Sunday readings in the English Congregation. Very rare. 1558. *
A little, quaint, old book. Not intrinsically worth the price, nor a tenth of it.

1073 Van Doren, W. H. – GOSPEL OF JOHN. 2 vols. in 1. Kregel Publications. ***
If men who read this volume do not preach the better for so doing, it is not Van Doren's fault; they must be Van Dolts by nature, though they may ignore the family name.

PARTS OF JOHN

(A selection of authors is all we can give.)

1074 Hildersham, Arthur – LECTURES ON JOHN 4. 1628, 1656. ***
A mass of godly teaching; but rather heavy reading.

1075 Turner, Samuel H. – ESSAY ON OUR LORD'S DISCOURSE AT CAPERNAUM. (John 6). 1851. *
Written with the immediate view of combating the errors of Cardinal Wiseman, who appeals to this chapter for proofs of "the real presence."

1076 Patterson, John B. – LECTURES ON JOHN 14, 15, AND 16. 1859. **
Solid discourses, containing much thought happily expressed. Yet withal somewhat laborious reading.

1077 Alexander, Thomas – GREAT HIGH PRIEST WITHIN THE VAIL. (John 17.) 1857. ***
Sound theology and honest exposition. Multum in parvo.

1078 Brown, John– EXPOSITION OF JOHN 17. 1850. ***
Dr. Brown is always deep, full, and overflowing.

1079 Burgess, Anthony – ONE HUNDRED AND FORTY-FIVE SERMONS ON JOHN 17. 1656. ***
A standard work by a great Puritan. Somewhat prolix.

1080 Landels, William – THE SAVIOR'S PARTING PRAYER FOR HIS DISCIPLES. (John 17.) 1872. **
Sermons of a high order; style admirable, but rather diffuse. To be estimated rather from a homiletical than an expository point of view.

1081 Newton, George – JOHN 17 UNFOLDED. 1660. Reprinted in Nichol's Commentaries. 1867. ***
If not one of the chief of the Puritans, Newton was but little behind the front rank in ability. Joseph Alleine was his assistant minister at Taunton. His writings are plain and profitable.

1082 Pierce, Samuel Eyles – EXPOSITION OF THE LORD'S PRAYER IN JOHN 17. 1812. ***
Always sweet as honey to those of strong Calvinistic views.

ACTS OF THE APOSTLES
See also "GOSPELS"

1083 Alexander, Joseph Addison – COMMENTARY ON THE ACTS OF THE APOSTLES. Klock and Klock (Kregel Publications). *******
In all respects a work of the highest merit.

1084 Alford, Henry – HOMILES ON THE FORMER PART OF THE ACTS OF THE APOSTLES. Chapters 1-10. 1858. *******
Not so good as his critical notes; but such an author always deserves attention.

1085 Arnot, William – STUDIES IN ACTS: The Church in the House. Kregel Publications. *******
Intended to be read in families on sabbath afternoons; but all who are acquainted with Dr. Arnot will know that even his simplest expositions are rich and full. He hath dust of gold.

1086 Baumgarten, M. – APOSTOLIC HISTORY. 3 vols., 1854. ******
"An exposition at once profoundly scientific and sublimely Christian, one of the most pressing wants of our times."–*Eclectic Review*. Alford calls it excellent, though somewhat fanciful.

1087 Bennett, James – LECTURES ON THE ACTS. 1847. ******
A good specimen of plain and popular pulpit exposition. Dr. Bennett fights very earnestly for the Congregationalist view of baptism, for which we do not blame him; for common humanity leads us to admire a man who struggles for a weak cause.

1088 Benson, George – HISTORY OF THE FIRST PLANTING OF THE CHRISTIAN RELIGION. 3 vols. , 1756. *****
Dull, but displaying considerable research. Benson was an Arian.

1089 Bonar, H. – LIGHT AND TRUTH. Vol. 3. See No. 6 *******

1090 Bouchier, Barton – MANNA IN THE HOUSE; or Daily Expositions of the Acts. 1858. ******
Superior family reading. Bouchier did not write for students, but for households, yet even the more advanced may learn from him.

1091 Brewster, John – LECTURES ON THE ACTS. 1830. *****
A sip of Howson or Hackett is worth a barrel of these weak and watery prelections.

1092 Calvin, John – *The Acts*, in CALVIN'S COMMENTARIES. Baker Book House; Wm. B. Eerdmans Publishing Co. *******
This forms the basis of the Calvin Translation Society's edition.

1093 Cook, F.C. – THE ACTS, WITH A COMMENTARY. 1866. ******
Contains many useful notes, instructive to fairly educated readers.

1094 Cradock, Samuel – THE APOSTOLICAL HISTORY, containing the Acts, labors, travels, sermons, of the apostles. 1762. *****
Tillotson, Reynolds, Doddridge and others highly commend the works of this Puritan writer. The style in which the *Apostolical History* is got up is most uninviting; the book is nearly all italics. Many modern works far excel it.

1095 Denton, W. – COMMENTARY ON THE ACTS. 2 vols., 1874. ***
A complete list of all authors upon the Acts will be found in this very learned and exhaustive work. We do not always agree with the author, but he has done his work thoroughly well.

1096 Dick, John – LECTURES ON THE ACTS. 1848. **
Interesting lectures upon selected portions of the Acts. This work has been reprinted in America, whence we obtained a copy of the second edition. This shows that it has been highly esteemed.

1097 Du Veil, C. M. – EXPLANATION OF THE ACTS. 1685. **
Claude's prefatory letter highly commends this work. The author defends the immersion of belivers with earnestness.

1098 Fawcett, John – EXPOSITION OF THE ACTS. 3 vols., 1860. ***
A fine series of expository discourses. Sometimes we differ.

1099 Ford, J. – THE ACTS, illustrated from ancient and modern times. 1856. See No. 955. **

1100 Gloag, Paton J. – COMMENTARY ON THE ACTS. Klock and Klock (Kregel Publications). ***
Dr. Hackett says of Dr. Gloag's work: "I have examined it with special care. For my purposes I have found it unsurpassed by any similar work in the English language. It shows a thorough mastery of the material, philology, history, and literature pertaining to this range of study, and a skill in the use of this knowledge, which places it in the first class of modern expositions."

1101 Gualtherus, Rodulphus – A HUNDRED THREESCORE AND FIFTEEN HOMELYES, or sermons vppon the Actes of the Apostles, made by Radulphe Gualthere of Tigurine, and translated from Latine by John Bridges. 1572. **
Full of Protestantism. The author judged that, as Luke who wrote Acts was a physician, his book was meant to be medicine to the Church.

1102 Hackett, Horatio B. – AMERICAN COMMENATRY. Hackett on Acts with Arnold and Ford on Romans in one volume. ***
Hackett occupies the first position among commentators upon the Acts. The Bunyan Library edition omits some of his most valuable critical observations.

1103 Hodgson, Robert – LECTURES ON THE FIRST SEVENTEEN CHAPTERS OF THE ACTS. 1845. *
Deficient in Gospel clearness, and in every other respect, except ardent churchism.

1104 Humphry, William Gilson – COMMENTARY ON THE ACTS. Second edition. 1854. *
Exegetical remarks upon the Greek text. Very good from a philological point of view, but professedly of an elementary character.

1105 Kelly, W. – INTRODUCTORY LECTURES TO THE ACTS. Believer's Bookshelf, Inc. *
By a man "who, born for the universe, narrowed his mind" by Darbyism.

1106 LANGE'S COMMENTARY ON THE HOLY SCRIPTURES. *Acts*, by Gotthard Victor Lechler. Edited by Dr. Philip Schaff. **
Adds nothing to our knowledge of the Acts; but the homiletical hints are useful.

1107 **Lightfoot, John – COMMENTARY ON ACTS.** Edited by J.R. Pitman. 1823. Vol. 8 of Lightfoot's *Works*. *
Few nowadays will care for this author, whose learning ran mostly in Talmudical channels. He was profound, but not always discreet.

1108 **MacBride, John David – LECTURES ON THE ACTS AND EPISTLES.** 1858. *
This author simply gives a continuous narrative. He has also written on the Gospels. We mention him that the student may not purchase his work as a commentary.

1109 **Maskew, T. R. – ANNOTATIONS ON THE ACTS,** with college and senate-house examination papers. 1847. *
A handbook to the Acts, viewing it simply as a Greek book; prepared for the use of students passing through the university.

1110 **Mimpriss, R.–THE ACTS AND EPISTLES,** according to Greswell's arrangement. 1837. **
A handy book for teachers.

1111 **Neander, J.A.W.–HISTORY OF THE PLANTING AND TRAINING OF THE CHRISTIAN CHURCH BY THE APOSTLES.** Translated by J.E. Ryland. 2 vols., 1851. **
The work rather of an historian than of a commentator. Bold, devout, learned and on the whole, sound. The result of wide research and deep learning.

1112 **Norris, J. P. – KEY TO THE ACTS.** 1871. **
A well-executed sketch of the Acts of the Apostles, giving the student a clear idea of the run of the Book. Like the same author's *Key to the Gospels* (No. 963), it would be most useful in Bible classes.

1113 **Olshausen, H.** See No. 964. **
Denton says that "this is a brief, hasty, and not well-digested supplement to Olshausen's volumes on the Gospels." He thinks all the German writers to be much overrated, and we are much of his mind.

1114 **Pyle, T. – PARAPHRASE OF THE ACTS.** 2 vols., 1795. *
This pile of printed paper may safely be left on the bookseller's shelves.

1115 **Stier, Rudolph – WORDS OF THE APOSTLES.** Klock and Klock (Kregel Publications). ***
Devout, scholarly, full of thought. To be used discreetly.

1116 **Stock, Eugene – LESSONS ON THE ACTS,** for Sunday school teachers and other religious instructors. 1874. ***
For half-a-crown the teacher may here obtain one of the most useful books known to us. Though produced for members of the Church of England, we recommend it heartily to ministers and others who are preparing addresses to the young.

1117 **Thomas, David – ACTS OF THE APOSTLES.** Kregel Publications. **
Many of the homiletic outlines strike us as "much ado about nothing." Still, if a man should read this work and get no help from it, it would be his own fault.

1118 **Thomson, James – EXPOSITION OF THE ACTS.** 1854. *
We fail to see much here of service to a preacher.

1119 **Trollopoe, W.** – COMMENTARY ON THE ACTS, with examination questions for the B.A. degree. 1854. *
Well-adapted to accomplish the design indicated in the title.

1120 **Vaughan, Charles** – STUDIES IN THE BOOK OF ACTS. Klock and Klock (Kregel Publications). ***
Not only does Dr. Vaughan expound his texts in the ablest manner, but he introduces passages of Scripture so aptly that he suggests discourses. Bating his churchianity, we cannot too highly commend him.

LIVES OF THE APOSTLES

1121 **Kitto, John** – *The Apostles and the Early Church,* in KITTO'S DAILY BIBLE ILLUSTRATIONS. Kregel Publications. ***

1122 **Baur, Ferdinand Christian** – PAUL, HIS LIFE AND WORKS. From the German. 2 vols., 1873-75. *
Of the very broad church school. Not at all to our mind.

1123 **Bevan, Joseph Gurney** – LIFE OF PAUL. 1807. *
For the Society of Friends. Contains nothing which adds to our information upon the life of Paul. It may have been useful in its day, but it is superseded.

1124 **Binney, Thomas** – PAUL: HIS LIFE AND MINISTRY. 1870. **
Mr. Binney says, "This work is strictly an outline of the life of Paul, and it is nothing more." It is a capital preparation for reading Lewin and Conybeare and Howson.

1125 **Blunt, Henry** – LECTURES ON THE HISTORY OF PAUL. 2 vols., sixth edition., 1835. **
Printed in such large and widely-leaded type that a very little matter goes a long way. Very good, but not striking.

1126 **Conybeare, W. J. and Howson, J. S.** – THE LIFE AND EPISTLES OF ST. PAUL. Wm. B. Eerdmans Publishing Co. ***
Far superior to any other work on the subject. It stands like some o'ertopping Alp, a marvel among scriptural biographies. We have not space to mention Howson's minor works connected with Paul, but they are all good.

1127 **Eadie, John** – PAUL, THE PREACHER. An expostion of his discourses and speeches, as recorded in the Acts. 1859. ***
Designed to give ordinary readers a juster and fuller conception of the doctrine and life-work of the Apostle. An able work.

1128 **Lewin, Thomas** – LIFE AND EPISTLES OF ST. PAUL. Second edition, much enlarged. 2 vols., 1875. ***
Dr. Gloag in his *Commentary on the Acts* says: "Two works are especially instructive, and deserve careful perusal. The *Life and Epistles of St. Paul,* by Lewin, and the classical work on the same subject by Conybeare and Howson. In the former, the historical connections of the Acts are chiefly stated, and in the latter its geographical relations."

1129 **Lyttleton, Lord George** – OBSERVATIONS ON THE CONVERSION AND APOSTLESHIP OF ST. PAUL, in a letter to Gilbert West. 1747. *
Gilbert West and his friend Lord Lyttleton, both men of acknowledged talents, had imbibed the principles of infidelity from a superficial view of the

Scriptures. Fully persuaded that the Bible was an imposture, they were determined to expose the cheat. Mr. West chose the Resurrection of Christ, and Lord Lyttleton the conversion of St. Paul, for the subject of hostile criticism. Both sat down to their respective tasks, full of prejudice, and a contempt for Christianity. The result of their separate attempts was that they were both converted by their endeavors to overthrow the truth of Christianity! They came together, not as they expected, to exult over an imposture exposed to ridicule, but to lament their folly, and to congratulate each other on their joint conviction, that the Bible was the Word of God. Their able enquiries have furnished two most valuable treatises in favor of revelation; one, entitled *Observations on the Conversion of St. Paul*, and the other, *Observations on the Resurrection of Christ*.

1130 MacDuff, J. R. – ST. PAUL IN ROME. 1871. **
Sermons preached in Rome, into which are ably introduced eloquent mention of the existing traditions and remains which associate the Apostle with that great city.

1131 Biscoe, Richard – HISTORY OF THE ACTS OF THE APOSTLES. Confirmed from other authors, and considered as full evidence of the truth of Christianity. 1840. **

1132 Paley, William (1743–1805) – HORAE PAULINAE. Numerous editions. The Religious Tract Society publishes the *Horae Paulinae*, with notes, and *Horae Apostolicae*, by Rev. T. Birks. **

1133 Tate, James – THE HORAE PAULINAE carried out and illustrated. 1840. **
Though not commentaried, the three works just mentioned are sources of information not to be neglected by the student of the Acts.

1134 Rivington, Francis – LIFE AND WRITINGS OF ST. PAUL. 1874. **
Nobody possessing Conybeare and Howson will need this work, though in the absence of better this would have been serviceable.

1135 Smith, Thornley – SAUL OF TARSUS. **
Thornley Smith always deserves attentive reading.

1136 Blunt, Henry – LECTURES UPON THE HISTORY OF ST. PETER. 1830. For remarks, see No. 1125. **

1137 Green, Samuel G. – THE APOSTLE PETER: His Life and Lessons. 1873. ***
Contains a large amount of needful information, condensed and well-arranged. Dr. Green is *the* writer on Peter's biography.

1138 Krummacher, F.W. – ST. JOHN THE EVANGELIST. **
The author's name is a sufficient guarantee. He has also written on Cornelius and Stephen.

1139 Goulburn, Edward Meyrick – ACTS OF THE DEACONS: Lectures on Acts 6—9. 1869. **
An interesting topic well-handled.

THE APOSTOLIC EPISTLES

1140 Benson, George – PARAPHRASE AND NOTES ON 1 AND 2 THESSALONIANS, 1 AND 2 TIMOTHY, PHILEMON, TITUS, AND THE SEVEN CATHOLIC EPISTLES. 2 vols., 1734. **
Benson has closely followed Locke's method, though scarcely with equal footsteps, and has paraphrased those epistles which Locke did not live to complete. In the consecutive reading of an epistle Locke and Benson are great assistants, but as Benson was an Arian he must be read with great caution. See No. 1148.

1141 Denton, W. – COMMENTARIES ON THE EPISTLES FOR SUNDAYS AND HOLY DAYS. 2 vols., 1869-71. **
Will be a treasure to Churchmen. Denton is a good author.

1142 Dickson, David – EXPOSITION OF ALL THE EPISTLES. 1659. ***
Dickson is a writer after our own heart. For preachers he is a great ally. There is nothing brilliant or profound; but everything is clear and well arranged, and the unction runs down like the oil from Aaron's head. In this volume the observations are brief.

1143 Ellicott, Charles – COMMENTARY ON ST. PAUL'S EPISTLES. 5 vols.; Galatians, Ephesians, Pastoral Epistles, Philippians, Colossians, Philemon, Thessalonians. 1861-64. ***
Dr. Eadie says, "Ellicott is distinguished by close and uniform adherence to grammatical canon, without much expansion into exegsis." Dr. Riddle thinks Ellicott to be in many respects without on English rival. For scholars only.

1144 Ferguson, James – EXPOSITION OF THE EPISTLES TO THE GALATIANS, EPHESIANS, PHILIPPIANS, COLOSSIANS, AND THESSALONIANS. 1659-74; 1 vol., 1841. ***
He who possesses this work is rich. The author handles his matter in the same manner as Hutcheson and Dickson, and he is of their class–a grand, gracious savory divine.

1145 Gloag, Paton J. – INTRODUCTION TO THE PAULINE EPISTLES. 1874. ***
Not an exposition, but an exceedingly valuable introduction, illustrating the design, date, and circumstances of the inspired letters.

1146 Jowett, Benjamin – EPISTLES TO THE THESSALONIANS, GALATIANS AND ROMANS. Greek and English, with critical notes. 2 vols., 1859. *
Professor Jowett's most unseemly attack on Paul, as an apostle, as a thinker, as a writer, and as a man, only proves his own incapacity for forming a just judgment either of the apostle or of himself.

1147 Kelly, William – INTRODUCTORY LECTURES TO THE PAULINE EPISTLES. Believer's Bookshelf, Inc. *
Of the same character as Mr. Kelly's other works. See No. 1220.

1148 Locke, John – PARAPHRASE AND NOTES ON THE EPISTLES
      TO THE GALATIANS, CORINTHIANS, ROMANS, AND
      EPHESIANS. 1733. **
      Anything from such a man is worthy of attention, and this piece, as a protest
      against rending texts from their connection, is most judicious. The paraphrase,
      though open to criticism, is executed with great candor, and really illuminates
      the text. See Benson, No. 1140.

1149 Lyth, John – THE HOMILETICAL TREASURY. Romans to Phil-
      ippians. 1869. *
      The plan of this book is surpassingly useful, but Dr. Lyth does not carry it out
      to our satisfaction. It is easy to divide an egg by letting it drop on the floor, and
      in this fashion this author divides texts.

1150 MacKnight, J. – TRANSLATION WITH COMMENTARY AND
      NOTES. 1816. *
      To be read with great caution. We do not admire this author.

1151 Marston, Charles Dallas – EXPOSITIONS ON THE EPISTLES.
      1868. **
      Expositions of each epistle as a whole. An admirable method of instruction.
      To do this in a popular style is as praiseworthy as it is difficult. Mr. Marston
      has succeeded.

1152 Paget, Alfred T. – ON THE UNITY AND ORDER OF THE
      EPISTLES OF ST. PAUL. 1851. **
      Suggests a rich vein for the student's own working. Few, we fear, will carry
      it out, but these will prize the Epistles more than others.

1153 Peile, T. W. – ANNOTATIONS ON THE APOSTOLICAL
      EPISTLES. For the use of students of the Greek text. 4 vols., 1848-
      52. *
      Anti-calvinistic in doctrine, and in style involved, obscure, and terribly
      parenthetical. The purchase of the volumes would be a heavy investment.

1154 Prichard, C. E. – COMMENTARY ON EPHESIANS, PHILIPPI-
      ANS, AND COLOSSIANS. 1865. **
      Not too diffuse. Among the notes are some admirable hints which may be
      worked out. The book is a small one for so large a subject.

1155 Slade, James – ANNOTATIONS ON THE EPISTLES. For the use
      of candidates for Holy Orders. 2 vols., 1836. *
      This is practically a continuation of Elsley's work (No. 954), which closed
      with the Acts. Notes dry and sapless, but from a literary point of view,
      respectable.

ROMANS

(Our space does not permit us to repeat the names of authors mentioned under
"Acts" and "Apostolic Epistles," but we urge the student carefully to refer
thereto.)

1156 Adam, Thomas – PARAPHRASE ON ROMANS 1 TO 11. 1774. *
      A poor paraphrase; very correct and evangelical, but thin as Adam's ale. We
      are disappointed, for the *Private Thoughts* of the same author are highly
      esteemed.

1157 **Anderson, Robert** – EXPOSITION OF ROMANS. 1837. **
      After the manner of Charles Bridges. Full of holy unction and devout
      meditation.

1158 **Brown, John** (of Wamphray) – EXPOSITION OF ROMANS.
      1766. **
      By a Calvinist of the old school. Heavy, perhaps; but precious.

1159 **Brown, John** (of Edinburgh) – ANALYTICAL EXPOSITIONS OF
      ROMANS. 1857. ***
      Dr. Brown's work must be placed among the first of the first-class. He is a great
      expositor.

1160 **Calvin, John** – *Romans,* in CALVIN'S COMMENTARIES. Trans-
      lated by Christopher Roodell. Baker Book House. ***

1161 **Challis, James** – TRANSLATION OF ROMANS, with notes.
      1871. **
      The translation is made in the current language of the day. The notes are mainly
      critical.

1162 **Chalmers, T.** – LECTURES ON ROMANS. 4 vols., 1827. **
      Our preferences as to expositions lie in another direction; but we cannot be
      insensible to the grandeur and childlike simplicity which were combined in
      Chalmers.

1163 **Edwards, Timothy** – PARAPHRASE WITH ANNOTATIONS
      ON ROMANS AND GALATIANS. 1752. *
      Watt calls this a judiciously compiled work from the best comments. We judge
      it to be poor as poverty itself.

1164 **Ewbank, W. W.** – COMMENTARY ON ROMANS, with transla-
      tion and notes. 2 vols., 1850. **
      A sound evangelical comment, very good and gracious. In condensed thought
      this work is not rich; it is adapted for general reading.

1165 **Ford, J.** – ROMANS. Illustrated from Church of England divines.
      1862. See No. 955. **

1166 **Forbes, John** – ANALYTICAL COMMENTARY. Tracing the train
      of thought by the aid of parallelism, with notes. 1868. ***
      We think Dr. Forbes carries the idea of parallelism further than it should go.
      It can only be applied strictly to poetical books, which Romans is not. He tries
      to bring out the other side of the truths taught in Hodge, Edwards, and Calvin;
      but we confess our preference of those authors to himself. The work will
      greatly edify those whom it does not confuse.

1167 **Fry, John** – LECTURES ON ROMANS. 1816. **
      Having no theory to serve in this instance, Fry writes to edification.

1168 **Godwin, John H.** – ROMANS. New translation with notes. 1873. **
      Such a book as students need while studying the Greek text in college.

1169 **Haldane, R.** – COMMENTARY ON ROMANS. Exposition with
      remarks on the commentary of Macknight and others. Kregel
      Publications. ***
      Dr. Chalmers styled this "a well-built commentary," and strongly recom-

mended it to students of theology. In his *Sabbath Readings* he writes: "I am reading Haldane's *Exposition of the Epistle to the Romans,* and find it solid and congenial food."

1170 **Hinton, J. Howard – EXPOSITION OF ROMANS.** 1863. *
Not believing in the constant parallelism of the Epistles, we care very little for this treatise, much as we esteem the author.

1171 **Hodge, Charles – ROMANS.** The Banner of Truth. ***
Hodge's method and matter make him doubly useful in commenting. He is singularly clear, and a great promoter of thought.

1172 **Kelly, William – NOTES ON THE EXPOSITION TO THE RO-MANS.** Believer's Bookshelf, Inc. *
Many of the remarks are admirable, but the theories supported are untenable.

1173 **Knight, Robert – COMMENTARY.** 1854. *
Not at all to our mind. The author often seems to us rather to becloud the text than to explain it.

1174 **LANGE'S COMMENTARY ON THE HOLY SCRIPTURES.** *Romans* , by J. P. Lange and F. R. Fay. See page 19, and No. 923. ***

1175 **Martyr, Peter – COMMENTARY ON ROMANS.** A most learned and fruitful commentary. 1568. **
Being in black letter, and very long, few will ever read it; but it contains much that will repay the laborious bookworm.

1176 **Olshausen, Hermann – STUDIES IN THE EPISTLE TO THE RO-MANS.** 1850. Klock & Klock (Kregel Publications). **
Nobody seems very enthusiastic as to Olshausen, but some authors have borrowed from his pages more than they have confessed. Personally we do not care for him, but many prize and all respect him.

1177 **Parr, Elnathan – A SHORT VIEW OF THE EPISTLE TO THE ROMANS.** (Chapter 1; 2:1-2; and 8—16.) This exposition forms nearly the whole of *The Works of Parr.* Fourth edition. 1651. ***
The style is faulty, but the matter is rich and full of suggestions. We regret that *The Works* is not complete, and is seldom to be met with except in fragments.

1178 **Plumer, William S. – COMMENTARY ON ROMANS.** With introduction on the life, times, writings, and character of Paul. Kregel Publications. **
Plumer is a laborious compiler, and to most men his works will be of more use than those of a more learned writer.

1179 **Pridham, Arthur – NOTES ON THE ROMANS.** Granary Classic (Kregel Publications). *
Sound and gracious, but somewhat dull.

1180 **Purdue, E.– COMMENTARY ON ROMANS.** 1855. *
Not important.

1181 **Robinson, Thomas – STUDIES IN ROMANS.** (Van Doren series of commentaries.) Kregel Publications. ***
A good book in a good style. Worth any amount to preachers.

1182 Stephen, John – EXPOSITIONS ON ROMANS. A series of lectures. 1857. **
Sound in doctrine, practical in tone; above mediocrity.

1183 Stuart, Moses – COMMENTARY ON ROMANS. **
Moses Stuart is judged to have been at his best in Romans and Hebrews. The present work is in some points unsatisfactory, on account of certain philosophical-theological views which he endeavors to maintain. Mr. Haldane denounced him as by false criticism "misrepresenting the divine testimony in some of the most momentous points of the Christian scheme." The charge was true.

1184 Terrot, C. H. – ROMANS. With introduction, paraphrase and notes. 1828. *
Anti-Calvinistic. Why do not such writers let Romans alone?

1185 Tholuck, A. F. – EXPOSITION OF ROMANS. 2 vols., 1842. **
Moses Stuart confesses his great obligations to this eminent divine, who far exceeds the most of his German brethren in spirituality, and is not behind them in scholarship; yet even he is none too orthodox nor too reverent in his treatment of Holy Scripture.

1186 Vaughan, Charles John – ROMANS. The Greek text with English notes. 1874. ***
Very valuable to students of the Greek. The result of independent study and honest labor.

1187 Walford, W. – CURAE ROMANAE. 1846. **
Walford makes comments of considerable value; he does not stand in the front rank, but his mediocrity is respectable.

1188 Wardlaw, Ralph – LECTURES ON ROMANS. 3 vols., 1861. **
Wardlaw interprets with great sobriety and spirituality, and we never consult him in vain, though we do not always agree with him.

1189 Willet, Andrew – HEXAPLA, that is, a sixfold commentary on Romans. 1611. See No. 142. **

1190 Williams, H. W. – EXPOSITION. 1869. **
This epistle has a fascination for Arminian writers. It affords them an opportunity for showing their courage and ingenuity. Mr. William's book is instructive.

1191 Wilson, Thomas – COMMENTARY ON ROMANS. 1627, 1653. **
Intended for the less-instructed among the preacher's hearers, and put into the form of a dialogue. It is very solid, but does not contain much which is very striking or original.

1192 Sclater, W. – A KEY TO THE KEY OF SCRIPTURE; or, An Exposition With Notes on Romans, Chapters 1, 2, and 3. 1611 and 1629. ***
An antique, but precious book.

1193 Morison, James – EXPOSITION OF THE THIRD CHAPTER OF ROMANS. 1866. **
A scholarly and exhaustive exposition. When we do not agree with Dr. Morison, we pay homage to his great learning and critical skill.

1194 Fraser, James – THE DOCTRINE OF SANCTIFICATION. Explication of Romans 6:1—8:4. 1830. ***
Dr. John Brown says: "Fraser's *Scripture Doctrine of Sanctification* is wellworth studying. The old Scotch divine is rude in speech, but not in knowledge."

1195 Elton, Edward – SUNDRY SERMONS UPON ROMANS 7, 8, AND 9. 1653. ***
The style is plain and homely, but the matter is of the choicest kind. This old folio is like an old skin bottle, with a rough exterior, but filled within with the product of the rarest vintage. Such books as this we never tire of reading.

1196 Kohlbrügge, H. F. – ROMANS 7 PARAPHRASED. 1854. **
An instructive rendering of this deeply experimental chapter.

1197 Binning, Hugh – THE SINNER'S SANCTUARY. Forty-eight sermons on Romans 8, 1670. Also vols. 1 and 2 of his *Works*. 3 vols., 1839. ***
The writer of Binning's Memoir says: "There is a pure stream of piety and learning running through the whole, and a very peculiar turn of thought, which exceeds the common rate of writers on this choice part of the Holy Scriptures."

1198 Horton, Thomas – FORTY-SIX SERMONS ON ROMANS 8. 1674. ***
Full of matter; well, but rather too formally arranged. The sermons are very prim and orderly.

1199 Winslow, Octavius – NO CONDEMNATION IN CHRIST. (On Romans 8.) 1860. **
Dr. Winslow is always sound and sweet; but his works are better adapted for general readers than for students. He is extremely diffuse.

FIRST AND SECOND CORINTHIANS
See also "APOSTOLIC EPISTLES"

1200 Billroth, Dr. Gustav (1808-1836) – COMMENTARY ON THE EPISTLES TO THE CORINTHIANS. 2 vols. **
To be prized for its criticism. The author tries to bring forth from each passage the sense which the Apostle intended it to convey. Observations and reflections there are none; but we are not among those who throw "the dry bones of criticism"— bones are as needful as meat though not so nourishing.

1201 Calvin, John – *Corinthians*, in CALVIN'S COMMENTARIES. Baker Book House; Wm. B. Eerdmans Publishing Co. ***
Tymme seems to have been constantly occupied in translating the Reformers, and to have done his work well.

1202 Hodge, Charles – 1 AND 2 CORINTHIANS. The Banner of Truth. ***
The more we use Hodge, the more we value him. This applies to all his commentaries.

1203 LANGE'S COMMENTARY ON THE HOLY SCRIPTURES. *Corinthians*, by C. F. Kluig. Edited by Philip Schaff. See page 19. ***

1204 Lothian, W. – LECTURES ON 1 AND 2 CORINTHIANS. 1828. *
This work must have done good service in its day, as in some degree an antidote to Macknight. It is good and sound; but the student need not distress himself if he cannot procure it, for it is not indispensable.

1205 Olshausen, Hermann – 1 AND 2 CORINTHIANS. 1851 Klock & Klock (Kregel Publications). **
Dr. Lindsay Alexander says that this commentary is highly esteemed for its happy combinations of grammatico-historical exegesis, with spiritual insight into the meaning of the sacred writers.

1206 Pridham, Arthur – NOTES AND REFLECTIONS ON 1 AND 2 CORINTHIANS. 2 vols., 1866. **
We do not always agree with Dr. Pridham, but we always admire the quiet, candid, and unaffected manner in which he writes.

1207 Robertson, Frederick W. – EXPOSITORY LECTURES. 1872 **
Robertson's doctrinal vagaries are well-known; yet he is a great thinker and a prompter of thought in other men. Read with discretion.

1208 Stanley, Arthur Penrhyn – CORINTHIANS. 1876. **
We do not advise the purchase of these volumes, for though Dean Stanley is an instructive writer, our perusal of his notes does not impress us with any sense either of their value or soundness.

1209 Colet, John – TREATISE ON 1 CORINTHIANS. With translation. 1874. *
A curiosity and nothing more. This same Dean Colet, the friend of Erasmus, wrote also on Romans.

1210 Pearce, Zachary – TRANSLATION OF 1 CORINTHIANS, with paraphrase and notes. In vol. 2 of *Commentary.* No. 966. **
We ought to value this work greatly, for the author was a renowned scholar; but we confess we do not think much of his production.

(The writers on small portions of these epistles are too numerous to be mentioned in our short catalog. Burgess, Branston, Thomas Fuller, Sibbes, Manton, Watson, and other masterly writers have all left a contribution to the expository stores of the Church of Christ.)

GALATIANS

(Do not forget to consult works from No. 1140 to 1155.)

1211 Bagge, Henry T. – GALATIANS. 1856. **
Simply a revised text and critical notes.

1212 Bayley, Sir E. – COMMENTARY ON GALATIANS. 1869 ***
Upon each portion there is a commentary, a paraphrase, and a sermon, and thus the author conveys a considerable amount of instruction. He is thoroughly evangelical, and his style clear.

1213 Brown, John – EXPOSITION OF GALATIANS. 1853. ***
Brown is a modern Puritan. All his expositions are of the utmost value. The volume on Galatians is one of the scarcest books in the market.

1214 Calvin, John – FORTY-TWO SERMONS ON GALATIANS.
1574. (A different work from his commentary.) *******

**1215 Eadie, John – COMMENTARY ON THE GREEK TEXT OF GA-
LATIANS.** 1869. *******
This is a most careful attempt to ascertain the meaning of the Apostle by
painstaking analysis of his words. The author is not warped by any system of
theology, but yet he does not deviate from recognized evangelical truth. As
a piece of honest grammatical exegesis the value of this commentary is very
great, though there is room to differ from it here and there.

1216 Edmunds, John – GALATIANS. With explanatory notes. 1874. *****
Thoroughly ritualistic. See remarks on this author's work on Thessalonians
(No. 1286).

1217 Godwin, John – GALATIANS. Translation with notes and doctrinal
lessons. 1871. ******
A helpful translation, with good textual notes.

1218 Haldane, James Alexander – EXPOSITION OF GALATIANS.
1848. ******
This work has never been popular, because the author in the third chapter
discusses the question of baptism. This is a fault of which we may say as the
Papist said of venial sin: "It deserved to be forgiven."

1219 Hawker, John – BIBLE THOUGHTS IN QUIET HOURS. Commentary on Galatians. 1874. ******
These "thoughts" are sound and edifying. The book does not profess to be a
thorough exposition.

1220 Kelly, William – LECTURES ON GALATIANS. *****
Mr. Kelly's authoritative style has no weight with us. We do not call these
lectures expounding, but confounding.

1221 LANGE'S COMMENTARY ON THE HOLY SCRIPTURES.
Galatians, by Otto Schmoller, *Ephesians, Philippians, and Colossians,* by Karl Braune. See page 19. *******

1222 Lightfoot, J. B. – COMMENTARY ON GALATIANS. Revised
text with introductions, notes, and dissertations. Hendrickson Publishers. *******
The Spectator says: "There is no commentator at once of sounder judgment,
and more liberal, than Dr. Lightfoot."

1223 Lushington, Thomas – THE JUSTIFICATION OF A SINNER:
The Main Argument of the Epistle to the Galatians. 1650. *****
A translation from Crellius, a Socinian divine, made by Lushington, who was
far gone towards the same error. We mention the book to warn our readers
of its character; for bad works of the Puritan are few.

1224 Luther, Martin – COMMENTARY ON GALATIANS. Kregel
Publications. *******
"I prefer this book of Martin Luther's (except the Bible) before all the books
that I have ever seen, as most fit for a wounded conscience."—Bunyan. This
is a great historic work, and is beyond criticism, on account of its great

usefulness. As a comment its accuracy might be questioned; but for emphatic utterances and clear statements of the great doctrine of the epistle it remains altogether by itself, and must be judged per se.

1225 **Olshausen, Hermann – COMMENTARY ON GALATIANS, EPHESIANS, COLOSSIANS, AND THESSALONIANS.** 1851. For remarks, see No. 964. **

1226 **Pearson, Samuel – SERMONS ON GALATIANS.** 1874. **
Discourses worthy of the successor of Spencer and Raffles.

1227 **Perkins, William – COMMENTARY ON THE FIRST FIVE CHAP-TERS OF GALATIANS,** with a supplement on the sixth chapter, by Ralfe Cudworth. 1604. **
Perkins was justly esteemed by his contemporaries as a master in theology. This commentary is deeply theological, and reads like a body of divinity. Truth compels us to confess that we find it dull.

1228 **Pridham, A. – GALATIANS.** 1872. **
Pridham is, we suppose, of the moderate Brethren school, but he is not carried away by any theory, being essentially a man of sober mind.

EPHESIANS
See also "APOSTOLIC EPISTLES"

1229 **Bayne, Paul – COMMENTARY ON EPHESIANS.** 1643, reprinted in Nichol's *Commentaries,* 1866. **
Sibbes says of this work: "The greatest shall find matter to exercise themselves in; the meaner, matter of sweet comfort and holy instruction; and all confess that he hath brought some light to this Scripture."

1230 **Calvin, John – SERMONS ON EPHESIANS.** Translated by A. Golding. 1577. ***
Not the same as exposition. The sermons are priceless.

1231 **Eadie, John – COMMENTARY ON THE GREEK TEXT OF EPHESIANS.** 1861. ***
"This book is one of prodigious learning and research. The author seems to have read all, in every language, that has been written upon the Epistle. It is also a work of independent criticism, and casts much new light upon many passages.

1232 **Graham, William – LECTURES ON EPHESIANS.** 1870. **
Dr. Graham is an earnest opponent of the German Neologians and frequently writes with their negations before his eye. He is a commentator of considerable learning and much spirituality of mind.

1233 **Hemminge, Nicholas – COMMENTARY ON EPHESIANS.** 1581. See No. 553. *

1234 **Hodge, Charles – COMMENTARY ON THE EPISTLE TO THE EPHESIANS.** Baker Book House. ***
Most valuable. With no writer do we more fully agree.

1235 **Kelly, William – LECTURES ON EPHESIANS.** See No. 1256. *

1236 Lathrop, Joseph – EXPOSITION OF THE EPISTLE TO THE EPHESIANS. In a series of discourses. 1864. **
These discourses are sure to be of the highest class. We have not been able to procure a copy.

1237 M'Ghee, R. – LECTURES ON EPHESIANS. 2 vols., fourth edition. 1861. **
Lively, warmhearted, extemporaneous sermons, full of good teaching. The preacher aimed to edify the many, rather than to write a critical work for the few, and he has succeeded.

1238 Newland, Henry – A NEW CATENA OF ST. PAUL'S EPISTLES. Commentary on Ephesians, in which is exhibited the results of the most learned theological criticisms, from the age of the early Fathers down to the present time. 1866. **
Used discreetly, this Catena of patristic, medieval, and modern Church interpreters, may be very helpful; without discretion it will mislead.

1239 Pattison, R. E. – COMMENTARY ON EPHESIANS. 1859. ***
A book to instruct intelligent, experienced believers. It is a model for a class-book, plain and yet profound.

1240 Perceval, A. P. – LECTURES ON EPHESIANS. 1846. *
Good, but not likely to produce headache by overloading the brain with thought.

1241 Pridham, A. – EPHESIANS. **
Style heavy, matter weighty.

1242 Pulsford, John – CHRIST AND HIS SEED. Central to all things: being a series of expository discourses on Paul's Epistle to the Ephesians. 1872. **
Contains a great deal of deep thought, but is too mystical and often too cloudy to be of much service to those who wish to explain Scripture.

1243 Ridley, Lancelot – COMMENTARIES ON EPHESIANS, PHILIPPIANS AND PART OF JUDE. Reprinted in Richmond's *Fathers.* *
John Bale wrote in 1543: "The commentary which that virtuous, learned man, Master Lancelot Ridley, made upon St. Paul's Epistle to the Ephesians, for the true erudition of his Christian brethren, hath my Lord Bonner here also condemned for heresy. But what the cause is I cannot tell, unless it be for advancing the Gospel as the thing whereby we are made righteous." Our author is equally fierce against Anabaptists and Papists, but is not much of a commentator.

1244 Turner, Samuel – EPHESIANS IN GREEK AND ENGLISH. With analysis and commentary. 1856. **
A learned American work; good, but not very attractive.

1245 Evans, James Harrington – CHRISTIAN SOLICITUDE, as exemplified in Ephesians 3. 1856. **
Harrington Evans was a great teacher. A more sound, earnest, and instructive divine never lived. This book consists of notes of sermons preserved by a hearer. It is well-worthy of study. His *Memoir* contains fragmentary remarks upon Ephesians 1.

1246 Rollock, Robert – AN EXPOSITION OF PART OF THE FIFTH AND SIXTH CHAPTERS OF ST. PAUL'S EPISTLE TO THE EPHESIANS. 1630. ******
This renowned Scotchman's writings generally come to us as translations from the Latin, and have been made preternaturally dull in the process of interpretation; but this appears to have been written in English by himself. It is practical to a high degree, and goes into minute details of the married life. It will not be much appreciated in these days, though Dr. McCrie styles Rollock's works "succinct and judicious."

PHILIPPIANS
See also "APOSTOLIC EPISTLES"

1247 Acaster, J. – EXPOSITORY LECTURES ON PHILIPPIANS. 1827. *****
Useful in showing the preacher how *not to do it*. By a violent effort we forced ourselves to read one lecture; but we have done nothing to deserve to read another. The author was domestic chaplain to an earl, meant well, and did his little best.

1248 Airay, Henry – LECTURES ON PHILIPPIANS. 1618, reprinted, with Cartwright on Colossians in Nichol's *Commentaries*, 1864. ******
Mr. Grosart says: "You will look in vain in this commentary for erudite criticism or subtle exegesis in the modern sense: but there seems to us to be an instructively true following up of the apostolic thoughts, and a quick insight into their bearings and relative force."

1249 Calvin, John – *Commentary on Philippians,* in **CALVIN'S COMMENTARIES .** Translated by Wm. Becket. Baker Book House; Wm. B. Eerdmans Publishing Co. ******

1250 Calvin and Storr – EXPOSITION OF PHILIPPIANS AND COLOSSIANS. By John Calvin and Gottlob Storr. Translated by R. Johnston. 1842. ******
A sort of sandwich, with Calvin for the meat, and Storr for very hard black bread. Students who can enjoy both spiritual exposition and stern criticism with equal relish will make fine expositors.

1251 Daillé, Jean – EXPOSITION OF PHILIPPIANS. Translated by Rev. James Sherman. 1841. This exposition, together with Daillé on Colossians, and Jenkyn on Jude, have been issued in one thick volume by Mr. Nichol of Edinburgh, 1863. ******
Written in a deliciously florid style. Very sweet and evangelical: after the French manner.

1252 Eadie, John – COMMENTARY ON THE GREEK TEXT OF PHILIPPIANS. 1859. *******
A standard work. Essential to the scholarly student.

1253 Eastburn, M. – LECTURES ON PHILIPPIANS. 1853. ******
Designed for family reading. Moderately good.

1254 Hall, Robert – EXPOSITION OF PHILIPPIANS. In 12 discourses. 1843. ******
Robert Hall does not shine so much upon the printed page as he did when he

blazed from the pulpit. These discourses were published after his death, from the notes of a hearer. They are good as sermons, but not remarkable as expositions.

1255 **Johnstone, Robert – LECTURES ON PHILIPPIANS.** With revised translation and notes on the Greek text. 1875. ***
A noble volume. A real boon to the man who purchases it.

1256 **Kelly, William – PHILIPPIANS AND COLOSSIANS.** 1869. *
Much that is excellent placed in "darkness visible."

1257 **Lange, J. P.** See No. 923, and also page 19. ***

1258 **Lightfoot, J. B. – COMMENTARY ON PHILIPPIANS.** Hendrickson Publishers. ***
Deservedly regarded as a standard work. The more instructed student will appreciate it.

1259 **Meyer, H. A. W. – CRITICAL AND EXEGETICAL HANDBOOK TO THE EPISTLES TO THE PHILIPPIANS AND COLOSSIANS.** See No. 928. **
No doubt wonderfully learned, but we cannot get on with it. Quotations from heretics we have happily never heard of before are of no great use to simple believers like ourselves.

1260 **Neat, Charles – DISCOURSES FROM PHILIPPIANS.** 1841. *
Strongly Calvinistic, and correct to a hair; but utterly devoid of originality either of thought or expression.

1261 **Neander, Johann August Wilhelm – PHILIPPIANS AND JAMES PRACTICALLY AND HISTORICALLY EXPLAINED.** 1851. **
Without dwelling upon the wording of the Epistle, Neander reproduces its spirit in other language, and so expounds it. The little work will be greatly appreciated by a certain order of minds.

1262 **Newland, H. – NEW CATENA. PHILIPPIANS.** 1860. See No. 1238. **

1263 **Pearce, James – PARAPHRASE ON PHILIPPIANS, COLOSSIANS, AND HEBREWS.** 1733. *
Had he but known the Lord, his writings would have been admirable. He conceals his Arianism, but it is fatal to his acceptance with believers. He wrote after the manner of Mr. Locke.

1264 **Robertson, J. S. S. – LECTURES ON PHILIPPIANS.** 1859. *
Lectures which will never set the Thames on fire.

1265 **Todd, James F. – APOSTLE PAUL AND THE CHURCH AT PHILIPPI.** (Acts 16 and Philippians.) 1864. **
A respectable work. The author is sound in doctrine and valorous in controverting error, and he says many good things; but he rather uses the text than expounds it. He deserves a reading; but men with whom money is scarce need not purchase this book.

1266 **Toller, Thomas – DISCOURSES ON PHILIPPIANS.** 1855. **
A very favorable specimen of plain, popular exposition. Nothing either deep, or new, or critically accurate; but sensible and practical.

1267 **Vaughan, Charles J.** – **EPISTLE TO THE PHILIPPIANS.** Klock & Klock (Kregel Publications). ✱✱✱
Deservedly esteemed. Dr. Vaughan gives a literal translation of his text from the original Greek, and then expounds it, believing it, as he says, "to be the duty of every Christian teacher to assist his congregation in drinking, not of the stream only, but at the spring of revealed truth."

1268 **Wiesinger, Lic. August** – **COMMENTARY ON PHILIPPIANS, TITUS, AND 1 TIMOTHY.** Continuation of the work of Olshausen. 1857. ✱✱
Many mistake this for Olshausen's. It is of the critical and grammatical school, and bristles all over with the names of the German band. We prefer the Puritanic gold to the German silver which is now in fashion.

COLOSSIANS

1269 **Bayne, Paul** – **COMMENTARY ON COLOSSIANS 1 AND 2.** 1634. ✱✱✱
On the first two chapters only. Edifying and very rare.

1270 **Byfield, Nicholas** – **EXPOSITION ON COLOSSIANS.** The substance of nearly seven years' week–day sermons. 1615 and 1617. Reprinted in Nichol's *Commentaries*, 1869. ✱✱✱
The author lived in intense pain, and died at 44, yet he produced quite a mountain of literature. He writes like an earnest, faithful man, reserved to keep back nothing of the counsel of God; but he too little studies brevity, and consequently he wearies most readers. He is always worth consulting.

1271 **Calvin, John.** See Nos. 1249 and 1250. ✱✱

1272 **Cartwright, Thomas** – **COMMENTARY ON COLOSSIANS.** 1612. Reprinted in Nichol's *Commentaries*. See No. 1248. ✱✱
This is but a small affair, consisting of scanty and second-rate "notes" by a hearer. Yet what there is of it has the true ring, and is rich in spirituality.

1273 **Daillé, Jean.** See No. 1251. ✱✱

1274 **Davenant, John** – **EXPOSITION OF COLOSSIANS.** Translated from the Latin, by Josiah Allport. 2 vols., 1831. ✱✱✱
"I know no exposition upon a detached portion of Scripture (with the single exception of Owen on the *Hebrews*) that will compare with it in all points. Leighton is superior in sweetness, but far inferior in depth, accuracy, and discursiveness."— Charles Bridges.

1275 **Eadie, John** – **COMMENTARY ON THE GREEK TEXT OF COLOSSIANS.** 1856. ✱✱✱
Very full and reliable. A work of the utmost value.

1276 **Elton, Edward** – **EXPOSITION OF COLOSSIANS.** Third edition. 1637. ✱✱✱
A Puritan work; strongly Calvinistic, popular, and very full.

1277 **Gisborne, Thomas** – **EXPOSITION OF COLOSSIANS.** 1816. ✱✱
Sermons which very much remind us of those of Henry Melvill, but with less of the gospel in them. Gisborne was a preacher of considerable repute, but he was more at home upon moral than spiritual topics.

1278 **Guthrie, Thomas – CHRIST THE INHERITANCE OF THE SAINTS.** Discourses from Colossians. 1859. **
Not so much an exposition as a series of brilliant discourses, or prose poems. Dr. Guthrie has only touched upon the first chapter.

1279 **Lightfoot, J. B. – COLOSSIANS AND PHILEMON.** A revised text, with introductions, notes, etc. 1875. ***
For remarks, see No. 1258. Lightfoot writes for scholars.

1280 **Milner, Joseph – SERMONS ON COLOSSIANS, 1 THESSALONIANS 5, AND JAMES 1.** 1841. **
Respectable sermons by the church historian.

1281 **Rollock, R. – LECTURES ON COLOSSIANS.** 1603. **
It is said that when this great divine died, the entire population of Edinburgh attended his funeral. His *Lectures on Colossians* were once very popular, but are now extremely scarce. The style is very simple and colloquial, and the matter far from profound.

1282 **Spence, James – DISCOURSES ON COLOSSIANS.** 1875. ***
A good specimen of honest, popular expounding. Intended for a congregation, but useful to the student.

1283 **Watson, Thomas – DISCOURSES ON COLOSSIANS.** 1838. *
Thoroughly evangelical and remarkably commonplace.

1284 **Wilson, Daniel – EXPLANATORY LECTURES ON COLOSSIANS.** 1845. **
By a famous modern evangelical, who shows much ability in wielding this Scripture against Tractarians and others. The work contains little original exegesis.

1285 **Lockyer, Nicholas – ENGLAND FAITHFULLY WATCHT WITH IN HER WOUNDS.** Lectures on Colossians 1. 1646. ***
Rich, full, simple. A fair specimen of plain Puritan preaching.

FIRST AND SECOND THESSALONIANS

1286 **Edmunds, J. – COMMENTARY ON 1 AND 2 THESSALONIANS.** 1858. *
For school teachers. The author's notion of a commentary, which he fully carries out, is contained in his preface. "My idea of the middleclass commentary is, that it should be in strict accordance with the doctrine and ritual of the church, should illustrate her ritual, and should recommend her to the esteem and affection of her children, by proving her adherence to the Word of God."

1287 **Jewell, John – EXPOSITIONS ON 1 AND 2 THESSALONIANS.** 1583. Reprinted 1811 and 1841. Also in his *Works*. **
Hooker calls Jewel "the jewel of bishops." This work is in the usual style of the first Reformers, but rather more lively than most of them. Many of the topics touched upon were peculiar to the times in which the exposition was written. It will serve as a good specimen of the preaching of the Fathers of the English Church.

1288 **LANGE'S COMMENTARY ON THE HOLY SCRIPTURES.** *Thessalonians,* by Drs. Auberlen and Riggenbach, translated by Dr.

Lillie; *Timothy, Titus, Philemon,* by Prof. Von Oosterzee; and *Hebrews,* by Dr. C. B. Moll. Edited by Philip Schaff. *******
"Lillie's Thessalonians will be found to be one of the best executed portions of the American edition of Lange. The translation is remarkably accurate and elegant, and the additions from his own researches, and the best English Commentaries, are carefully selected and valuable."— Dr. Philip Schaff.

1289 **Lillie, John – LECTURES ON THESSALONIANS.** 1863 *******
Remarks on the preceding will apply here.

1290 **Rollock, Robert – LECTURES ON THE EPISTLE TO THE THESSALONIANS.** 1606. ******
For remarks, see No. 1246.

1291 **Sclater, William – EXPOSITION ON 1 AND 2 THESSALONIANS.** 1627. ******
Sclater is antique; but, in the usual Puritanic manner, he gives very instructive disquisitions upon a vast variety of topics suggested by the text.

1292 **Patterson, Alexander Simpson – COMMENTARIES ON 1 THESSALONIANS, JAMES, AND 1 JOHN.** 1857. ******
Notes of discourses, with much in them. Hints may be gleaned here in abundance by students who open their eyes.

1293 **Phillips, J. – THE GREEK OF THESSALONIANS EXPLAINED.** 1751. *****
Short, but not particularly sweet.

1294 **Bradshaw, W. – A PLAINE AND PITHY EXPOSITION OF 2 THESSALONIANS.** 1620. *****
As we cannot get a sight of this, perhaps some reader will present us with a copy.

1295 **Manton, Thomas – EIGHTEEN SERMONS ON 2 THESSALONIANS,** concerning Antichrist. 1679. *******
Here Manton smites heavily at Popery. Richard Baxter wrote a commendatory preface to this valuable exposition.

1296 **Squire, John – A PLAINE EXPOSITION ON 2 THESSALONIANS: 1-13,** proving the Pope to be the Antichrist. 1630. ******
Squire works out the point of the Pope's being Antichrist with very great cogency of reasoning. The exposition of the Epistle is lost in the point aimed at; but that point is of the utmost importance.

PASTORAL EPISTLES

1297 **Calvin, John – SERMONS ON THE EPISTLES OF ST. PAUL TO TIMOTHY AND TITUS.** Translated from the French, by L. T. 1579. *******
Quite a different work from Calvin's *Commentaries.*

1298 **Fairbairn, Patrick – THE PASTORAL EPISTLES.** Greek text, translation, introductions, and expository notes. 1874. *******
What with a good translation, full defense of the apostolic authorship of the Epistles, fruitful comments, and profitable dissertations, this volume is about as complete a guide to the smaller Epistles as one could desire.

FIRST AND SECOND TIMOTHY
See also "PASTORAL EPISTLES"

1299 Bickersteth, E. See No. 1386. **

1300 Patterson, Alexander – COMMENTARY ON TIMOTHY AND TITUS. 1848. **
See our remarks on No. 1292.

1301 Slade, Henry Raper – PULPIT LECTURES ON THE EPISTLES TO TIMOTHY. 1837. *
Utter rubbish. Dear at a gift.

1302 Wiesinger, L. A. See No. 1268. **

1303 Pinder, John H. – THE CANDIDATE FOR THE MINISTRY. Lectures on 1 Timothy. 1837. *
Of no consequence.

1304 Barlow, John – EXPOSITION OF 2 TIMOTHY 1 AND 2. 1632. ***
By a master is Israel. Thoroughly practical, deeply experimental, and soundly doctrinal.

1305 Hall, Thomas – COMMENTARY ON 2 TIMOTHY 3 AND 4. 1632–1658. ***
Hall is often found in union with Barlow, completing the Commentary on 2 Timothy, as he completed Amos (No. 840). He is a masterly expositor of the old-fashioned school.

TITUS
See also "PASTORAL EPISTLES"

1306 Graham, W. – TITUS. 1860. **
Dr. Graham endeavors to make criticism intelligible, and the results of learning really edifying. We have our doubts as to some of his criticisms, and he is quite dogmatic enough, but on the whole good.

1307 Taylor, Thomas – COMMENTARY ON TITUS. 1619. Reprinted 1668. Also in *Works*. ***
The title page calls Thomas Taylor "a famous and most elaborate divine." He was a preacher at Paul's Cross during the reigns of Elizabeth and James I., and a voluminous writer. This commentary will well-repay the reader.

PHILEMON

1308 Attersoll, William – COMMENTARY ON PHILEMON. Second edition. 1633. ***
A long comment upon a short epistle. The pious author labors to keep his text, and succeeds in bringing out of it a mass of quaint practical teaching.

1309 Cox, Samuel – *Philemon*, in THE PRIVATE LETTERS OF ST. PAUL AND ST. JOHN. 1867. ***
Such exposition as this adds interest to the epistles, and makes their writers live

again before our eyes. Mr. Cox delivered this work in public on certain week evenings. Happy are the people who are thus instructed.

1310 Dyke, Daniel – PHILEMON. A most fruitful exposition upon Philemon. 1618. **
Dyke's remarks are memorably practical and full of common sense. He abounds in proverbs. The work is not very valuable as an exposition of the words, but excels in making use of them.

1311 Jones, William – COMMENTARY ON PHILEMON, HEBREWS, AND 1 AND 2 JOHN. 1636. ***
Very lively, sprightly, colloquial lectures, by a Suffolk divine, who thinks the Brownists and Dissenters were not persecuted. "Christ was whipped, that was persecution; Christ whipped some out of the temple, that was no persecution." Despite his intolerance he says some uncommonly racy things.

1312 Lightfoot, J. B. See No. 1279. ***

HEBREWS

1313 Brown, John – HEBREWS. The Banner of Truth . ***
Dr. David Smith says of this work... "There is not a single instance of carelessness in investigating the true meaning of a text, or of timidity in stating the conclusion at which the author had arrived." What more could be said in praise of any exposition?

1314 Calvin, John – *Hebrews*, in CALVIN'S COMMENTARIES. Translated by Clement Cotton. Baker Book House; Wm. B. Eerdmans Publishing Co. ***

1315 Dale, R. W. – THE JEWISH TEMPLE AND THE CHRISTIAN CHURCH. Discourse on Hebrews. 1871. **
Among modern divines few rank so highly as Mr. Dale. Daring and bold in thought, and yet for the most part warmly on the side of orthodoxy, his works command the appreciation of cultured minds.

1316 Delitzsch, Franz – COMMENTARY ON HEBREWS. 2 vols. 1868. **
Remarks formerly made upon Delitzsch apply here also (Nos. 412 and 724).

1317 Dickson, David – SHORT EXPLANATION OF HEBREWS. 1635, 49; 1839. ***
This is generally to be found in connection with the author's *Matthew* (No. 1033.) We need say no more than– get it, and you will find abundance of suggestions for profitable trains of thought.

1318 Duncan, David – EXPOSITION OF HEBREWS. 1731. **
"An excellent condensation of Dr. Owen's valuable work, and giving the pith and marrow of the great commentator."

1319 Ebrard, John H. A. – COMMENTARY ON HEBREWS. 1853. **
This is intended as a continuation of Olshausen, but it is an improvement thereupon. Ebrard is at once learned and spiritual, and we prefer him to almost any other author whose works the Messrs. Clark have issued.

1320 **Gouge, William – COMMENTARY ON HEBREWS.** Kregel Publications. ***
We greatly prize Gouge. Many will think his system of observations cumbrous, and so, perhaps, it is; but upon any topic which he touches he gives outlines which may supply sermons for months.

1321 **Haldane, James Alexander – NOTES ON EXPOSITION OF HEBREWS.** 1860. ***
A posthumous work, and issued, not as a finished exposition, but as "Notes of an intended exposition." Very valuable for all that.

1322 **Howard, J. E. – HEBREWS.** A revised translation with notes. 1872. *
Contains a few suggestive observations; but is a small affair in all respects.

1323 **Jones, W.** See No. 1311. **

1324 **Jones, W. – FOUR LECTURES** on the relation between the Old and New Testaments as set forth in Hebrews. 1811. *
Very little of it, and bound up with a work of an ingenious, but fanciful character.

1325 **Knox, J. Spencer – THE MEDIATOR OF THE NEW COVENANT.** Sermons on Hebrews. 1834. **
Thirteen sermons on select passages. Mediocrity highly polished.

1326 **Lange, J. P.** See No. 1288. ***

1327 **Lawson, G. – EXPOSITION OF HEBREWS,** wherein the Socinian comment is examined. 1662. **
Richard Baxter says: "I must thankfully acknowledge that I learned more from Mr. Lawson than from any divine that ever I conversed with."

1328 **Lindsay, W. – LECTURES ON HEBREWS.** 2 vols., 1867. ***
One of those great expository works with which the Scotch ministry has so frequently enriched the church. We wonder if any one ever read this excellent exposition through; we should not like to be sentenced to do so.

1329 **Lushington, Thomas – THE EXPIATION OF A SINNER.** Commentary on Hebrews. 1646. *
This work was published anonymously, and is charged with Socinianism.

1330 **M'Caul, Joseph B. – HEBREWS.** A paraphrastic commentary with illustrations from Philo, the Targums, etc. 1871. **
Mr. M'Caul attacks the gentlemen of the higher criticism with great plainness of speech and some asperity. We hardly think his work will attain a great circulation; it has so much Hebrew, Greek, Latin, and German in it, that only men of learning and leisure can use it.

1331 **MacLean, A. – PARAPHRASE AND COMMENTARY ON HEBREWS.** 2 vols., 1847. ***
One of the most judicious and solid expositions ever written.

1332 **Nelson, Robert – COMMENTS ON HEBREWS.** 1868. *
By a thoughtful and devout man, but we cannot endorse some of his interpretations. The taint of a certain modern school appears in passages such as this: "Had Paul been preaching holiness of life as essential to seeing the Lord, would he not have been advocating the very principle on which the law was based." We are afraid of this covert Antinomianism; its presence eats as doth a canker.

1333 Newton, Adelaide L. – HEBREWS COMPARED WITH THE OLD TESTAMENT. 1872. **
Devout, simple, and instructive. The authoress was an invalid, and died ere she had finished her work. She worked out a good idea with far more of expository matter than could have been expected of her.

1334 Owen, John – EXPOSITION OF HEBREWS. 4 vols. Abridged edition, reprinted in 1 vol., entitled *Hebrews, the Epistle of Warning.* Kregel Publications. ***
Out of scores of commendations of this colossal work we select but one. Dr. Chalmers pronounced it "a work of gigantic strength as well as gigantic size; and he who has mastered it is very little short, both in respect to the doctrinal and practical of Christianity, of being an erudite and accomplished theologian."

1335 Parry, Thomas – HEBREWS. In a series of lectures. 1934. *
So feeble that we wonder how it got through the press. A sermonized paraphrase.

1336 Patterson, Alexander Simpson – COMMENTARY ON HEBREWS. 1856. **
Lectures delivered in the course of the author's ministrations. Excellent for the public; the student should consult other authors for learning; but Patterson has savor and spirituality.

1337 Pridham, A. – HEBREWS. 1862. **
Rather mystified with expressions peculiar to "dispensational truth." Whatever that may mean; but devout, candid, sober, and sound.

1338 Sampson, Francis S. – COMMENTARY ON HEBREWS. 1856. *
A respectable production, but we know many which we value far more. As a set of lectures to a college class these comments would be of great value, but the author did well not to print them, although it was natural and fitting that his surviving colleague should do so.

1339 Sampson, G. V. – HEBREWS. Translation, with notes. 1828. *
Dr. Kendrick says that Sampson is candid and sensible, but scarcely grapples with the difficult points of the Epistle. Perhaps he was not strong enough.

1340 Saphir, Adolph – EPISTLE TO THE HEBREWS. 2 vols. in 1. Kregel Publications. **
Mr. Saphir has always something to say worthy of the attention of spiritual minds. His mind finds a track of its own, but he is never speculative. We always enjoy his remarks, though he is not especially terse or brilliant.

1341 Steward, George – ARGUMENT OF THE EPISTLE TO THE HEBREWS. 1872. **
Unhappily the author died before he had quite completed this "argument." The work is most helpful.

1342 Stuart, Moses – COMMENTARY ON HEBREWS. 1837, 1853. ***
We are constantly differing from Moses Stuart, but are bound to consult him. He is one of the greatest of American scholars, and this is one of his best comments.

1343 Tait, William – MEDITATIONES HEBRAICAE. 2 vols., 1855. **
A noteworthy series of lectures. If Gouge, Owen, and others, had not done all for Hebrews that one could well-need, this would have been of first-class value; and though we have much better it is still a worthy companion to them.

1344 Tholuck, A. F. – COMMENTARY ON HEBREWS. 2 vols., 1842. **
Delitzsch speaks highly of this work; but, for our part, we understand the Epistle better without Tholuck than with him. Clouds of smoke and volleys of hard words destroy our equanimity.

1345 Turner, Samuel H. – HEBREWS. In Greek and English, with commentary. 1852. **
Carefully done. Written for those who really wish to understand the Epistle.

1346 Williams, H. W. – EXPOSITION OF HEBREWS. 1872. **
The author has evidently been a diligent reader and student. Apart from its Wesleyan peculiarities, we can commend this book as edifying and instructive, though we do not place it in the first class.

PARTS OF HEBREWS

1347 Deering, Edward – TWENTY-SEVEN LECTURES ON HEBREWS 1-6. 1590. ***
Mainly aimed at the errors of the Church of Rome, and at the practical questions of the Reformation period. A learned but antiquated set of lectures.

1348 Montague, George – HORAE HEBRAICAE. An attempt to discover how the argument of the Epistle to the Hebrews (1-4:11) must have been understood by those therein addressed. 1835. **
A peculiar book, altogether *sui generis*, written by a man who did his own thinking. The Duke would be an unreliable guide, but he frequently strikes out new paths, and suggests novel trains of thought.

1349 Anderson, James – DISCOURSES ON THE 11TH AND PART OF THE 12TH CHAPTERS OF HEBREWS. 2 vols., 1839-43. *
Good church sermons. Of very slight value for commenting purposes.

1350 Manton, Thomas – SIXTY-SIX SERMONS ON HEBREWS 11. In vol. 3 of Manton's *Works*. ***
Exhaustive. Manton piles up his matter heaps upon heaps.

1351 Perkins, William – A CLOUD OF FAITHFUL WITNESSES. Commentary on Hebrews 11. 1622; and *Works*, vol 3. **
Good in its day, but now superseded. Very many points are discussed which would now be regarded as ridiculous: as for instance, *whether a man may travel in a foreign country*. It is terribly prosy.

1352 Andrews, G. – SERMONS ON HEBREWS 12. 1711. **
Thoroughly Scotch. Sound, but somewhat prolix and commonplace.

1353 Phillips, W. Spencer – THE TRIUMPHS OF A PRACTICAL FAITH. (On Hebrews 11.) 1840. *
Cloudy discourses on the cloud of witnesses. Will quicken no one's pace.

1354 **Sylvester, Matthew – THE CHRISTIAN'S RACE AND PA-TIENCE.** Sermons on Hebrews 12. 2 vols. 1702–1708. **
Not of the first class; yet respectable sermons.

CATHOLIC EPISTLES

1355 **Ebrard, J. H. A.** See No. 1387. ***

1356 **LANGE'S COMMENTARY ON THE HOLY SCRIPTURES.**
James, by Professor Van Oosterzee. *Epistles of Peter,* by Dr. C. F.
Fronmüller. *Epistles of John,* by Dr. K. Braune. *Epistle of Jude,* by
Dr. C. F. Fronmüller. Edited by Dr. Philip Schaff. **
In his comment on the First Epistle of John, Dr. Braune teaches baptismal
regeneration in a very decided manner. This plague-spot of sacramenta-
rianism should put the reader on his guard.

JAMES

1357 **Adams, John – EXPOSITION OF JAMES.** 1867. **
Good, plain discourses for which the author acknowledges his indebtedness to
various eminent writers who have discussed the Epistle. Our readers had better
make similar discourses of their own—*if they can.*

1358 **Hemminge, Nicholas – A LEARNED AND FRUITFUL COM-MENTARY UPON JAMES.** 1577. *
The price which this book fetches is preposterous. It is hard antique reading.

1359 **Jacobi, Bernard – LECTURES ON JAMES.** 1838. **
A good, simple, practical set of expository lectures. Safe in doctrine, or the
Religious Tract Society would not have issued it.

1360 **Johnstone, Robert – JAMES.** The Banner of Truth. ***
A very useful, scholarly, and readable book.

1361 **Manton, Thomas – JAMES.** The Banner of Truth. ***
In Manton's best style. An exhaustive work, as far as the information of the
period admitted. Few such books are written now.

1362 **Mayer, John – PRAXIS THEOLOGICA:** or, The Epistle of James
Resolved, Expounded and Preached Upon. See pages 16 and 17. **

1363 **Neander, J. A. W. – JAMES PRACTICALLY EXPLAINED.**
Translated by Mrs. Conant. 1852. **
See also No. 1261.

1364 **Nelson, Robert – JAMES.** 1872. *
Setting out with the notion that the Epistle is only written to the Jews, this
author's remarks are too much warped by this and other theories to be of any
value to students.

1365 **Stier, R.** See No. 972. ***

1366 **Patterson, A. S. – COMMENTARY ON JAMES.** 1851. See remarks
on No. 1292. **

1367 Turnbull, Richard – EXPOSITION OF JAMES AND JUDE. 1592, 1605. *
Old and occupied with Popish controversies. Good, solid, and tedious.

1368 **Wardlaw, Ralph – LECTURES ON JAMES.** 1862. ***
The lectures are noteworthy specimens of expository preaching. They were Wardlaw's last work, and are fully up to the mark.

First and Second Peter

1369 **Ames, William – EXPOSITION OF THE EPISTLES OF PETER.** 1641. *
Too much divided and subdivided, chopped up and cut into dice pieces and laid in order; for, after all, there is very little meat in it. It is an analysis, and little more.

1370 **Benson, George – EPISTLES OF PETER.** 1742. *
The author was an Arian. "Benson possessed considerable learning, but no great portion of genius." This is a paraphrase with notes.

1371 **Lillie, John – LECTURES ON 1 AND 2 PETER.** 1869. ***
Dr. Phillip Schaff says: "Though very different from the immortal work of Robert Leighton on the *First Epistle of Peter,* these lectures breath the same reverential spirit and devotional fervor, while they are much more full and thorough as an exposition."

1372 **Luther, Martin – COMMENTARY ON FIRST AND SECOND PETER AND JUDE.** Translated by Thomas Newton. Kregel Publications. ***
In Luther's racy style. One of his best productions.

1373 **Nisbet, Alexander – 1 AND 2 PETER.** The Banner of Truth. ***
A judicious and gracious Scotch commentary, after the style of Dickson and Hutcheson.

First Peter

1374 **Alley, William – EXPOSITION OF 1 PETER.** (In *Poore Man's Librarie.*) 1560. *
The exposition on Peter is mainly occupied with the questions and controversies of the Reforming period. Do not buy it.

1375 **Brown, John – 1 PETER.** The Banner of Truth. ***
The epistle is divided into paragraphs, and these are made the themes of discourses. Thus Dr. Brown produced what is substantially a commentary, and one of the best. It affords us a grammatical interpretation, together with an exposition, at once exegetical, doctrinal, and practical. It is a standard work, and the indices increase its value.

1376 **Byfield, Nicholas – COMMENTARY UPON 1 PETER 1, 2, 3.** 1637. **
Byfield is an able and pious divine, but he is not very vivacious, and neither in manner nor matter is he at all original.

1377 Kohlbrügge, H. F. – SERMONS ON 1 PETER. 1853. ******
Strictly orthodox and deeply spiritual. No German neology may be expected from this author. He is very happy in his practical remarks.

1378 Leighton, Robert – COMMENTARY ON FIRST PETER. Kregel Publications. *******
Dr. Henry Mills thus wrote of Leighton's works: "There is a spirit in them I never met with in any other human writings, nor can I read many lines in them without being moved." We need scarcely commend this truly heavenly work. It is a favorite with all spiritual men.

1379 Rogers, John – FRUITFUL EXPOSITION ON ALL THE FIRST EPISTLE OF PETER. 1650. *******
Rogers was a true Boanerges. His style is earnestly practical and wisely experimental. This is one of the scarcest and liveliest of the Puritan expositions.

1380 Steiger, Wilhelm – EXPOSITION OF 1 PETER. Translated by Dr. Fairbairn. 2 vols., 1836. ******
Steiger was a sound German divine. His criticism is good, but like all the Germans he is far too fond of dragging in learned names.

1381 Gomersall, R. – SERMONS ON ST. PETER 2:13–16. 1634. *****
Teaches absolute submission to rulers. Only worth notice from its age.

SECOND PETER

1382 Adams, Thomas – COMMENTARY ON THE 2ND EPISTLE OF PETER. 1633. New Edition, revised by Rev. James Sherman, 1839; included in Nichol's *Commentaries.* 1862 *******
Full of quaintness, holy wit, bright thought, and deep instruction. We like Adams better in commenting than in preaching. His great work is quite by itself, and in its own way remains unrivalled. We know no richer and racier reading.

1383 Symson, Archibald – EXPOSITION ON THE SECOND EPISTLE GENERAL OF ST. PETER. 1632. ******
Abundance of matter, pithily expressed. Symson is among the oldest and rarest of the English divines.

1384 Brown, John – 2 PETER CHAPTER 1: Parting Counsels. The Banner of Truth. *******
We always think of Brown as a Puritan born out of due time. Everything he has left us is massive gold. He is both rich and clear, profound and perspicuous.

1385 Wilson, William – SECOND EPISTLE OF PETER. ******
"Thoughtful and fresh in its matter, fine and polished in its style, laying hold of us at once, and tightening its grasp on our sympathies the longer we read." *British and Foreign Evangelical Review.* (Too laudatory.)

EPISTLES OF JOHN

1386 Bickersteth, Edward – EXPOSITION ON THE EPISTLES OF JOHN AND JUDE, AND OF PAUL TO TIMOTHY. 1853. *****
Notes taken by his children of Mr. Bickersteth's expositions at family prayer.

Simple, devout, soundly evangelical, and, we must add, superficial and commonplace.

1387 Ebrard, J. H. A. – COMMENTARY ON THE EPISTLE OF ST. JOHN. With an appendix on the Catholic Epistles. 1860. ***
Dr. Robert S. Candlish, in his *First Epistle of John*, says: "I must acknowledge my obligation to Dr. Lücke. But it is Dr. Ebrard who has helped me most. Ebrard is especially valuable, and for an English reader, acquainted with theology, very easily intelligible."

1388 Hawkins, Thomas – COMMENTARY ON JOHN'S EPISTLES. 1808. ***
Very excellent. The writer has upon every verse something to say worth the saying.

1389 Lücke, G. C. F. – EPISTLES OF JOHN. 1837. **
Dr. Graham, of Bonn, says that "Lücke is impartial, learned, and critically in earnest; yet the attentive reader soon discovers a very decided anti-evangelical tendency. I say anti-evangelical in our sense of the word, for in Germany he has done much to overthrow the cold kingdom of rationalism and unbelief." Graham is severe, and a discount may be allowed from this judgment. Let it serve as a warning.

1390 Shepherd, R. See No. 1069. *

FIRST JOHN

1391 APOSTOLIC INSTRUCTION. Exemplified in the First Epistle of John. Anonymous. 1840. ***
Upon two chapters only, but thoroughly good, and full of sweetness and light.

1392 Binning, Hugh – FELLOWSHIP WITH GOD, or Twenty-eight Sermons on 1 John 1 and 2:1–3. In his *Works*, vol. 2, See No. 1197. 1833. ***
Milk for babes, and meat for men; calls to backsliders, and comforts for mourners. "There is no speaking," says Durham, "after Mr. Binning; truly he had the tongue of the learned, and knew how to speak a word in season."

1393 Calvin, John – *First Epistle of John* and *Epistle of Jude*. Catholic Epistles. in **CALVIN'S COMMENTARIES.** Reprint of C. T. S. edition. Baker Book House; Wm. B. Eerdmans Publishing Co. ***

1394 Candlish, Robert – FIRST EPISTLE OF JOHN. Complete 1 vol. edition. Kregel Publications. ***
We set great store by these lectures. A man hardly needs anything beyond Candlish. He is devout, candid, prudent, and forcible.

1395 Cotton, John – COMMENTARY ON THE FIRST EPISTLE OF JOHN. 1656. ***
Calamy puts his imprimatur upon this book, and speaks of the author's name as "deservedly precious among the saints of God." In doctrine and experience he is a noble teacher.

1396 Graham, W. – THE SPIRIT OF LOVE. Commentary on 1 John. 1857. **
Graham is sound and vigorous, and does not mince matters in dealing with

semi-skeptics; hence he brings upon himself violent reviews from opponents. *The Library Churchman* denounces his book as containing "controversy without argument, criticism without proof, citation without reference, a show of scholarship without the fruits of it, and denunciation without decorum." To say the least of it, this review is far too severe.

1397 Handcock, W. J. – EXPOSITION OF 1 JOHN. 1861. *
The author has carefully studied the original, and has his own ideas as to its meaning; but either he has not the power of communicating them, or else we are slow of apprehension. Very frequently we are at a loss to know what he means.

1398 Hardy, Nathaniel – FIRST EPISTLE OF JOHN UNFOLDED AND APPLIED. 2 vols. 1656-59. Reprinted in Nichol's *Commentaries*. 1865. *****
The Editor of Nichol's edition says, "This exposition is only a fragment. It was intended to consist of five parts, corresponding generally with the five chapters of the Epistle; but only two of them were accomplished. In matter, the sermons are purely evangelical; in spirit, they are earnest and affectionate; in manner, they are eloquent and impressive." This is rather too ardent a commendation.

1399 Morgan, James – EXPOSITION OF 1 JOHN. 1866. ***
Dr. Robert Candlish says that this is a work "of great practical interest and value," and that had it appeared at an earlier date, "he might have abstained from issuing" his own lectures on this Epistle. We are glad to possess both works.

1400 Neander, J. A. W. – FIRST EPISTLE OF JOHN EXPLAINED. Translated by Mrs. Conant. 1852. ****
Mrs. Conant in her preface says: "The treasures of genius and learning which enrich his more scientific works, here seem vivified by a new element, and melt, under the fervor of his inner spiritual life, into a glowing stream of eloquent practical instruction."

1401 Patterson, A. S. – COMMENTARY ON 1 JOHN. 1842. See No. 1292. **

1402 Pierce, Samuel Eyles – EXPOSITION OF 1 JOHN, in 93 sermons. 2 vols., 1835. *****
This devout author was highly Calvinistic, but withal full of spiritual power and unction. He loved the deep things of God, and wrote upon them in a gracious manner.

1403 Stock, John – EXPOSITION OF 1 JOHN. 1865. ***
Written by a well-instructed man of God. For spiritual teaching the work is second to none. *Robert Candlish* prized it greatly.

1404 Cox, Samuel – ST. JOHN'S LETTER TO KYRIA and ST. JOHN'S LETTER TO CAIUS. See No. 1309. ***

1405 Jones, W. See No. 1311. *****

JUDE

1406 Bickersteth, E. See No. 1386. *

1407 Gardiner, F. – THE LAST OF THE EPISTLES. Commentary on Jude. 1856. ******
An interesting, straightforward, instructive commentary.

1408 Jenkyn, William – EXPOSITION OF JUDE. 2 vols., 1652, 1656. See No. 1251. *******
Earnest and popular, but very full, and profoundly learned. A treasure–house of good things.

1409 Luther, Martin. See No. 1372. *******

1410 McGilvray, Walter – LECTURES ON JUDE. 1855. ******
Vigorous, popular addresses by a Free Church divine.

1411 Manton, Thomas – COMMENTARY ON JUDE. Kregel Publications. *******
Manton at first gave up all idea of printing this book on Jude, when he found that Jenkyn had taken up the subject; but he afterwards changed his mind. He tells us: "I consulted with my revered brother's book, and when I found any point at large discussed by him, I either omitted it or mentioned it very briefly; so that his labors will be necessary to supply the weaknesses of mine." Manton's work is most commendable.

1412 Muir, William – DISCOURSES ON JUDE. 1822. *****
Sermons which do not rise above mediocrity.

1413 Oates, Samuel – EXPLANATION OF JUDE IN FORTY-ONE SERMONS. 1633. ******
Of the conforming Puritan style, full of quaintness and singularities of learning. A book by no means to be despised.

1414 Perkins, William – EXPOSITION OF JUDE. 1606. ******
Perkins was regarded by his contemporaries as a paragon of learning, but his writings fail to interest the generality of readers.

1415 Turnbull, Richard – EXPOSITION OF JUDE. See No. 1367. *****

1416 Willet, Andrew – A CATHOLICON. Gathered out of the catholic Epistle of Jude. 1614. *******
This book is in the Museum, but we cannot procure a copy.

REVELATION

(The works upon Revelation are so extremely numerous (Darling's list contains 52 columns), and the views entertained are so many, so different, and so speculative, that after completing our list we resolved not to occupy our space with it, but merely to mention a few works of repute. As for the lucubrations upon parts of the book, they lie at the booksellers "thick as leaves in Vallambrosa." Numbers of these prophecyings have been disproved by the lapse of time, and others will in due season share their fate. The following remarks may help the student, and at the same time prove the difficulty of making a selection.

Davidson distinguishes a fourfold manner of apprehending apocalyptic prophecy:

1. *Preterists.* The prophecies contained in the Apocalypse were fulfilled with the destruction of Jerusalem and the fall of heathen Rome. This is the view of Bossuet, Grotius, Hammond, Wetstein, Eichhorn, Ewald, De Wette, Lücke, and others, among whom is the American expositor, Moses Stuart.

2. *Continuists.* The Apocalyptic prophecies are predictive of progressive history, being partly fulfilled, partly unfulfilled. Thus Mede, Brightman, Isaac Newton, Woodhouse, Cunningham, Birks, Elliott (and many Germans).

3. *Simple Futurists.* According to these, only the first three chapters relate to the historic present of the Seer, all else having reference to the absolute future of the Lord's appearing. Thus, Burgh, Maitland, Benjamin Newton, Todd, and others.

4. *Extreme Futurists.* Even the first three chapters of Revelation are a prophecy relative to the absolute future of Christ's coming being a prediction of the condition of the Jews after the first Resurrection. Kelly, and some Irish authors.)

1417 Bengel, John Albert – EXPOSITION OF THE APOCALYPSE. Introduction to his *Exposition of the Apocalypse*, with his preface to that work, and the greatest part of the conclusion of it, and also his marginal notes on the text, which are a summary of the whole exposition. Translated from the High Dutch by John Robertson. 1757. *
This great author was rather too precise in his dates. The end of the 42 months was settled for the 21st of May, 1810, and the destruction of the beast for June 18th, 1836. When so princely an expositor maunders in this fashion it should act as a caution to less able men.

1418 Bonar, Horatious – LIGHT AND TRUTH, vol. 5. See No. 6. ***

1419 Brightman, Thomas – THE REVELATION OF ST. JOHN. 1644. 1611. See Nos. 649 and 775. *
Brightman's admirers called him "the English Prophet," and this work they styled the "Apocalypse of the Apocalypse;" but it survives only as a noteworthy monument of the failure of the most learned to expound the mysteries of this book. Ellicott says "his commentary is one of great vigor both in thought and language, and deservedly one of the most popular with the Protestant churches of the time."

1420 Burgh, William (or De Burgh) – AN EXPOSITION OF THE REVELATION. 1857. **
Good in its own time.

1421 Cowper, William – PATHMOS; or, a Commentary on the Revelation. 1619; and in *Works,* 1629. **
The simple piety and vigorous style of Cowper have preserved his old-fashioned work, and will preserve it.

1422 Cradock, Samuel – EXPOSITION OF REVELATION. 1696. *
Dr. Doddridge and Job Orton were very fond of this old author. We are not.

1423 Cumming, J. – APOCALYPTIC SKETCHES. 2 vols. **
Here the views of Elliott are admirably popularized.

1424 Daubuz, Charles – A PERPETUAL COMMENTARY ON THE REVELATION. Abridged by Peter Lancaster. 1730. **
Subsequent writers have drawn much from this work. We have heard it highly commended by competent judges. There is also a larger unabridged edition, which we have not seen. This is said to be still more valuable.

1425 Durham, James – A LEARNED AND COMPLETE COMMEN-TARY. 1788. Original edition, 1658. **
After all that has been written, it would not be easy to find a more sensible and instructive work than this old-fashioned exposition. We cannot accept its interpretations of the mysteries, but the mystery of the gospel fills it with sweet savour.

1426 Elliott, C. B. – HORAE APOCALYPTICAE; or, A Commentary on the Apocalypse, critical and historical. 4 vols., 1862. ***
The standard work on the subject.

1427 Garratt, Samuel – COMMENTARY ON THE APOCALYPSE. 1866. **
This author mainly follows Elliott, but differs as he proceeds. He is an esteemed author.

1428 Fuller, Andrew – EXPOSITORY DISCOURSES. 2 vols., 1815. Also in *Works*. **
Fuller is too judicious to run into speculations. The work is both condensed and clear. Fuller called Faber "the Fortune-teller of the church," and there are others who deserve the name.

1429 Glasgow, James – APOCALYPSE TRANSLATED AND EX-POUNDED. 1862. **
We do not care much for the translation, and think some of the interpretations speculative and forced; yet the work is important.

1430 Hengstenberg, E. W. – THE REVELATION EXPOUNDED FOR THOSE WHO SEARCH THE SCRIPTURES. Translated by Patrick Fairbairn. 2 vols., 1851–52. **
Highly esteemed by the best judges.

1431 Mede, Joseph – A KEY TO THE APOCALYPSE. (A translation of Mede's *Clavis Apocalyptica* by R. Bransby Cooper.) 1833. **
There are several other works on the Apocalypse by this author, who, says Elliott, "was looked upon and written of as a man almost inspired for the solution of the Apocalyptic mysteries. Yet I think his success was at first overestimated as an Apocalyptic expositor."

1432 Newton, Benjamin Wills – THOUGHTS ON THE APOCALYPSE. 1853. **
Of the futurist school. Condensed and instructive.

1433 Rogers, George – LECTURES ON THE BOOK OF REVELATION. 4 vols., 1844–51. **
Not half so well-known as it ought to be: a mass of judicious remarks. We do not subscribe to the author's system of interpretation, but his expositions always command our respect.

1434 **Stuart, Moses** – A COMMENTARY ON THE APOCALYPSE. 2 vols., 1845; 1 vol., 1847. **
Stuart rejects the historical interpretations generally given; but his textual criticisms and his primary disquisitions are very helpful. This work has laid us under great obligations.

1435 **Vaughan, C. J.** – LECTURES ON THE REVELATION. 2 vols., 1875. **
Does not grapple with the difficulties, but inculcates the lessons of the Book. A sensible course.

1436 **Williams, Isaac** – THE APOCALYPSE, with notes and reflections. 1873. **
Considering the High Church school to which he belongs, this author is marvellously rich in exposition. The whole is tinged with the medieval spirit.

1437 **Woodhouse, John Chappel** – THE APOCALYPSE. Translation with notes. 1805. **
Bishop Hurd says, "This is the best book of the kind I have seen." We give no opinion, for we are too much puzzled with these Apocalyptic books, and are glad to write...

FINIS

A CLASSIC BIBLE STUDY LIBRARY

for Today

Recommended by:
Charles H. Spurgeon
Warren W. Wiersbe
Cyril J. Barber
David W. Brookman
Wilbur M. Smith
Peter M. Masters
and others

CONTENTS

SECTION IV – OTHER SUBJECTS

PUBLISHER'S PREFACE

A Classic Bible Study Library for Today features an extensive collection of recommendations by well-known, respected church leaders. These are comments on over 300 classic books from famous past (Charles H. Spurgeon, Wilbur M. Smith, Merrill C. Tenney, etc.) and present (Warren W. Wiersbe, Cyril Barber, Peter M. Masters, J. I. Packer, etc.) church spokesmen.

These books are all published by Kregel Publications, and are "classics" because they are "works of enduring excellence" (Webster), and they persistently speak to the needs of believers, from generation to generation. Some of these great biblical studies have never been surpassed. They stand above all others for their commitment to the authority of the Scriptures and as models of theological insight and application.

Pastors, Bible students, professors, and Sunday school teachers seeking to build quality, "classic Bible study" libraries will find *A Classic Bible Study Library for Today* an excellent resource. Here is a handy listing, in biblical order, of some of the greatest biblical studies ever produced, along with comments for each title. With the multitude of books available today, readers will find this a dependable guide to choosing those works which possess the timeless quality of commitment to the authority and proclamation of the Word of God. These classics will lead you in practical application and assist you in your teaching and preaching ministry.

The recommendations come from a diverse group of superbly qualified scholars, bibliophiles, pastors, professors and evangelists. Under each title, the source of the quote is named, and each quote is followed by a source code set in bold typeface. A quick reference to the Source Code List (p. 259) will provide more detailed information on the source of each quote.

Periodicals and individuals quoted infrequently are not listed individually in the Source Code List. Their full names are given before each quote. Individuals quoted frequently show only the last name before the quote, and detailed source information is in the Source Code List. Complete Author and Subject Indexes are included to further assist you in using this section.

SECTION I
BIBLE TRANSLATIONS
AND
WORKS ON THE WHOLE BIBLE

BIBLE TRANSLATIONS

Rotherham, Joseph Bryant – THE EMPHASIZED BIBLE
BARBER – A literal translation of the Greek and Hebrew texts, with particular stress upon the grammatical emphasis of each verse by use of diacritical marks. ...of help...to pastors whose knowledge of Greek and Hebrew is limited. B

CUSTER – ...the ease with which the emphasized words can be spotted in a passage is a great help in perceiving where the stress in a sermon should fall for a given passage. For the pastor whose Greek and Hebrew are only a dim memory of student days, this version can bring to his mind the grammatical emphasis that only a critical knowledge of Greek and Hebrew can provide. I

LOCKYER – In its class, it is incomparable. It constitutes one of the most valuable contributions to Bible study ever conceived. N, DD

Way, Arthur S. – THE LETTERS OF PAUL AND PSALMS
BARBER – ...clarifies the meaning and is stimulating and challenging. DD

SMITH – ...This is not what is called a literal translation, but it is an attempt, by one who was a master of classical Greek, to give us in chaste, beautiful language exactly what Paul meant by his profound, inexhaustible, powerful sentences.... This volume has been a choice treasure in the library of thousands of ministers who are acquainted with it. W

Weymouth, Richard Francis – THE NEW TESTAMENT IN MODERN SPEECH
BARBER – A most readable translation that combines a lucid style with grammatical accuracy. Old, familiar phrases take on new significance. B

BOLLIER – ...noted for its carefulness in rendering the shades of the Greek tenses. E

DANKER – ...noted for awareness of tenses and...displays exquisite literary taste. J

LOUIS PAUL LEHMAN – ...a treasure-house...the plethora of new translations, paraphrases, and accompanying materials, does not eliminate the need for works of proven value.... DD

MERCHANT – ...achieves a high level of accuracy.... R

COMMENTARIES AND OTHER WORKS ON THE WHOLE BIBLE

Gray, James M. – HOME BIBLE STUDY COMMENTARY

BARBER – The thoroughness and soundness of Gray's teaching continue to make this an important work for the lay church-worker. C

WIERSBE – A very fine, one-volume commentary on the entire Bible. James M. Gray was a godly man and a fine Bible student. I recommend this to keep handy on your shelf. DD

Kitto, John – KITTO'S DAILY BIBLE ILLUSTRATIONS (2 vols.)

BARBER – While not intended to be a commentary, the material in these volumes is excellent. The originality of Kitto's thought and his extensive research and commitment to the truth make this indispensible for the expository preacher. ...heartily commended to all who wish for a deeper understanding of God's inspired Word. B, C

BROOKMAN – Kitto was a tremendous expositor, providing the minister with several illustrations of several texts of Scripture. Practical. G

MASTERS – Dr. Kitto was beyond any shadow of doubt a genius in the writing of magnificent character studies, the reconstruction of confusing biblical events, and the unravelling of problem passages. Where many commentaries disappoint, Dr. Kitto excels. He maintains an exceptional level of original thought so that even in the treatment of familiar passages something new and challenging will frequently be suggested. ...well worth having...are worth their weight in gold to preachers. P, Q

SPURGEON – ...not exactly a commentary, but what marvelous expositions you have there! You have reading more interesting than any novel that was ever written, and as instructive as the heaviest theology. The matter is quite attractive and fascinating, and yet so weighty, that the man who shall study those two volumes thoroughly will not fail to read his Bible intelligently and with growing interest. Y

McNicol, John – McNICOL'S BIBLE SURVEY

BARBER – An impressive synopsis of the books of the Bible. C

BIBLIOTHECA SACRA – ...outlines are simple and helpful...useful in presenting synthetic reviews of each Bible book. DD

Slemming, C. W. – BIBLE DIGEST
BIBLE DIGEST CHARTS

BIBLIOTHECA SACRA – For each book [of the Bible], after a short introduction, Slemming gives a résumé of the contents of the Bible book, which presents a good overview of the book. DD

V. RAYMOND EDMAN – ...a splendid overview of the Bible. I find that a careful study of it along with the Bible is most helpful in opening up the contents of each book. DD

Williams, George – STUDENT'S COMMENTARY ON THE
HOLY SCRIPTURES

BARBER- – A comprehensive one-volume Bible commentary. Thoroughly conservative.... DD

HARRY BULTEMA – ...thoroughly trust-worthy for old and young, because it is fundamental in all the great doctrines, evangelical and evangelistic, premillennial and dispensational; the author is sane and pious throughout, while his style is always pungent and as clear as a bell. In this whole splendid volume, in which more truth is found than in any other volume of our day, is not found one dark sentence. DD

GRACE THEOLOGICAL JOURNAL – ...It is fresh, spiritual and inspiring. The devotional flavor is refreshing.... DD

CARL F. H. HENRY – ...holds solid evangelical views of the inspiration and authorship of the Scriptures, and of the great central doctrines. ...has provided a useful and stimulating volume. DD

Godet, Frederic L. – STUDIES IN THE OLD TESTAMENT

BARBER – ...covers a wide range of subjects including angels, the plan and development of life on earth. ...[Godet] is always worth consulting. c

Hengstenberg, E. W. – CHRISTOLOGY OF THE OLD TESTAMENT (4 vols. condensed into one)

BARBER – A first-rate study of Christ as He appears in type and prophecy in the Old Testament. Of great value to preachers. B

BROOKMAN – A complete examination of all major Messianic passages of Scripture in the Old Testament. This classic work refutes several of the radical views of liberal scholars. Excellent. G

MASTERS – ...a successful abridgement of the acclaimed (but formidable) work. The original work wasted much print repudiating dead and forgotten unbelieving scholars. This abridgement clips out most of these portions, preserving all the vital arguments of Hengstenberg as he traces the Messianic passages through the Old Testament. This...abridgement...is the most usable edition available.... The foundation stone in the preacher's library.... P

SAMUEL J. SCHULTZ (as quoted by Merchant) – ...essential for twentieth-century theology. It is especially helpful and reliable from an evangelical perspective. For the student of the New Testament it provides an enriching background. R

SMITH – The greatest work that has ever been written on the Messianic prophecies of the Old Testament, though we do not agree with all of its interpretations. ...one of the most valuable works on prophecy ever written, filled with learning, a powerful answer to rationalism, confirming the student in his faith, and ever deepening his holy regard for the miracle of Messianic prediction.... Nothing has been written to compare with this in vastness of learning, and the firmness with which the writer sets forth his own convictions on the many disputed points of Messianic interpretation. DD, W, U

SPURGEON – This great work deals with a most vital theme in a masterly manner; it has always been held in high esteem. Y

Newell, William R. – STUDIES IN THE PENTATEUCH

BROOKMAN – ...draws out spiritual truths from the books of the Pentateuch. It also offers valuable facts and excellent material helps for sermon preparation. G

WIERSBE – Valuable for your library. DD

Thomas, W. H. Griffith – THROUGH THE PENTATEUCH: Chapter by Chapter

BARBER – Well-outlined and contains helpful thoughts on the text. B

BROOKMAN – These valuable notes take the form of a connected commentary on the Pentateuch. A helpful introduction to each book plus the excellent homiletical material will give the minister devotional insights into the Pentateuchal writings. Evangelical. G

R. K. HARRISON – ...among that elite group of authoritative expositors of God's Word in the twentieth century. A man of brilliant intellect, enormous energy, and profound Christian faith.... A lucid and uncomplicated analysis of the Pentateuch. The author's clear, crisp, straightforward style, joined as it is with wisdom, both theological and devotional, give his expository works classic status. DD

WIERSBE – Griffith Thomas excels in spiritual depth, practicality and a simplicity of expression that make the most profound truths come alive with excitement. DD

GENESIS

Alford, Henry – GENESIS AND EXODUS 1–25

BARBER – A rare work; buy it while it is available. C

BROOKMAN – [A] reprint work...by an outstanding biblical writer. G

SPURGEON – The works of this eminent scholar are too well known and appreciated to need even a word from us. Y

Bush, George – NOTES ON GENESIS (2 vols.)

BARBER – ...enriching comments on the text; sidelights drawn from...a thorough knowledge of the...culture. [Includes] devotional application. C

BROOKMAN – This volume contains rich expository notes based upon the original text. Of practical value to the pastor with little or no knowledge of Hebrew. G

Candlish, Robert – STUDIES IN GENESIS

BARBER – Expository messages rich in their devotional emphasis, containing helpful theological discussions. Thoroughly conservative and of special value to the pastor. ...remains one of the best works for pastors.... B, C

BROOKMAN – ...a very important, classic work on Genesis. It has a treasure-house of sermon suggestions and teachings. These are expository messages, thoroughly conservative, rich in devotional emphasis and contain many theological discussions that will be of special value to ministers. Doctrinal and biographical. G

CUSTER – A rich devotional and practical expositon. I

MASTERS – ...full of suggestions for preachers. One of the very few Old

Testament commentaries which will help in the preparation of evangelistic addresses.... Spurgeon's favorite Genesis commentary will doubtless be the immediate favorite of many preachers today. P
SPURGEON – We venture to characterize this as THE work upon Genesis, so far as lectures can make up an exposition; we have greatly profited by its perusal. It should be in every biblical library. Y

Delitzsch, Franz J. – A NEW COMMENTARY ON GENESIS (2 vols.)
BARBER – A critical commentary on the Hebrew text that holds to the Mosaic authorship of Genesis but leaves room for final redaction in the post-exilic period. Advocates an early form of the documentary hypothesis, and holds to the "long day" theory of creation. The treatment of chapters 12-50 is greatly superior to the material in volume one and is essential whenever anyone preaches on the lives of Abraham, Isaac, Jacob, and Joseph. Deserving of careful reading. B, C
CHILDS – ...by far the most profound commentary from a conservative theological perspective.... His penetration of theological issues and often sensitive handling of the biblical text is of a high order. H
DOUGLAS MOO – ...[is] separate from the Keil and Delitszch series; this is a classic theological expression. S
SMITH – ...in some ways the greatest commentary on Genesis in any language.... W

Strahan, James – HEBREW IDEALS IN GENESIS
BARBER – A rich and rewarding study. Does not permit critical considerations to mar his work. B
BROOKMAN – A classic reprint dealing with the heart and spirit of the people and events in Genesis. Then these Hebrew ideals are related to the ideals of life today. This is a valuable character study. G
SMITH – ...not as well known in this country as it deserves to be...rich blessings...are in store for the reader. ...the [devotional] classic on Genesis... [is] one of the most precious volumes on the deeper aspects of the teaching of Genesis.... W, U, X
ALEXANDER WHYTE (as quoted by Wilbur M. Smith) – I have read it in proof [form], and again and again since it was printed. Let that fine piece of evangelical scholarship be in every home. X
WIERSBE – One of my favorite books.... I think every preacher ought to have this in his library and use it faithfully. One of the most valuable studies of Genesis to appear in this century. It has enriched my life and ministry, and I am sure it will enrich yours as well. DD

Thomas, W. H. Griffith – GENESIS: A Devotional Commentary
ALLISON – He is able to picture the original setting of Bible events in such colorful terms that the reader feels transported to that place and time, to relive the Bible experience. A
BARBER – Well outlined, and contains helpful thoughts on the text. Possibly the most helpful devotional exposition of Genesis available.

Pastors will find the material on Abraham, Isaac, Jacob, and Joseph to be unsurpassed. B

BROOKMAN – A highly recommended devotional commentary on Genesis. This author has mastered all the relevant literature pertaining to this book, making it truly sound in biblical scholarship. G

KAISER – ... carefully weaves the book's purpose, plan, unity, values, and doctrines into a beautiful, but challenging tapestry.... It can be used as a basis for an individual devotional on the text or as a teaching block of text.... Thomas must be commended and thanked a thousand times over for his laboring in the text in order to guide us into a realization of how that text applies to us today. For this the whole church can be grateful to our Lord. DD

PACKER – The author's clear, crisp, straightforward style, joined as it is with wisdom, both theological and devotional, gives his expository works classic status. DD, Y

WIERSBE – A helpful devotional commentary. Griffith Thomas excels in spiritual depth, practicality and a simplicity of expression that make the most profound truths come alive with excitement. BB, DD

EXODUS

Meyer, F. B. – DEVOTIONAL COMMENTARY ON EXODUS
BARBER – Excellent devotional commentary. D

BROOKMAN – This commentary is both devotional and expositional. It will be extremely helpful in sermon application. Meyer was a leading British Baptist preacher in his time. G

FAIR – You will find this work descriptive, directive, and above all, devotional. Although not exhaustive nor critical, this commentary will be an extra special help to the hungry soul, the busy pastor, the pressured evangelist, the weighted missionary, and the searching scholar. DD, K

MASTERS – ...there is an abundance of material here, with a great deal of application. This must be rated as the best life of Moses in print. O

Murphy, James G. – COMMENTARY ON EXODUS
BARBER – Is not abreast of the latest archaeological discoveries, but the treatment of the text reveals painstaking exegesis and is helpful to expositors. Ranks as one of the best general works ever produced on Exodus. B, C

BROOKMAN – Murphy was an Irish Presbyterian scholar of the 19th century. He had a keen knowledge of the Hebrew language. This work is a treasure in spite of its age. It will be useful to all expositors in sermon preparation. G

SPURGEON – The result of laborious study by a scholar of ripe learning. Y

JOURNEYINGS OF THE CHILDREN OF ISRAEL

Ritchie, John – FROM EGYPT TO CANAAN
FAIR – ...a wealth of knowledge, excitement, and challenge await you in

this small but dynamic volume. Here are rich nuggets of scriptural principles to apply to your life.... DD, K

THE BAPTIST BULLETIN – These studies were originally published in the late 1800's, but for the serious student of Old Testament types, they are as current as today.... New Christians who are serious about Bible study will find these helpful. They could be used for a discipleship program. DD

Wagner, George – PRACTICAL TRUTHS FROM ISRAEL'S WANDERINGS

BARBER – A welcome reprint. C

BROOKMAN – The author draws out similarities between Israel's wanderings in the wilderness and a Christian's pilgrimage through life. A classic reprint of 384 pages. G

SPURGEON – A book which we have read with great pleasure and profit, and very heartily recommend. Y

WIERSBE – [Contains] rich veins of gold that others have ignored or neglected. I rejoice that [this] classic is available again for people who are serious about Bible study. ...you [will] find insights from the Scriptures that can enrich your life and ministry.... DD

THE TABERNACLE

Kurtz, John Henry – THE SACRIFICIAL WORSHIP OF THE OLD TESTAMENT

BARBER – Thoroughly conservative and evangelical, Kurtz's treatment even today makes rewarding reading and serves as an effective counterbalance to other more liberal works whose viewpoints continue to recur in modern discussions. B

Ritchie, John – THE TABERNACLE IN THE WILDERNESS

FAIR – ...practical, simply-stated truths, yet deeply enriching.... What a thrilling parallel between the Old Testament tabernacle and a Christian's life is given here! DD, K

Soltau, Henry W. – THE HOLY VESSELS AND FURNITURE OF THE TABERNACLE

BARBER – ...designed to give a correct exposition of the texts relating to the Tabernacle and its furniture, and to present the typical teaching with regard to Christ and His work. B

BROOKMAN – Very helpful exposition giving the most correct delineation from Scripture of the contents of the Tabernacle that has ever appeared. The furniture and vessels used in the Tabernacle are all treated in their typical significance for the believer's instruction, and the riches of the Old Testament economy are unfolded for the New Testament saint. G

MASTERS – This famous old work has ten color plates with devotional comments and some lessons drawn. B

SPURGEON – A series of sumptuous pictures, executed in the best style of art, impressing the mind far more vividly than any letter-press could do.y
WIERSBE – ...an excellent volume. BB

Soltau, Henry W. – THE TABERNACLE, THE PRIEST-HOOD, AND THE OFFERINGS

BARBER – A classic study sufficiently detailed to be helpful. Avoids typology and fanciful spiritualization, and expounds the Scripture with reverence and clarity. B

BROOKMAN – A classic, comprehensive study unfolding the beauties and glories of the Lord Jesus Christ as portrayed in the Jewish ritual. This work avoids extreme and fanciful spiritualization often found in many books on typology. Contains a wealth of direct, practical teaching regarding the daily life of the Christian and the maintenance of communion with God. G

MASTERS – ...packed with information and suggested practical application. Worth any commentary on Exodus and Leviticus. Extremely readable and a very good value. o

SPURGEON – Richly suggestive. Exceedingly well worked out in details; but not so wire-drawn as to prevent thought on the reader's part. y

WIERSBE – ...an excellent volume. BB

LEVITICUS

Bush, George – NOTES ON LEVITICUS

BARBER – A book that pastors will find exceedingly useful. ...this study of Israel's Levitical code provides an indispensable basis for an examination of the New Testament Book of Hebrews. B, c

BROOKMAN – This work shows the beauty of God's redemption as revealed in the Book of Leviticus. These are some of the best notes on Leviticus in print. G

SPURGEON – The author read extensively to produce this volume. In his later years he became a Swedenborgian, but there is no trace of that leaning in this or his other comments. y

Kellogg, Samuel H. – STUDIES IN LEVITICUS

ALLISON – Kellogg gives more emphasis to the historical impact that Jewish civil laws had upon their worship. A

BARBER – Perhaps the finest exposition of this portion of God's Word ever to come from the pen of man. An exemplary study.... Should be in every pastor's library. B, c

BROOKMAN – An outstanding commentary on Leviticus.... In this work, Kellogg staunchly defends Mosaic authorship and ably treats Jewish ceremonial law in all its aspects. G

DOUGLAS MOO – Magnificent old classic. Readable, well-studied, evangelical, and quite helpful for the pastor. s

SAMUEL J. SCHULTZ (as quoted by Merchant) – A very helpful commentary, providing helpful insight and understanding concerning the details of the religion of Israel.... R

WIERSBE – ...a classic. DD

Seiss, Joseph A. – GOSPEL IN LEVITICUS

BARBER – Expository sermons by a nineteenth-century Lutheran pastor. Although valuable, not as thorough or as helpful as Kellogg's work. B

BROOKMAN – ...in this standard evangelical work on Leviticus, the author has been able to clearly define and explain how the Book of Leviticus points forward to Christ. He gives the symbolism of the Book of Leviticus new meaning. The work is critical, doctrinal, practical, and expository. G

SPURGEON – Twenty-one very admirable lectures, founded upon Bush and Bonar, but containing much original matter. Y

NUMBERS

Heslop, William G. – NUGGETS FROM NUMBERS

BROOKMAN – This concise work unfolds several biblical truths from the Book of Numbers. Heslop has a series of ...helpful books on the Old Testament. Evangelical. G

DEUTERONOMY

Cumming, John – THE BOOK OF DEUTERONOMY

BARBER – Of special value due to the fact that there are so few homiletical studies of Deuteronomy. ...a series of "homely" expositions for general readers. Old-fashioned, but lively (almost conversational) and furnishing a constant flow of spiritual applications. ...abounds in warmly evangelical, personal lessons. B, C

BROOKMAN – ...the best-known of Dr. Cumming's more than 200 expositions of many of the books of the Bible. It is a classic...containing homely expositions rather than a verse-by-verse commentary. G

SPURGEON – Pretty, popular, profitable. Y

HISTORICAL BOOKS

Bush, George – NOTES CRITICAL AND PRACTICAL ON JOSHUA AND JUDGES

BROOKMAN – A valuable classic reprint that will enhance sermon preparation. Even though this work was published in 1852, it is still loaded with rich expository thoughts on the books of Joshua and Judges. G

Garstang, John – JOSHUA—JUDGES

BARBER – In spite of its age and adherence to the documentary hypothesis, this work contains some valuable information on the historic background to Joshua-Judges, Joshua's military campaigns, the settlement of the tribes, and the period of the Judges. ...possessed of a freshness and vitality seldom found in works of this nature. B, C

BROOKMAN – ...an older work that deals with the text along with several color maps, charts and photographs [which] accurately reveal the historical context and archaeological finds for the books of Joshua and Judges. G

SAMUEL J. SCHULTZ (as quoted by Merchant) – ...offers archaeological interpretation that is still valuable. R

SMITH – ...the most important single volume devoted to the exposition of any one portion of the Old Testament that has been written out of an exhaustive knowledge of all the archaeological work that has been done up to the time of publication.... This is truly a monumental work, not devotional or expository, but of a strictly historical nature, illuminating many Old Testament passages heretofore rather obscure. W

Meyer, F. B. – CHOICE NOTES ON JOSHUA—2 KINGS

FAIR – ...very clear.....plain, practical, precise, perceptive and profitable.... K, DD

BROOKMAN – The design of this book is to make understandable [and] accessible notes from the books of Joshua to Second Kings. This work will bring new understanding, insight and challenge. A chapter-by-chapter study. Devotional. G

Newell, William R. – STUDIES IN JOSHUA—JOB

BROOKMAN – Popular studies with an excellent synopsis of the historical books. It is written in a clear manner, and surveys each book giving key ideas and insight[s]. G

WIERSBE – Valuable for your library. DD

JOSHUA
See also "HISTORICAL BOOKS"

Scroggie, W. Graham – JOSHUA IN THE LIGHT OF THE NEW TESTAMENT

BROOKMAN – ...Scroggie shows the believer's position in Christ and his walk with God as illustrated in the study of Joshua's life. An important reprint. G

WIERSBE – Valuable.... How that man could preach and teach the Word of God! DD

JUDGES
See also "HISTORICAL BOOKS"

Kirk, Thomas & Lang, John Marshall – STUDIES IN THE BOOK OF JUDGES (*Samson: His Life and Work* and *Gideon and the Judges,* 2 vols. in one)

BARBER – [Kirk & Lang] provide a satisfying work that covers the material and shows to readers how the incidents of the Old Testament find a parallel in our day. c

BROOKMAN – One of the best treatments on the Book of Judges, giving accurate geographical and historical data and excellent biographical descriptions on the life of Samson. Devotional and exegetical. G

Wiseman, Luke H. – PRACTICAL TRUTHS FROM JUDGES

BARBER – ...contains a wealth of practical material; applications are offered to encourage and challenge us today. c

BROOKMAN – A valuable classic reprint study that presents a general overview of the period of the Judges along with an in-depth study of the lives of Barak, Gideon, Jephtah, and Samson. The author shows extensive research.... G

SPURGEON – Mr. Wiseman in this work tells "of Gideon and Barak, of Samson and of Jephthah," and he does it in a powerful style. He was one of the best preachers in the Wesleyan body. A man of fullness, and judiciousness; in fact, a wise man. Y

WIERSBE – [Contains] rich veins of gold that others have ignored or neglected. I rejoice that [this] classic is available again for people who are serious about Bible study. ...you [will] find insights from the Scriptures that can enrich your life and ministry.... DD

RUTH
See also "HISTORICAL BOOKS"

Heslop, William G. – RUBIES FROM RUTH

BROOKMAN – ...This work... [contains] over 116 pages of biblical truths from the Book of Ruth. G

FIRST SAMUEL
See also "HISTORICAL BOOKS"

Deane, William John & Kirk, Thomas – STUDIES IN FIRST SAMUEL *(Samuel and Saul: Their Lives and Times* and *Saul: The First King of Israel,* 2 vols. in one)

BARBER – ...provide[s] the kind of practical application that will delight every devout Bible student. c

BROOKMAN – Devotional and practical. G

FIRST AND SECOND CHRONICLES
See also "HISTORICAL BOOKS"

Bennett, William H. – AN EXPOSITION OF CHRONICLES

BARBER – Commentaries on Chronicles are few and far between. This work meets a need. c

BROOKMAN – ...a painstaking study which is at once understandable, generally reliable, and capable of providing rich insights into the Books of Chronicles. G

JOB
See also "HISTORICAL BOOKS"

Gibson, Edgar Charles – THE BOOK OF JOB

BARBER – A valuable exposition....perceptive and edifying.... Deserves a place in the library of every pastor. **B, C**

BROOKMAN – Not only is this commentary rich in word studies, but the author's outline is also very thorough, giving one an immediate familiarity with Job. **G**

CHILDS – ...[has] long been used by pastors with great profit. **H**

Thomas, David – THE BOOK OF JOB

MASTERS – ...this must be the very best work of David Thomas.... A big book, but composed in a manner which makes it very usable in personal devotions. Thomas uses exciting, graphic and moving prose as he explains each passage, and constantly makes spiritual applications. The pastor who thumbs through this volume is unlikely to resist buying it. **P**

PSALMS

Clarke, Adam – ANALYTICAL STUDIES IN THE PSALMS

BARBER – Prefaced with a comprehensive introduction to the Psalms, their nature, scope, and use in Israel's worship. Complete with outlines based on the Hebrew text, notes on the text, and exegetical comments. ...exceedingly helpful for preachers. ...these brief analyses of each Psalm breathe the confidence of one whose reliance was established on the unchanging character of God. **C, DD**

BROOKMAN – An excellent treatment of the Book of Psalms, featuring homiletical outlines and practical applications. This classic study...presents an analysis of each Psalm and its relationship to the canon of Scripture. **G**

W. E. VINE – ...a comprehensive and useful volume. It affords [me] a very great pleasure to commend this work to servants of God. **DD**

WIERSBE – I only wish I had known about this book earlier in my ministry.... I know of no other book, apart from Scroggie's on Psalms, which unlocks the meanings found in the Psalms. [Clarke] accomplishes this feat with excellent results. **DD**

Cox, Samuel – THE PILGRIM PSALMS

BARBER – His works are among the best that have come down to us. This book could easily form the basis for a series of expository messages. **B**

BROOKMAN – An excellent series of expository studies covering Psalms 120-124. It is probably some of the best expositions on these Psalms to be found anywhere in print. Cox was an outstanding expository preacher.**G**

SPURGEON – This will be greatly valued by intelligent readers. A noble series of sermons would be pretty sure to grow out of its attentive perusal. Samuel Cox is a great expositor. **Y**

Dickson, David – COMMENTARY ON THE PSALMS (2 vols.)

BARBER – A richly devotional exposition by a Scottish Covenanter of the seventeenth century...exhibit[s] a vibrancy of faith and a care in exposition that is refreshing. **B, C**

CHILDS – The exegesis is warm, vigorous, bold, and devotional...is highly recommended. **H**

GRIER – Spurgeon termed this "a rich volume, dropping fatness." **L**

MASTERS – ...filled with deep reflections, doctrinal observations and applications to the spiritual life. Very important...highly stimulating to preachers. **P**

SPURGEON – Invaluable to the preacher. Having read and re-read it, we can speak of its holy savor and suggestiveness. We commend it with much fervor. **Y**

WIERSBE – ...will rejoice your soul. **BB**

Meyer, F. B. – CHOICE NOTES ON THE PSALMS

FAIR – ...a classic in its brevity and beauty of clarity. [It] will give delight and blessed learning. Meyer is pastorally at his best in this brief commentary. **K, DD**

Meyer, F. B. – THE SHEPHERD PSALM

BARBER – A warmly devotional exposition. **B**

BROOKMAN – Meyer has put together a warmly devotional exposition on Psalm Twenty-three. This work will aid the minister that attempts to do a series of messages on this important Psalm of the Old Testament. **G**

PHILLIP KELLER – This...book, if read with an open and receptive spirit, will enrich the reader's life. Read...and rejoice in its green pastures. **DD**

Smith, George Adam – FOUR PSALMS (23, 36, 52, and 121)

F. F. BRUCE – ...it illustrates the gifts of linguistic and geographical knowledge and religious insight which [Smith] brought to the exposition of Scripture. Its reappearance is...welcome. **DD**

Spurgeon, C. H. – PSALMS (*The Treasury of David* condensed into one volume)

BARBER – A classic in its field. Richly rewarding, deeply devotional, and pleasingly relevant. Provides not only the thoughts of the great "Prince of Preachers" of the last century, but also an abundance of quotations taken from the writings of those who have preceded him in the ministry of the Word. **B**

GRIER – Preachers and teachers will find much useful material [here].... **L**

ROBERT G. LEE – Reading this condensation, one has the joy of a diver who, "standing naked for the plunge, rejoices when he comes up with hands filled with pearls." [Contains] the wealth of the spiritual riches of God's truth and the wonder of God's gospel.... This condensation...brings us the assembled sweetness of many fields into one garden of rare and radiant blossoms and fruitage. **DD**

LOCKYER – ...a success.... The selection...in no way detracts from Spurgeon's original work. **N, DD**

MASTERS – ...a one-volume edited and abridged edition of *The Treasury of David*...for those who would like the Treasury in shortened form for the purpose of, say, private devotions, this is an ideal size and a very fine piece of work. B

PROVERBS

Arnot, William – STUDIES IN PROVERBS
BARBER – Perceptive studies of selected verses in the Book of Proverbs. [They] provide both practical instruction and spiritual direction. B, C
BROOKMAN – The author's aim was to be doctrinal, spiritual and practical. A classic work. G
MASTERS – A fine companion for daily Bible study, with some good points to stimulate preachers also. P
SPURGEON – We wish Dr. Arnot had gone steadily through the whole book, for his mind was of an order peculiarly adapted for such a task. Those passages which he dilates upon are set in a clear and beautiful light. For a happy blending of illustrative faculty, practical sound sense, and spirituality, Dr. Arnot was almost unrivalled. Y
WIERSBE – ...a gold mine of spiritual truth. BB

Lawson, George – EXPOSITION OF PROVERBS
BARBER – ...rich, rewarding insights...in this able Scot's warm devotional exposition. DD
BROOKMAN – This practical classic on Proverbs will bring a source of spiritual strength, wisdom and direction for every minister and Bible student of the Word of God. Devotional. G
MASTERS – This practical treatment...has a charm of its own. P
SPURGEON – A thoroughly sound and useful commentary. Lawson wrote popularly and vigorously. Y

ECCLESIASTES

MacDonald, James – THE BOOK OF ECCLESIASTES
BARBER – Perhaps the finest work produced on Ecclesiastes in the nineteenth century. Clear, authoritative, reliable. An excellent work. Buy it. B, C
BROOKMAN – MacDonald does not slight the demands of scholarship, but in a clear, readable way, draws out and then applies the teaching of the Book of Ecclesiastes. G
SPURGEON – Thoroughly exegetical, with excellent "scopes of argument" following each division. Y

SONG OF SOLOMON

Durham, James – EXPOSITION OF THE SONG OF SOLOMON
BROOKMAN – Durham understands the Song of Solomon as an allegory of

the relationship between Christ and the believer. G

SPURGEON – Durham is always good, and he is at his best upon the Canticles. Y

ISAIAH

Bultema, Harry – COMMENTARY ON ISAIAH

BARBER – Brief and to the point. C

THE BAPTIST BULLETIN – ...the author writes from a premillennial, pretribulational viewpoint in language clear and readable.... The book is a delight to read.... DD

THE BAPTIST STANDARD – ...with evangelistic zeal seasoned with the clarity and concern of the prophet, Bultema unfolds the spiritual insights of Isaiah and distinctly enlightens applications of these truths to your life today. This evangelistic classic is most applicable for today. DD

Kelly, William – AN EXPOSITION OF ISAIAH

BARBER – This is a work that can be recommended to serious Bible students. It is non-technical, accurate, and well worth the time spent on mastering its contents. An excellent treatment. B, C

BROOKMAN – This classic exposition...defends the unity of Isaiah with sound, conservative scholarship. Premillennial. G

SPURGEON – This eminent divine of the Brethren school sometimes expounds ably, but with a twist towards the peculiar dogmas of his party. Y

JEREMIAH

von Orelli, Hans Conrad – THE PROPHECIES OF JEREMIAH

BARBER – A moderately conservative, exegetical and expository work. B

DANIEL

Anderson, Sir Robert – THE COMING PRINCE

BARBER – Focuses upon Daniel's prophecy of the seventy weeks, and traces its chronological development through to the time when Messiah was "cut off" at the end of the sixty-ninth week. Provides reconstruction of the chronology, and deals with the times of the Gentiles, the tribulation period, and the Second Advent of Christ. B

BROOKMAN – One of the most detailed works ever written on Daniel's Seventieth Week and the coming Antichrist. G

WIERSBE – ...an excellent study. BB

Gaebelein, Arno C. – THE PROPHET DANIEL

ALLISON – ...one of the leading premillennial, dispensational works on Daniel. A

BARBER – A chapter-by-chapter treatment of the visions and prophecies of Daniel which presents the essence of the predictive ministry of the prophet and expounds the prophecy in an enlighting and helpful way from the premillennial perspective. DD

Pusey, Edward B. – DANIEL, THE PROPHET

BARBER – An extensive, scholarly treatment. Ably defends the authorship and integrity of Daniel's prophecy. Amillennial. B

BROOKMAN – ...a classic conservative work. G

SPURGEON – To Dr. Pusey's work on Daniel all subsequent writers must be deeply indebted, however much they may differ from him in other departments of theological study. Y

Wright, Charles H. – STUDIES IN DANIEL'S PROPHECY

BROOKMAN – Wright was an outstanding writer on the Old Testament. This classic work places special emphasis on the historical aspects of the Book of Daniel. Amillennial and conservative. G

THE MINOR PROPHETS

von Orelli, Hans Conrad – THE TWELVE MINOR PROPHETS

BARBER – A most valuable study by a moderately conservative German theologian. B

BROOKMAN – The meanings of Hebrew words are brought to light by a simple but full English explanation. This classic work is based upon sound scholarship. Conservative. G

MOO – A very usable and easy-to-read work. Thoroughly researched and evangelical....s

AMOS

Cripps, Richard S. – COMMENTARY ON AMOS

ALLISON – ...his practical comments on the text are helpful. A

BARBER – Not abreast of the latest archaeological material. The exposition, however, is very full...deserving of close study. B, C

BROOKMAN – This full exposition contains many practical applications to the needs of today. Conservative. G

OBADIAH

Marbury, Edward – OBADIAH AND HABAKKUK

BROOKMAN – Marbury's work on Obadiah and Habakkuk is a true classic.... This work will be of great benefit to every minister and Bible student. G

SPURGEON – Far more lively than Rainolds. His spirituality of mind prevents his learning becoming dull. He says in the preface, "All my desire is to do all the good I can," and he writes in that spirit. Y

JONAH

Burn, Samuel C. – THE PROPHET JONAH

BARBER – All things considered, this is one of the best expositions on this Old Testament book for the preacher. C

BROOKMAN – Every minister will be able to glean some homiletical treasures from this practical work. G

Exell, Joseph S. – PRACTICAL TRUTHS FROM JONAH

BARBER – A capable devotional commentary...based on sound scholarship. c

BROOKMAN – This verse-by-verse exposition deals with the practical aspects of the Book of Jonah. Exell was an excellent devotional writer. Conservative. G

MASTERS – ...exactly what its title claims, and worthily adds to the fine treatments which Jonah has attracted. B

SPURGEON – Mr. Exell, in a very unpretending but able way, brings to light the practical lessons of Jonah. Paxton Hood calls these readings "admirable," and we concur in the verdict. Y

WIERSBE – [Contains] rich veins of gold that others have ignored or neglected. I rejoice that [this] classic is available again for people who are serious about Bible study. ...you [will] find insights from the Scriptures that can enrich your life and ministry.... DD

Kirk, Thomas – JONAH: HIS LIFE AND MISSION

BARBER – It is difficult to think of any devout Bible student failing to receive blessing from a perusal of this fine work. c

BROOKMAN – ...expository, fresh, and suggestive. Kirk has an intriguing way of making Bible characters come alive. Conservative. G

HABAKKUK

Marbury, Edward – OBADIAH AND HABAKKUK

BROOKMAN – Marbury's work on Obadiah and Habakkuk is a true classic.... This work will be of great benefit to every minister and Bible student. G

SPURGEON – Here Marbury holds the field alone among old English authors, and he does so worthily. There is about him a vigorous, earnest freshness which makes his pages glow. Y

ZECHARIAH

Baron, David – COMMENTARY ON ZECHARIAH: His Visions and Prophecies

BARBER – ...a helpful elucidation of the messianic prophecies contained in this book. B

BROOKMAN – ...one of the best commentaries on the Book of Zechariah. G

CUSTER – ...thorough premillennial exegesis by a Hebrew-Christian, who knows both the language and the customs of his people. The work is warmly devotional and gives a clear portrait of Israel's place in God's prophetic program. I

WALTER C. KAISER, JR. – One of Baron's crowning achievements....Baron has given us a rich treat of theology and exegesis in this study. Few...are as adept as he is in tracing the inner connections between the sections of this prophecy and its organic unity, logic, and thrust.... It would appear that he literally lived with this Scripture.... By any fair standards of comparison, this work is still one of the monumental statements of all time on the meaning and significance of Zechariah. DD

SMITH – In some ways I believe this is the greatest volume devoted entirely to the exposition of any one of the Minor Prophets in our language. When one has Baron's work he needs little else on Zechariah...not only a work of great scholarship, but one that is exceptionally rich devotionally, warm with spiritual teachings, so that the entire volume not only illuminates the mind, but enriches the soul.... Indeed, here is a volume that should be in every Bible student's library, one not as well-known as it ought to be, but of the very first importance in understanding this portion of the prophetic Scriptures.... W, X

WIERSBE – A recognized Hebrew-Christian scholar whose commentary is *the* commentary on this book. It is hard to find a good commentary on Zechariah. David Baron has given us one of the best. BB, DD

Wright, Charles H. – ZECHARIAH AND HIS PROPHECIES

BARBER – ...these extensive studies translate, introduce, and treat the visions of this neglected Old Testament prophet. Amillennial. C

BROOKMAN – Dr. Wright's exposition is both scholarly and conservative. G

SECTION III
NEW TESTAMENT

Barnes, Albert – BARNES' NOTES ON THE NEW TESTAMENT

MASTERS – As the publishers state, every word of Barnes is included. This is a beautiful production and frankly makes nonsense of the multi–volume edition. His "Notes" are full of information, and he summarizes the views of all the key expositors up to his time. Regular users grow very attached to these notes, which are especially valuable to preachers. Dr. Barnes had particular skill when it came to summarizing opposing views on controversial passages (such as Romans 7). For these problem passages he has a clarity generally unmatched by others. **P, Q**

SPURGEON – Everybody has this work, and therefore can judge for himself, or we would both commend and criticize. **Y**

WIERSBE – ...a detailed commentary...most satisfactory. **DD**

Bengel, John Albert – NEW TESTAMENT COMMENTARY
(2 vols.) (Original title: *The Gnomon of the New Testament*)

BARBER – ...contains valuable insights into the Greek of the New Testament and is still sought after...[it] is worthy of repeated consultation. **B, C**

DANKER – ...anticipates and influences considerably both German and English scholarship of the next century and combines perspicuity with brevity in a most remarkable manner. In a single line of Bengel's comment there is frequently more spiritual freight than garrulous predecessors and contemporaries packed into a page. *Gnomon* is the Latin term, now adopted into English, for the pin, or style, of a sundial. Bengel's comments are just that: his style points the student directly to the timely meaning of the text and is not simply the dress of thought, tailored to fit some fixed fashion.... **J**

A. T. ROBERTSON – ...one of the great commentaries of the New Testament for scholarly and spiritual insight. **DD**

PHILIP SCHAFF – A marvel of condensation and spiritual insight; must remain a classic. **DD**

SPURGEON – ...the scholar's delight. He selected the title *Gnomon* as modest and appropriate, intending it in the sense of a pointer or indicator, like the sundial; his aim being to point out or indicate the full force and meaning of the words and sentences of the New Testament. He endeavors to let the text itself cast its shadow on his page, believing with Luther that "the science of theology is nothing else but grammar exercised on the words of the Holy Spirit." The editor...says in his preface: "It is quite superfluous to write in praise of the *Gnomon* of Bengel. Though modern criticism has furnished many valuable additions to our materials for New Testament exegesis, yet, in some respects, Bengel stands out still...among all who have labored, or who as yet labor in that important field. He is unrivaled in felicitous brevity, combined with what seldom accompanies that excellence, namely, perspicuity. Terse, weighty, and suggestive, he often, as a modern writer observes, 'condenses more matter into a line, than can be extracted from pages of other writers'." ...the pioneer of true biblical criticism. Y

MARVIN R. VINCENT – [Bengel] must always stand preeminent for his keen and deep spiritual insight and for that marvelously terse and pithy diction with which, as a master key, he so often throws open by a single turn, the secret chambers of a word. DD

WIERSBE – One of the sets I use often in my library...a fine book.... Old, yes, but filled with good treasures for the careful student of the Word of God. DD

Doddridge, Philip – EXPOSITION OF THE FOUR GOSPELS (2 vols.)

SPURGEON – The late Dr. Barrington, Bishop of Durham, in addressing his clergy on the choice of books, characterizes this masterly work in the following terms: "I know no expositor who unites so many advantages and perspicuity of his composition, the utility of his general and historical information, the impartiality of his doctrinal comments, or, lastly, the piety and pastoral earnestness of his moral and religious applications." Y

Fairweather, William – BACKGROUND OF THE GOSPELS

BARBER – A very important older work tracing the historical and doctrinal themes of the intertestamental period and the preparation of the Greco-Roman world for the coming of Christ. Provides all that the busy pastor could desire. An indispensable work. Will handsomely repay the busy pastor each time he uses it. B, C

BROOKMAN – Fairweather...traces historically and religiously the interval beginning with the Maccabean revolt and ending with the destruction of Jerusalem. G

Godet, Frederic L. – STUDIES IN THE NEW TESTAMENT

BARBER – ...these studies cover differences in the four Gospels, the person and work of Christ, the leading apostles, and the structure of the Book of Revelation. C

Hort, F. J. & Hort, A. F. – EXPOSITORY AND EXEGETICAL STUDIES (Includes: *Prolegomena to Romans and Ephe-*

sians, Epistle of St. James, First Epistle of St. Peter, The Apocalypse of St. John 1-3 and *The Gospel According to St. Mark.*)
BARBER – ...the reissuing of all of [Hort's] works in one handy volume is extremely fortuitous. c

Zahn, Theodor – INTRODUCTION TO THE NEW TESTAMENT (3 vols.)
BARBER – ...Zahn's work is...extensive and contains a mine of valuable material. It should be consulted by all students of the New Testament. c
CUSTER – The...classic in the field.... I
DANKER – ...impressive for its profound learning. J
SMITH – ...without doubt the greatest New Testament scholar in the world during the latter part of the 19th century, and a thorough conservative. His work is the most important of its kind ever to be published, and if a Bible student really wants to master the difficult but important problems relating to the literature of the New Testament, this is the one volume to study. w

LIFE OF JESUS CHRIST
See also "CHRISTOLOGY"

Arnot, William – PARABLES OF OUR LORD
BARBER – These devotional studies are rewarding. Preachers will find them helpful. B, C
BROOKMAN – ...a concise, practical study of the 30 most widely-known parables of Christ. Every pastor will find a lot of helpful devotional material in these...pages. G
MASTERS – His style is intensely spiritual and practical, and these pages are filled with observations and reflections not seen in other works. This volume will prove of enormous help to preachers alongside the formal commentaries, and it also makes excellent devotional reading...of great value to preachers. Particularly helpful in stimulating evangelistic thoughts. P, Q

Arnot, William – LESSER PARABLES OF OUR LORD
BARBER – A valuable resource...in spite of its vintage. B, C
BROOKMAN – ...a classic on the lesser-known parables. One will discover the varied theological and biblical concepts embedded in these parables. G

Blaikie, William G. – THE PUBLIC MINISTRY OF CHRIST
BARBER – ...reverent and devout. We are glad that this volume is available again, so that it can direct the activities of a new generation of pastor-teachers. c

Farrar, F. W. – THE LIFE OF CHRIST
BARBER – A reverent treatment. The literary excellence of this work, as well as its historic reliability, places this study only slightly behind Edersheim for overall value and reliability. B

BROOKMAN – A work that is highly regarded by C. H. Spurgeon. This well-illustrated edition of the life of Christ has been well-accepted for years. G
SPURGEON – *The* work upon the subject. Fresh and full. Y

Fraser, Donald – THE METAPHORS OF CHRIST

BARBER – A must for all who desire to know how Christ used metaphors to communicate truth to His hearers. This study may well serve as a model of good communication even today. Excellent. C

Habershon, Ada R. – STUDY OF THE MIRACLES

BARBER – A helpful supplement to Trench's masterly treatment. Premillennial. B
BROOKMAN – The author reveals the reasons for the miracles and their application for daily life. Conservative. G

Habershon, Ada R. – STUDY OF THE PARABLES

BARBER – A perceptive treatment by a capable Hebrew-Christian writer. B
SMITH – I do not know of any work on the parables which brings forth so much new, fresh, suggestive and often profound truth as the volume by Miss Habershon. She was one of the deepest Bible students and clearest writers on biblical subjects of her day.... W

Innes, Alexander T. & Powell, Frank J. – THE TRIAL OF CHRIST (2 vols. in one)

BARBER – Two British [lawyers] examine the trials of Jesus Christ from different...points of view. The result is a pair of legal monographs that are deserving of a place in every zealous Christian's library. Highly recommended. C
BROOKMAN – An excellent combination of two works that trace the order of events of Christ's trials and death. G

Laidlaw, John – STUDIES IN THE MIRACLES OF OUR LORD

BARBER – An unusually complete and satisfying exposition. One of the best presentations of this kind of material. ...it deserves a place in the library of every pastor. Highly recommended. B, C

Liddon, Harry P. – THE DIVINITY OF OUR LORD

BARBER – ...a standard treatment on the subject for more than a century...the information presented is of such a nature that it strengthens the reader's faith and also grounds his belief in the "impregnable rock of Holy Scripture." Excellent. Preachers will have call to refer to this book often. B, C
BROOKMAN – A classic reprint on the Divinity of Christ. G
GRIER – Still valuable, though delivered over a century ago. L
C. W. GROGAN (as quoted by Merchant) – ...a great classic on the subject.... The wedding of scholarship and devotion in it makes it heartwarming as well as instructive. R
SMITH – This monumental, scholarly work is undoubtedly the greatest treatment by any one author of the preeminently important subject of the

deity of our Lord Jesus Christ that was ever written in the English language.... The truths here touched upon are presented in a noble style, every page revealing a profound acquaintance with all relevant literature. A minister really commits a professional sin when he permits literature of an ephemeral and secondary nature to absorb the precious hours of his mornings, when such a great work as this stands before him pleading for a close study, with the promise that his whole life will thereby be enriched, and his convictions concerning the Lord Jesus Christ deepened, strengthened, and broadened. w

Liddon, H. P. & Orr, James – THE BIRTH OF CHRIST *(The Magnificat* and *The Virgin Birth of Christ,* 2 vols. in one)

SMITH – The Magnificat is treated exhaustively in a series of four sermons....w

Maclaren, Alexander & Swete, Henry B. – THE POST-RESURRECTION MINSTRY OF CHRIST *(After the Resurrection* and *The Appearances of Our Lord After the Passion,* 2 vols. in one)

BARBER – ...deserving of careful consideration. They have been described as "brilliant and effective," evidencing "mastery of the subject matter," and being representative of the finest scholarly and suggestive material ever written on this long-neglected aspect of Christ's ministry. c

BROOKMAN – An excellent combination on the post-resurrection appearances of Christ by two outstanding authors. These two books have been uniquely blended together to form a valuable study on this subject. G

Marsh, F. E. – WHY DID CHRIST DIE?

BARBER – A Christ-centered, scriptural exposition of the atonement. B

BROOKMAN – A sound exposition of the various practical and theological aspects of the atonement. Four common errors regarding the atonement are examined carefully. This work has some excellent homiletical values. G

McIntosh, Hugh – IS CHRIST INFALLIBLE AND THE BIBLE TRUE?

BARBER – This work has long been buried in oblivion because the author dared to expose (through their own writings!) some of the leading scholars of his day: George Adam Smith, William Robertson Smith, John Watson, et al. Nor does he hesitate to take on the different European schools of thought whose views, in modified form, still are being taught today. What remains is a powerful, well-reasoned apologetic for a belief in the inspiration and inerrancy of Scripture. B

Milligan, William – THE ASCENSION OF CHRIST

BARBER – Combines excellence in presentation with accuracy in interpretation to make this study of Christ's post-resurrection and present heavenly ministries a book that all Christians will enjoy reading. c

Moule, H. C. G. & Orr, James – THE RESURRECTION OF CHRIST (*Jesus and the Resurrection* and *The Resurrection of Jesus*, 2 vols. in one)
BARBER – ...provides pastors and students with a rare combination of excellence in exposition coupled with a clear enunciation of theological truth. c

Ramsay, William H. – THE EDUCATION OF CHRIST
BARBER – An informative, historical study that makes a unique contribution to our knowledge of the time. B
EDWARD M. BLAIKLOCK – Its pages will serve as an introduction to the man, and his insight into that strong interweaving of place and time, of stage and circumstance, which were part of his [Ramsay's] contribution to ancient studies. They may never be separated again. DD

Schilder, Klass – CHRIST CRUCIFIED
BARBER – Theologically accurate, abounds in suggestive insights, and provides exegetical illumination for a score of Easter sermons. B
BROOKMAN – Schilder's works on the life of Christ are loaded with sermon material. This study on the crucifixion of Christ is a classic. G

Schilder, Klass – CHRIST IN HIS SUFFERING
BARBER – A classic treatment on the passion of Christ. Deserves a place in every pastor's library. B
BROOKMAN – This classic work deals with Christ's distress during the beginning stages and ends with Gethsemane. G

Schilder, Klass – CHRIST ON TRIAL
BARBER – Covers the events of the night of His betrayal to His condemnation. A learned, accurate treatment. B
BROOKMAN – This classic work covers the events of the night of Christ's betrayal to His actual condemnation. c

Stier, Rudolf E. – THE WORDS OF THE RISEN CHRIST
BARBER – An extensive study revealing the author's mystical leanings, thorough familiarity with ascetic literature, and unique ability to present Greek concepts and word studies in a pleasing manner. Abounds in suggestive material for a series of sermons. B, c

Taylor, William M. – THE PARABLES OF OUR SAVIOR
BARBER – ...may be consulted with profit by all.... c
BROOKMAN – For expository preaching ideas on the parables, this classic reprint is a must. This work is considered to be an extremely practical exposition that offers an evangelistic thrust to the Parables. G
WIERSBE – ...be sure to obtain his volumes on the parables and miracles of Christ. They are among the finest you will ever read. cc

Thomas, W. H. Griffith – CHRISTIANITY IS CHRIST
BARBER – Centers on the person and work of Christ, vindicates the uniqueness of His character and mission, establishes the credibility of the

gospel records, and deals convincingly with the meaning of and need for His bodily resurrection. A most important volume. B

BROOKMAN – ...[a] good older work. G

CHARLES C. RYRIE – It is concise yet complete. It is simple yet thorough. It is straightforward and sobering. It is faithful to the Bible. ...Altogether it is a fine apologetic for the Christian faith. DD

MATTHEW

Morison, James – THE GOSPEL ACCORDING TO MATTHEW

BARBER – A practical and devotional, phrase-by-phrase commentary. In many instances, provides helpful comments on textual problems. B

BROOKMAN – ...Morrison was an outstanding expository preacher who influenced the spiritual awakening in several parts of Scotland in the 1800's. [An] excellent devotional, phrase-by-phrase commentary.... G

SPURGEON – We differ greatly in doctrinal views from Dr. Morison, but we set a great price upon his Matthew and Mark, which deserve the utmost praise. Y

Powell, Ivor – MATTHEW'S MAJESTIC GOSPEL

WIERSBE – Don't overlook this fine book. It is filled with treasures of sermon ideas and spiritual truths to help you in your ministry. DD

Thomas, W. H. Griffith – OUTLINE STUDIES IN MATTHEW

BARBER – This work contains nearly 500 pages of homiletical and expository outlines. B

DONALD K. CAMPBELL – ...sound interpretation and practical application of truth.... Those who preach and/or teach the Bible will be helped by these studies, as they observe the method of a biblical scholar who possessed a rare, homiletical gift. DD

PACKER – The author's clear, crisp, straightforward style, joined as it is with wisdom, both theological and devotional, gives his expository works classic status. DD, Y

WIERSBE – ...shows...his scholarship, devotion to Christ, and ability to analyze and outline Scripture. Griffith Thomas excels in spiritual depth, practicality and a simplicity of expression that make the most profound truths come alive with excitement. BB, DD

MARK

Alexander, Joseph Addison – COMMENTARY ON MARK

BARBER – A heartwarming study that does not adequately explain the theme of Mark's gospel, but still is worth consulting. Devotional. B, C

BROOKMAN – This classic reprint is one of the best older works on the Gospel of Mark. Alexander gives a good defense of Mark as an independent witness to the life of Christ. G

CUSTER – An old but helpful exposition. I

GRIER – A helpful exposition. L

MASTERS – …provides the most lucid commentary available…a fine commentary. P, Q

SPURGEON – Alexander expounds Mark as an independent record, and does not constantly tell us to "see Matthew and Luke." Hence the book is complete in itself, and the author's learning and care have made it invaluable. Y

Morison, James – THE GOSPEL ACCORDING TO MARK

BARBER – A very full, devotional treatment. The overall strength of this exposition far outweighs its syntactical deficiencies. …a commentary all expositors and students of the Word will want to own. Buy it! B, C

BROOKMAN – …devotional. …a companion volume to Morison's commentary on Matthew. G

SPURGEON – A deeply learned work; we know of none more thorough. Differing as we do from this author's theology, we nevertheless set a high price upon this production. Y

Powell, Ivor – MARK'S SUPERB GOSPEL

WIERSBE – Don't overlook this fine book…. It is filled with treasures of sermon ideas and spiritual truths to help you in your ministry. DD

Swete, H. B. – COMMENTARY ON MARK

ALLISON – Reviewers recommend this more than any other commentary on Mark…. Be sure to consult this classic…. A

BARBER – Long regarded as one of the finest exegetical treatments available. B, C

CUSTER – The most thorough commentary on the Greek text of Mark. I

SMITH – For one who is able to follow the Greek text, this volume will be found to be one of the richest commentaries on any New Testament book ever published in our language. It is simply packed with a wealth of material, with exhaustive analyses, and fine, accurate, compact definitions. W

TENNEY (as quoted by Merchant) – A commentary of solid worth…. R, AA

WIERSBE – …a scholarly commentary you should buy. BB

LUKE

Godet, Frederic L. – COMMENTARY ON LUKE

ALLISON – His commentary is an invaluable resource for studying any portion of Luke, and you are apt to return to it again and again. A

BARBER – An exhaustive, technical commentary that ably defends the cardinal doctrines of the Christian faith while expounding the text. Deserves a place on the shelf of every pastor. B

BROOKMAN – A minister needs to read Godet slowly, but the rewards are worth the extra effort. All of his commentaries have now become standard works in the field of biblical exposition. G

CUSTER – An exhaustive, technical commentary. I

MASTERS – A great classic…. B

Moo – …a classic in the field. s

SPURGEON – Dr. F. B. Meyer says: "To an immense erudition, to a living piety, Godet unites a profound feeling of reality; there is here a vivifying breadth, an ardent love for the Savior, which helps the disciple to comprehend the work, the acts, and the words of his Divine Master." Y

WIERSBE - I recommend [it]. BB

Powell, Ivor – LUKE'S THRILLING GOSPEL

WIERSBE – Don't overlook this fine book. It is filled with treasures of sermon ideas and spiritual truths to help you in your ministry. DD

Thomas, W. H. Griffith – OUTLINE STUDIES IN LUKE

BROOKMAN – Thomas developed these practical sermon outlines from his personal devotional life. It is not a verse-by-verse section outline of Luke's Gospel. G

PACKER – …a Bible teacher of first rank. His books are pressed down and running over, potent to clear the heads and warm the hearts of those who love the Bible and its Christ. [His books have] classic status…Bible students seeking refreshment and teachers seeking resources will both be delighted…. The author's clear, crisp, straightforward style, joined as it is with wisdom, both theological and devotional, gives his expository works classic status. DD, T

WIERSBE – Griffith Thomas excels in spiritual depth, practicality and a simplicity of expression that make the most profound truths come alive with excitement. DD

Van Doren, William H. – GOSPEL OF LUKE

MASTERS – …[provides] lists of ideas, explanations and applications under every word of every verse. (The word "hypocrite", for example, gives rise to a complete list of all biblical hypocrites, and a penetrating description of all types of hypocrites and their characteristics.) Very important for stimulating thought…. Q

SPURGEON – Well named "suggestive"; it is all suggestions. It teems and swarms with homiletical hints. Y

SUGDEN – It is impossible to pursue this volume without adding to one's knowledge and spiritual stature…. Van Doren has the gift of sending you on a quest for treasure that hitherto you were unaware of…. A priceless volume. DD, Z

JOHN
See also "OUR LORD'S PRAYER"

Godet, Frederic L. – COMMENTARY ON JOHN'S GOSPEL

BARBER – A monumental work by a great theologian and an able defender of the faith. Thorough and exhaustive without being elaborate and verbose…. No preacher should be without it. B, C

BROOKMAN – …exhaustive…. From a theological and Christological standpoint, Godet has written one of the best works available in print today. G

CUSTER – A very thorough exposition. I

MARTIN – ...has a rich vein of spiritual worth, with practical applications. O

SMITH – ...from a theological standpoint, and for going to the uttermost depths of the profound teachings recorded in the fourth Gospel, Godet is the supreme work.... Here are some of the finest pages of Christology to be found anywhere; in some paragraphs, truths are so brilliantly set forth that, once read, they will never leave the reader's mind and heart. W

Hengstenberg, E. W. – COMMENTARY ON JOHN   (2 vols.)

BARBER – This study, by the same person who gaves us his now famous *Christology of the Old Testament* [see comments, p. 13], is rich in insights, and treats with rare piety the life and labors of Christ. A rewarding work that will handsomely repay the time spent reading it. B, C

BROOKMAN – ...[a] well-balanced, massive commentary on John's Gospel, Hengstenberg develops the life and works of Christ brilliantly from the apostle's writings. This work is a classic.... G

SPURGEON – Like others of this author's works: solid, but dry. Y

Powell, Ivor – JOHN'S WONDERFUL GOSPEL

WIERSBE – Don't overlook this fine book. It is filled with treasures of sermon ideas and spiritual truths to help you in your ministry. DD

Thomas, David – GOSPEL OF JOHN

MASTERS – Another extremely useful mass of preaching suggestions. P

Van Doren, William H. – GOSPEL OF JOHN

MASTERS – A most important and successful work. (See entry under Luke.) Its value to preachers cannot be exaggerated. Q

SPURGEON – If men who read this volume do not preach the better for so doing, it is not Mr. Van Doren's fault; they must be Van Dolts by nature, though they may ignore the family name. Y

SUGDEN – ...different. As you travel over terrain that is familiar, you suddenly realize that you are being confronted with truths that somehow you have missed.... Exhaustive without being exhausting. He provides sound, reliable exposition of the text, accented with refreshing insights for application to daily living. DD, Z

ACTS

Alexander, Joseph – COMMENTARY ON THE ACTS OF THE APOSTLES   (2 vols. in one)

BARBER – An exhaustive, thorough exposition that gives valuable help on the meaning of Greek words, defends Stephen's accuracy of chronology in Acts 7, and provides preachers with an abundance of usable material. A warmly devotional treatment. Reformed. B, C

BROOKMAN – [Alexander's] concern...is to promote an exhaustive understanding of the text of Acts and of its message as a whole. G

GRIER – Sound and sober exposition. L

MASTERS – The clear, concentrated note-style of Alexander is perfect for Acts...a most useful and informative commentary. Q

Arnot, William – STUDIES IN ACTS: The Church in the House

BARBER – ...provocative as well as edifying. C

MASTERS – In the short, homely, and somewhat devotional homilies of this work, there are numerous deep reflections which will help the preacher. Dr. Arnot took very unusual texts and drew thoughts from them. Q

SPURGEON – ...all who are acquainted with Dr. Arnot will know that even his simplest expositions are rich and full. He hath dust of gold. Y

Gloag, Paton J. – CRITICAL AND EXEGETICAL COMMENTARY ON THE ACTS (2 vols.)

BARBER – A thorough exposition based on careful exegesis. Particularly praiseworthy is the writer's handling of critical problems. Warmly recommended. B, C

BROOKMAN – This thorough exposition on the Book of Acts shows a lot of research by an older Scottish Presbyterian minister. The author was not afraid to tackle any problem in the text. G

SPURGEON – Dr. Hackett says of Dr. Gloag's work: "I have examined it with special care. For my purposes I have found it unsurpassed by any similar work in the English language. It shows a thorough mastery of the material: philology, history, and literature pertaining to this range of study, and a skill in the use of this knowledge, which places it in the first class of modern expositions." Y

Laurin, Roy L. – ACTS: Life in Action

BARBER – ...brings out practical applications.... C

BILLY GRAHAM – I have read every book [Dr. Laurin] has ever written. ...many of the thoughts which I use in my preaching have come from [him]. DD

Powell, Ivor – THE AMAZING ACTS

WIERSBE – Don't overlook this fine book. It is filled with treasures of sermon ideas and spiritual truths to help you in your ministry. DD

Stier, Rudolph – THE WORDS OF THE APOSTLES

BARBER – A comprehensive analysis of the speeches and sermons of the Book of Acts. Deserves a place in every expository preacher's library. A must for every student.... B, C

SPURGEON – Devout, scholarly, full of thought. To be used discreetly. Y

Vaughan, Charles John – STUDIES IN THE BOOK OF ACTS

BARBER – A series of sermons accompanied by a paraphrase of the Greek text and providing some penetrating insights into the Scriptures. Excellent as example of exposition. This is a work of rare merit, and it will be appreciated by those who use it wisely. B, C

BROOKMAN – These expository messages on the Book of Acts contain some outstanding examples of good biblical preaching. G

SPURGEON – Not only does Dr. Vaughan expound his text in the ablest manner, but he introduces passages of Scripture so aptly that he suggests discourses. Y

Walker, Thomas – ACTS OF THE APOSTLES

SMITH – ...I consider this the greatest commentary on the Book of Acts written from a missionary standpoint that has been published in our language. The author was a careful student of the Greek text.... Each chapter concludes with a most helpful summary of the teachings of that particular portion of the Word of God. I have never seen this book listed in any bibliography, but it is a treasure house indeed, with much material not to be found in any other commentary on Acts. x

SUGDEN – ...a remarkable exposition...has been of tremendous value in my own personal ministry.... I am confident that a great company of those who minister the Word of God will be grateful for the republishing of this refreshing volume.... DD, z

WIERSBE – ...written by a missionary to India, this older work is worth many of the newer books combined. BB

LIVES OF THE APOSTLES, ETC.

Bruce, A. B. – THE TRAINING OF THE TWELVE

BARBER – Unequalled in its field. Shows how Christ disciplined and trained His disciples for the position of apostleship. A most rewarding study. B

BIBLIOTHECA SACRA – Many Christian leaders today still concur with W. H. Griffith Thomas who regarded this volume as "one of the great books of the nineteenth century." It is directed more toward an ongoing life of obedience to Christ than toward the "instant discipleship" that characterizes much of the late twentieth century Christianity. This classic continues to be "must reading" for every Christian. DD

BROOKMAN – ...this work...has never been equaled. This classic, learned, practical and inspiring book on the twelve apostles is a must for every minister's library. G

CUSTER – A unique study...not only helps the expositor to instruct his people but also helps him to see his own responsibility before his Lord. I

TED ENGSTROM (as quoted in Jones) – One of the most helpful books on leadership that I've come across.... Without a doubt...one of the finest biblical approaches, and the best teaching known concerning management principles emphasized by the Lord Jesus Christ. M, DD

HOWARD HENDRICKS – A significant book that helped me greatly in the whole area of discipleship. DD

SMITH – ...There is nothing quite as important on the life of our Lord as related to the training of the twelve apostles as this volume. ...fresh and inspiring...a classic resource.... It has never been equalled. ...it will still be found fresh and inspiring. DD, W

WIERSBE – [A] classic that will help you study and preach about the twelve apostles.... This is one book that every pastor ought to take with him on a long holiday and read carefully, not only for insights into the hearts and minds of the apostles, but also for an understanding of the Master's methods with His men. One of the greatest books on discipleship ever written. CC, DD

Chadwick, W. Edward – THE PASTORAL TEACHING OF PAUL

BARBER – ...a rare and valuable volume that every minister should own and refer to repeatedly. c

WIERSBE – I rejoice that this work...is now available to a generation of ministers who read what these chapters present. [Several of these sections] are musts for the pastor who truly wants a spiritual ministry. I know of no volume that treats the "images" of the minister as this one does.... DD

Eadie, John – THE WORDS OF THE APOSTLE PAUL

BARBER – Recommended. c

BROOKMAN – ...this study will be valuable to all who seek to understand Paul's discourses and speeches as contained in the Book of Acts. Eadie clearly demonstrates some of the secrets of the early church's dynamic witness. G

SPURGEON – Designed to give ordinary readers a juster and fuller conception of the doctrine and life-work of the apostle. An able work. Y

Farrar, Frederic W. – THE LIFE AND WORK OF PAUL (2 vols.)

BARBER – ...a priceless asset.... c

SMITH – ...brilliantly written.... v

Godet, Frederick L. – STUDIES IN PAUL'S EPISTLES

BROOKMAN – ...still helpful. It is a remarkable treatise on the Epistles of Paul. This work is a classic and contains many excellent discussions. G

MacDuff, J. R. – THE FOOTSTEPS OF ST. PETER

BARBER – This study...is one of the best and deserves a place in every preacher's library. c

BROOKMAN – This account of the life of Peter [is] one of his finest expositions. ...a practical work.... G

Thomas, W. H. Griffith – THE APOSTLE JOHN: His Life and Writings

BARBER – A lucid study of the Johannine writings that includes a biographical sketch of the apostle and an extensive analysis of the gospel, epistles, and Revelation. c

BROOKMAN – This outline study is loaded with great teaching and preaching material. G

ARTHUR L. FARSTAD – ...a full book, a fine book, and a finely tuned book.... I recommend it heartily to all who wish to learn or teach [this subject]. DD

PACKER – The author's clear, crisp, straightforward style, joined as it is with wisdom, both theological and devotional, gives his expository works classic status. DD, T

WIERSBE – Has all the merits for which the author is noted (see comments under Matthew). Griffith Thomas excels in spiritual depth, practicality and a simplicity of expression that make the most profound truths come alive with excitement. CC, DD

Thomas, W. H. Griffith – THE APOSTLE PETER: His Life and Writings

BARBER – Drawing heavily upon Peter's natural characteristics, the writer shows how these were transformed by the Holy Spirit. A timely, devotional study. B

BROOKMAN – ...excellent for devotional study or homiletical use. These outline studies include each event in Peter's life and every verse or chapter in his Epistles. G

PACKER – The author's clear, crisp, straightforward style, joined as it is with wisdom, both theological and devotional, gives his expository works classic status. DD, T

JOHN F. WALVOORD – ...will provide much insight into the noble character of the Apostle Peter...a great work. DD

WIERSBE – ...a good survey of his life that...often [shows] the interesting relationships that exist between Peter in life and his Letters. Griffith Thomas excels in spiritual depth, practicality, and a simplicity of expression that make the most profound truths come alive with excitement. BB, DD

ROMANS

Godet, Frederic L. – COMMENTARY ON ROMANS

ALLISON – ...this commentary on Romans still holds real historical interest. A

BARBER – This exhaustive and technical commentary provides an excellent treatment of the argument of the epistle. The author surveys the varying theories, refutes theological liberals who differ with him on important points of doctrine, and adequately defends his views. A valuable addition to a pastor's library. B, C

BROOKMAN – ...exegetical and theological. A true classic. G

MASTERS – ...a great commentary on the Greek text of Romans.... P

WIERSBE – ...a classic commentary. BB

Haldane, Robert – COMMENTARY ON ROMANS

BARBER – ...has enjoyed a widespread ministry since its first appearance. Brought about a genuine movement of the Spirit.... B

SPURGEON – Dr. Chalmers styled this "a well-built commentary," and strongly recommended it to students of theology. In his "Sabbath Readings" he writes: "I am reading Haldane's *Exposition of the Epistle to the Romans*, and find it solid and congenial food." Y

Laurin, Roy L. – ROMANS: Where Life Begins

BILLY GRAHAM – I have read every book [Dr. Laurin] has ever written.... Many of the thoughts which I use in my preaching have come from [him]. DD

Luther, Martin – COMMENTARY ON ROMANS

BARBER – ...this significant commentary deserves repeated consultation. C

DONALD GREY BARNHOUSE – The fact that Wesley was saved through the instrumentality of Luther's *Romans* gives us sufficient warrant to maintain this old work in modern form. Beyond question, Luther's *Romans* is one of the great books of Christian history and well deserves the devotional reading by believers. DD

CHILDS – ...Luther's robust and profound commentaries offer an inexhaustible resource for the proclamation of the gospel. H

MASTERS – A great classic. Perhaps every preacher should have at least this commentary by Luther. He loved this epistle, and his unique and distinctive style is most effective here. P

DUKE McCALL – ...obviously a "must" for every preacher's library. DD

J. THEODORE MUELLER – Luther's *Romans* deserves general study, not only because of its vast devotional material, but also because of its clear and sharp emphasis on salvation by grace through faith in Christ. Fraught with profound thoughts, it witnesses everywhere to the sincere piety of the great Reformer. DD

JOHN WESLEY – In the evening I went very unwillingly to a society in Aldersgate Street, where one was reading Luther's Preface to the *Epistle to the Romans*. About a quarter before nine, while he was describing the change which God works in the heart through faith in Christ, I felt my heart strangely warmed. I felt I did trust Christ, Christ alone, for my salvation; and an assurance was given me that He had taken my sins away, even mine, and saved me from the law of sin and death. DD

Moule, H. C. G. – THE EPISTLE TO THE ROMANS

BARBER – One of the finest and most helpful expositions available today. Deeply devotional, based upon a very careful exegesis of the text, and abounding in practical truths. Should be read often and studied in a spirit of true devotion. B, C

CUSTER – Probably the finest, most helpful exposition of Romans in print. He is intensely devotional but writes with real scholarship and insight. His sympathy with the thought and phraseology of Paul is remarkable...combine[s] real scholarship with devotional warmth. I

MASTERS – He frequently says in a sentence what others say in several paragraphs. The tone is warm throughout and there is good application. P

SMITH – Moule was a perfect combination of a great scholar and a great saint, which, incidently, is a rare combination to come upon. Dr. Griffith Thomas, some years ago, said of this work: "It is no exaggeration to say that for a combination of profound scholarship and equally profound spirituality, this book on Romans is unequalled, and if anyone can only afford to buy one book on this epistle, let him by all means obtain this one." W

TENNEY (as quoted by Merchant) – A most valuable commentary. R, AA

Olshausen, Hermann – STUDIES IN THE EPISTLE TO THE ROMANS

BARBER – ...may still be read with profit. C

Plumer, William S. – COMMENTARY ON ROMANS

BARBER – Contains brief extracts from other commentators together with Plumer's own analysis of the text. C

MASTERS – ...he collects material from everyone else so his work reflects all the great divines up to that time. He includes considerable additional information about the Apostle Paul. Plumer's commentary is easily the best on Romans in terms of suggestion to preachers for it is packed with practical application.... Every chapter is concluded with long strings of numbered doctrinal and practical remarks. Truly, this is a "preachers" commentary. Q

Pridham, Arthur – NOTES ON ROMANS
SPURGEON – Sound and gracious, but somewhat dull. Y

Robinson, Thomas – STUDIES IN ROMANS
SPURGEON – A good book in a good style. Worth any amount to preachers. Y
MASTERS – ...a word-by-word commentary which concentrates into terse notes the views of all leading commentators and supplements them with numerous applications, ideas and "leads" to stir the thinking of preachers.... The sheer quantity of information, doctrinal observation and spiritual suggestion against individual words would fill five or six volumes if written up in a more formal style. I have frequently used and proved this...volume over twenty years and warmly recommend it as a great aid to preachers. A wonderful commentary, highly recommended. DD, P, Q

Scroggie, W. Graham – SALVATION AND BEHAVIOR (Romans 1—8; 12—15)
BARBER – Brief devotional studies. Recommended. C
WIERSBE – Valuable.... How that man could preach and teach the Word of God! DD

FIRST AND SECOND CORINTHIANS

Brown, John – THE RESURRECTION OF LIFE: 1 Corinthians 15
BARBER – A rich, full, expository treatment that includes a lengthy essay on our Lord's resurrection. B
BROOKMAN – ...a thorough, expository, and practical exposition.... In addition, it contains some helpful footnotes. G

Edwards, Thomas C. – FIRST CORINTHIANS
BARBER – One of the truly great commentaries on the Greek text. Of inestimable value. Remains one of the best discussions extant. This work is truly meritorious and deserves a place...in the library of every pastor's library. B, C
BROOKMAN – ...a rich, verse-by-verse, conservative exposition. G

Godet, Frederic L. – COMMENTARY ON FIRST CORINTHIANS
ALLISON – ...restores a treasure to the hands of modern Bible students. ...he offers some of the best background information on the cultural and moral climate of Corinth. A

BARBER – Scholarly, exegetical comments on the text and theme of the epistle make this work one of the outstanding treatments of all time. B
BROOKMAN – Godet's commentary on First Corinthians is one of the best in print today. A careful reading of this exegetical work will pay rich dividends. G
MASTERS – ...Godet was best known for his works on Luke and this epistle.... Full of exegetical help, very technical, yet endowed with practical comment. P

Laurin, Roy L. – FIRST CORINTHIANS: Where Life Matures
BILLY GRAHAM – I have read every book [Dr. Laurin] has ever written.... Many of the thoughts which I use in my preaching have come from [him]. DD

Laurin, Roy L. – SECOND CORINTHIANS: Where Life Endures
BARBER – With genuine devotional warmth, Laurin explains how life endures and matures in accordance with the plans and purposes of God. C
BILLY GRAHAM – I have read every book [Dr. Laurin] has ever written.... Many of the thoughts which I use in my preaching have come from [him]. DD

Olshausen, Hermann – FIRST AND SECOND CORINTHIANS
BARBER – Said W. Lindsay Alexander, "Highly esteemed for his happy combinations of grammatico-historical exegesis, with spiritual insight into the meaning of the sacred writings." B
PHILIP SCHAFF (as quoted by Barber) – Pays careful attention to the theological exposition.... C

Scroggie, W. Graham – THE LOVE LIFE: A Study of 1 Corinthians 13
BARBER – A valuable, devotional work. B
WIERSBE – Valuable. How that man could preach and teach the Word of God! DD

GALATIANS

Luther, Martin – COMMENTARY ON GALATIANS
ALLISON – ...this commentary gives us an intimate view of the Bible study that shaped Luther's life-work. A
JOHN BUNYAN – I do prefer this book...excepting the whole Bible, before all books I have ever seen. DD
CHILDS – ...Luther's robust and profound commentaries offer an inexhaustible resource for the proclamation of the gospel. H
MASTERS – A fine reprint of this classic. P
SPURGEON – This is a great historic work, and is beyond criticism, on account of its great usefulness. As a commentary, its accuracy might be questioned; but for emphatic utterances and clear statements of the great doctrine of the epistle it remains altogether by itself, and must be judged per se. Y

EPHESIANS

Moule, H. C. G. – STUDIES IN EPHESIANS
ALLISON – Here is a good devotional commentary. A
BARBER – A devotional masterpiece full of comfort and exhortation. B
BROOKMAN – ...valuable for Bible students today. G
CUSTER – A warmly devotional exposition. I
MASTER – A much more devotional work...a useful companion.... P
SUGDEN – ...anything [Moule] writes will bless you. Z
TENNEY (as quoted by Merchant) – [A] profound commentary. R, AA
WIERSBE – ...a standard commentary [on this book]. ...helpful in the
Greek, very devotional and very practical. BB, DD

Powell, Ivor – THE EXCITING EPISTLE TO THE EPHESIANS
WIERSBE – Don't overlook [this] fine book. It is filled with treasures of
sermon ideas and spiritual truths to help you in your ministry. DD

Robinson, J. Armitage – COMMENTARY ON EPHESIANS
BARBER – ...one of the finest exegetical treatments to be found anywhere.
The writer's paraphrase of the Greek text is particularly valuable.... By
all means obtain it. B, C
BRANSON – Helpful, with history, exegesis, and theology. F
MARTIN – Students of Greek will find [this] edition indispensable.... O
MOO – ...one of those older commentaries which is perennially useful. The
author's viewpoint, arguments and exegetical conclusions are always
worth weighing. S
TENNEY (as quoted by Merchant) – One of the most useful works on
Ephesians. R, AA

Westcott, Brooke Foss – EPISTLE TO THE EPHESIANS
BARBER – A widely acclaimed work. Deserving of the same attention given
his other works. B, C
BROOKMAN – For those who want to do some serious exegetical study on
Ephesians, Westcott's commentary is a must. G
CUSTER – A...very valuable study. I

PHILIPPIANS

Hutchinson, John – AN EXPOSITION OF PHILIPPIANS
BARBER – ...traces with care the unfolding of Paul's thought and applies
the principles that are laid bare to the needs of believers. This is an
excellent volume, perspicuous and practical. C

Laurin, Roy L. – PHILIPPIANS: Where Life Advances
BILLY GRAHAM – I have read every book [Dr. Laurin] has ever written....
Many of the thoughts which I use in my preaching have come from [him].
DD

Meyer, F. B. – DEVOTIONAL COMMENTARY ON PHILIP-PIANS

BARBER – Textual messages, devotional and edifying. **B**
BROOKMAN – This verse-by-verse devotional commentary is inspirational and challenging. It is a series of textual sermons that exhibit a combination of thorough scholarship and practical application. **G**
MASTERS – Full of application.... **P**
WIERSBE – ...a helpful study. **BB**

Moule, H. C. G. – STUDIES IN PHILIPPIANS

BARBER – A beautifully written, deeply devotional treatment expounding the affectionate character of this epistle and relating its message to the lives of believers. **B**
SUGDEN – ...anything [Moule] writes will bless you. **Z**
TENNEY (as quoted by Merchant) – Precipitates the beauty and light of the Scriptures. **R, AA**
WIERSBE – ...a helpful study. ...very devotional and very practical. **BB, DD**

Vaughan, Charles John – EPISTLE TO THE PHILIPPIANS

BARBER – Twenty-one messages based upon a detailed exegesis of the text and containing some valuable thoughts. Excellent. **B, C**
BROOKMAN – Vaughn's expository messages on this epistle are considered classic. Ministers will welcome this valuable reprint for help in preparing a series of sermons on the Book of Philippians. **G**
SPURGEON – Deservedly esteemed. Dr. Vaughan gives a literal translation of his text from the original Greek, and then expounds it, believing it, as he says, "to be the duty of every Christian teacher to assist his congregation in drinking, not of the stream only, but at the spring of revealed truth." **Y**

COLOSSIANS AND PHILEMON

Cox, Samuel & Drysdale, A. H. – THE EPISTLE TO PHILEMON (2 vols. in one)

BROOKMAN – ...good examples of Bible exposition. The comments in these books are extremely helpful. **G**

Eadie, John – COLOSSIANS

BARBER – First published over a century ago, this rich and inspiring exposition is one that preachers who have a knowledge of Greek will appreciate for its insights and detailed explanations. **B**
BROOKMAN – This work is valuable for its exposition and its study of the original text. A helpful, classic reprint. **G**
CUSTER – A very thorough expositon of the Greek text. **I**
WIERSBE – ...a standard commentary. **BB**

Laurin, Roy L. – COLOSSIANS: Where Life Is Established

BILLY GRAHAM – I have read every book [Dr. Laurin] has ever written.... Many of the thoughts which I use in my preaching have come from [him]. **DD**

Moule, H. C. G. – STUDIES IN COLOSSIANS AND PHILEMON

ALLISON – Evangelical readers will prefer this volume. A

BARBER – Moule was known for his saintliness and evangelical fervor. These studies bear testimony to his ability as an expositor. They deal adequately with the text and deftly apply the message of these epistles. One of the most reverent and delightful of expositions extant. By all means buy it. B, C

BROOKMAN – Moule's commentary on the English text. ...a valuable, practical exposition. G

CUSTER – Warmly devotional exposition. I

MASTERS – A very useful "second commentary" with devotional application. P

SUGDEN – ...anything [Moule] writes will bless you. Z

TENNEY (as quoted by Merchant) – [A] rewarding and glowing commentary. R, AA

WIERSBE – ...a deeply devotional commentary based on a profound knowledge of the Greek text. BB, DD

Nicholson, William – COLOSSIANS: Oneness With Christ

BARBER – ...combines outstanding scholarship with deeply devotional spirit. G

BROOKMAN – Here are some valuable expository lectures. ...a combination of outstanding scholarship and an excellent devotional tone. Highly regarded by Dr. Wilbur M. Smith. G

CUSTER – Rich devotional expositions...combine[s] real scholarship with devotional warmth. I

JAMES M. GRAY – The feast of my own soul in the perusal of [this book] I am impatient to share with as large a constituency of my fellow-brethren as I can possibly reach, for such teaching, as to its deep insight into spiritual things, its rigor of appeal, its heavenly unction, its grace of manner and beauty of diction, is not commonly met with in this day or any other day. DD

SMITH – ...in no other book in our language are there such wonderful expositions on certain passages in this Epistle. ...these lectures came from the heart and mind of an intellectual and spiritual giant; they will communicate power and inspiration to every one who carefully, expectantly reads them. W

Scroggie, W. Graham – STUDIES IN PHILEMON

BARBER – A rewarding and in-depth study. One of the best ever produced on this epistle...remains one of the best ever written on...Philemon. B, C

BROOKMAN – A worthy devotional and expositional study on Philemon by a gifted writer. This is a rewarding in-depth study of a very neglected book of the Bible. Conservative. G

WIERSBE – Valuable...How that man could preach and teach the Word of God! DD

Thomas, W. H. Griffith – STUDIES IN COLOSSIANS AND PHILEMON

CUSTER – Devotional expositions. I

PACKER – The author's clear, crisp, straightforward style, joined as it is with wisdom, both theological and devotional, gives his expository works classic status. DD, T

WIERSBE – [From] one of the spiritual giants of his day [comes] one of the best expositions available, not only for the advanced student, but also for the average believer who wants to gain a working knowledge of [these] important epistles.... Deeply spiritual and very practical. Griffith Thomas excels in spiritual depth, practicality and a simplicity of expression that make the most profound truths come alive with excitement. BB, DD

THESSALONIAN EPISTLES

Marsh, F. E. – PRACTICAL TRUTHS FROM FIRST THESSALONIANS

SUGDEN – ...a wealth of enrichment for our spiritual lives. I am personally grateful that this volume...has been made available.... DD, Z

Milligan, George – PAUL'S EPISTLES TO THE THESSALONIANS

BARBER – A brilliantly written, critical study that must of necessity take second place to more recent works. However, it is worth consulting. Amillennial. B, C

BROOKMAN – ...an outstanding New Testament writer. This exegetical work includes a good summary on the person of the Antichrist. G

CUSTER – The best commentary on the Greek text. I

THE PASTORAL EPISTLES

Fairbairn, Patrick – THE PASTORAL EPISTLES

BARBER – ...this old standard treatment shows how pastors may use the Greek text to aid their exposition. A fine work in spite of its age. B

BROOKMAN – Fairbairn writes with a pastor's heart. This classic exposition will always be a helpful guide to the Pastoral Epistles. ...conservative. G

CUSTER – A thorough exposition. I

MASTERS – ...an outstanding work.... The notes and comments here stand in a class of their own. P

SPURGEON – What with a good translation, full defense of the apostolic authorship of the Epistles, fruitful comments, and profitable dissertations, this volume is about as complete a guide to the smaller epistles as one could desire. Y

Liddon, H. P. – THE FIRST EPISTLE TO TIMOTHY

BARBER – A competent treatment based upon a grammatical analysis of the Greek text. Excellent. Serves as a model of good expository preparation. B

BROOKMAN – Even though it is based on the Greek text, a minister without a knowledge of the original language can still profit from this book. G

Moule, H. C. G. – STUDIES IN SECOND TIMOTHY

BARBER – A delightful devotional commentary. C

BROOKMAN – ...a devotional classic worth consulting. G

WIERSBE – A fine [commentary]...helpful in the Greek, very devotional and very practical. DD

SUGDEN – ...anything [Moule] writes will bless you. Z

Rowland, Alfred – STUDIES IN FIRST TIMOTHY

THE ENGLISH CHURCHMAN (as quoted by Barber) – We may say it is a work of no ordinary value, and Christians will find it a rich feast. It is needless, of course, to say that [this study] is a work of a scholar; it is also the work of a whole-hearted believer and its design was intended for the use of all who love the Lord in simplicity and truth. C

Stock, Eugene – PRACTICAL TRUTHS FROM THE PAS-TORAL EPISTLES

SMITH – ...every pastor ought to study these fifty chapters carefully. W

WIERSBE – No book on pastoral theology, based on the Pastoral Epistles, contains more practical application, and is more of a delight to read. DD

Taylor, Thomas – AN EXPOSITION OF TITUS

BARBER – A Puritan commentary that readily explores the inner reality of Paul's letter to his youthful associate. C

BROOKMAN – ...extensive...it will still be helpful to the Bible student and minister. G

SPURGEON – The title page calls Thomas Taylor "a famous and most elaborate divine." He was a preacher at Paul's Cross during the reigns of Elizabeth and James I and a voluminous writer. This commentary will well repay the reader. Y

HEBREWS

Anderson, Sir Robert – TYPES IN HEBREWS

BARBER – A rewarding study that evangelical Christians can ill afford to neglect. C

Bruce, A. B. – THE EPISTLE TO THE HEBREWS

BARBER – An exhaustive interpretation of the epistle based on the premise that it is a formal defense of the Christian faith. Preachers will find this a most helpful exposition. B, C

Bullinger, E. W. – GREAT CLOUD OF WITNESSES IN HEBREWS 11

BARBER – An extensive expository treatment frequently provides discerning explanations of Greek words and their origin. Preachers will find these studies helpful. B

BROOKMAN – A complete exposition of Hebrews chapter 11 dealing with the heroes of the faith. ...is still very helpful. G

WIERSBE – Bullinger was a great student of the Word of God...a must for your library. I know of no other book on Hebrews 11 in the English language that contains more solid spiritual teaching and practical truth. **DD**

Edwards, Thomas C. – THE EPISTLE TO THE HEBREWS
BARBER – An excellent, easy-to-follow discussion of the purpose of the epistle. Serves to give laypeople as well as those looking for a theological development of a central theme exactly what they need. **B, C**
BROOKMAN – [Edwards] blends careful exposition and application. **G**

Moule, H. C. G. – STUDIES IN HEBREWS
WIERSBE – A fine [commentary]...helpful in the Greek, very devotional and very practical. **DD**
SUGDEN – ...anything [Moule] writes will bless you. **Z**

Owen, John – HEBREWS (7 vols. condensed into one)
ALLISON – Thomas Chalmers called this commentary "a work of gigantic strength as well as gigantic size." **A**
LOCKYER – ...a mine of truth. The most outstanding of Owen's works. **DD, N**
MASTERS – The major contribution on Hebrews.... Though hard to believe, the greatly shortened version retains all the rich argument and sense of the expository parts of the 7-volume original work. With such a paperback available, it simply makes no sense for preachers NOT to have Owen on Hebrews. **P**
SMITH – The most exhaustive work ever written on Hebrews is *The Exposition of the Epistle to the Hebrews*, by that great Puritan divine, John Owen.... **DD**

Saphir, Adolph – EPISTLE TO THE HEBREWS
BARBER – Expository studies by a converted Jew. **C**
CUSTER – Fervent, warmhearted messages on Hebrews by a converted Jew. **I**
LOCKYER – Without doubt, Saphir's most satisfying *Epistle to the Hebrews* is a masterpiece.... We most heartily commend this...to all Bible lovers. **DD, N**
SMITH – ...one of the finest expository works in our language, exceptionally rich from a devotional standpoint, and should stand on the shelves of every Bible student's library. **W**
SPURGEON – Mr. Saphir has always something to say worthy of the attention of spiritual minds. His mind finds a track of its own, but he is never speculative. We always enjoy his remarks, though he is not specially terse or brilliant. **Y**
WIERSBE – ...excellent. **DD**

JAMES

Johnstone, Robert – LECTURES ON JAMES
ALLISON – It is a good introduction to James for a beginning Bible student. **A**

BARBER – One of the few works of its kind. Makes rich, rewarding reading. Suitable for both pastor and informed layperson. A must for the expository preacher. B, C

BROOKMAN – Johnstone brings together a balanced exposition, both practical and exegetical, on this important epistle. Very helpful.... G

CUSTER – A strong exposition. I

MASTERS – ...derived from sermons and is very readable and strongly applied.... A most valuable commentary. Q

SPURGEON – A very useful, scholarly, and readable book. Y

WIERSBE – I have enjoyed using [this] work. BB

Stier, Rudolf E. – COMMENTARY ON JAMES

BARBER – ...of value to preachers as well as laypeople. C

BROOKMAN – ...helpful. ...a series of expository messages on the Epistle of James. G

SPURGEON – No one can be expected to receive all that Stier has to say, but he must be dull indeed who can not learn much from him. Read with care; he is a great instructor. Y

FIRST AND SECOND PETER

Leighton, Robert – COMMENTARY ON FIRST PETER

ALLISON – This classic commentary on 1 Peter deserves notice from every reviewer.... Leighton's comments are largely devotional and practical. A

BARBER – One of the best expository works on 1 Peter. Leighton provides his reader with the results of his vast learning without ostentation: his theology is accurate and his eloquence unmatched. Devotional. B

BROOKMAN – This valuable work is unparalleled.... Leighton gives the reader a balance of thorough exposition with a warm devotional application. G

MASTERS – No commentary has ever been praised as highly as this for its spirit of reverence and fervor. It was of Leighton's works that Dr. Mills wrote the oft-quoted lines, "There is a spirit in them I never met with in any other human writings, nor can I read many lines in them without being moved." Kregel is to be commended for this fine edition of "the immortal work" of Archbishop Leighton (Schaff). P

SPURGEON – We need scarcely commend this truly heavenly work. It is a favorite with all spiritual men. Y

WIERSBE – A classic commentary that ought to be in every library. Not only does he give us good explanatory material, but he also gives us wonderful spiritual food. This book has been a great help to me personally in my Bible study. DD

Luther, Martin – COMMENTARY ON FIRST AND SECOND PETER AND JUDE

BARBER – These studies challenge the spiritual laxity of our times and call us back to the principles that led to the Reformation. C

CHILDS – ...Luther's robust and profound commentaries offer an inexhaustible resource for the proclamation of the gospel. H

MASTERS – Simple exposition, very practical; a pastor's heart evident in meaningful communication with his people. Q
SPURGEON – In Luther's racy style. One of his best productions. Copies are scarce as white elephants... Y

EPISTLES OF JOHN

Candlish, Robert – FIRST EPISTLE OF JOHN
BARBER – Expository messages presenting a moving portrait of Christ and the believer's relationship to Him. A true classic. B, C
BROOKMAN – ...the classic work on the First Epistle of John. It is clear, concise and practical. G
CUSTER – An exhaustive exposition of surprising fervency. ...combine[s] real scholarship with devotional warmth. I
MASTERS – Without a doubt the best available work on First John. This volume towers above the others.... This "commentary" is actually a series of 46 brilliant lectures. They are highly readable and literally full of experimental material. This is an essential commentary for preachers and teachers. Q
SMITH – ...I have been frequently amazed to find how few ministers, even those who have been preaching for some years, have ever heard of this work.... These lectures go to the very depths of the truths set forth in this precious, inexhaustible, and not always easily understoood Epistle of the Beloved Apostle. Some pages here seem to be almost perfect. The book will search one's heart, it will lift him up into new heights, where he will see with greater clearness than ever before some of the precious privileges and obligations of the child of God. It is a work to turn to frequently for inspiration and strength.... My own opinion is that the richest exposition of the First Epistle of John is still that series of lectures [of] the *First Epistle of John*. ...this volume became very scarce in the early part of our century, but fortunately it has since then been reprinted. W, X
SPURGEON – We set great store by these lectures. A man hardly needs anything beyond Candlish. He is devout, candid, prudent, and forcible. Y
WIERSBE – If you have not read Candlish's remarkable exposition on 1 John, by all means do—prayerfully. CC

Laurin, Roy L. – FIRST JOHN: Life at Its Best
BILLY GRAHAM – I have read every book [Dr. Laurin] has ever written.... Many of the thoughts which I use in my preaching have come from [him]. DD

Lias, John J. – THE FIRST EPISTLE OF JOHN
BARBER – A conservative and scholarly exposition defending the genuineness of the epistle and containing some valuable exegetical insights. One of the finest exegetical and expository works for preachers. B, C

JUDE

Manton, Thomas – COMMENTARY ON JUDE
BARBER – ...very extensive, as can be seen from the fact that this exposition covers 375 pages. B

BROOKMAN – Manton's work on Jude is a classic. G
CUSTER – An exhaustive...exposition. I
MASTERS – ...[a] full and rewarding Puritan commentary.... P
SPURGEON – Manton's work is most commendable. Y

REVELATION

Bullinger, E. W. – COMMENTARY ON REVELATION
BARBER – ...offers a uniquely different interpretation of the Apocalypse. C

Hendley, Jesse – THE FIFTH HORSEMAN OF THE APOCALYPSE
JERRY VINES – ...one of the finest Bible scholars, teachers, and evangelists of our day. These messages...are storehouses of Bible information. DD

Scott, Walter – EXPOSITION OF THE REVELATION OF JESUS CHRIST
BARBER – ...gives evidence of intensive research, careful exposition, and an awareness of God's plan for the future. Strongly typological. B
SMITH – If I were asked what one volume I would suggest for the layreader for an understanding of the Book of Revelation, I would recommend the work by Walter Scott.... DD
WIERSBE – ...among the commentaries I keep nearby.... A classic treatment of the English text. BB, DD

Seiss, Joseph A. – THE APOCALYPSE: Exposition of the Book of the Revelation
BARBER – An exhaustive, premillennial exposition by a well-known Lutheran writer of the past century. B
CUSTER – Powerful messages.... I
SMITH – ...the most famous expository work on Revelation in our language, and no minister intending to preach an extended series of sermons from the Book of Revelation can afford to be without it. ...sane, suggestive, reverent, and, on the whole, dependable. There is no man in the English world today, as far as we know,...who is equipped both with a knowledge of the Word and a gift of oratory, to deliver such a series of lectures as these which are found in these some five hundred pages. U
WIERSBE – ...a helpful commentary. BB

Swete, H. B. – COMMENTARY ON REVELATION
BARBER – A masterful exposition of the Greek text. Amillennial. B
CUSTER – Strong analysis of the Greek text. I
MARTIN – ...well regarded.... N
MASTER – A classic exposition (amillennial) of the Greek text.... Technical and suited to students of New Testament Greek. O
SMITH – On the Greek text of Revelation, there is nothing equal to [Swete]. His knowledge of the meaning of the Greek words is unparalleled among interpreters of his day. He knows how to compress much in a small place...one of the greatest that will ever be written.... DD, V

Tatford, Frederick A. – THE REVELATION
BARBER – This...work, ably correlates the writings of Moses, Balaam, Isaiah, Jeremiah, Ezekiel, and other biblical writers with the text of the Book of Revelation. The result is an amazing synthesis of eschatological thought, and one of the finest expositions for laypeople ever written. c
BROOKMAN – A clear, sound, premillennial introduction to the events of the Book of Revelation. G

Tucker, W. Leon – STUDIES IN REVELATION
FAIR – ...one of the most well-structured commentaries...on Revelation that has ever been published.... Prayerfully and carefully written...contains a goldmine of handy and rare information.... DD, K

SECTION IV
OTHER SUBJECTS

BAPTISM

Carson, Alexander – BAPTISM
BARBER – A full discussion on the proper subjects of baptism, as well as a vigorous plea for the immersion of believers…a welcome and important contribution…. B, C
GRIER – …remains one of the strongest and ablest statements…. L

BIBLE CHARACTERS

Blaikie, William G. – HEROES OF ISRAEL
BARBER – A valuable acquisition. C
BROOKMAN – This volume covers the Bible characters mentioned in the Book of Genesis and the narrative parts of Exodus and Numbers. The graphic pen-portraits contained within this work will be welcomed by ministers preaching on Bible characters. G

Edersheim, Alfred – PRACTICAL TRUTHS FROM ELISHA
BARBER – …this book is worthy of diligent reading. C
BROOKMAN – A classic…giving a complete scriptural account of the life and work of the prophet Elisha, featuring thorough research, solid exposition and spiritual application. G
SPURGEON – This author is always interesting, showing close acquaintance with Jewish customs, and knowing how to utilize his information. Y
WIERSBE – [Contains] rich veins of gold that others have ignored or neglected. I rejoice that [this] classic is available again for people who are serious about Bible study. …you [will] find insights from the Scriptures that can enrich your life and ministry…. DD

Hamilton, James – MOSES, THE MAN OF GOD
BARBER – …this work deserves a place on the bookshelf of every pastor. B
BROOKMAN – This delightful handling of the life of Moses will enlighten

any minister or Bible student. This valuable classic reprint will prove invaluable to the minister's library. G

SPURGEON – Beautiful as a poem, like everything which fell from Dr. Hamilton's pen. It would be impossible to study it without profit. Y

(ALSO ON MOSES, SEE MEYER:
A DEVOTIONAL COMMENTARY ON EXODUS
UNDER *EXODUS* ABOVE)

Kirk, Thomas – THE LIFE OF JOSEPH

BARBER – Of utmost value for the pastor who preaches on Bible characters...a work that preachers will want to refer to again and again. B, C

BROOKMAN – This is an excellent treatment of the great life of Joseph. Kirk shows diligent research, painstaking detail and considerable insight in these studies. The homiletical helps are abundant in this volume. G

MacDuff, John R. – ELIJAH, THE PROPHET OF FIRE

BROOKMAN – ...MacDuff's books are still eagerly sought after today. This classic reprint on the life of Elijah is a must for ministers desiring to preach on this Bible character. G

Matheson, George – Bible Portraits Series
PORTRAITS OF BIBLE WOMEN
PORTRAITS OF BIBLE MEN (1st series)
PORTRAITS OF BIBLE MEN (2nd series)
PORTRAITS OF BIBLE MEN (3rd series)

WIERSBE – In this series...this...blind scholar-preacher saw more than most of us who see! No evangelical writer, including the great Alexander Whyte, surpasses Matheson in...Bible biography. BB, DD

Vander Velde, Frances – WOMEN OF THE BIBLE

BARBER – ...this volume has stood the test of time. Thirty-one stimulating, imaginative, and devotional studies of women of the Old and New Testaments. Ideal material for discussion groups. Should be consulted when teaching or preaching on the women of the Bible. B, C

Whyte, Alexander – BIBLE CHARACTERS FROM THE NEW TESTAMENT (2 volumes)

ALLISON – Whyte has a colorful way of recreating Bible characters. Though he did not have access to the discoveries of archaeologist in this century, Whyte did have a brilliant imagination and a marvelous gift for narrative writing. This book is a joy to read. A

BARBER – An epochal work that increases in value the more it is used. B

BROOKMAN – This is one of the best books on Bible characters to be found anywhere. G

GRIER – Whyte has much that is striking and illuminating.... L

BEN HADEN – Through the Scriptures I first met the characters of the Bible. But only through Alexander Whyte have I come to know them. Next to the Bible I find *Bible Characters* by Alexander Whyte the greatest help in understanding the men and women in God's Word. ...My life is richer for reading this man. *Bible Characters* is biography at its best. DD

DAVID R. MAINS – In his *Bible Characters*, Whyte's imaginative skills amaze and delight. Time and again, you are convinced he must have known these people personally, and if not these specific men and women, then certainly he understood human nature intimately well. DD

SMITH – For the study of Bible biographies, you should secure...a marvelous series by Alexander Whyte, one of the great preachers in the world of a generation ago.... No one has analyzed these characters so vividly and penetrating as Whyte. Every page is edifying and suggestive. ...if I can stir up a few of my younger friends...to gather to themselves everything that Whyte has ever written which they can secure...and I know that they in turn were being daily refreshed. ...there is nothing to compare with it in the English language, and I doubt if there is in any language. Some of these chapters will send one weeping to one's knees; others will make one shudder; others will drive one into the pulpit to preach with new power, new conviction, and new fervor. ...By all means lay hold of this set, and do not let it collect dust, but read the pages, and let them mold, and master and mature you. Oh, for more men like Whyte today! U, V, W

WIERSBE – *Bible Characters* is a collection of the great preacher's messages which focus on one key aspect of the subject's personality and use that to illumine his life. BB

BIBLE STUDY

Bullinger, E. W. – NUMBER IN SCRIPTURE

WIERSBE – I find myself referring to this work. One need not agree with all of Bullinger's views to benefit from his work. DD

SUGDEN – ...a great book. Z

Burton, Ernest DeWitt – SYNTAX OF THE MOODS AND TENSES IN NEW TESTAMENT GREEK

BARBER – ...is still of inestimable value to students of Greek and contains one of the best treatments on the translation of direct and indirect discourse available. B, C

DANKER – ...clamors for attention. ...still holds the field as a lucid presentation of an often elusive subject. J

Spurgeon, Charles Haddon – COMMENTING AND COMMENTARIES: A Reference Guide to Book Buying (Newly Updated Edition)

BARBER – ...An extensive catalog of Bible commentaries and other expository works. Of particular value for its listing of works from the time of the Reformation to the middle of the nineteenth century. Emphasis is placed on those works making relevant application of truth to life. B, C

CHILDS – ...I consider Charles H. Spurgeon's *Commenting and Commen-*

taries a real classic...he...had much skill and common sense in discerning the enduring qualities of excellence. H

SMITH – Every minister ought to have in his library Charles H. Spurgeon's famous, helpful and fascinating work, *Commenting and Commentaries.* ...a remarkable piece of work for anyone preaching to such great audiences as Spurgeon, whose sermons were published every week, and who continued for years to edit the *Sword and Trowel.* ...the most widely used bibliography of commentaries on the Scriptures.... There are over [1,400] volumes listed in this unique annotated bibliography. U, W

Wilson, William – NEW WILSON'S OLD TESTAMENT WORD STUDIES (New edition keyed to *Strong's Concordance* and *The Theological Wordbook of the Old Testament*)

BROOKMAN – ...a valuable tool for both the Hebrew student and those who do not have a working knowledge of the language, offering an aid for the understanding of word meanings and help in understanding difficult passages. It is both an exhaustive dictionary and a concordance in that significant English words are translated from more than one original Hebrew word have a listing of major Scripture references coded to each original Hebrew word used. The book is arranged in English alphabetical order, giving every Hebrew word its literal English meaning. G

WIERSBE – One of the most helpful Hebrew concordances that I have. It's a wonderful shortcut to help me in getting to those Hebrew words. This new edition is one hundred times more useful than it was before. DD

SUGDEN – ...the greatest book that has been published recently.... Z

BIBLIOLOGY

Gaussen, Louis – DIVINE INSPIRATION OF THE BIBLE

BARBER – A classic defense of the conservative view and authority of the Scriptures. Contains a valuable subject index. B

SMITH – ...still probably the most important treatment of the subject of inspiration to appear in modern times.... It is solid matter, difficult to read, but distinctly worth all the mental labor its study will demand. U

Saphir, Adolph – DIVINE UNITY OF SCRIPTURE

BARBER – ...readers of Scripture will benefit greatly from this discussion. C

SMITH – ...a classic work. V

CHRISTOLOGY
See also "LIFE OF JESUS CHRIST"

Anderson, Sir Robert – THE LORD FROM HEAVEN

BARBER – A study of the deity of Christ, with particular emphasis on His messiahship and His role as "King of kings and Lord of lords".... A refreshing study of Christ's deity.... B, C

Andrews, Samuel J. & Gifford, Edwin Hamilton – THE IN-CARNATION OF CHRIST (*Man and the Incarnation* and *The Incarnation: Phil. 2:5-11 & Psalm 110*, 2 vols. in one)

BARBER – Indispensable to a minister's library. c

BROOKMAN – An excellent combination of two classic works on the incarnation. This book shows that Jesus Christ is the incarnate Son of God—very God and very man. G

Dalman, Gustaf H. – THE WORDS OF CHRIST

BARBER – A series of studies on a wide variety of themes ranging from a consideration of God's theocracy to the evasive modes post-exilic Jews used in referring to God. Includes Jewish eschatological belief and essays dealing with "Son of Man," "Son of God," "Christ," and the Semitic idea of kingship inherent in the "Son of David." B, c

BROOKMAN – An excellent volume.... G

Delitzsch, Franz & Gloag, Patton J. – THE MESSIANIC PRO-PHECIES OF CHRIST (*The Messianic Prophecies of Christ* and *The Messianic Prophecies*, 2 vols. in one)

BARBER – These books...make available works that were virtually unobtainable. c

Harris, John – THE TEACHING METHODS OF CHRIST

BARBER – ...this work can only be described as indispensable. The pedagogical truths that Harris draws from the pages of the New Testament are deserving of careful study and close emulation. All pastors and teachers should be thoroughly familiar with this book. c

BROOKMAN – This thoroughly written work deals with studies on Christ's teaching methods and the training of His disciples. A carefully written work. G

Horne, Herman Harrell – TEACHING TECHNIQUES OF JESUS: How Jesus Taught

BARBER – Pastors today need to learn from the teaching techniques of Jesus Christ. This book is designed to stimulate such a study and deserves a place on every pastor's desk. B

THE PRARIE OVERCOMER – It's a classic. For Christian leaders it is "must" reading, because it deals with the whole process of how Jesus trained His disciples. DD

Ramsay, William H. – THE EDUCATION OF CHRIST

BARBER – An informative, historical study that makes a unique contribution to our knowledge of the time. B

EDWARD M. BLAIKLOCK – Its pages will serve as an introduction to the man, and his insight into that strong interweaving of place and time, of stage and circumstance, which were part of his [Ramsay's] contribution to ancient studies. They may never be separated again. DD

Thomas, W. H. Griffith – CHRISTIANITY IS CHRIST

BARBER – Centers on the person and work of Christ, vindicates the unique-

ness of His character and mission, establishes the credibility of the gospel records, and deals convincingly with the meaning of and need for His bodily resurrection. A most important volume. **B**
BROOKMAN – ...[a] good older work. **G**

Vine, William E. – THE DIVINE SONSHIP OF CHRIST
BARBER – These studies in Christology draw information from both Testaments and relate the information to the nature of Christ, His work, and the benefits of the believer's union with Him. Stimulating. **C**

CHURCH MINISTRIES

Hiscox, Edward T. – PRINCIPLES AND PRACTICES FOR BAPTIST CHURCHES
BAPTIST BULLETIN – By all means get a copy of this manual. No pastor's library is complete without it. **DD**
BIBLICAL EVANGELIST – This book...has long been considered the classic in its field. We cannot imagine a Baptist pastor's library not containing this book, but if yours does not: *get it!* **DD**
REVIEW AND EXPOSITOR – ...a classic and a valuable resource for understanding Baptist church order, discipline and ministry. **DD**
MASTERS – ...the only handbook of its kind. ...it teems with definitions and is complete with résumé of Baptist history.... Every pastor should have one. **O**

Westing, Harold J. – MULTIPLE CHURCH-STAFF HANDBOOK
BARBER – ...an in-depth, practical, sagacious handbook. ...his material can be applied to churches of all sizes. **C**
DONALD L. BUBNA – ...excellent help for developing a multiple staff. Readers will get handles on goal setting, role clarification, conducting staff meetings and leadership retreats.... Pastors will find this volume very helpful in getting started right with their team. **DD**
KENNETH O. GANGEL – Surpasses all other major texts on multiple church-staff ministry and should become the new standard. **DD**

DEVOTIONAL / CHRISTIAN LIFE

Bonar, Horatius – WHEN GOD'S CHILDREN SUFFER
GRIER – Written primarily for members of God's family under the chastening rod. **L**
GEORGE SWEETING – ... is an important book to help us understand human suffering. **DD**

Bunyan, John – THE PILGRIM'S PROGRESS (Large Print)
BARBER – A vivid allegory describing the experiences of a soul from the time when he is first awakened to his need of Christ until he reaches the heavenly city at the end of his earthly pilgrimage. First published in 1678. **B**

PAUL BECHTEL (as quoted by Merchant) – A book that both children and adults have loved for some three hundred years. Every Christian ought to read this book often. R

BROOKMAN – A classic allegory of the Christian life by an excellent devotional writer. G

CUSTER – The greatest Christian classic, second only to the Bible itself. Spurgeon read it a hundred times; Alexander Whyte preached and later published a famous series of sermons on Bunyan's characters. No preacher should be ignorant of this masterpiece. I

GRIER – [This] masterpiece by Bunyan should be in every home. L

DONALD T. KAUFFMAN – Anyone who tastes of the Pilgrim's experiences…will find here tremendous substance for meditation and clear light for all kinds of situations. DD

WIERSBE – …it stands next to the Bible as an all-time religious best-seller and has been translated into scores of languages.…Read it leisurely, with your heart and mind wide open. Let the book become spiritual medicine to your soul. CC

Fénelon, Francois de Salignac de la Moth – SPIRITUAL LETTERS TO WOMEN

ELISABETH ELLIOT – Fénelon…needs to be recalled in a time of supreme self-seeking, self-expression, self-indulgence and self-analysis. His example of utter submission to authority needs to be studied…. His call to simplicity needs to be heard…. DD

Havergal, Frances Ridley – KEPT FOR THE MASTER'S USE (Large Print)

WILLIAM J. PETERSON – Taking the words of her beloved hymn, "Take my life and let it be," the author shows what they truly mean to every Christian… DD

Henry, Matthew – THE SECRET OF COMMUNION WITH GOD

BARBER – Writes about maintaining unbroken fellowship with the Lord throughout the day. Simple and practical, and based solidly on the Word. B

PAUL BECHTEL (as quoted by Merchant) – The famous Bible commentator writes about the secret of beginning, continuing, and ending each day with God…. It is a guide to help discipline the mind and direct the heart, and should be read to bring spiritual refreshment to many needy hearts. R

BROOKMAN – …a good devotional work. G

MASTERS – …[includes] many valuable pieces of counsel. Q

SHERWOOD WIRT – Matthew Henry was not a theoretician of the devotional life…he took a practical position on the Christian's daily walk with God…. I am honored to commend this treasure from the past to men and women everywhere who are seeking to investigate and understand the "mystery of serious godliness." DD

a' Kempis, Thomas – IMITATION OF CHRIST (Large Print)

BARBER – …first published in 1441.…he explores the nature of spirituality with clarity, and he writes of the beauty of Christ's life with enriching simplicity. B

BECHTEL (as quoted by Merchant) – Issued in thousands of editions and translated into hundreds of languages, no book of devotion has been so widely read as this one since its appearance in 1441. Although a' Kempis tends to be a bit ascetic, he is a profound explorer of the inner life and writes with beautiful simplicity. R

WILLIAM J. PETERSON – Few books have found such universal acceptance.... [It] has become the part of the lives of millions who refer to it constantly for guidance, consolation, spiritual strength and inspiration. DD

Maclaren, Alexander – VICTORY IN FAILURE

WIERSBE – ...MacLaren has left us a wealth of sermonic material that can enrich us for eternity. You will find your own spiritual life challenged and strengthened.... DD

Meyer, F. B. – THE GIFT OF SUFFERING

MERRILL WOMACH – I believe it is one of the greatest books ever written on the subject of "why Christians suffer." DD

Murray, Andrew – ABIDE IN CHRIST (Large Print)

BARBER – A deeply devotional study. B

BROOKMAN – An excellent devotional study from a great writer on the Christian life. G

CUSTER – Warm-hearted meditations on living in fellowship with the Son of God, based on John 15:1-12 and other suitable passages. I

WILLIAM J. PETERSON – ...one of the first books [Andrew Murray] wrote... ....there are 31 short chapters so you can read them one a day for a month. This will give you time to meditate. DD

Newton, John – OUT OF THE DEPTHS

GRIER – 14 autobiographical letters showing God's amazing grace, followed by a further account of Newton's life. Abridged from the original. L

HERBERT LOCKYER – ...this remarkable Christian classic, in its new dress, has come to the kingdom for such as time as this. ...we certainly need a spiritual magnet to draw us up out of the depts of sin, fear, depression and rumors of war; the reissue of Newton's soul-stirring volume provides such a magnet. N, DD

Smith, Wilbur M. – THEREFORE STAND

BARBER – An apologetic for biblical Christianity that was one of the best works available when it first appeared. B

BROOKMAN – This work has never been superseded. It stands among the best in the field of apologetics. Evangelical. G

HAROLD J. OCKENGA – The influence of Dr. Smith's...writings...will go on to benefit young women and men, who wish to proclaim the Lord. Many are the testimonies of those who have been established through his positive teaching. DD

Stalker, James – THE EXAMPLE OF JESUS CHRIST

BROOKMAN – ...an excellent work. G

EVERETT F. HARRISON – Reading Stalker brings both pleasure and profit.

From time to time the reader encounters a compelling observation about Christ that leads him to say to himself, "Why didn't I think of that?" Let those scattered observations serve as stepping stones into the edifice itself that Stalker has built for us. DD

Stalker, James – LIVING THE CHRIST LIFE

MALCOLM CRONK – Stalker reveals insights that are timeless and expresses them in a way to be readily grasped and remembered. ...Such reading is bound to be richly instructive and inspiring. DD

Tileston, Mary W. (comp.) – GREAT SOULS AT PRAYER (Large Print)
DAILY STRENGTH FOR DAILY NEEDS (Large Print)

WILLIAM J. PETERSON – I highly recommend them. And one of the easiest and most enjoyable ways of establishing such a habit is to begin with [these books]. DD

THE GODHEAD

Bickersteth, Edward H. – THE TRINITY

BAPTIST EXAMINER – ...a veritable gold mine of inspiration and information relative to the trinity.... No one could even doubt nor question the teachings of the Scriptures as to the trinity after using this book. DD

BARBER – Deals with the biblical evidence for belief in the one eternal Godhead of the Father, Son and Holy Spirit. An important contribution. B, DD

BROOKMAN – ...it is one of the most valuable treatments ever published on the Trinity. Conservative. G

CHRISTIANITY TODAY – ...should be required reading for all theological students, and would well serve as a refresher course in Christology for pastors.... DD

MASTERS – Bickersteth's unique treatment of the Trinity, complete with proof-texts; parallel column presentation of the persons of the Godhead, and extensive references. There is nothing quite like it. O

WALTER L. WILSON – There is no book like it in our language.... As you read the marvellous unfolding of the personality of these great Three, you will be led to worship God as you never did before. This book is a tonic to the soul. It is the only book...that describes in detail each of the persons of the Trinity. It presents in parallel columns the marvellous deity of each one. This book has no competition. DD

Jukes, Andrew – NAMES OF GOD

BARBER – ...these devotional studies center in the Old Testament...edifying to read. B

MASTERS – The most famous work on the names of God. The significance of Jehovah, El Shaddai, etc., is here brought out as the Divine names of both testaments are expounded. A very wordy book, but the intrepid reader will appreciate the strikingly original thought which Jukes never fails to produce. O

Wood, Nathan R. – THE TRINITY IN THE UNIVERSE
G. CAMPBELL MORGAN – ...startling, challenging, scholarly, sane, courteous.... Will surely make men stop, look and listen. DD

HISTORY

Josephus, Flavius – COMPLETE WORKS OF JOSEPHUS
(Whiston translation)
BARBER – A classic! Valuable as a guide to the study of the Old Testament, and helpful in understanding the history of the Jewish people.... This classic should be in every Christian's library. B, C
BROOKMAN – A complete, accurate documentation of Jewish history. It contains the first known reference to Jesus Christ by a secular historian. A classic for understanding Jewish culture and thinking. G
WILLIAM SANFORD LASOR – The best complete English translation of Josephus. We are, therefore, grateful to Kregel Publications.... DD

Maier, Paul L. – JOSEPHUS: The Essential Writings (*Jewish Antiquities* and *The Jewish War*, edited and condensed)
F. F. BRUCE – Dr. Maier is an authority on Josephus and on first century Christianity.... I am delighted to welcome this abridged edition which preserves the essential Josephus. I commend it warmly to all fellow students of the New Testament. DD
CARL B. HOCH, JR. – This new work will fill a significant need for those who have found the Elizabethan English and fine print of the Whiston edition intolerable and the astronomical price of the Loeb edition unaffordable.... Not only is this volume a very readable retranslation into modern English of the text of Josephus, but it is also an edited edition which removes (successfully in the reviewer's opinion) material which is extraneous to a free-flowing narrative and to the use of Josephus for Jewish and Christian backgrounds.... Dr. Maier is well-qualified to produce a volume of this type. I commend his new work to all readers highly. DD

THE HOLY SPIRIT

Baxter, Ronald E. – GIFTS OF THE SPIRIT
JOHN F. WALVOORD (In *Bibliotheca Sacra*) – Readers will find this a helpful, understandable, and carefully thought-through presentation of the gifts of the Spirit, so essential for effective Christian service. DD
VOICES – Exploding the myths surrounding the subject, Baxter presents a meticulous, rewarding study of the biblical teaching on spiritual gifts. DD

Bickersteth, Edward H. – THE HOLY SPIRIT
BARBER – A complete study of the personality of the Godhead and the divine work of the Holy Spirit. B
UNITED EVANGELICAL – This is a very valuable contribution to our enlightenment of the Holy Spirit's ministry. It is scholarly, yet understandable by laymen. DD

Biederwolf, William Edward – STUDY OF THE HOLY SPIRIT

BARBER – ...this brief, conservative study covers the important aspects of the Paraclete's person and work. c

MASTERS – ...as positive and humble as its title. [Biederwolf] gives the student his "homework" already done, assembling all the references to the Holy Spirit: baptism, filling, etc. Highly recommended as the finest work of its kind. Has outstanding chapters on the Sealing, Anointing, Communion, Baptism and Filling of the Spirit. o

Bullinger, E. W. – WORD STUDIES ON THE HOLY SPIRIT

BARBER – Bullinger provides a penetrating study of the biblical teaching. Ultradispensational. c

WIERSBE – ...unique in that it is both a concordance and a concise commentary on every verse in the New Testament that uses the word "spirit" (*pneuma*). One of the older works that had a steady ministry and is sure to last. DD

Gardiner, George E. – THE CORINTHIAN CATASTROPHE

OHIO INDEPENDENT BAPTIST – ...clearly answers the arguments proposed by today's charismatic adherents. It would be well for pastors to make this easily understood book available to their people. DD

W. WILBERT WELCH – ...Gardiner has put his finger on the Corinthian problem. In a very splendid way he answers the matter of the Corinthians seeking and displaying the showy gifts. DD

Koch, Kurt E. – SPEAKING IN TONGUES? (formerly *Strife of Tongues*)

BARBER – Provides the author's closely reasoned evaluation of the biblical teaching on tongues, summarizes the teaching of leaders in the history of the Christian church, carefully sifts the evidence of "case histories," and provides the author's statement of the "biblical counterpart." B

CONCORDIA – A helpful contribution to the writings on the "tongues" movement. DD

COVENANTER WITNESS – ...a stimulating analysis of the "modern tongues movement" .... It is well worth the few minutes it takes to be read. DD

Marsh, F. E. – EMBLEMS OF THE HOLY SPIRIT

BAPTIST BIBLE TRIBUNE – Most practical and lucid discussion of the subjects we have been privileged to read. DD

BIBLIOTHECA SACRA – Sane in the interpretation of symbols, and warmly devotional and heart-warming in the application of the truth concerning the scriptural teaching on the Holy Spirit's work. DD

CHRISTIANITY TODAY – The detailed explanations of the symbols of the Holy Spirit...are done with a freshness and originality seldom excelled, plus sound exegesis. DD

JOHN F. WALVOORD (as quoted by Merchant) – ...[an] important...study of the many figures in the Bible speaking of the Holy Spirit. Q

GEORGE WILLIAMS – Excellent little book. DD

Morgan, James – THE BIBLICAL DOCTRINE OF THE HOLY SPIRIT

BARBER – This is a work of solid erudition. c

EVANGELICAL CHRISTIAN (as quoted by Barber) – Controversy and criticism are avoided. Scripture ideas are unfolded in a clear and popular way, so as not only to inform the judgment, but also to purify the heart. c

Owen, John – THE HOLY SPIRIT

BARBER – One of the outstanding books of all time. Presents a learned and spiritual analysis of the names and titles of the Spirit, His nature and personality, and His varied works and influence. B

BROOKMAN – An outstanding one-volume study on the person and work of the Holy Spirit. This extensive work contains 356 pages. G

GRIER – ...[it] should not be neglected.... L

MASTERS – Another completely successful condensation of a renowned classic...the whole of Owen's reasoning on the Holy Spirit in one magnificent volume. o

JOHN F. WALVOORD (as quoted by Merchant) – ...a theological classic, this work is one of the most thorough treatments of the subject.... R

Schwab, Richard C. – LET THE BIBLE SPEAK...ABOUT TONGUES

JOSEPH C. ALDRICH – A thorough treatment of the tongues issue.... DD

EARL D. RADMACHER – ...the finest balance of careful scholarship and practical application that I have seen on the subject. If I were to pick one book to give to a person to read [about tongues] that is THE book. DD, c

JOHN F. WALVOORD – True to the Scriptures...should be helpful to Christians seeking biblical answers to this important subject. DD

Thomas, W. H. Griffith – THE HOLY SPIRIT

BARBER – [These lectures] have won the admiration of theologians in all parts of the English-speaking world. [They] survey the work of the Spirit in biblical revelation, historical interpretation, theological formulation, and modern application. B

PACKER – The author's clear, crisp, straightforward style, joined as it is with wisdom, both theological and devotional, gives his expository works classic status. DD

SUGDEN – All [Griffith Thomas'] writings bear the stamp of heaven and true greatness on them. His zenith of Bible exposition is certainly reached in this work! Each of the thirty-two chapters is like an "...apple of gold in a picture of silver." DD, z

WIERSBE – Griffith Thomas excels in spiritual depth, practicality and a simplicity of expression that make the most profound truths come alive with excitement. DD

Unger, Merrill F. – NEW TESTAMENT TEACHING ON TONGUES

BAPTIST BULLETIN – A thorough, scholarly, and biblical study.... DD

COVENANTER WITNESS – Thorough, convincing.... DD

INNER WITNESS – ...a gold mine.... Thoroughly scriptural and eminently scholarly. DD

MASTERS – Typically clear and easy presentation.... o

HOME AND FAMILY

Barber, Cyril & Aldyth – YOU CAN HAVE A HAPPY MARRIAGE

H. NORMAN WRIGHT – In the midst of many volumes written for married couples, there is a refreshing quality to this work...it is far more biblical in its content than many others which have been completed before. c

RAY C. STEDMAN – [Cyril and Aldyth Barber] blend together contemporary case histories...and patriarchal examples of the good and bad in marriage. The sections at the close of each chapter...will prove extremely valuable to any individual or couple who seriously seeks to follow a biblical example in marriage. DD

Barber, Cyril & Aldyth – YOUR MARRIAGE HAS REAL POSSIBILITIES

GRACE THEOLOGICAL JOURNAL (quoted by Barber) – [They] have given us a thoroughly biblical look at the marriage relationship in a style conductive to personal/couple devotional study or use by a group. They present Bible couples as models to emulate or avoid, including interaction questions to stimulate thought and discussion.... No other work presently in print deals with marriage in quite the same way. c

RAY C. STEDMAN – [Cyril and Aldyth Barber] blend together contemporary case histories...and patriarchal examples of the good and bad in marriage. The sections at the close of each chapter...will prove extremely valuable to any individual or couple who seriously seeks to follow a biblical example in marriage. DD

MUSIC MINISTRY

Osbeck, Kenneth W. – 101 HYMN STORIES
101 MORE HYMN STORIES

BARBER – Osbeck['s]...handling of the material is excellent. [These two books] make delightful devotional reading. Preachers will also find that the material presented can be used to enhance the worship service. We are grateful to him for his research and for making the benefits of his study available in such a pleasing way. c

BROOKMAN – Excellent for devotional readings, sermon illustrations and bulletin inserts. G

WIERSBE – I appreciate these books...they are filled with good illustrative material about the great hymns and gospel songs so familiar to our people. DD

PRAYER

Dods, Marcus – THE PRAYER THAT TEACHES TO PRAY

CUSTER – A fervent, eloquent, and powerful exposition of the Lord's Prayer. Although the reader may not agree with everything here, he will be struck with more devotional inspirational thoughts per page than he would think possible. I

MILLIE DIENERT – When you finish these pages, I'm sure you will agree with me that valuable lessons have been gleaned from them. For every Christian this book is a necessary reading and for every teacher and preacher, it's a must! DD

Rainsford, Marcus – OUR LORD PRAYS FOR HIS OWN: Thoughts on John 17

BARBER – Timely, relevant, devotional thoughts on John 17. ...the greatest classic ever written on Christ's high priestly prayer.... B, C

BROOKMAN – These extensive studies on John 17 are timely, relevant and devotional. This work is considered to be one of the greatest classics ever written on Christ's high priestly prayer. G

JOHN W. CAWOOD (as quoted in Jones) – ...it makes one bow in awe to Christ. It is a rare book, worth reading more than once. M

CUSTER – Powerful devotional messages on every verse of John 17. I

MASTERS – ...an exceedingly warm treatment of John 17.... These pages teem with what used to be called elevated spiritual thought. As a spiritual refresher it is magnificent and is a source of stimulation for preachers with so much original material. It expounds evangelical unity in a totally spiritual rather than organizational manner.... P

SMITH – ...one of the great devotional classics of our language. There are many volumes on this exceptionally rich chapter from the fourth Gospel, but none can begin to compare with the one by Rainsford. Occasionally I have given copies of this book to friends, and I have never failed to have them say to me that it is the greatest devotional volume they have ever had in their hands. This book will lead one to the throne of grace; it is a book to place at the bedside to read for the refreshing of one's soul late at night or early morning. Words fail to describe the wealth these pages will convey. U

W. H. GRIFFITH THOMAS – ...Deals with the "Holy of Holies" of our Lord's earthly life, and those who prayerfully read it through, Bible in hand, will find ample reward in its exposition of doctrine and its application of truth to mind and heart. DD

WIERSBE – ...obtain this work. BB

Saphir, Adolph – OUR LORD'S PATTERN FOR PRAYER

BARBER – Fervent messages that expound the text and edify the reader. Frequent digressions into matters of theological importance make fascinating reading. ...a must for every believer. B, C

BROOKMAN – This classic reprint is a thorough work on "The Lord's Prayer." It will be difficult to find a more complete and exegetical book than Saphir on this important study. Each section is systematically outlined for ease of understanding. Practical. G

WIERSBE – ...one of the best on [this] very special portion of Scripture. Saphir...blends pastoral warmth with good exegesis. ...I especially appreciate the insights he gives from Jewish lore and custom. Best of all, Saphir magnifies the person of our Lord Jesus Christ, so that the reading of this book is almost an experience of worship. DD

Scroggie, W. Graham – HOW TO PRAY

BARBER – Deals effectively with such topics as adoration, confession, petition, intercession, and thanksgiving. c

Scroggie, W. Graham – PAUL'S PRISON PRAYERS

WIERSBE – Valuable.... How that man could preach and teach the Word of God! DD

PROPHECY

Anderson, Sir Robert – FORGOTTEN TRUTHS

BAPTIST MESSENGER – ...cherished truths, brought to focus. DD
BARBER – Insightful. c
CALVARY REVIEW – We are indebted to the late Robert Anderson for his great classic.... DD

Andrews, Samuel J. – CHRISTIANITY AND ANTI-CHRISTIANITY IN THEIR FINAL CONFLICT

BARBER – Highly acclaimed, yet long out-of-print, this work deserves to be studied by every professing Bible student. c
BROOKMAN – A great work on the study of the Antichrist and the apostasy of the last days. Highly recommended by Wilbur M. Smith. G
SMITH – ...the late Dr. James M. Gray, who knew how to separate chaff from the wheat, and had an almost uncanny ability to discover the important books which a minister ought to have in the avalanche of literature that continually pours from the press, said, "After the Bible, a concordance, a Bible dictionary, and, perhaps, a...Bible Handbook, the book I would recommend as indispensable for the library of the pastor, missionary or Christian worker of today, is *Christianity and Anti-christianity in Their Final Conflict,* by Rev. Samuel J. Andrews. ...you must read this book. Here are no wild fancies, no foolish setting of times and seasons, no crude and sensational interpretations of prophecy, but a calm setting forth of what the Bible says on the most important subject for these times." U

Baron, David – ISRAEL IN THE PLAN OF GOD

BROOKMAN – This book deals with the four major passages of Scripture that deal exclusively with Israel's history. G
LIBRARIAN'S WORLD – ...an excellent commentary; challenging, scholarly, and directed toward the more serious Bible student. DD
PULPIT HELPS – The reader will not want to miss any of the inspiring details of this exposition. DD
JOHN F. WALVOORD – ...will contribute much insight. DD

Baron, David – TYPES, PSALMS, AND PROPHECIES

BARBER – Provides a pleasant blending of sound interpretation with true spiritual instruction. Succeeds in highlighting much of the New Testament's teaching on Christ and God's plan for His people. Preachers especially, will welcome...this fine work. c

Bultema, Harry – MARANATHA! A Study of Unfulfilled Prophecies

BARBER – ...this is an important treatise, which Bible students of all persuasions will appreciate. c

BELIEVER'S MAGAZINE – ...the book reads of prophecy well, and deals thoroughly with its importance and influence on daily living.... A very helpful book.... DD

BIBLIOTHECA SACRA – This is a very important document for anyone interested in the premillennial interpretation of Scripture. Readers will find it a mine of information.... The author has done an exceedingly careful piece of work that deserves study by those who wish to be informed in this area of doctrine. DD

Ironside, H. A. & Ottman, F. C. – STUDIES IN BIBLICAL ESCHATOLOGY (*The Great Parenthesis* and *God's Oath*, 2 vols. in one)

BARBER – [*The Great Parenthesis*] surveys the interval between the sixty-ninth and seventieth weeks of Daniel's prophecy and other "gaps" between events predicted in God's Word. A valuable treatise. [*God's Oath*] draws together the biblical data in support of a belief in a future, literal, Davidic (millennial) kingdom. Builds upon a careful, consistent, literal interpretation of Scripture. B

BROOKMAN – ...two important eschatological studies.... G

Keith, Alexander – CHRISTIAN EVIDENCES: Fulfilled Bible Prophecy

THOMAS CHALMERS (quoted by Barber) – It is recognized in our halls of theology as holding a high place in sacred literature, and it is found in almost every home and known as a household word throughout the land. c

SPURGEON – Horne says, "The multiplied editions which have been required within a very few years sufficiently attest to the high estimation in which Mr. Keith's work is deservedly held." And we may add that the improvements and additions have increased its value, and that fresh editions have shown that it is still appreciated. Y

Peters, George N. – THE THEOCRATIC KINGDOM (3 vols.)

BARBER – ...ranks as one of the greatest studies on the interpretation of the prophetic word ever produced. Discourses at length on the theocratic kingdom concept contained in the Scriptures. Sometimes laborious, but no one can claim to have a thorough grasp of this subject until he has interacted with this treatise. Indispensable and highly recommended. Espouses a midtribulation rapture. B

BROOKMAN – A truly monumental work on the study of Bible prophecy. This work is a classic.... Highly recommended by Wilbur M. Smith. Premillennial. G

LEWIS SPERRY CHAFER (quoted in *Prairie Overcomer*] – ...the greatest work on prophetic interpretation ever written.... DD

MOO – A classic of historic premillennial theology. R

DWIGHT D. PENTECOST – Without question this work will be carefully studied by all serious students of the prophetic Scriptures since it embodies the most exhaustive, scholarly, reverent treatment of the questions of the kingdom of our Lord available today. DD

SMITH – ...this [is] without question the greatest work on the Second Advent of our Lord Jesus and the many subjects relating to the Second Advent, ever published in our language....there is no work in the English language that deals with this...important subject with such depth, clearness, and understanding.... What a tragedy that a vast amount of learning like this should be hardly known to the Christian world within half a century after it is published! U

Pink, Arthur – THE ANTICHRIST

BARBER – A very capable synthesis of the biblical evidence surrounding the person and work of the Antichrist. A work of exceptional merit. B

BIBLICAL EVANGELIST – ...one of the most thorough studies of this theme written in the twentieth century. DD

Powell, Ivor – WHAT IN THE WORLD WILL HAPPEN NEXT?

BAPTIST BULLETIN – You will be challenged by this fine presentation of biblical prophecy. DD

CHRISTIAN BOOKSELLER – ...written with an uncommon humbleness not normally found in books written about prophecy. A text for both pastor and student of prophecy. DD

PROPHETIC WITNESS – A readable and worthwhile book. DD

WIERSBE – Don't overlook [this] book.... [It is] filled with treasures of sermon ideas and spiritual truths to help you in your ministry. DD

Tatford, Frederick A. – GOD'S PROGRAM OF THE AGES

BARBER – Stressing the imminency of the Second Advent, these studies survey the scope of prophecy from a premillennial point of view. The writer demonstrates remarkable charity...dealing with those whom he disagrees. B

SALVATION

Anderson, Sir Robert – THE GOSPEL AND ITS MINISTRY

BARBER – A complete survey of Bible doctrine. Contains a clear definition of terms, with excellent illustrations. Ideal for Bible study groups. B

Anderson, Sir Robert – REDEMPTION TRUTHS

BARBER – ...show[s], as well as man can, the marvels of God's plan for our redemption. Well done; stimulating. C

Denney, James – BIBLICAL DOCTRINE OF RECONCILIATION

BARBER (quoting Alexander Whyte) – "Read it again and again, and then preach its doctrine all your days...I do not know any modern book that has so much preaching power in it." Well conceived and executed. This book deserves careful reading. B, C

BROOKMAN – Most all of Denny's works are of the utmost value. G

Denney, James – THE DEATH OF CHRIST

BARBER – A definitive study that...includes the writer's work on *The Atonement and the Modern Mind.* Superior to the abridged version by R. V. G. Tasker. B

BROOKMAN – ...an older classic work. G

G. W. GROGAN (as quoted by Merchant) – One of the greatest books on the subject in English and long regarded as a classic exposition of the evangelical doctrine of the atonement. R

CARL F. H. HENRY – The message of Denney's forceful volume... is as much needed today as it was at the beginning of our century. [It] has lost none of its truth and fascination with the passage of time and serves to remind us of our incomparable debt the Redeemer. DD

Salmond, Stewart D. – BIBLICAL DOCTRINE OF IM-MORTALITY

BARBER – This "excellent study deserves an honored place in every Christian's library. What [Salmond] has written underscores the believer's hope. His work, therefore, should be studied by all who wish to be faithfully instructed in the Bible's teaching on this important subject." C

BROOKMAN – An excellent study of the biblical teaching of immortality. G

Westcott, Frederick Brooke – THE BIBLICAL DOCTRINE OF JUSTIFICATION

BROOKMAN – An important work that is based upon Paul's Roman and Galatian letters. This volume is thorough in exegesis. G

SCIENCE

Pember, G. H. – EARTH'S EARLIEST AGES

BAPTIST BULLETIN – A most revealing study of an oft-neglected subject. DD

G. H. LANG – It is with every confidence that I commend to my fellow-servants of Christ this illuminating treatise. I know of none other on its theme to be compared with it in spiritual value. DD

INNER WITNESS – Its pages burn with revealing truth and illumination...you need a copy in your library for reading and reference. DD

PROPHETIC WITNESS – ...will prove extremely valuable to the Bible student. DD

SERMONS, OUTLINES AND ILLUSTRATIONS

Evans, Christmas – SERMONS AND MEMOIRS OF CHRIST-MAS EVANS

BAPTIST BULLETIN – This volume is well worth reading by pastors, teachers and lay folk everywhere. DD

BEREA BANNER – You have never heard good preaching until you have read these sermons.... Buy, beg, borrow, but obtain this book. You will never be the same after you read it! DD

BIBLICAL EVANGELIST – We warmly recommend this good volume! DD

BRITISH COLUMBIA FELLOWSHIP BAPTIST MESSENGER – These books will feed the soul and encourage the heart as they are fully digested. DD

WIERSBE – These sermons will be a turning point for many in their ministry of preaching. I rejoice that this rare volume is back in print. You will not be the same after reading this book. DD

Finney, Charles G. – Finney Memorial Library
 GOD'S LOVE FOR A SINNING WORLD
 GUILT OF SIN
 PREVAILING PRAYER
 SO GREAT SALVATION
 TRUE AND FALSE REPENTANCE
 TRUE SAINTS
 TRUE SUBMISSION
 VICTORY OVER THE WORLD

BAPTIST BIBLE – ...well organized, logical, and practical. DD

BARBER – A collection of sermons by a great revival preacher. These messages speak to the conditions within the church, and also relate to the world in general. B

CALVARY REVIEW – ...hard-hitting messages.... It will be impossible for the reader to avoid self-evaluation and examination. DD

Lockyer, Herbert – LAST WORDS OF SAINTS AND SINNERS

BARBER – Recounts the testimonies of those whose simple faith in Christ was sufficient for the crises confronting them. Also contains the testimony of those who turned to Christ in their final hours. Provides source material and illustrations for sermons. B

BROOKMAN – Lockyer is an extremely practical writer on many subjects. This work provides helpful resource material in sermon preparation. G

Powell, Ivor – Outlines and Illustrations
 BIBLE CAMEOS
 BIBLE GEMS
 BIBLE HIGHWAYS
 BIBLE NAMES OF CHRIST
 BIBLE PINNACLES
 BIBLE TREASURES
 BIBLE WINDOWS

BAPTIST BULLETIN – ...Christians will find these readings profitable. Concise, imaginative and stimulating.... DD

BAPTIST EXAMINER – ...brief, but highly informative and suggestive studies. DD

WIERSBE – Don't overlook these fine books...they are filled with treasures of sermon ideas and spiritual truths to help you in your ministry. DD

Proctor, F. B. (ed.) – **TREASURY OF QUOTATIONS ON RELIGIOUS SUBJECTS**

LOUIS PAUL LEHMAN – ...[a] treasure chest of centuries [which contains] the

air of immortality.... A masterpiece of the classification of material....
The power and beauty of language come glistening from the pages....
Gems of thought which can run, walk, creep and sit down, as well as soar.
Thoroughly Christ-centered. **DD, Y**

PROPHETIC NEWS AND ISRAEL'S WATCHMAN – This time-saving and practical
volume will introduce minds to otherwise unattainable writings
and...stimulate great thoughts.... Preachers, librarians, students, teachers,
writers and speakers will save hours of labor...by keeping this
welcome resource book within reach. **DD**

Whitesell, Faris D. – 65 WAYS TO GIVE EVANGELISTIC INVITATIONS

BARBER – Unique because it is the only work of its kind. **B**

PREACHING – While there are many books about the mechanics of sermon
preparation, there is very little help on the mechanics of giving a public
invitation.... [This]...is the most complete book in print. **DD**

ROBERT G. LEE – ...a most helpful book...of great worth.... Will give
courage to the timid, skill to the awkward, prompting to the perplexed,
help to the hesitant and effectiveness to the ineffective in the matter of
giving Gospel invitations.... Deserves a wide sale and reading and
practice. **DD**

SWORD OF THE LORD – This is an excellent little book and is written in a
manner that is interesting and motivational. We recommend it. **DD**

Wiersbe, Warren W. (comp.) – CLASSIC SERMONS ON FAITH AND DOUBT

BARBER – Recommended. **C**

PROPHETIC WITNESS – ...will enrich and bless the reader. **DD**

SWORD OF THE LORD – ...they will greatly bless the hearts of those who read
them. We recommend the book. **DD**

Wiersbe, Warren W. (comp.) – TREASURY OF THE WORLD'S GREAT SERMONS

BROOKMAN – ...helpful collection of 122 outstanding sermons from 122 of
the greatest preachers with a short biographical description of each
preacher. Excellent. **G**

CHRISTIAN REVIEW – ...a sermon library in one volume.... **DD**

EMPHASIS MAGAZINE – A rewarding volume. **DD**

EVANGELICAL BAPTIST – ...a worthwhile gift for a pastor or a young person
training for the ministry. **DD**

INTEREST – ...a great volume to put into the hands of young preachers—an
ideal gift! **DD**

PULPIT HELPS – It's doubtful if any preacher can fail to benefit from the
reading and study of such a treasury as this. **DD**

SPIRIT BEINGS

Gilpin, Richard – BIBLICAL DEMONOLOGY: SATAN'S TEMPTATIONS

BARBER – ...ably explores Satan's person and work...of particular value for

Gilpin's analysis of the way Satan tempts the saints. A rare and edifying study. c

Koch, Kurt E. – THE DEVIL'S ALPHABET

ALLIANCE WITNESS – ...highly recommended for ministers, church libraries and alert Christians. DD
BARBER – A review of forty-seven forms of superstition, fortune-telling, magic, and spiritism. B
LUTHERAN ALERT – ...a handy handbook. DD

Koch, Kurt E. – OCCULT ABC

AUSTIN RECORD – ...an interesting and scholarly work, probably a very necessary work, showing the pitfalls the unwary must avoid. DD
BARBER – A must for those who work with teens and those in college. Should be in every church library. c

Nevius, John C. – DEMON POSSESSION

BAPTIST BULLETIN – ...an important contribution to an understanding of what Satan is doing in the world. DD
LIBRARIAN'S WORLD – The classic volume on the subject.... DD
PRAIRIE OVERCOMER – Dr. Nevius' presentation of his subject is balanced both by biblical insight and personal experience. DD
MERRILL F. UNGER – ...a classic. ...it reads like a page from the Gospels. DD

TYPOLOGY
SEE ALSO "THE TABERNACLE"

Baron, David – TYPES, PSALMS, AND PROPHECIES

BARBER – Provides a pleasant blending of sound interpretation with true spiritual instruction. Succeeds in highlighting much of the New Testament's teaching on Christ and God's plan for His people. Preachers especially will welcome...this fine work. c

Habershon, Ada R. – STUDY OF THE TYPES

BARBER – A detailed, devotional study of the Old Testament types and their fulfillment in the New Testament. DD
BROOKMAN – ...full of useful hints, thoughts and illustrations.... G
WIERSBE – A classic treatment. CC

Jukes, Andrew – THE LAW OF THE OFFERINGS

BARBER – Beginning with a defense of biblical typology, the writer analyzes the five offerings of the Levitical system and discusses the typical significance of each. B
BROOKMAN – This work is a classic on the typological significance of the offerings mentioned in Leviticus, showing how each clearly points to some particular aspect of the redemptive work of Christ. The author clearly defines the significance of this Judeo-religious rite and its application to the New Testament church. G
MASTERS – No one else explains the significance of the Levitical offerings (in relation to Calvary) as well as Jukes does here.... Suddenly...it bursts

into life with several superb chapters which are practically essential to the study of Leviticus. P

SPURGEON – A very condensed, instructive, refreshing book. It will open up new trains of thought to those unversed in the teaching of the types. Y

Keach, Benjamin – PREACHING FROM THE TYPES AND METAPHORS OF THE BIBLE

BROOKMAN – Every pastor will glean sermonic material from this classical reprint.... Keach gives a complete analysis of the spiritual significance of each type and metaphor along with its practical application for today. G

LOCKYER – ...believers throughout the Christian world should know of and revere the witness and work of Benjamin Keach. I am not ashamed to confer how deeply in debt I am to the most substantial studies of this renowned expositor. N

MASTERS – ...packed with rich suggestion for preachers. Those who can catch (and update) the spirit of this great preacher will derive much stimulation. O

SPURGEON – This is a vast cyclopedia of types and metaphors of all sorts, and was once very popular. It is a capital book, though too often the figures not only run on all-fours but on as many legs as a centipede. Y

SOURCE CODE LIST

(All quotes taken from the following sources are used by permission.)

A. Allison, Joseph D. *Bible Study Resource Guide*, revised edition. Grand Rapids: Sagamore Books, 1984.

B. Barber, Cyril J. *The Minister's Library*, vol. 1. Chicago: Moody Press, 1985.

C. Barber, Cyril J. *The Minister's Library*, vol. 2. Chicago: Moody Press, 1985.

D. Barker, Kenneth L., Waltke, Bruce K. (comp.), Zuck, Roy B. (ed.). *Bibliography for Old Testament Exegesis and Exposition*. Dallas: Dallas Theological Seminary, 1975

E. Bollier, John A. *The Literature of Theology: A Guide for Students and Pastors*. Philadelphia: The Westminster Press, 1979.

F. Branson, Mark Lau. *The Reader's Guide to the Best Evangelical Books*. San Francisco: Harper & Row Publishers, Inc. 1982.

G. Brookman, David W. *Basic Books for the Minister's Library*. Shippensburg, PA: Destiny Image Publishers, 1986.

H. Childs, Brevard S. *Old Testament Books for Pastor and Teacher*. Philadelphia: The Westminster Press, 1977.

I. Custer, Stewart. *Tools for Preaching and Teaching the Bible*. Greenville, SC: Bob Jones University Press, Inc. 1981.

J. Danker, Frederick W. *Multipurpose Tools for Bible Study*. St. Louis: Concordia Publishing House, 1966.

K. Fair, J. Arnold. Respected Bible professor, pastor, and author.

L. Grier, W. J. *The Best Books: A Guide to Christian Literature.* London: The Banner of Truth, 1968.

M. Jones, Charles E., ed. *The Books You Read.* Harrisburg, PA: Executive Books, 1986.

N. Lockyer, Herbert, Sr. Late author of many books including *Last Words of Saints and Sinners.* Grand Rapids: Kregel Publications, 1969.

O. Martin, Ralph P. *New Testament Books for Pastor and Teacher.* Philadelphia: The Westminster Press, 1984.

P. Masters, Peter M. Pastor of Metropolitan Tabernacle in London, and author of *The Preacher's Library.* London: Wakeman Publishers Ltd, 1979.

Q. Masters, Peter M. Pastor of Metropolitan Tabernacle in London, and author of *Survey of Bible Commentaries.* London: Metropolitan Tabernacle, 1983.

R. Merchant, Harish, ed. *Encounter With Books: A Guide to Christian Reading.* 2nd printing, 1971. Intervarsity Press, P. O. Box 1400, Downers Grove, IL 60515.

S. Moo, Douglas, ed. *An Annotated Bibliography on the Bible and the Church.* Deerfield, IL: Trinity Evangelical Divinity School, 1986.

T. Packer, J. I. Respected professor and author of numerous works, including *Knowing God.*

U. Smith, Wilbur M. *A Treasury of Books for Bible Study.* Boston: W. A. Wilde Co., 1960.

V. Smith, Wilbur M. *Chats From a Minister's Library.* Boston: W. A. Wilde Co., 1951.

W. Smith, Wilbur M. *Profitable Bible Study.* Boston: W. A. Wilde Co., 1951.

X. Smith, Wilbur M. *The Minister in His Study.* Boston: W. A. Wilde Co., 1973.

Y. Spurgeon, Charles Haddon. *Commenting and Commentaries.* Grand Rapids: Kregel Publications, 1988.

Z. Sugden, Dr. Howard F. Respected pastor, conference speaker and author of several books, including *What Does the Bible Say About...?* Grand Rapids: Kregel Publications, 1987.

AA. Tenney, Merrill C. Respected professor and author of many works including *New Testament Survey,* and editor of *The Zondervan Pictorial Bible Encyclopedia.*

BB. Wiersbe, Warren W. *Listening to the Giants,* including "A Basic Library for Bible Students." Grand Rapids: Baker Book House, 1980.

CC. Wiersbe, Warren W. *Walking With the Giants.* Grand Rapids: Baker Book House, 1976.

DD. Recorded recommendations and printed forewords, prefaces, covers, jackets, and periodicals.

AUTHOR INDEX

Thompson, Henry 66
Thomson, James 145, 150
Thornton, J. 90
Thrupp, Joseph Francis 85,
108
Tileston, Mary W. 245
Tittmann, K. C. 146
Todd, James F. 164
Toller, Thomas 164
Topsell, Edward 64, 122
Townsend, George 48, 134
Townson, Thomas 137
Traheron, Bartholomew 146
Trapp, John 9, 14, 43
Trapp, Joseph 137
Tregelles, S. Prideaux 119
Trench, T. Chenevix 137, 141,
142
Trollopoe, William 134, 150
Troughton, W. 91
Tucker, W. Leon 235
Tucker, William Hill 85
Tudor, Richard 57
Turnbull, Richard 89, 174,
178
Turner, Samuel H. 51, 162,
172
Tweedie, W. K. 126
Tyler, Thomas 101
Tyng, Stephen 64

Udall, John 114, 122
Umbreit, Friedrich 76
Unger, Merrill F. 248
Upjohn, W. 142

Van Doren, William H. 145,
147, 217, 218
Van Hagen, Mrs. Henry 76
Van Oosterzee, J. J. 55
Vander Velde, Frances 238
Vaughan, Charles John 151,
157, 165, 181, 219, 227
Verney, Lady 112
Vince, Charles 66
Vine, William E. 242
Von Gerlach, Otto 46
von Orelli, Hans Conrad 205,
206

Wagner, George 56, 76, 197
Wake, W. R. 85
Walford, William 85, 157
Walker, Thomas 220
Wall, William 43, 134
Ward, Richard 144
Wardlaw, Ralph 54, 98
Warner, Richard 51
Warren, Israel 137
Watson, Richard 137
Watson, Thomas 128, 166
Way, Arthur S. 189
Weemse, John 57, 59
Weiss, Benjamin 85, 102, 108
Wells, Edward 43, 119
Wemyss, Thomas 76
Wesley, John 134
Westcott, Brook Foss 137,
226
Westcott, Frederick Booke
254

Westing, Harold 242
Weymouth, Richard Francis
189
Whateley, William 51, 57
Whedon, D. D. 134
Whish, J. C. 113
Whitby, Daniel 134
White, Frank H. 58
White, John 52
White, Samuel 113
Whitesell, Faris D. 256
Whyte, Alexander 238
Wiersbe, Warren W. (comp.)
256
Wieseler, Karl 137
Wiesinger, Lic. August 165,
168
Wilcocks, Thomas 10, 71, 85,
98, 108
Willard, Samuel 90
Willet, Andrew 10, 51, 55, 60,
65, 94, 119, 157, 178
Williams, George 191
Williams, H. W. 157, 172
Williams, Isaac 53, 87, 138,
139, 181
Williams, Rowland 110
Wilson, Daniel 166
Wilson, Joseph 119
Wilson, Thomas 43, 157
Wilson, William 85, 134, 175,
240
Winslow, Octavius 95, 158
Wintle, Thomas 119
Wiseman, Luke H. 62, 201
Wodrow, Robert 119
Wolfendale, J. 121
Wood, Nathan R.
Wood, William 119
Woodford, Samuel 86, 108
Woodhouse, John Cappel 181
Woodward, Henry 69, 70
Wordsworth, Charles 22, 43
Worsley, John 134
Wright, Abraham 48, 86
Wright, C. H. H. 51, 64
Wright, Charles H. 206, 208
Wright, M. 108

Ycard, Fr. 102
Yound, Loyal 102
Young, John 140
Young, Robert 43

Zahn, Theodor 211
Zillwood, J. O. 86

SUBJECT INDEX

The Decalogue

Deuteronomy

Devotional / Christian Life

Ecclesiastes (See also "Books of Solomon")

Elijah, Elisha, etc.

Ruth Expounded 63
Ruth's Recompense 63
Ruth, in Hebrew 64
Six Lectures (Philpot) 64
Six Lectures on the Book of Ruth (Price) 64
Story of Ruth 64

Salvation
Biblical Doctrine of Immortality 254
Biblical Doctrine of Justification 254
Biblical Doctrine of Reconciliation 253
Death of Christ, The 254
Gospel and Its Ministry, The 253
Redemption Truths 253

Samuel, Saul, David
Critical History of the Life of David, A 66
David 66
David, King of Israel: The Divine Plan and
Lessons of His Life (Blaikie) 65
David, The King of Israel (Krummacher)
66
David: His Life, and Its Lessons 66
Davidica 66
Discourses on the History of David 66
Historical Account of the Life and Reign of
David, An 66
History of Samuel, The 65
Life and Reign of David, The 66
Lights and Shadows in the Life of King
David 66
Samuel, Saul, and David in Kitto's Daily
Bible Illustrations 65
Samuel, the Prophet 65
Saul, The First King of Israel 65
Shepherd King, The 66
Whole History of King David, The 66

Science
Earth's Earliest Ages 254

Sermons, Outlines and Illustrations
Bible Cameos 255
Bible Gems 255
Bible Highways 255
Bible Names of Christ 255
Bible Pinnacles 255
Bible Treasures 255
Bible Windows 255
Classic Sermons on Faith and Doubt 256
God's Love for a Sinning World 255
Guilt of Sin 255
Last Words of Saints and Sinners 255
Prevailing Prayer 255
Sermons and Memoirs of Christmas Evans
254
65 Ways to Give Evangelistic Invitations
256
So Great Salvation 255
Treasury of Quotations on Religious Subjects 255

Treasury of the World's Great Sermons 256
True and False Repentance 255
True Saints 255
True Submission 255
Victory Over the World 255

Solomon's Temple
Orbis Miraculum 67
Solomon's Temple Spiritualized 67
Temple, The: Its Ministry and Services 67

Song of Solomon
Beauty of the Word in the Song of Solomon
108 (Wright)
Bowels Opened 107
Bride of Christ , The 107
Brief Exposition, A 103
Brief Outline of an Examination of the Song
Of Solomon, A 103
Canticles of the Song of Solomon, The 103
Christ and His Church 106
Commentary (Burrowes) 103
Commentary, A (Littledale) 106
Commentary on the Canticles (Brightman)
103
Commentary on the Canticles (Ibn Ezra)
105
Commentary on the Canticles, A (Homes)
105
Conversion of Solomon, a Direction to
Holiness of Life, The 103
Discourses upon Solomon's Song 107
Dissertation on the Song of Solomon, A 104
Essays Towards a Literal or True Radical
Exposition 107
Exposition (Robotham) 107
Exposition (Stuart) 107
Exposition (Wilcocks) 108
Exposition of the Book of Solomon's Song,
An 104
Expositon of the Divinely Prophetic Song
of Songs, An 102
Exposition of the Song of Solomon, An
104, 204
Failure and Discipline: Thoughts on Canticles 107
Fifteen Sermons on the Song of Solomon
105
Intercourses of Divine Love Betwixt Christ
and His Church, The 103
Love's Intercourse Between the Lamb and
His Bride 105
Meditations 106
Metrical Meditations on the Canticles 106
Mirror of Divine Love, The 104
New Translation (Fry) 104
New Translation (Percy) 107
New Translation (Thrupp) 108
New Translation, A (Williams) 108
Nymphas. A Paraphrastic Exposition 106
Outlines of a New Commentary on Solomon's Song 105